EDDY JOKOVICH
DAVID LEWIS

POLITICS, PROTEST, PANDEMIC

THE YEAR THAT CHANGED AUSTRALIA

Politics, Protest, Pandemic: The year that changed Australia
ISBN: 978-0-6481644-8-7
ISBN (Amazon): 979-8-7372030-8-5

©2021 Eddy Jokovich & David Lewis

All rights reserved. No part of this book may be reproduced in any form or by any electronic or mechanical means, including information storage and retrieval systems, without written permission from the authors, except for the use of brief quotations in book reviews and promotional material.

April 2021. Published by New Politics, an imprint of ARMEDIA Pty. Ltd.

New Politics
PO Box 1265, Darlinghurst NSW 1300
www.newpolitics.com.au

Published and produced on the land of the Wangal people.

Email: info@newpolitics.com.au

 @NewPoliticsAU

Production: ARMEDIA

Cover photograph: Black Lives Matter protesters, Parliament House in Canberra, 5 June 2020. (AAP Image/Mick Tsikas)

 A catalogue record for this work is available from the National Library of Australia

Contents

About the authors 6

Introduction: Politics, Protest, Pandemic 8

1. Corruption as the new normal in federal politics 16
2. Continuing politicisation of the Australian Federal Police 22
3. Reforming Australian politics and improving democracy 30
4. The coronavirus appears: How will it affect the economy? ... 38
5. Breaking conventions and what it means for democracy 45
6. Is the media slowly turning against the Prime Minister? 50
7. A failure of government 57
8. The end of neoliberalism but what will replace it? 63
9. The mysterious case of the Ruby Princess 72
10. Politics and coronavirus: The issues flying under the radar ... 78
11. Pell Mal 85
12. Government performance during the coronavirus crisis 89
13. The bigger picture of the Turnbull and Murdoch battle 97
14. Back to school and the vexed question of opening up 105

15. It's on: The Eden–Monaro byelection 116
16. Mismanaging the relationship with China 120
17. The bad luck of being in opposition during a crisis 128
18. When will black lives matter? 135
19. Morrison: He's no Bob Hawke 146
20. The cruel and brutal RoboDebt scheme 155
21. The closure of Murdoch's regional newspapers 160
22. Branch stacking in Victoria 163
23. Opening up too quickly 169
24. The new McCarthyism in Australia 172
25. Barbarians at the gate and reaching for their guns 182
26. Are we really all in this together? 186
27. Reading the tea leaves in Eden–Monaro 192
28. The release of the Palace Letters 198
29. A prime minister at the football: Let's drink to that 207
30. The ghosts of Margaret Thatcher and Ronald Reagan 212
31. Coronavirus politics fails to act in the public interest 219
32. The ongoing scandals in New South Wales 226
33. COVID-style shape shifting and blame games 229
34. Stimulus support and the post-pandemic economy 237
35. When money means absolutely everything in Canberra 243
36. The return of Parliament and a crisis in aged care 246
37. The continuing saga of Australia's border wars 253
38. An international infrastructure program gets a belting 258

39. The interfering vested interests 263
40. Recycled political stories that are too good to be true 268
41. Chaos and corruption in the Coalition 273
42. The NBN revisited 278
43. Unrealistic Budget expectations and lost opportunities 281
44. Albanese and his Budget Reply 289
45. The Morrison recession 295
46. The continuing corruption in New South Wales 304
47. Investigating News Corporation 312
48. Going postal: A deflection to cover up corruption 318
49. The end of Trump and a change for Australian politics 324
50. Sex in the city and the private lives of politicians 330
51. A Queensland victory for sensibility and decency 338
52. Murdoch petition sealed and delivered 342
53. Not flying the Indigenous flag 344
54. Mr Morrison goes to Tokyo and returns empty handed 347
55. Cormann takes on the OECD 357
56. Pizza lockdown in South Australia 363
57. Afghanistan and the political killing season 367
58. The hard right-wing agenda and bad habits 372
59. Labor's lack of success since federation 382
60. A most dramatic year in politics 387
61. Incumbency and the year ahead 395

About the authors

Eddy Jokovich is editor of *New Politics*, and co-presenter of the monthly New Politics Australia podcast. He has worked as a journalist, publisher, author, political analyst, campaigner, war correspondent, and lecturer in media studies at the University of Technology, Sydney and the University of Sydney; has a wide range of experience working in editorial and media production work and is Director of ARMEDIA, a publishing and communications company specialising in public interest media.

 @EddyJokovich

David Lewis is co-presenter of the monthly New Politics Australia podcast, historian, musicologist, musician and political scientist based in Sydney. His lecturing and research interests include roots music, popular music, Australian, UK and US politics and crime fiction. He has published in *Music Forum Australia*, *Eureka Street*, *Quadrant*, *Crikey* and has edited several books.

 @dlew919

New Politics Australia is a monthly podcast, providing analysis and opinions on Australia politics. It can be found at Apple and Google podcasts, Amazon Audible, Spotify and SoundCloud.

About the authors

ALSO BY EDDY JOKOVICH + DAVID LEWIS

DIVIDED OPINIONS

THE NEW POLITICS ANALYSIS OF THE 2019 YEAR IN AUSTRALIAN POLITICS

As the mainstream media struggles to retain audiences and survive under new business models and shrinking revenue streams, independents are filling in the gaps left behind by the older mastheads. New Politics is one of the more important voices appearing in this new landscape, and *Divided Opinions* presents some of the best work from the monthly podcast, and a selection of articles published during 2019. Guaranteed to make you think; aggravate, or inform and enlighten—and maybe all at once—this is a must-read analysis of one of the most dynamic years ever in Australian politics.

Available in paperback and ebook.

Divided Opinions: The New Politics analysis of the 2019 year in Australian politics
ISBN: 978-0-6481644-5-6
ISBN (Amazon): 978-1-6611355-7-7
338 pages

Introduction: Politics, Protest, Pandemic

Politics, Protest, Pandemic: The year that changed Australia is the story of the year in Australian federal politics, told through a collection of extended essays from the New Politics Australia podcast series, and a selection of political essays published online.

The 2020 year was one of the most dramatic in human history, shaped by a coronavirus pandemic that influenced society in so many different ways, combining the fields of health, politics, economics, business and education into the one area that proved to be difficult for many governments around the world to manage.

Incumbency during a time of crisis was considered to be beneficial for political leaders and this was shown to be the case in Australia, with the Queensland Government returned at the October 2020 election, and the Western Australia Government returned at their March 2021 election, a result which saw the WA Liberal Party reduced to only two seats in a Parliament of fifty-nine seats. Certainly, those governments did hold political advantages but a mysterious and invisible coronavirus isn't the sole panacea for political difficulties: governments still need to provide competent management and offer safety to the electorate and, in the case of these two governments, they were rewarded for their efforts.

The opposite occurred in the United States Presidential election: early in 2020, US President Donald Trump was expected to be re-elected, only for those expectations to dissipate throughout the year, primarily due to mismanagement of the coronavirus pandemic, and

Introduction: Politics, Protest, Pandemic

an indifference which at the time of the November election, had led to over 10 million infections and the deaths of over 245,000 people. A crisis can be beneficial to political leaders but the defeat of Trump proved the electorate is prepared to punish incumbents when there is mismanagement of such critical health and economic issues.

The ashes and smoke particles from the 2019/20 bushfires season were still lingering in the air when the political year commenced and it seemed the damage to the Prime Minister's credibility was so severe—after he surreptitiously went overseas for a family holiday at the height of the bushfires season—that there were some considerations about if he would be able to survive and discussions within the Liberal Party focused upon whether it was time—yet again—to choose new leadership.

But the one crisis which seemed to ruin the tenure of Scott Morrison was replaced by another—the coronavirus pandemic—and this dramatically reversed his political fortunes and changed the discussions from how tenuous his hold on the leadership was, to one where journalists in the mainstream media were suggesting the Labor Party should forget about winning the next federal election, and start campaigning for the election after that—in 2025, or even further ahead in 2028. That's how fickle politics can be: events can make the world change dramatically, and it's wise to show caution when viewing these events through a political prism.

The year also commenced with further allegations of corruption and misappropriation of Commonwealth funds in the so-called 'sports rorts' scandal, where over $250 million from sports infrastructure programs was directed to Coalition-held seats in the 2019 federal election, in many cases, towards unwarranted and unwanted projects.

Corruption was a continuing theme throughout 2020, with further revelations of the federal government paying ten-times over the market valuation for land in western Sydney owned by Liberal Party donors; the NSW Premier in a secret relationship with a former politician extracting commissions from government land deals; a $3.9 million payment made by the federal government which was outside of the purview of Freedom of Information laws; millions of dollars paid to Foxtel without public justification; corporations reaping larger-than-expected profits and paying dividends and bonuses to senior executives after receiving JobKeeper subsidy payments—no questions asked, and no answers provided.

Anthony Albanese started the year as the preferred prime minister in opinion polls—and that was to be expected after Morrison's poor handling of the bushfires crisis—but his role as Leader of the Opposition receded into the background, once the coronavirus pandemic arrived. It seems a crisis has no time for political leaders and parties who are outside of government, and Albanese found it difficult to gain political traction and media attention throughout the year, leading to media speculation as to whether he would lead the Labor Party to the next election.

Albanese's intention was to support the public interest, as well as provide as much political support and cover for the federal government to create stimulus packages and cushion a quickly-deteriorating economy and reduce ever-increasing unemployment queues. Of course, this was the best series of events for the public and the economy, but left Albanese without any political capital, or credit for acting in a responsible manner.

State Liberal opposition leaders in Victoria, Queensland and Western Australia saw matters differently and, in conjunction with the mainstream media, directed hostile campaigns against Labor Premiers Daniel Andrews, Mark McGowan and Annastacia Palaszczuk, calling for borders and the economy to open up immediately—and quite often, reversing their positions as soon as the circumstances changed. Morrison and his senior leadership team also attacked the Labor premiers, even going as far as supporting Clive Palmer's court challenges to Western Australia's border closures, and demanding Queensland and Victoria urgently end their respective lockdown strategies, even through Liberal premiers in South Australia and Tasmania had engaged in exactly the same closures and lockdowns. The shock of the onset of the coronavirus pandemic encouraged the federal government to use the mantra of "all in this together" and, as the year progressed, it was evident not everyone was part of this rhetoric.

Political protest and action was also a theme throughout the year. The blacks lives matter movement was ignited after George Floyd was murdered by a police officer, and the movement spread from the streets of Minneapolis to over 400 cities across the world, including in Australia.

But far from the passive support and encouragement shown by Morrison to anti-vax/5G/lockdown protests in May, where he understood "the frustrations that they're feeling", the Prime Minister suggested the black lives matter protests organised several weeks later would place "the economic recovery at risk", were "politically-driven left-wing agendas", and instructed NSW Police to charge protestors. Again, not everyone was "all in this together", and Morrison offered his musings according to his political biases.

The coronavirus pandemic was most certainly a combined health and economic issue, but it also provided an existential crisis. What is purpose of government? What is the purpose of the economy? What is the purpose of society? Human history has been littered with salient points that change the course of that history and it's only after those points have occurred that humanity has a full perspective and understanding of these events. World War I was one of those points, as was World War II. Fundamental changes occurred during the post-war period: cities, communities, societies and countries were rebuilt, guided by Keynesian economic thinking, until the onset of neoliberalism in the late 1970s and early 1980s, which fast-tracked economic development and technological change, but also privatised essential social services, as well as creating a larger barrier between the super-wealthy capital classes and working classes.

Neoliberalism has failed. As an economic ideology, it was teetering after the global financial crisis in the late 2000s, but bailed out by the United States government and the European Union, hoping to continue with the easier option of unsustainable growth and endless productivity drives. This pandemic has offered an opportunity for the world to reassess a future pathway over the next decade or two, and new economic thinking and strategies are required to navigate world economies through this precarious path. Which political parties will be able to successfully guide their national economies? In Australia, Morrison has pushed forward the notion of 'snap-back', hoping to return the economy to pre-COVID-19 conditions but this seems to be offering false hope to the electorate. Sometimes, prevailing circumstances dictate a set of economic responses—as was the case in the post-World War II period—and perhaps this expectation of returning to the economy of yesteryear offers comfort to the electorate, even if this means the unpalatable truth is pushed further down the political road.

Primarily, the electorate is after solutions from their political leadership, and the leaders who fail to deliver, are the ones likely to suffer at the time of an election. Morrison—and many of his ministers—have the habit of making public announcements and promises, only for those promises to remain undelivered, or re-announced in a different form. And, if there's anything that goes wrong, deflections are offered, as are excuses and mistruths: it seems there's always someone else to blame, rather than accepting the responsibility for errors and ensuring they are not repeated.

In the latter part of the year, there were revelations senior male ministers were engaged in inappropriate relationships with young staff members. Other allegations implied against the Attorney-General, Christian Porter, and aired by the ABC *Four Corners* program, exploded onto the scene in early 2021, when the full details of an alleged rape in 1988 were made public. There was also an allegation of a rape committed by a ministerial staffer in Parliament House just before the 2019 federal election, and the details of this incident were revealed in February 2021.

Other incidents of sexual misbehaviours by ministerial staffers were also revealed, which brought up the question: is Parliament House a safe workplace for women? It seems there are serious issues there and the federal government will need to make reforms within its own system if it is to match public expectations and the way the rest of the community is expected to behave.

This book primarily offers insights into the performances of the Liberal–National Coalition and the Labor Party throughout the year. It was a dramatic year in which no-one really understood what the final outcome would be, and this is still a delicate issue for 2021 and beyond.

Vaccines for coronaviruses have been created and that is one of the biggest breakthroughs in medical history. There is still some way to go in this area but the discovery of the vaccine is a game-changer for the field of medicine, despite varying efficacy of some versions of the vaccine, and the issues caused by the AstraZeneca version, where rare blood clots resulted from a small number of vaccinations.

It was said that developing a vaccine to coronaviruses was close to impossible and, if it was to be developed, it would take many years, if at all. Twelve months after the coronavirus pandemic commenced, a vaccine became available to the public: there was an international will to make a vaccine, and the vaccine was developed.

While there were successes in the field of medicine, politics was disappointing. An opportunity to find constructive responses in the public interest was available to political leaders, but the opportunity to point score and seek political benefit always seems to be greater. Politics in Australia had become too tribal and these divisions are eagerly exploited by a conservative mainstream media and key political players, including Prime Minister Morrison.

The rollout of the vaccines seemed to coincide with a political timetable—the completion schedule of October 2021 fitted in neatly to expectations Morrison planned to call an early federal election to exploit the anticipated success of this rollout—but the political party which prioritises politics and places its own interests first is in peril of losing control of its agenda and is destined for failure. There is now a shortage of vaccines and there is no schedule offered for when Australia's population will be fully vaccinated; there is confusion about whether these vaccines are safe, primarily because the federal government placed vested interests ahead of the public interest. And it will suffer politically for acting in this way.

Australia is still at the crossroads, with no clear direction of which way it will proceed. The country has handled the pandemic well: coronavirus cases are in single digits across the country, and these have mainly been caused by overseas passenger arrivals. If there was a choice of residing in Australia, or in one of the many countries with thousands of new cases reported every day, most of the electorate would choose to live here.

But there are still many areas needing attention: long-term economic issues need to be resolved; climate change and environmental issues are still largely neglected by a federal government, which sees more merit in a 'gas-led recovery' than investing in a renewables energy future. The structure of federation placed a handbrake on Morrison's initial desire to place more emphasis on the economy, rather than health, and the responses of the premiers and chief ministers were the ones which stopped Australia replicating the severe outbreaks, caseloads and deaths that occurred in the United States, and many parts of Europe.

Politics in this country needs to change, but the system itself is unclear about where it needs to start. The simple act of increasing female representation within the Liberal and National parties created a raucous response from the existing male members, unwilling to relinquish their privilege, or in the case of Morrison, saying he didn't "want to see women rise only on the basis of others doing worse".

A constant theme within *Politics, Protest, Pandemic* is the belief that Australia currently has the wrong type of federal government at the wrong time. Australia's Constitution is outdated, created in 1901 and not fit-for-purpose in 2021; a political system which makes it difficult for women, migrants and community interests to engage and be an active part of that system; vested interests taking prominence over public interests; endless corruption, media manipulations, mismanagement; a hostile mainstream media which seems to be more intent on holding the public to account, rather the federal government.

It has been said that a government should "never let a good crisis go to waste" but it's often forgotten that these are words from British Prime Minister, Winston Churchill, mentioned towards the end of World War II. It took many years for the changes implemented at this time—the Bretton Woods agreement, the International Bank for Reconstruction and Development, the International Monetary Fund, as well the creation of the United Nations—to come to full fruition in the latter part of the 1950s and the 1960s. The leadership towards the end of World War II comprised Churchill, Franklin Roosevelt, John Curtin, among many others around the world. In comparison, during 2020, the world leadership comprised Boris

Johnson, Donald Trump and Scott Morrison. Trump has departed the scene—for the time being—but the leadership of Johnson and Morrison remains.

An opportunity to reform world economics and communities—or, at least, install the first building blocks of change—was missed during 2020 but that's not to suggest the opportunity has been lost forever. Finding the right vaccines was critical in reducing the impact of the coronavirus all around the world and, through human endeavour, those vaccines were found.

The French philosopher, Henri Bergson, believed solutions to all of the problems in society do exist; the issue for humanity is how to find those solutions. The same resolution is evident in the political sphere: the solutions to the many problems that exist in Australia's political system are there and available.

It's just a matter of choosing the right kind of leadership that can find and implement those solutions.

April 2021

Corruption as the new normal in federal politics

11 February

Most of Australia has been hibernating through the holiday period but politics, just like rust, never sleeps and there were reports during the break that the Prime Minister's 2019 election victory wasn't as miraculous as he claimed, with much of the credit going to two sports funding programs worth a quarter of a billion dollars—programs used as a cash splash on marginal and Coalition-held seats.

The two programs—the Community Sport Infrastructure program worth $100 million, and the little-known Female Facilities and Water Safety Stream program worth $150 million—used no guidelines, there was no tender application process, no forms and, essentially, were slush funds used for political purposes.

Since its inception in August 2018, the Morrison government has quickly become one of the most secretive governments in federal history, and it's also a government where very few of its members take responsibility for their actions, an unacceptable situation for a country based upon openness and democratic principles. Democracy needs transparency. Ultimately, the voters decide which political party will form government and the voters cannot do this effectively if they're not properly informed. Democracy is built on pillars of honesty, of transparency, and the communication of fairness. Some of these concepts are malleable, depending on who is in office, and the concept of democracy will be different to different people.

The Australian federal system has existed for almost 120 years, most of these years have seen open, honest and diligent governments—that's not to suggest there was a golden age of democratic propriety before September 2013 when the current Liberal–National Government returned to office, but it does seem democratic practices have been reduced and corruption in government has become significantly worse.

Governments of all persuasions will use incumbency and many programs and projects to gain political advantage—that's the nature of politics, and the electorate has come to expect that. But it becomes a problem for the political system if the electorate accepts that all sides of politics will engage in this behaviour and excusing the practice in this way means corrupt behaviours will continue.

A similar event occurred during the infamous 'white board' affair in 1993, where the Labor Minister for Sport at the time, Ros Kelly, allocated $30 million of sports and recreational grants towards marginal seats, and the only 'documentation' that existed was a list of grant allocations drawn up on a large white board in her parliamentary office. Kelly did resign as minister and then left Parliament altogether. That incident was twenty-seven years ago but even taking inflation into account, this modern-day event is far more scandalous. The government can't just keep pushing the message that all sides of politics engage in this kind of behaviour, and the allocation of $250 million from these two programs needs to be investigated.

In Kelly's case, all of the allocations of funds to marginal seats came from within her own department, based on her own actions. In the 'sports rorts' affair, it has been overt and all the evidence points to the Prime Minister's office being involved. And in both cases, the question is: why would they act in this way? To gain political advantage and to maintain their position in government is the primary reason.

It was right for Kelly to resign and leave Parliament in the 1990s; these actions should not be tolerated in any form. But it's now becoming more evident that this kind of behaviour is becoming more tolerated by government and the media: blatant favouring of safe Coalition seats and swinging seats. Some of the arguments put forward by the government have also been ridiculous, suggesting that because the seats of Mayo in South Australia and Warringah in New South Wales didn't return a Liberal member of Parliament, this was the evidence to prove the rorting didn't actually occur.

In those seats, the Liberal Party candidates, Georgina Downer and Tony Abbott respectively, could have walked around handing out $50,000 cheques to every voter and they still wouldn't have won in those two seats. They were very close seats, and it was only a handful of seats in the final election result anyway. No safe or even moderately swinging Labor seat received a grant, which is appalling: the government of the day is meant to govern for every member of the community, not just the people who voted for it.

In the seat of Mayo during the 2019 election campaign, Downer was announcing and handing out large celebrity cheques of $127,000 to local bowling clubs, even though she wasn't the local member of Parliament for that seat: she was only the candidate. Her rival in Mayo, the sitting member Rebekha Sharkie, asked the Australian National Audit Office to investigate the Community Sport Infrastructure fund, and that's what uncovered this scandal.

ANAO found that the entire fund was open to corruption, was corrupt and that there was a lack of correct documentation. The Office also suggested the application of both funds were possibly illegal and found that so many of the funded programs were either ineligible or not worthy for consideration.

The ANAO response was scathing, but Scott Morrison decided to ignore that report and commissioned the Secretary of Prime Minister and Cabinet Philip Gaetjens, a long-term Liberal Party apparatchik and insider, to do his own investigations, which did find the Minister responsible for the funding, Victoria Senator Bridget McKenzie, breached parliamentary standards on a 'technicality' but completely exonerated the government. The government made a decision to hide this report, so the contents are not in the public domain: a government that decides to hide reports to cover up mismanagement of funds and other misbehaviours is not acting in the public interest.

If the report was thorough and clear, why wouldn't the government release it? The fact that they haven't released a report suggests that there isn't a report to release, and Gaetjens reputation has been used and discarded to follow the government line. But the final result is the Minister for Sports, Bridget McKenzie, has been forced to resign on a 'technical issue' of providing a grant to a gun club that she was actually a member of. It's more obvious, however, that she was sacrificed to stop the government bleeding on this issue and to also to stop the track leading all the way back up the Office of Prime Minister and Cabinet and the Liberal Party election campaign team, which is where all of these decisions would have been made in the lead-up to the 2019 federal election.

It's difficult to accept a Senator from Victoria would have been able to know which marginal seats should be pork-barrelled in Western Australia or New South Wales, without gaining the knowledge from a central campaign office. And it's also difficult to accept the Prime Minister would not have been involved in the allocations of these grants.

There is a clear link between government grants from these two funding programs and key marginal seats. And during the 2019 election campaign, Morrison toured every one of those marginal seats, close to the time these funding allocations were announced. There's also a clear link between the misappropriation of funds within this community sport infrastructure program and the Prime Minister's office, and his own seat of Cook in the Sutherland Shire.

In the Shire, local soccer clubs commenced building new facilities before the grant had been announced—having the Prime Minister as the local member in this electorate provides many advantages, especially when compared to the humble backbencher. But it's not a good look politically, and the management of this $100 million fund is concerning.

But that was a model of excellence compared to the other program caught up in this scandal—the female facilities and water safety stream program awarded close to $150 million in the lead up to the 2019 election campaign. It was a relatively unknown program, without guidelines, tendering protocols or application forms.

In some cases, the recipients of these grants—some were up to $20 million—only found out they had been awarded the funds through the media, or through a social media announcement made by the local Liberal Party candidate. In other cases, funds were awarded to local government areas where the money or projects were not wanted, or to organisations who were unaware of the fund, or the fact that they were even eligible.

$120 million of that $150 million fund went to the building of fourteen public swimming pools, all in Coalition-held seats or in highly marginal seats. There were no checks and balances. There was no indication as to whether these were valuable or worthy community projects. This was akin to an open-ended slush fund where Liberal Party candidates—whether they were sitting members of Parliament or not—could nominate whichever project in whichever area fitted into the electoral demands of the Liberal Party.

This is not to disparage the notion of local pools and government funding into community resources, but it does become a question of applying limited resources to the areas and regions that need them the most. In some less affluent areas, there are communities where their sports facilities are either non-existent or rudimentary, soccer fields that easily flood and become unplayable. In another region, there's an ice rink that also acts as a community hub and a meeting place for teenagers that's in a state of total disrepair. But these are in safe Labor seats and if these organisations applied for funding—if they'd somehow found out about the existence of these funds—they wouldn't have received funding anyway.

Basketball courts, skateboarding parks: all of these facilities used by the community, along with other shared facilities such as community halls or senior citizen centres, should be funded fairly on a needs basis. Is the $50 million funding of the Mosman Yacht Club, in one of the most affluents areas in Sydney, of more value to the community than the much-need overhaul of a football park in a downtrodden part of inner city Fitzroy in Melbourne? Many people would suggest this is inequitable and, without any guidelines to compare different projects in different areas around the country, it's fair to say that these were projects that were addressed on partisan political needs.

In addition to the total of $250 million in these two sports-related funds, there was also a $200 million regional jobs and investment scheme available to government ministers to allocate prior to the 2019 federal election. Within this fund, there were twelve projects deemed to be ineligible—at least this project did contain guidelines—

and of course, all of these funded projects were awarded in highly marginal states. There was also a Liberal Party donor—Nolan Meats—which received a $5.5 million job and investment grant, even though the organisation was deemed ineligible by both the infrastructure department, and the ANAO.[1]

Close to half a billion dollars within three programs, for ministers and Coalition backbenchers to allocate towards their own political needs. It's evident that with the expectation the Coalition was likely to the lose the 2019 election, outgoing members were keen to deliver government funding to as many of their friends in the electorate as possible. And if the Coalition ended up winning the election—which is what they achieved with the undoubted support of these pork-barrelling programs—it would have been considered a bonus.

Much of this funding was allocated to some of the most affluent parts of Australia, many of which were not needed or even asked for, while other areas which needed the funding the most, went without. A better system for allocating these funds needs to be found, one without whim or the interference of ministers or backbenchers in from government. But it's also obvious reforms to these processes won't be coming from the current government, the main beneficiary of these corrupted processes.

*

---

1 *The Guardian*, 11 February 2020, 'Coalition donor received $5.5m grant despite potentially being ineligible'. https://www.theguardian.com/australia-news/2020/feb/11/coalition-donor-received-55m-grant-despite-potentially-being-ineligible

Continuing politicisation of the Australian Federal Police

11 February

A few weeks after he became Labor leader in 2019, Anthony Albanese claimed he hadn't seen any corruption during his time in politics—and he's been in federal politics since 1996—he was ridiculed for the comment at the time, but he might be a little bit too close to the action to see this, because anyone can see from any far-away vantage point that political corruption is rife in Canberra and barely a day goes by where there isn't news about another government minister involved in some kind of malpractice that would generally land anyone else outside of politics in jail.

This time, the corruption seems to involve the Australian Federal Police, and their decision to drop the forgery case against the error prone, ineffective and incompetent Minister for Energy and Emissions Reduction, Angus Taylor.

The allegations of forgery relate to the incident in September 2019, where Taylor leaked a forged annual report of the Sydney City Council to the *Daily Telegraph*, claiming the Council expenses for overseas travel was $15.9 million, when it was actually only a small fraction of this amount. Taylor's actions were intended to humiliate the Lord Mayor of Sydney, Clover Moore, and highlight a hypocrisy on demands for climate change action, while expending so many funds on carbon-intensive international air flights. The problem for Taylor was: it wasn't actually true.

Here we have a federal minister releasing forged documents into the public domain to attack a political opponent at a local government level, and a Liberal Party staffer—Josh Manuatu—who has publicly admitted to obtaining the documents, yet the Australian Federal Police suggested there is no case to answer. It's a potential criminal case where there is a culprit, evidence, a victim, criminal intent, and at least two people who are part of a conspiracy, yet the law enforcement agency is essentially saying: move on, nothing to see here. There are many parts of this incident that don't add up.

Democracy can be a discussion point about all those lofty principles that need to exist at the apex of the system—politics and law enforcement—but the heart of the democratic system needs to be based on trust. There needs to be honest law enforcement, and there also needs to be good and enforceable laws. The Shadow Minister for Education, Tanya Plibersek, was recently criticised for suggesting schoolchildren should recite the national pledge, part of which included the words 'law abiding', something which the early Labor members at the time of federation were not, when they were protesting against laws which made unionism illegal.

But, essentially, her message was clear: democracy needs to be built on good and just laws and underneath that, there needs to be a trust that the institutions are working in the best interests for most people, whether the institution is that of the prime minister, the Parliament, the court system, government departments, the police or judicial systems. These are the institutions that need to be completely unimpeachable.

And, of course, this is a difficult process—maintaining democratic institutions is onerous and tedious but is essential for the good workings of a community. The American crime novelist, Raymond Chandler, suggested the problem with policing and law enforcement is that a community needs to attract the best people for these roles, but there's not too much in it for these "best people", so "we have to work with what we get". Most serving police and law enforcement officers are hard-working and law-abiding and have very difficult tasks and work to carry out. But a corrupt police force is a real threat to democracy.

The police forces in Queensland and New South Wales in the 1970s and 1980s; the police forces in Victoria and Western Australia in the 1970s through to the 1990s—all were found through state-based corruption inquiries to have substantial elements of corruption within their ranks. At the time, this was deemed to be a serious problem for democratic governments and the judiciaries. At the federal level, the Australian Federal Police since 1917 (as the Commonwealth Police) has had a cozy relationship with federal governments but even more so since 2013, when the Liberal–National Coalition returned to office. This hand-in-glove relationship was highlighted when the Prime Minister at the time, Tony Abbott, preferred to reside onsite at the Australian Federal Police barracks in Canberra, which was not a good look, and a reminder of the tin-pot banana republics of South America, rather than an open and robust democratic system.

Police forces, whether it be at a state or federal level, should be able to arrest and prosecute a case against any citizen who has broken a law, whether that be a citizen at the lower echelons, or a prime minister, or a minister of the Crown. And above all, the actions of law should be seen to be impartial and fair and, it seems that in the case of Taylor, these principles have not been applied.

The subject of these attacks by Taylor, Clover Moore, believed the incident had a corrosive effect on democracy:[2]

> "I think there's tremendous harm and I think it's about standards of ministers and standards of what the public expect of their ministers on. For them [the Australian Federal Police] to think there's no harm there, I think is extraordinary. And they seem to be happy to go after journalists, but to not investigate where this originated. It came out of his [Taylor's] office, signed by him, crossed out the 'Lord Mayor' and wrote 'Clover', signed it 'Angus Taylor,' with this outrageous allegation.
>
> No response from Sussan Ley [Minister for the Environment] at all over all of this time. And for the AFP to say: 'we're not going to investigate further, we don't think it's important,' I think it's a real failure in their processes. And I think people will question their *modus operandi*—'really? Why do they go after some things, not others.' Some people seem to think that they're

---

2   ABC News, 'Clover Moore says AFP decision disappointing, but not surprising', 7 February 2020. https://youtu.be/hw7NYst09Fk

pleasing their political masters. And I have no evidence of that but that's what it's looking like."

The original case of forgery was presented by the Labor Party to NSW Police, which is another clearly politicised entity, and they passed the case onto the Australian Federal Police. The result from their investigation was a short media statement, where they claimed there was a low level of harm, and the case was not worth pursuing. But there was a high level of harm to the political reputation of Clover Moore, and there was a high level of harm to the fabric of the political system and democratic ethics and practices.

There were no details released about whom the Australian Federal Police actually spoke with during their investigation, or any evidence they collated. Therefore, it's not possible to know whether they questioned the other player in this act of forgery, Josh Manuatu. Manuatu is a former president of the Young Liberals, considered to be a rising star within the federal Liberal Party and was previously adviser to Liberal Party Senator for Tasmania, Eric Abetz. During the police investigation, Manuatu was shafted off to Canberra, where he became the campaign director of the Canberra Liberals, and was allocated to a new minister within a different portfolio.

It's quite a bizarre scenario where official documents have been doctored and presented to the public as fact by a federal government minister—an official crime—a political operative has admitted obtaining the doctored documents, before being shunted away and out of the limelight, and no further questions have been asked about where the doctored documents originated from, who altered the documents, and why they were used to attack a political opponent.

NSW Police have suggested it's unclear whether this incident is a federal or state matter but have also implied they have other more important issues to deal with—serious crime—and to continue pursuing the case would take away resources from these other important matters they need to deal with. But this incident is also an important issue.

If there is a precedent where federal ministers can fabricate official documents and place them in the public domain without any sanction, why wouldn't they attempt it a second time? It's a clear case of police interfering with the course of justice and encouraging continued corruption within government, and a clear case of the respective state and federal police forces being too close to the Liberal Party, and the behaviours of these organisations suggest there is a strong case of corruption here.

Obviously, police officers as private citizens are allowed to have their own political views and perspectives. Some will vote for the Liberal Party; some will vote for the Labor Party: Australian Greens; National Party, or One Nation, and some will be apolitical—in other words, a political reflection of the rest of the community. And provided their personal political views do not impinge upon the proper performance of their duty, this is perfectly acceptable.

But it seems the political beliefs of some members of the Australian Federal Police and NSW Police, especially senior members in the upper reach of management, are preventing the proper performance of policing duties. It might not be personal political ideology driving these issues, but the politicised public service acting under the threat of a soft kind of blackmail, in terms of contracts not being extended, deserved promotions not made and senior positions awarded to those who do the 'right thing' by the government of the day.

It could actually be a case where the Australian Federal Police and NSW Police have realised that too many resources and funding may be put into an investigation that will ultimately be fruitless, and the possibility that everyone involved is somehow genuinely innocent and it was a cluster of bureaucratic bungles that resulted in fabricated figures, rather than a conspiracy. But that's highly unlikely and at the heart of this issue is a complete lack of transparency by all the parties concerned, and final decisions that have been favourable to both the federal government and the NSW Government.

And the cloak of secrecy, where the final decisions seems to favour the government of the day is the antithesis of a normal functioning democracy, where government needs to be held at arms' length from the police forces. There have been raids on union offices, in particular, the CFMEU, where investigations found nothing. There were also raids on the homes of journalists to investigate leaks coming out of the Department of Home Affairs, inspecting the underwear and personal items of journalists.

Aside from the fact the Australian Federal Police shouldn't be involved in these types of activities, these are actions taken to protect the government, or produce results that are favourable to the government, and actions not taken that may result to unfavourable results or embarrassment to the government. That is not a case of justice being served or being seen to be served and these actions are proof that the Australian political system is moving dangerously close to some fairly distasteful political systems from other countries that Australian governments have been highly critical of in the past.

There have been historical precedents for this type of government-sanctioned action, but they have been few and far between. The Menzies government arrested two journalists from the *Bankstown Observer*, Ray Fitzpatrick and Frank Browne, in 1955 over the right of privilege of the Australian Parliament and freedom of speech issues.[3] The Menzies government acted in this way once in sixteen years, which is not to excuse it or to suggest it was the correct course of action, but it's an action that has become more frequent and politically biased in more recent times.

The Abbott–Turnbull–Morrison governments have a higher rate of these actions that any other government. Whether a minister forged these official documents or whether a political staffer or someone else provided that document to the minister is immaterial. Although some have argued that within the big picture, this is really not a big issue and it's time to move on to the more substantive issues, but if all issues are placed within this concept of the 'bigger picture', then nothing in political life matters, and political corruption will be allowed to continue. These are all important issues for many people outside of the political system, if the system is to hold the confidence of the people within the electorate.

The upshot is that if an official and public document has been forged and placed into the public domain to attack a political opponent, it's up to the legal and law enforcement fraternity to decide whether a crime has been committed or not, not the political establishment. That is one important factor: but the biggest issue of all is there have been no consequences, and no responsibility for an illegal act has been taken by anybody.

Corruption exists when the mechanisms in place to combat corruption are either too weak to enforce, or don't exist in the first instance. And the recent behaviours of federal ministers also helps to

---

[3] Australian Parliament House, 'Fitzpatrick and Browne after 60 Years'. https://www.aph.gov.au/About_Parliament/Senate/Powers_practice_n_procedures/pops/pop64/c01

explain why the federal government has been so lax in implementing a permanent national crime and corruption commission. It was promised by Morrison in November 2018, and eighteen months later, the public is still waiting for it to arrive.

The initial iteration of the New South Wales Independent Commission Against Corruption in 1989 is the model the federal government should look to. It was established by one of the better Attorneys–General of New South Wales, John Dowd, and modelled on the Hong Kong ICAC. But since the time it was initiated by the Liberal–National Greiner government, it has been curtailed by successive governments once their own members started being found in breach of the regulations on corruption. More recently, the NSW Berejiklian government created a shortfall of $3.94 million to the ICAC operational budget. Combating corruption takes up resources and costs money, and the obvious result from funding cutbacks to a crime and corruption commission is that less crime and corruption will be uncovered. It's an unacceptable situation.

And this is not the type of crime and corruption commission the federal government would want to see implemented on the national level which, at the state level, ended the political careers of two Liberal Premiers; Nick Greiner in 1992, and Barry O'Farrell in 2014. If a national crime commission was created with the same powers as the NSW ICAC, Angus Taylor would be one of the first Parliamentarians to be forced out of office. The member for New England, Barnaby Joyce, would follow soon after. The Minister for Sports, Bridget McKenzie, would definitely have been forced to resign, not just from her position, but from Parliament as well. Even the Prime Minister, Scott Morrison, probably wouldn't last long if a national crime and corruption commission was allowed to investigate his involvement in the 'sports rorts' affair, or even if they went back further to investigate his malfeasance during his time as the managing director of Tourism Australia.

The 'problem' of the New South Wales ICAC was that it was a very well-funded body, part of an election promise by Greiner, who won the 1988 election for the Liberal Party. It was doing its job too well and found that Greiner was guilty of corruption in offering a Liberal-turned-independent member, Terry Metherell, an executive position at the Environmental Protection Authority, in exchange for leaving Parliament. A Court of Appeal did overturn the ICAC's finding of corruption, but the damage had already been done to Greiner, having already vacated Parliament. And the Liberal Party has never forgiven the ICAC for this finding, even though it was a body they initially created, and offers further explanation for their reluctance to create such a body at a federal level.

If a national commission of crime and corruption is created by this federal government, based on historical evidence, it would prefer to see a neutered body with low levels of funding and fewer powers, than the 1989 model of the New South Wales ICAC. But the public is demanding a body on a federal level that does have authority, rather than a paper tiger that is purely for show, takes no action against political friends, or decides to drop investigations when it's politically convenient for the government of the day for problems to just disappear. This would go a long way to restoring confidence in the political system, where justice is not only being seen to be done but acted upon in an open and transparent manner, with the requisite independence.

*

Reforming Australian politics and improving democracy

11 February

With trust in the political system at an all-time low, not just in Australia, but across most of the democratic world, it's important to look at all the ways the political system can be improved to reverse this decline of public trust. Some on the fringes of the community have asked the question: how many people are needed to start a revolution, but that might be taking the process too far. By the way, it's not so much a fixed number, but according to Occupy activists, there are six *types* of people needed to change a society: activists, intellectuals, artists, insiders, supportive elites, the masses.[4] That seems to cover just about everyone, except for the most obvious: control of the military and armed forces but, as it's unlikely for this scenario to develop, it's best to focus on smaller achievable goals—reforming Parliament Question Time, although achieving this small task is almost as difficult as implementing a revolution.

It might not be apparent to the electorate, but Parliament Question Time is at the apex of political accountability in the Westminster system of politics and it's no coincidence that the fall in political standards can be directly attributable to the decline in the standards of Question Time.

---

4   *Alternet*, '6 People You Need to Start a Revolution', Sara Robinson, 2012. https://www.alternet.org/2012/04/6_people_you_need_to_start_a_revolution

It wasn't so long ago that Question Time could provide to the general viewer, a reasonable understanding of the events in federal politics, and an opportunity to see the issues of the day scrutinised by other members of Parliament, but it has descended into the theatre of irrelevancy, obfuscation, political point scoring, grandstanding and political spin.

Historically, Question Time has been the focus of the ideological differences between the major parties, and produced moments of classic political theatre, and a reminder of this occurred during the battles between former Prime Minister, Paul Keating, and his opponent in the early 1990s, the Liberal Party Leader of the Opposition, John Hewson:[5]

> **John Hewson:** I refer the Prime Minister to his hopeless attack on Fightback! at the Press Club today...
>
> [Government members interjecting...]
>
> **Speaker:** Order! The Leader will get to the question.
>
> **Hewson:** I ask the Prime Minister: if you are so confident about your view of Fightback!, why will you not call an early election?
>
> **Opposition members:** Resign! Resign!
>
> **Speaker:** Order!
>
> **Paul Keating:** The answer is, mate, because I want to do...you... slowly. There has to be a bit of sport in this for all of us. In the psychological battle stakes, we are stripped down and ready to go. I want to see those ashen-faced performances; I want more of them. I want to be encouraged. I want to see you squirm out of this load of rubbish over a number of months. There will be no easy execution for you. You have perpetrated one of the great mischiefs on the Australian public with this thing, trying to rip away our social wage, trying to rip away the Australian values which we built in our society for over a century.

---

5   Parliament of Australia, Hansard, 15 September 1992.
    https://parlinfo.aph.gov.au/parlInfo/search/display/display.
    w3p;adv=yes;orderBy=customrank;page=0;query=%22do%20you%20slowly%22%20
    Dataset:hansardr,hansardr80;rec=3;resCount=Default

Hewson interjecting...

Speaker: The Leader of the Opposition!

Keating: If you think I am going to put you out of your misery quickly, you can think again.

A probing opposition or, sometimes, a probing government backbencher worried about a concern in their seat or a genuine concern highlighted by one of their constituents, asking government ministers difficult questions and receiving pertinent and correct answers and, if they are unable to answer them during Question Time, putting them on notice: that's the essence of Question Time and parliamentary scrutiny.

But the Question Time of today, questions are barely answered, quite often given short shrift or ridiculed by the government, and the issues raised are never revisited. There was a time when political aficionados would watch Question Time from beginning to end, and be quite annoyed when the allocated one hour of time expired. Nowadays, it's difficult to gain a sense of the overall strategy from either side; it's ineffective, it's missing the flow of debate, the cadence and cleverness of speech, it's irrelevant. More importantly, it's missing that opportunity for accountability and scrutiny of government actions and performances.

Question Time has been a formal part of the Australian Parliament since the 1960s and it needs reform quickly if public confidence is to be restored in the institution of Parliament. But where would be the best place to start? The wider part is a more educative process and providing an education for how government actually works and, alongside this, reforms to the mainstream media, which is how many people receive their political news and information. The other factor which not much can be really done about is there are very few good parliamentary speakers who can stand up, provide a concise and honest answer, revealing as much information as possible, without incriminating or creating problems for the government. That is a fine balance that requires a delicate skill and perhaps it's a case where public speakers of this kind no longer exist.

There have been some suggestions that a great improvement to the Parliament would be the appointment of an independent Speaker of the House, similar to the appointment made in the British House of Commons. In Australian politics, the Speaker of the House is provided by the party of government and, of course, they will side with the government and makes rulings that favour the government.

The former Liberal Party member of Parliament, Bronwyn Bishop, became the Speaker of the House in 2013 and proceeded to act as one of the most partisan speakers in Australian history. She also breached protocols by sitting in the Liberal Party room meetings and the standards of Parliament improved once she was forced to resign over the misuse of parliamentary entitlement spending. The current speaker, Tony Smith, is a marginally better manager of Parliament, but he's still a highly partisan political player.

An incumbent government providing the Speaker of the House from their own party is not a formal rule, it's only a protocol, and a rule that could easily be amended. In the British Parliament, the appointed Speaker of the House is obliged to shed their political party membership and relinquish all formal ties with not just the incumbent government party, but any political party at all. The other point about the British independent Speaker of the House is that it's usually the crowning to a distinguished political career for a second tier, but prominent parliamentarian.

There have only been two independent Speakers of the House in federal parliament: Frederick Holder, who resigned from the Free Trade Party upon his appointment in 1901; and Peter Slipper, who was appointed by Labor Prime Minister Julia Gillard in 2011, and resigned from the Liberal Party upon his appointment.

Littleton Groom fashioned himself as an 'independent' speaker in the 1920s, even though he was a member of the Nationalist Party government. His refusal to use his tie-breaking vote on a Bill that would end federal government involvement in conciliation and arbitration processes, led to the collapse of the government, triggering the 1929 election, an election which saw the Prime Minister, Stanley Bruce, lose government, as well as his own seat. But aside from these few examples, federal Parliament had been managed by highly partisan Speakers of the House.

One other critical reform is to end the technique of 'Dorothy Dix' questions, where backbenchers ask their own side of politics, usually the government, a favourable question that is then used to attack the opposition. Any member of Parliament has a right to ask any other a question of scrutiny, but it's both a painful and predictable form of parliamentary tactic, a ridiculous practice and shows a distinct contempt for all of Parliament.

> "Thank you, Mr Speaker. My question is for the Minister for Home Affairs. Will the Minister update the house on steps the government is taking to keep the Australian community safe from the threat of terrorism…"

> "My question is to the Prime Minister: Will the Prime Minister advise how the government is getting on with the job of supporting all Australians to realise their aspirations to secure their future…"

> "Will the Prime Minister update the House on further action the government has taken this week to deliver on its priorities…"

> "Will the Minister outline to the House how the Morrison government is backing Australian women who choose to have more choices about how they live their lives…"

> "Will the Deputy Prime Minister update the House on the actions being taken to deliver the government's $100 billion infrastructure program…"

> "Will the Prime Minister kindly outline to the House how the government is getting on with the job of delivering its plan to keep Australia safe and secure…"

> "Can the Treasurer update the House on how the Morrison government's certain and stable fiscal management will keep our economy resilient in the face of future challenges…"

> "Will the Minister update the House on the Morrison government's approach to setting and meeting our consistent and responsible emissions reduction targets…"

> "My question to the Minister for Industrial Relations: Will the minister inform the House of the contributions made by militant unions to political parties in recent years. Is the Minister concerned that law breaking unions are funding the activities of political parties…"

These are all real questions offered in Question Time that have been drawn up in the parliamentary tactics room, provided to government backbenchers, who then proceed to take turns to ask these questions of the Prime Minister and other senior ministers. There is no accountability, it's a process purely used to promote and spruik the performances of the government, results in vainglorious speeches, and used to leverage attacks against the opposition. These are not questions of inquiry; they are a complete bastardisation of Parliament and designed to avoid scrutiny.

If 'Dorothy Dix' were no longer permitted by the Speaker of the House, or if a ruling was introduced to bar questions asked of the same side of politics, there would be a major improvement in the quality of Question Time and, as a result, the performance of Parliament. Of course, it's naïve to suggest this would be the sole solution to a decaying Parliament, as it's only human nature for a government to debauch the initiation of better processes, and swing them towards its own advantage. But it would be a start.

Another key reform for consideration is introducing questions from the community. There have been some rebuttals to this idea, on the basis that members of Parliament are meant to ask questions that are presented to them by the community anyway, but involving the community directly into Parliament would offer a new way for the electorate to engage in the political process. But whatever reforms are introduced, it's evident that all sides of politics would need to give something up to achieve a better system and, with the way the current system is managed, that's a very unlikely outcome.

A more likely driver of change is the combination of a large and strong crossbench, and a hung Parliament, where a minority government would be held hostage to changes requested by these crossbenchers. But given that federal Parliament has only seen a minority government on two occasions since 1940—2010 to 2013, and 2018 to 2019—these opportunities are minimal, although it has to be remembered the current Morrison government only holds office by one seat. One byelection loss during this parliamentary term, and the government slides back into a minority position.

The first day of Parliament for 2020

One issue that can never be underestimated is the ability for the National Party, to create problems for its senior Coalition partner, the Liberal Party. It was the first day of the 2020 parliamentary year, and it was a day set aside to commemorate the victims from the recent bushfire season, which claimed thirty-four lives, destroyed over eighteen million hectares of land, and caused over $100 billion of fire-related damage. But the member for New England, Barnaby Joyce, decided to display his tin-ear to the sufferings of the Australian community and thought this was the best day to launch a leadership challenge against the incumbent, Michael McCormack.

If Joyce is considered a viable leadership contender for the National Party—and by virtue of the Coalition agreement, becoming the Deputy Prime Minister—there is something very wrong with the National Party, but it also highlights the ineffectiveness of the current leader.

Aside from the paucity of intellect or lack of understandings of community concerns shown by the National Party, the heart of all of these issues and as a backdrop for Parliament in Canberra—both literally and metaphorically—is climate change.

Climate change was a massive issue during the 2019 holiday break and didn't drop off as a serious agenda item leading into 2020, although there have been some concerns developing internationally, with a serious outbreak of a coronavirus in the Chinese city of Wuhan. But with the smoke now starting to dissipate from many Australian cities, it may reduce some of the pressure on the federal government, although it will continue to affect politics in different ways. It's an issue splitting the National Party and there is the so-called 'modern' Liberals group that is calling for climate change as an issue that needs to be addressed effectively, at odds with the more conservative factions of the Liberal Party.

The Labor Party also has its pro-coal lobbyists, such as Joel Fitzgibbon and Richard Marles, and it seems that in the management of divergent viewpoints with Labor, the Leader of the Opposition, Anthony Albanese, is in a similarly invidious position British Labour leader Jeremy Corbyn found himself on Brexit—'leave' people in the north of England and Labor remainers in the south of England, where good compromises were made by Corbyn, which simply weren't taken up by the rest of the electorate, something which was replicated by Bill Shorten with the issue of coal during the 2019 Australian election campaign.

There is a distinct schism, politically at least, in the mining states of Western Australia and Queensland. Within these two states, Labor only holds eleven of the forty-six federal seats, whereas in the rest of Australia, it holds fifty-seven seats of the remaining 105. It's obvious, albeit a rather simplistic approach, but making up significant ground in the states of Queensland and Western Australia, while holding seats in other areas, is Labor's clearest pathway back into office. It needs to develop strategies and policies that attracts people in those mining communities but, at the same time, doesn't alienate those people who don't live in those mining communities. But it's a difficult task that lies ahead for Labor.

Morrison also has similar problems in trying to bridge that gap in the more progressive parts of Australia, but as the incumbent, he doesn't need to make up ground, he simply needs to hold ground, and this makes it a problem for Labor to resolve, not the Liberal–National Coalition.

*

The coronavirus appears: How will it affect the economy?

12 March

Unless people have been hiding in a petri dish, everyone would have heard about the coronavirus that has now been found in over 100 countries around the world, prompting the World Health Organization to define the outbreak as a pandemic.[6]

There hasn't been a run on the banks yet, but in scenes reminiscent of *The Walking Dead*, there has been a run on toilet paper and essential supplies in many supermarkets, and facemasks have become the most common bodywear in many cities.

It is a real national health crisis and great care does need to be taken, but it's fast becoming an economic issue and a political headache for the federal government. The Prime Minister, Scott Morrison, was the one who announced a Budget surplus in the lead-up to the 2019 election and claimed superior Liberal Party economic management would be able to withstand any external influences.

The economy was facing problems before the onset of the bushfire season and the coronavirus, and it's likely Morrison will end up having the recession former Prime Minister Kevin Rudd managed to avoid during the global financial crisis in 2008. What will the economic result be for this government? A Budget surplus and a

---

6 World Health Organization, 'WHO announces COVID-19 outbreak a pandemic, March 2020. https://www.euro.who.int/en/health-topics/health-emergencies/coronavirus-covid-19/news/news/2020/3/who-announces-covid-19-outbreak-a-pandemic

recession, or a budget deficit that at least holds up the economy and averts an economic collapse?

For many years, the Liberal Party pointed out how the Rudd government made mistakes in its stimulus program during the global financial crisis, without ever articulating what these mistakes actually were. But the global financial crisis was never fully comprehended in Australia, because the main effects of it largely bypassed the local economy. The directive from the Secretary of the Department of the Treasury at the time, Ken Henry, was to 'go hard, go early, and go households' and, as history has shown, it was the correct course of economic action.

Australia was one of four developed economies to avoid a recession during the global financial crisis, along with Israel, Poland and South Korea.[7] Other economies around the world were almost destroyed, such as the Greek economy, and bankers in Iceland were actually sent to jail. Britain hasn't fully recovered and with its exit from the European Union, will take many more years to stabilise its economy. The United States economy, in so many ways, is still recovering from the global financial crisis. Despite the public clamourings made by the Liberal Party, Australia performed very well at that time and if there are counter arguments to this, it's always best to analyse the facts and figures, rather than bending towards uninformed opinion.

The Abbott, Turnbull and Morrison governments all prided themselves on being better economic managers and their measure for better economic management was focused on producing a surplus. In economic terms and national management of the economy, either a surplus or deficit is not relevant: it's more a question of which areas the finances are spent on and whether a surplus or a deficit fits into the economic circumstances of the time. But the Coalition government has defined its success on delivering a Budget surplus, and that's what it needs to be judged on. The political messaging at the time from the Treasurer, Josh Frydenberg, was a Budget surplus would be delivered, irrespective of the circumstances, and irrespective of the 'global headwinds' he kept on referring to.

And, of course, it would be churlish to not accept the catastrophic effects of the recent bushfire season, as well as any effects that may

---

7   Eurostat Conference, European Commission, The Accounts of Society National Accounts at the Service of Economic and Monetary Policy Making, 2014.

arise from the impending coronavirus outbreak, but a government that made a virtue of delivering a Budget surplus, as well as gaining substantial political benefit from this virtue, can't just turn around and point to excuses for its poor economic management.

Morrison is mindful of the harsh and incessant political criticisms made by the Liberal Party opposition during the global financial crisis, and has tried to differentiate the economic decisions his government is making today, even though they will be identical to the policies Labor implemented in 2008. At the beginning of the global financial crisis, Labor released an immediate stimulus package which sent $10 billion directly into pensions and middle-income families. And, of course, this is exactly what the Liberal Party has initiated now, because that is what the economic circumstances of the time require.

Labor went one step further at the time, where several months later, they released a package of $42 billion, which included the Building the Education Revolution program, the home insulation scheme, further one-off payments to families, as well as small business tax breaks. But the Liberal Party during this time in 2008 and 2009, pilloried Labor and then spent the best part of the next decade arguing how Labor completed wasted its stimulus spending, and how they initiated a course of action unrequired by the electorate and by the economy. The evidence suggests otherwise but in 2020, the Liberal–National Coalition is following exactly the same course of action as Kevin Rudd back in 2008. Why? Because the economic circumstances of the time require a great deal of government intervention within the economy, and clinging to the Coalition's neoliberalist ideals of low government spending would have destroyed the Australian economy.

Morrison and Frydenberg have been choosing their terminology very careful, using the terms 'support package', rather than 'stimulus', and avoiding all references to Budget surplus, even though it's the phrase Morrison was shouting from the rooftops in the lead-up to the 2019 election:[8]

---

8   Parliament of Australia, Scott Morrison media conference, 27 November 2018. https://parlinfo.aph.gov.au/parlInfo/search/display/display.w3p;query=Id%3A%22emms%2Fbroadcast%2F834352%22;src1=sm1

> **Morrison:** "What I'm here today to announce is that, before we go to the next election, we will be handing down a budget and it will be a surplus budget. It will be a budget which is the product of the years of hard work of our government, of successive treasurers and prime ministers, that has ensured that we have stayed on track to deliver a balanced budget, a surplus budget, which is what we promised the Australian people we would do. It is absolutely our intention to have the Budget before the election and to deliver a surplus budget—a surplus budget that we promised we would deliver; a surplus budget that we will deliver and only a Coalition government would have been able to deliver."

Politics, rather than action, is what the Liberal Party seems to do best and their current approach seems to be waiting around and adopting a 'go soft, go late, and go business' approach, which is the opposite of Labor's action during the global financial crisis.

Morrison has downplayed the effects of the global financial crisis, trying to make it seem like it was nothing like the problems he's now facing, when in fact, as a global economic event, the global financial crisis was far worse and far more prolonged. And, of course, a media that is so concentrated and supportive of conservative governments will amplify the message promoted by Morrison, and diminish whatever credible economic measures the Labor government took at that time.

The criticisms of the Labor government spending from 2008 didn't just arrive from the Liberal Party, it was strongly driven by conservative media outlets, especially from News Corporation. At the time, barely a day went by before a breaking story appeared on the front pages of *The Australian* about alleged misappropriations of payments or maladministration of funds within the Building the Education Revolution scheme: there were great criticisms about the building of school halls, of outdoor learning environments and new quadrangles, as if to suggest schools were not deserving of these facilities. Twelve years later, these resources are still there, and still being used by those schools. They're great community resources.

Despite the barrage of complaints that arose from the Coalition opposition and conservative media at that time, many economists agree it was the correct course of action. It kept Australia out of recession, it kept people in employment, and this was a very important factor in keeping the economy afloat.

Australia avoided recession during the global financial crisis but perhaps it's a case where the community needs to experience a recession just to understand living through dire economic circumstances. The last recession in Australia occurred during 1990–91 and because it occurred almost thirty years ago, many people have either little recollection or experience of that: a shortage of cash, retrenchments, social security restrictions, higher prices and high interest rates. These were difficult times, but the combination of the reforms that were made leading up to that recession and the recession itself, created the platform for a much stronger economy and a recession-free period for twenty-nine years.

Technically, a recession is two consecutive quarters of negative growth in gross domestic product, although it feels the economy is already in a recession—and the Australian economy recently narrowly avoided the first part of that equation. The December 2019 quarter showed growth in GDP of just 0.5 per cent, a sure signal of a staggering economy, especially in the context of the inclusion of the Christmas retail spending period and, since then, the economy has also endured the effects of national bushfires, a downturn in spending and retail and, of course, the onset of a coronavirus pandemic.

The March 2020 quarter, in all probability, will show negative growth in GDP, as will the June 2020 quarter: those two events fulfil the technical definition of recession. Sometimes in economics, it's not just the data and statistics that appear in spreadsheets or balance sheets: there are other factors, such as consumer sentiment, confidence in the economy, unemployment and the likelihood of being able to pick up a new job if one has been lost.

Morrison has announced people on Newstart benefits and pensioners will receive a $500 bonus payment; half of the wages for apprentices will be paid until the end of 2020. There have been discussions about wage subsidies for other workers in the economy, but this is funding that should be provided now, rather than later. Money needs to start flowing upwards through the economy, rather than sending it at the top through the business community, hoping that it will filter through to other parts of the economy. This is not how stimulus spending works.

And the economy, as far as all the indicators are concerned, is not looking very good, and has not looked very good for some time. Morrison has had the good political fortune of being able to blame a staggering economy on the onset of coronavirus, which is something the media has been quite keen to support him on. However, politicians, especially prime ministers, create their own fortune and exploit these issues wherever they can: that's the nature of politics. Morrison tends to handle any situation politically and that's where many of his problems arise, and evidence of this can be seen in his handling of the bushfires in late 2019, which was calamitous for his leadership and for his credibility.

Morrison doesn't handle a crisis well: his natural instinct is to score political points, and he tends to get lost when he's in a position where he cannot behave politically and seek opportunity. During the time of the Christchurch massacre in 2019, he was lost for words because it was an inopportune time to attack Labor, and it went against his natural instinct. During the bushfires, he went on the attack against climate change actions, renewable energy and the Labor Party, but it wasn't what the public wanted to hear. The electorate expects the prime minister of the day to face up to all adversities, whatever they may be, and rise above the fracas of day-to-day politics and meaningless political point scoring.

It's evident that Australia has the wrong type of political leadership in government, at exactly the wrong time. Australia is on the edge of a financial and economic precipice but it would be more beneficial for a government to proceed with the task at hand, support the economy, support the community, and refrain from political point scoring, opportunism, or attacking their political opponents. That's how politics is played out in this country, unfortunately, but it would be better to put that aside for the time being.

Perhaps with experience, Morrison will learn from his mistakes of the past, but has equivocated on dealing with coronavirus effectively, and it seems he's more concerned at this stage about making sure he can get to the football over the weekend, claiming "the fact that I would still be going on Saturday speaks not just to my passion for my beloved Sharks; it might be the last game I get to go to for a long time".⁹

It suggests a prime minister not focusing on the essence of his job: in his first few media conferences after the coronavirus commenced, he was racing his words. He was struggling and he didn't seem across the subject at all. He has calmed down somewhat, but a prime minister more intent on going to watch a game of rugby league is probably not the prime minister the country needs in a time of crisis.

The last series of prime ministers that have been called up to handle a difficult crisis—Bob Hawke, Paul Keating, Kevin Rudd, John Howard—have all managed well, or at least offered a public persona of being in control during a crisis, even if behind closed doors, they've been hiding a ball of stress and nerves. Most prime ministers seem to be able to publicly handle a crisis in a way that Morrison hasn't, although he is improving. And, the current crisis, might be the turning point where he actually grows into being a prime minister worthy of the title.

*

---

9   *7 News*, 'Scott Morrison will not attend the Cronulla Sharks over fears attendance would be misinterpreted', Katina Curtis, 13 March 2020. https://7news.com.au/lifestyle/health-wellbeing/pm-warns-of-challenging-months-ahead-c-742482

Breaking conventions and what it means for democracy

12 March

It's an issue that keeps appearing and at a time when the federal government hoped the scandals from the Sports Funding programs might disappear from the public domain, another reference to it appeared in Senate estimates hearings to remind the electorate just how corrupt the entire funding program was.

The revelations about the obscene amounts of funds that were diverted to marginal seats in the lead-up to the 2019 election were made several months ago, but there are new details about how funding was released after the election was announced, and during the time the government had moved into caretaker mode. It might not seem like a big deal to the electorate, but why is the caretaker convention so critical?

Essentially, when an election is called, all ministerial positions become vacant: technically, for at least thirty-five days, the minimum duration of an election campaign, Australia has a nominal prime minister who still has to do the day-to-day work of the prime minister. There may be a diplomatic issue, a trade issue or a national emergency that appears during an election campaign and whoever is the prime minister at the time the election is called, essentially acts in the role until the election is resolved and declared.

And that makes the caretaker convention more understandable. The convention also exists so binding decisions are not made by an incumbent government that would require a new incoming government to implement those decisions, and also to provide the opposition with a more equal platform during an election campaign to offer its perspectives to the electorate. It's not a law, it's a protocol, and it's essential for a functioning democracy to adhere to these protocols, especially when there's a government in office that sails so close to the legal winds. And because these conventions are not law, the only repercussions that exists for government and ministers who break these conventions are political, rather than legal.

In Australia, it's generally the conservative side of politics which breaks these kinds of conventions—not always, but usually. Successive Australian governments have excelled in removing components of the British Westminster system they like and quietly removing the areas they don't but it is ironic how these conventions have been smashed by conservative governments. They will go to extreme lengths to protect conservative institutions such as the monarchy or the Constitution but quite happy to break longstanding conventions when it suits them politically.

Incidents such as these relate to accountability and responsibility, and it seems there will be no repercussions within this sport funding scheme, which now involves Senator McKenzie and the Prime Minister. Grants were amended and approved fifteen minutes after the election was actually called, and it might be suggested that fifteen minutes after the deadline is not such a big deal, but where is the line to be drawn? That day afterwards, or even the following week? Protocols exist for good reasons, and there needs to be punitive actions taken against those who broke the protocols.

However, the only punishment meted out to McKenzie was for her to lose her ministerial position, and there was also an attempt by the Senate to censure her. McKenzie's Liberal counterpart, Senator Eric Abetz, was ever so helpful, using all sorts of legal contortions to suggest McKenzie shouldn't be censured at all, because she was unaware she didn't have the legal authority to authorise these funding applications, and she was unaware that funds could be altered after the election was called. The electorate would be right to assume ignorance of the law can never be a defence against crime and also have an expectation that politicians elected to Parliament would be competent enough to know the limitations of their powers, especially ministers of the Crown.

And this deception, and the win-at-every-cost approach goes to the heart of many of the problems of this government. There are members of Parliament who don't know what their job descriptions are, and they're unsure about how to do their jobs with competence—this is great worry at the pinnacle of the democratic system: ministers who are unclear about their roles are more likely to engage in corruptive practices. These ongoing rorts are brutal and corrupt political behaviours without any theoretical underpinning to it, and suggests the Australian Parliament needs to move into a twenty-first century mode of thinking that is more suited to the times, and more suited to serving the public, rather than vested interests. When protocols and conventions keep being broken, as has been occurring in Australia, British and the United States, and if there are no consequences, it's obvious there needs to be a rethink of how the business of politics is carried out.

Another example of corruption occurred on the day before the announcement of the 2019 federal election, where the government made an 'act of grace' payment of $3.9 million through a Cabinet office policy committee, but no details have been released about what this payment was for, and to whom it was paid to. The Prime Minister has refused to answer questions about it, the file is secret and there is no freedom of information access. The application was lodged with the Department of Foreign Affairs and Trade on 6 January 2017 but was approved by the Minister for Finance, Mathias Cormann on 10 April 2019. Certainly, there can be a case for Cabinet-in-confidence in specific privacy matters, but for such a matter to remain a complete secret and hidden from the public is not good for democracy. Governments that keep issues hidden from the public usually engage in this practice to hide embarrassment for themselves or cover up corruption—otherwise they would have no difficulties in releasing information.

Morrison is also the only permanent member to this Cabinet office policy committee, effectively creating a one-person Cabinet. This process has a precedent, where after the 1972 election, Gough Whitlam and Lance Barnard created a two-person Cabinet. However, on this occasion, the election had been held in early December, the counting of the votes hadn't been completed and, although the Labor Party had officially won the election, there were several close seats still being processed and Whitlam was unsure about which candidates had won their seats—this was an anomaly, but made sense at the time because Labor had just returned to office after a twenty-three-year hiatus, and they were keen to start the process of government.

Morrison, on the other hand, had none of these issues to deal with, except for the inherent Liberal Party philosophy that government should be broken down and reduced to a bare minimum. But a $3.9 million payment that nobody knows anything about—except for the fact it was made the day before the election date was announced—is a process that is open to corruption and is a continuing theme for this government.

This is a government that cherishes its secrecy, and the continuing decay of openness and accountability. This $3.9 million payment is not as extreme but similar to the $30 million payment made to Foxtel by this government in 2016. To this day, the public is unaware about how this money was spent—aside from vague public statements that it was to be used to promote women's sport, to which there is no evidence to support this—and the government refuses to release any details about this matter. Will the public ever find out how any of these funds have been spent? It's unlikely to be a payment that would be beneficial to the public, considering the Morrison government recently reduced or removed funding to women's shelters and the National Family Violence Prevention and Legal Services Forum, the peak body for Aboriginal and Torres Strait Islander victims and survivors of domestic violence, and has a habit of cancelling programs that offer no electoral benefit to the Liberal–National Coalition.

And it is also a question of the government's priorities—a $345,000 contract for the television celebrity Scott Cam to promote trades and apprenticeships, when all he has managed in the three months since he was appointed is several social media messages.

Ultimately, the electorate will decide what kind of resonance these issues have, because they are the ones who decide whether a government stays or goes when it comes to the next election, and whether they believe $30 million paid to a private enterprise such as Foxtel, or $345,000 paid to television celebrities is money well spent.

And, ultimately, it is up to the electorate to decide whether the point has been reached where conventions and protocols don't seem to be relevant anymore. But for a government to break long established codes and standards of behaviour creates very dangerous precedents, and it's unclear whether new laws need to be implemented, or whether there comes a point where the Governor–General needs to intervene somehow: of course, this is a sensitive issue for Australian politics, considering the interventions of the Governor–General in 1932 and 1975. But this is an intervention that is unlikely and, as it stands, Australia will continue to be managed by 'second-rate people' but survives through luck and good fortune, as described in Donald Horne's *The Lucky Country*. Although it's an abstract concept and intangible, luck is a finite resource, and Australia's luck could run out soon.

And based on the panic-buying, fighting and hoarding of toilet paper that has been seen all around Australia because of the onset of coronavirus, the luck may have already run out.

*

Is the media slowly turning against the Prime Minister?

12 March

There has been a slight change in the way the mainstream media has been dealing with Scott Morrison in 2020, and after all the support they seemed to offer him both as a new Prime Minister in 2018 and in the lead up to the 2019 election, the combination of his poor management of national emergencies, misleading the public, and simply not answering questions has started a slow turning of the tide against the Prime Minister.

Morrison's media management strategy is very similar to the strategy used by former Queensland Premier, Joh Bjelke-Petersen: mislead, fabricate stories, not answer questions, or divert all the attention back onto the Labor Party. It's easier to do this in state politics that has a smaller focus of attention, but it's more difficult to hide from poor political performance on the national stage and reality always does have the habit of catching up, even if it does take some time to get there.

Journalists are detecting Morrison's low level of competence, and are starting to take him to task over breaking long-established protocols and conventions, not answering questions, and telling open-faced lies. Morrison is strong on deflection and avoiding accountability and responsibility, and this makes him a very difficult politician to lay a glove on, but the electorate expects prime ministers to stand up in the face of adversity, and at least be a little bit above playing political games. Is he slowly being found out by the media?

Morrison seems to be steeped in all the protocols of public relations, but he's not terribly good at the role of prime minister, and the public record up to this point reflects this. He's good at developing a quick three-word slogan, but whether the slogan is effective is an entirely different issue. Morrison lacks substance; it seems he doesn't cope well in a crisis, as can be seen with his management of the bushfires crisis late last year. He lacked gravitas; he seemed untrustworthy.

Of course, he will have his defenders, as most prime ministers do. Most people in the electorate will be satisfied with the performance of a prime minister, provided their own way of life is not affected too much, and their economic circumstances are favourable but, with the economy heading towards an inevitable recession, that perception may change.

The press gallery should be holding the government of the day to account, as well as the opposition, and because Liberal–National Coalition reflects the conservatism of the business owners of the mainstream media, this has tended not to happen ever since they returned to office in 2013. But because of fatally falling media consumption numbers and falling revenues, perhaps the media owners have realised that defending these unpopular political figures is not a sustainable business model, especially if they're excluding half of the electorate whose views are not being reflected in what they publish. Ideologically, conservative media owners find it difficult to publish material they dispute or disagree with but, business-wise, more alternative perspectives, especially those that critically assess and criticise Morrison's performances might lead to more people purchasing their newspapers, watching their news television programs, or listening to news radio again. There has been a slight switch in the way Morrison is now being reported within the media, but that may be put on hold with the onset of the coronavirus.

The former leader of the Liberal Party, John Hewson, observed that on just the average day, Morrison will not deal with any crisis issues or political problems but, rather, respond with a three-word slogan or, if it's a good day, a four-word slogan, that runs in the media and provides a fig leaf of cover to whatever the issue of the day is. It's clever political marketing but the issue is that the problems remain and are never effectively resolved.

For all of these flaws in Morrison's performances and leadership, he did win the last federal election in May 2019. And according to recent opinion polling—with the caveat that pollsters were highly inaccurate at the last election—Morrison is preferred prime minister when compared to the Labor leader, Anthony Albanese, and holds the same electoral lead in two-party preferred voting as recorded at the last election. One issue here is how the electorate receives news and information about politics, and how this material shapes their political opinions. According to Roy Morgan polling, the internet is Australia's main source of news,[10] above traditional media such as television, radio and newspapers.

Shock jocks such as Alan Jones and Ray Hadley remain popular, but in terms of audience share, in a Sydney population of over five million, their listenership is 120,000. Other influencers within new media are becoming more prominent however; the political commentator Jordan Shanks-Markovina (Friendly Jordies) has over 470,000 YouTube subscribers. Increasingly, the electorate is finding other avenues to receive their political messaging—Facebook, Twitter, Reddit—and legacy media has had to play catch-up. The more obvious solution to the financial woes of legacy media would be to provide a more comprehensive news coverage from all sides of politics and different political prisms, not just operating as a public relations company solely for the political needs of the Liberal–National Coalition.

And the ongoing issue in political reportage is the Canberra press gallery, which is moribund and should be injected with fresh faces and new reporters. Essentially, federal political news is reported by the same group of ten or so journalists, acting within a Canberra-based group think bubble, that fail to place very much pressure on Morrison. But Morrison is a prime minister who does not handle political pressure very well and, as a front runner, performs when the issues are running in his favour, and crumbles when they are not. If he's subjected to tougher media scrutiny and questioning, he flusters, he fumbles, shirks responsibility and deflects to talk about

---

10 Roy Morgan, 'It's official: Internet is Australia's main source of news; TV remains most trusted', 21 August 2020. http://www.roymorgan.com/findings/8492-main-sources-news-trust-june-2020-202008170619

other issues or looks for someone else to blame, as can be seen in this exchange with the ABC's *7.30* host, Leigh Sales:[11]

> **Leigh Sales:** You won't release the Gaetjens report into the sports rorts. Your office tried to conceal when you were on holidays in Hawaii in December. The government cited national security to avoid answering a question under FOI about whether Pastor Brian Houston was invited to a White House dinner, although you've finally admitted this afternoon that he was invited. Why all the secrecy on stuff that on the surface would seem to be not that big a deal?
>
> **Scott Morrison:** Well, those things aren't that big a deal that you've talked about. And I'm always focused on the...
>
> **Sales:** But why the secrecy then?
>
> **Morrison:** Leigh, I'm just focused on the things that I took to the Australian people. And I know...
>
> **Sales:** No, no, I just want to know: why the secrecy? You're not answering what I'm asking.
>
> **Morrison:** Leigh, well I've disclosed the issues you've referred to. So, I mean, in relation to one of those matters, I mean, I could have been more candid at the time about it. I wish I was, but frankly, it wasn't a big deal...
>
> **Sales:** But you want—you go back to the trust question—you want Australians to trust you, does this excessive secrecy help that?
>
> **Morrison:** No. Well, I don't accept—I don't accept the assertion you're putting to me Leigh. I mean, you're making accusations like the Labor Party...
>
> **Sales:** No, no, I gave you three concrete examples.
>
> **Morrison:** These are these are minor matters, Leigh, that I don't think go to the issues you're talking about...
>
> **Sales:** That's my point.

---

11 Prime Minister of Australia, Interview with Leigh Sales, ABC Television, *7.30*, 3 March 2020. https://www.pm.gov.au/media/interview-leigh-sales-730-abc

> **Morrison:** If you want to join in on the accusations that the Labor leader makes in Parliament every day, well, you can join in...
>
> **Sales:** I'm not interested in what the Labor leader's got to say. I'm putting to you three examples.
>
> **Morrison:** Well, there's an uncanny resemblance between the allegations Leigh.

In this exchange, Morrison doesn't like the question from a journalist, so his immediate inclination is to make accusations that she is siding with the Labor Party: he ran out of space to deflect and to obfuscate, he was under pressure, caught out and his only response was to claim the journalist was biased against him and doing the work of the opposition.

It's a technique the former Prime Minister, Malcolm Turnbull, used to deflect serious questions; it was also a technique used by Bjelke-Petersen. And it's also Morrison's inclination to reduce his appearances on this type of program where there is a possibility he will be caught out, and increase his appearances on Liberal Party-friendly outlets such as Sky News, and Sydney radio station, 2GB.

There has been an increase in scrutiny through other media outlets, in particular, Network 10 and the journalist, Peter van Onselen, who has been running many high-pressure news reports about federal sports funding frauds and scandals, and other related corruption such as the mismanagement of water allocations in the Murray–Darling Basin. And for his efforts in exposing these misdemeanours by government, the 'Independent. Always' *Sydney Morning Herald*—surely now an ironic tagline—has accused van Onselen of being 'left-wing' and "dishing up the biggest load of tripe",[12] for essentially doing the traditional task of a journalist—holding power to account, and publishing the news governments want to close down.

And, to add to the political confusion, Minister for Home Affairs, Peter Dutton, has labelled extreme Islamic fundamentalists as 'left-wing', and the Senator for New South Wales, Concetta Fierravanti-

---

12 *Sydney Morning Herald*, 'Network Ten's political drift to left of The Guardian makes no business sense', Stephen Brook, February 2020. https://www.smh.com.au/business/companies/network-ten-s-drift-to-the-political-left-of-the-guardian-makes-no-business-sense-20200223-p543h5.html#comments

Wells has mentioned that she feels affronted when people refer to her as 'right-wing', even though her entire political career has been built on pushing forward the more extremist right-wing positions of the Liberal Party. It just seems that these political players in federal politics no longer understand who they are anymore.

These left–right dynamics are tedious and have become more problematic in a post-Cold War world, where the traditional divisions along social and economic paths have become more complex and more diffused, and it's a paradigm that is breaking down. These dynamics may still be useful in overall political positioning of particular politicians or public figures, but the world has become far more complicated over the past thirty or so years, and certainly far more complicated since the French Revolution in 1789, which is when the left–right divide first became popular—the parliamentarians who wanted more radical change in society sat in the left chamber of the Parliament; those who wanted less change or no change at all sat in the right chamber. The dynamic of today is not so much a left–right divide, but a four-way shift of libertarianism versus authoritarianism, and communitarianism versus individualism.

Dutton's claim that Al Qaeda and Islamic terrorism is a left-wing movement—given their approach to women's rights, worker's rights, religion and law is, by any standard, a classic right-wing agenda—is laughable but, also, in keeping with Morrison's strategy of political division and obfuscation of any issue, it's just another way of manipulating the media messaging and making a link between extremist terrorism with the opponents of the Liberal Party. It's a disturbing tactic.

But these definitions tend to be peripheral and certain parts of the media are starting to attack each other: the shrinking base of revenue is becoming more difficult to share, but there also needs to be an understanding that when the media smells the blood of a prime minister in the water, they'll put aside their ideological biases and became aggressive onlookers calling for change. The media turned against former Prime Minister, Tony Abbott, very rapidly in 2015 when it became evident that after two years in office, he just wasn't up to the job. Had the media scrutinised Abbott far more significantly, Australia would not have had two years of wasted and meandering government, although it seems the media repeated this mistake with Turnbull, and now continuing this mistake with Morrison.

There is a federal election due in 2022 and, given the effects of the coronavirus so far in 2020, it's difficult to imagine the state of the Australian society in two years' time. As always, economic performance is critical and if the poorly performing economy doesn't improve, or at least if there isn't a roadmap put forward for a transition into a new kind of economy, it will be difficult for the government to succeed at this election. But a government—and the performance of the economy—can only be scrutinised effectively, if the opposition performs its work effectively and, up to this point of the parliamentary term, the Labor Party hasn't been effective in placing pressure upon the Prime Minister.

But it also has to be remembered, former Prime Minister Paul Keating won the 1993 election during the end point of recession, poor economic performance, high interest rates and an unemployment rate of 11.4 per cent. Economic factors do matter, but there are many other issues that come into play during election campaigns. After his performances during the recent bushfires, there were some murmurings about Morrison's ability to lead the Liberal Party to the next election—Abbott was prime minister for two years, Turnbull was prime minister for three years. It's now coming up to two years for Morrison, but the onset of the coronavirus has solidified his faltering position within the Liberal Party and his challenger in the 2018 leadership ballot, Peter Dutton, has largely been invisible in recent times.

But while Morrison is safe for the time being, political leaders not only have to deal with external crises, but internal ones as well from within their own political party, and while these have been put aside temporarily, there's always a chance they can quickly reappear when least expected.

*

A failure of government

25 March

The coronavirus crisis is continuing to have detrimental effects all over the world and it's likely to be a health, political and economic issue that will need to be managed for some time to come. Governments have been doing their best to manage the crisis, but it seems some countries are doing better than others. The Australian government has been dragging its feet, both on the economic and health fronts, and it seems that it's directing its actions based on ideological pursuits, rather than putting that all aside, and working out what is the best outcome for the entire community.

Its economic action has been slow—two stimulus packages have been announced, but not a cent has actually been received by anyone yet, and its messaging on health outcomes has been contradictory and confusing. Governments of all persuasions need to rise to the occasion in a time of crisis but it seems this government is going to exhaust all other options before embarking on the correct course of action. Is this the right government for the times, or does Australia need something different?

There's an expectation for the Prime Minister to rise to the occasion but he hasn't, as yet, been able to. Scott Morrison failed the community when it came to the management of the bushfires season; he failed the community when it came to the floods on the eastern seaboard, and he's failing the community when it comes to the management of all the issues that are arising from the onset of the coronavirus.

There have been revelations that it was Australian Border Force that was responsible for allowing passengers off the *Ruby Princess* cruise ship that was docked in Sydney Harbour, without adequate health checks, and that resulted in over 900 coronavirus infections among the passengers and crew from this ship.[13] The damage to the Australian community could be immense, especially when looking at the experience of the United States, where it took three months for the first 100,000 coronavirus cases to develop, one month for the next 100,000 cases and, after that, only three more days for the third batch of 100,000 cases.

The coronavirus is a highly contagious disease and can get out of hand very quickly, but Australian Border Force and NSW Health ignored all of these warnings coming in from overseas and decided to allow 2,647 passengers to disembark from the *Ruby Princess*, walk the streets of Sydney and travel all over Australia. This was a highly irresponsible act by the federal and NSW governments, at a time when they should be taking extreme caution and protecting their citizens.

Australia should have gone into a lockdown much earlier and should have closed down schools earlier as well. There has been a wide range of arguments presented for schools remaining open, such as frontline workers who didn't have the option of staying at home with their children, and would need their children to go somewhere, safely—but this also placed teachers at risk. Perhaps the best balance was achieved by keeping school numbers to an absolute minimum and implementing social distancing protocols, but it would have been best for them to close completely. Businesses should have been fully closed, and public transport should have been fully closed.

Morrison has been announcing mixed messages, suggesting people should stay at home but, if they still have employment, they should go to work, because, in his words, "everyone who has a job in this economy is an essential worker". Who is to make the call on what defines the 'essential' worker? Of course, these are difficult decisions that need to be made but the community calls on governments in a time of crisis to make difficult decisions, and the right decisions

---

13 State of New South Wales, 'Report: Special Commission of Inquiry into the Ruby Princess', Brett Walker SC, August 2020. https://www.rubyprincessinquiry.nsw.gov.au/report

in the best interests of the community—that's the main reason why governments exist. But mixed messaging coming from the prime minister of the day is not in anyone's interests.

The coronavirus has created a unique set of problems, but the federal government has made a series of mistakes and errors in the management of the economy and health, primarily because it needs to act in a manner it is ideologically opposed to, to resolve these problems. Ideologically, the Liberal–National Coalition is opposed to community lockdowns, it is opposed to stimulus spending to support the community. And with a prime minister at the helm who is always looking for personal marketing opportunities and avenues for attacking his political opponents, it has been difficult for the community to receive clear and consistent health information.

Primarily, the coronavirus is a health crisis but it's a health crisis creating an economic crisis, not just in Australia, but global economies as well. And when there's an economic downturn, people lose their jobs: in this case, this massive job shedding is not happening over several months or several weeks, it's happening over a matter of days. Many people are losing their jobs and losing their jobs quite quickly and, of course, if people are losing their jobs, they won't have an income and they'll be seeking support from the government. That's where Centrelink comes into effect, the government's human and welfare support agency.

There was a mishap during the week where Centrelink's website—and most people have been told to access the website, rather than going to a Centrelink office in person—had a severe outage, and the Minister for Human Services, Stuart Robert, blamed the outage on hackers, rather than taking responsibility for the issue. When it was pointed out that it wasn't because of hacking or a denial of service event, but because the government had failed to invest in a website that could make it easier for people to access government benefits, Robert simply responded by shrugging his shoulders, saying: "my bad".

'My bad' is slang street term from the 1970s and popularised in the 1995 movie, *Clueless*, which in Robert's case, seemed quite appropriate. But does the electorate want a minister quoting inane pop cultural references from the 1990s when something goes wrong, or a minister who can take responsibility for problems and resolve them?

Australia's Westminster system of government suggests that ministers take responsibility for all actions of their department, even if the minister didn't create the action in the first instance. But this is a federal government that has trashed the concept of Westminster tradition: the minister always held the responsibility and, of course, when everything went well, the minister would receive all the praise, the glowing reviews in the media, and promotion for doing their job effectively. But, if there was mistake within the department; if they acted improperly, or if there were senior public servants engaged in impropriety, the minister would be forced to resign: it was a tension within the position that ensured they would always perform to their maximum abilities, as well as ensuring their underlings always kept the community interest at heart.

The Australian federal system currently doesn't engage in this system of Westminster ministerial responsibility, and this possibly explains the delays and incompetence of the management of the coronavirus by the federal government. If ministers face little pressure or scrutiny, they have little incentive to perform with competence.

The public service does have a large role to play here, but they act under the direction of ministers, and the government. Stimulus funding should have already been delivered to businesses and individuals but has been withheld so far. This compares with the Rudd government's response during the global financial crisis in 2008, when money was sent out to people as soon as possible—this, of course, caused political problems where money was sent to people who had died, but the reasoning was that this political cost—and financial cost—was a price that needed to be paid to sustain and rescue the economy from collapse. Targeted spending would have taken too long to implement and would have been too late to stop the economy plunging.

The Morrison government is dithering about how to spend stimulus funding and it's difficult to understand the delays. There have been two stimulus packages announced to the value of $189 billion, which are still sitting in the government coffers—even though the Labor opposition offered their legislative support for packages. It's also instructive to compare the behaviour of the Labor

Opposition in 2020—providing as much support to the government to provide stimulus—with the Liberal Party opposition in 2009, when they voted against the Rudd government's $42 billion stimulus package. Tony Abbott actually missed this vote because he had been drinking too much wine the previous night and had fallen asleep in his parliamentary office.[14] And the Liberal Party continued to rail against Labor's stimulus package for the next decade, only dialling down the crescendo when they realised they would need to take exactly the same course of action to stop the economy collapsing during the coronavirus pandemic.

In 2020, the Labor Party has fully supported the government's stimulus packages, and they also provided *carte blanche* to the government to spend $40 billion in immediate funding in whichever way they wished to. Labor's response had been economically sustainable and politically sensible as well, and an example of what a mature political party in opposition should do when the country is in crisis. Yet, even with this political support, the federal government is hesitating to spend money at this critical time.

It's clear they wish to the avoid the political problems they highlighted of the Labor Party during the time of the global financial crisis. The Liberal Party's response at that time was not to give support to the Labor Party, which was acting in the best interests of the community and the economy. The Liberal Party behaved in a politically negligent and irresponsible way, where it opposed everything and, once they returned to government in 2013, implemented the Royal Commission into the Home Insulation Program in 2014, essentially to besmirch the reputations of former Prime Ministers Kevin Rudd and Julia Gillard, the Minister for Environment, Peter Garrett, and the leader of the Labor Party after these events, Bill Shorten. Although the Royal Commission found there were some shortfalls within the management of the Home Insulation Program, it also determined that Garrett was a diligent minister, and Rudd had no case to answer. The Royal Commission was essentially a political witch hunt instigated by conservatives, at a cost of $20 million.

---

14 *Sydney Morning Herald*, 'Tony Abbott admits missing key vote in Parliament because he was drunk and passed out', Fergus Hunter, 25 August 2017. https://www.smh.com.au/politics/federal/tony-abbott-admits-missing-key-vote-in-parliament-because-he-was-drunk-and-passed-out-20170825-gy3vs4.html

But the Liberal–National Coalition mainly seeks to score political points against opponents and avoid scrutiny wherever possible. Parliament did sit for one day during this past week, and there was a proposal presented by the Labor leader, Anthony Albanese, to amend standing orders so Parliament could meet in a different way during the coronavirus pandemic, including using online services such as Skype or Zoom conferencing and webinars. As expected when there is a government in office that avoids scrutiny and accountability, the proposal was rejected, even though given the circumstances and the technology that is currently available, there would be an expectation that if the rest of the community is expected to work as much as they can, then politicians should be able to as well.

The government argued their case that opening up Australian Parliament House would create a high-level health risk, even though the Prime Minister has insisted schools should be open, early education centres and childcare centres should remain open, as well as close-contact businesses such as hairdressing salons. If these are to remain open, why can't Parliament remain opened for business as well?

And if there are unreasonable health risks for Parliament, why the resistance to adopting internet-based solutions so the actions of government can continue to be scrutinised and held to account? Parliament will remain closed until August—another five months—and for a functioning democracy, this is unacceptable. It means the decisions made by Australian Border Force in their management of the *Ruby Princess* debacle in Sydney Harbour cannot be scrutinised. It means the key actions of the federal government, which seem to be well hidden within the creation of the National Cabinet, cannot be known, or assessed as to whether they are decisions made in the best interests of the community. Or if the $189 billion in stimulus spending—whenever it commences—is effective.

Morrison's ideological view of government is to reduce its role in society and reducing all scrutiny of its actions is aligned with this viewpoint. But this is a time where community is looking towards government for strong resolutions and leadership, and reducing accountability is the antithesis of what is needed at this critical point of time.

*

The end of neoliberalism but what will replace it?

25 March

Modern history has shown that in times of crisis, the world does have the ability to stop, reassess the direction it's heading towards and develop strategies for a better future. After World War I, over a hundred years ago, the Paris Peace Conference resulted in the creation of the League of Nations. The League failed in its primary purpose, which was to prevent further war, and after World War II ended in 1945, the United Nations was created, new terms of monetary relations between North America, Western Europe, Australia and Japan were introduced through the Bretton Woods agreement, as well as the International Bank for Reconstruction and Development, and International Monetary Fund.

The mode of thinking at that stage was the need to control speculative financial capital, a need to consolidate Keynesian economic thinking, and stabilise world economies—an economic thinking that existed until the onset of neoliberalism in the early 1980s and now, there have been calls among leading economists for new economic thinking and philosophies more suited to the current circumstances.

In 1945, the world had leaders such as Winston Churchill, Franklin Roosevelt and John Curtin—among many others—great national figures in their respective countries. In 2020, the world leadership comprises Boris Johnson, Donald Trump and Scott Morrison—it's a question that needs to be asked again—does Australia have the right leadership? And internationally, is the right leadership in place that will be able to create a new financial and economic structure to guide the world through this crisis?

It's evident the market model, based on the notion that local and global markets alone can solve all the economic, social and political problems, is failing. The marketplace alone cannot cope with a pandemic. The marketplace alone cannot cope with natural disasters. And this failure is precisely what Karl Marx predicted almost two centuries ago. Marx wasn't right on some areas of economic and social thinking, but he was certainly correct on the relationship between the real value of money and labour. With currency traders and bankers, and others who don't deal in actual tangible products and services, money and value has been based on more intangible and esoteric values, such as contracts for difference, hedging funds, and virtual stock markets, where it's almost a high-level technical form of sports gambling.

It was these forms of money-making high-end capitalism that created the conditions for the global financial crisis during 2007–08, along with issues in the subprime lending market in the United States, but the onset of the coronavirus, and the slowdown in the global economy has accelerated discussions about the need for new economic thinking.

There possibly will be a move towards Keynesian economic thinking, although it's also evident that those who have benefited the most from the previous forty years of economic neoliberalism will be keen to hang on to that privilege and power for as long as possible.

There have been a range of neoliberalist and libertarian economists, such as the economics editor for *The Australian*, Adam Creighton, coming out recently to ridicule Keynesian economics and government interventions into the economy, suggesting that an economic philosophy that's only required during a time of crisis such as at the end of World War I, the Great Depression, or at the end of World War II, is not an economic philosophy worth having.

But that is the nature of implementing economic ideas that are suitable for the times, and adopting certain economic ideas is not just a remedy implemented for one or two years, but for an entire generation. The economic disasters of the twentieth century were largely committed by the excesses of capitalism and liberalist economic policies. The Great Depression was caused, essentially, by the preceding decade of free market economics. Government intervention in world economies was essentially part of the post-war recovery period and many countries around the world implemented Keynesian thinking between 1945 and the late 1970s. The neoliberalist economic approaches since the 1980s have generated better economic conditions overall, albeit with a very uneven spread and at a massive cost to the environment, but when neoliberalism crashes, it crashes badly and detrimentally affects many more people than it benefits. With many developed economies now supporting wages through direct government subsidies, a new economic thinking is required.

The most successful economic phase in history has been that period between the late 1940s, up to the early 1970s: wages were high—prices were also high, but the higher wages catered for these prices. Interest rates were fair, and employment was close to full capacity—anyone who wanted a job was more than likely to have one, unlike the modern day policy objective of a 5 per cent unemployment rate to push wages down. Access to credit was more widely available, although it was mainly available to men, and severely restricted to women. Women required their husband's approval if they were married and could be refused access to credit if they were unmarried. Although the Australian economy between 1991 and 2020 has been more stable and avoided the 'boom-or-bust' cycle of the 1960s and 1970s, the post-World War II era has been the most sustainable in terms of stability, equity, nation building and economic expansion.

What kind of economy is Australia looking at in the near-to-medium future? The technical definition of a recession is two consecutive quarters of negative growth of gross domestic product, but the technical definition of an economic depression is far more severe: twelve consecutive quarters of negative growth—three years—or a GDP decline of 10 per cent. Since federation in 1901, Australia has experienced three recessions as of March 2020—the late 1920s, early 1970s, early 1980s and the early 1990s—and one economic depression in the early 1930s.

Two economic historical words that are not heard very often today are 'Bretton Woods', the name of the economic conference held in 1944, towards the end of World War II in the United States, a conference that developed the international monetary system that essentially still exists today.

At the start of the global financial crisis in 2008, the French President at the time, Nicolas Sarkozy, suggested it was time for the world community to develop new accords and instigate new international financial systems, labelling this accord as 'Bretton Woods Mark II' and recommending "we must rethink the financial system from scratch".[15] In 2010, the Greek Prime Minister, Georgios Papandreou, also suggested the creation of "a new global financial architecture",[16] so it's clear that there has been some thinking about new economic responses to severe economic conditions, but how does the global community start this process? Should Australia look at international responses, or should it look to the intellectual and economic resources available locally?

Ken Henry was the Secretary of the Department of the Treasury at the time of the global financial crisis and had the intellectual and economic capacity and credentials to offer key economic advice to the government of the day. But who is available with the right links to this government, and who has the gravitas to influence an ideologically-driven Liberal–National Coalition? The public service has been politicised. The Liberal Party does not have the capabilities, and the political party more likely to be attracted to progressive modes of economic thinking—the Labor Party—is in opposition and doesn't currently have the economic firepower to develop these ideas.

The Prime Minister keeps rejecting the idea of a comprehensive National Cabinet that could include federal Labor leadership, or greater economic thinkers, possibly because he realises his own inadequacies could be exposed and his weaknesses would become apparent. It's still the early days of this crisis, but Morrison will be doing his best to be seen to be doing things, and he has created

---

15 *New York Times*, 'At Davos, Sarkozy Calls for Global Finance Rules', Katrin Bennhold, 27 January 2010. https://www.nytimes.com/2010/01/28/business/global/28davos.html

16 *Mediterranean Quarterly*, 'A New Global Financial Architecture: Lessons from the Greek Crisis', George Papandreou, Fall 2010, Duke University Press.

the National COVID-19 Coordination Commission to advise the government on actions to anticipate and mitigate the economic and social impacts of the global COVID-19 pandemic. With such a high level commission, it would be fair to assume that such a task force would be comprised of high level economics practitioners and intellectuals, developing strategies and lateral approaches to the economic difficulties Australia is facing, along with highly credentialled health experts and doctors in the field of epidemiology and public health, and experts that could traverse the two spheres of health and the economy.

But the Commission is headed by Neville Power, who was CEO of Fortescue Metals up until 2017, and is currently the Chair of Perth Airport Corporation. A former mining executive who has experience in mining and airports: is this the right person for such a high-powered commission? The other members of the Commission are Greg Combet, Jane Halton, Paul Little, Catherine Tanna, David Thodey—all former political operatives, mining executives and business people—and supported by the Secretaries of the Department of the Prime Minister and Cabinet, Philip Gaetjens, and Home Affairs, Mike Pezzullo.

Where are the epidemiologists? The economists? The critical thinkers? Again, the government is playing this crisis through the prism of politics—including a former Labor politician, Combet, to avoid accusations of partisanship—and not understanding the full gravity of the crisis. The coronavirus is not only a health and economic crisis, it's also an existential crisis. What is the purpose of government? What is the purpose of the economy? What is the purpose of community?

Australia would have been better served by a collection of thinkers and intellectuals, such as the Global Business Network, which provided advice to the South African government in the early 1990s for a peaceful transition to a post-apartheid world, or the Club of Rome, an organisation comprised of former heads of state and government, United Nations administrators, high-level politicians and government officials, diplomats, scientists, economists, and business leaders, dedicated to resolving economic, social, environmental and political problems around the world.

This might be beyond what the Australian political system is capable of, but the community, through its representatives, needs to be able to stop, sit still, draw breath and think what the Australian community is all about and how it can fulfil its full potential. What is this project of 'Australia' meant to represent, the so-called 'Team Australia', a pithy nationalist phrase conservative politicians like to espouse?

The pre-COVID system of neoliberalism is in its death throes, the system where people were expected to ride the avalanche or be crushed by it. In *His Last Bow: Some Reminiscences of Sherlock Holmes*, a collection of stories written by Arthur Conan Doyle, Holmes says "there's an east wind coming, such a wind as never blew. It will be cold and bitter, Watson and a good many of us may wither before its blast".

He was, of course, speaking about the onset of World War I and, in this case, Conan Doyle was absolutely correct, albeit the story was written in 1917 with the benefit of hindsight. Nothing in the world was the same after World War I and the impacts of the coronavirus has the potential to be revolutionary in the fullest sense of the term. Of course, it depends on the duration of this pandemic and if it only for a short period of time, politics and economy will go back to business as usual. And going back to 'business as usual' would mean that the changes that are required to stabilise the world economy probably will never occur. But if this pandemic continues for a longer term—which is highly possible—it means the economy will slow down, the community will slow down, and society will slow down.

Sydney, at present, is a city under lockdown and most people, as far as possible, have been restricted to their homes. This is a once-in-a-century opportunity of community introspection and provides time to rethink the future in terms of economics, health, education, supply chains of goods and services, and technology. Human history has provided many examples where conflicts and times of crisis have also created opportunities for positive and creative solutions to the many problems faced by the world. And the worst result would be for this opportunity to be wasted in the haste to return to a world that was malfunctioning and not producing the best outcomes for its citizens.

But the chances of missing this opportunity are great: the systems in place means countries, states and territories can't just remove the leaders that are not up to delivering in these new circumstances and changed environments: in a democratic system, judgement appears in the form of election day and, up until that time, the community has to accept the leadership at the time and hope they can do the best according to their abilities.

Internationally, the British Prime Minister, Boris Johnson, is looking at a decade in power, after the crushing election defeat of Labour at the 2019 election. There is an election in the United States in November this year, and after the clown-show performances of President Donald Trump, their political system may wish to return to some semblance of normality through the election of the Democrats candidate, Joe Biden: he may not be the greatest candidate for the Democrats, but he may be the one to trigger an end to four years of political mayhem in the United States.

Closer to home, Morrison doesn't need to face the electorate until 2022, but holds onto government narrowly—the Coalition has a four-seat majority in Parliament, but losing one member through resignation or a forced byelection will push it into a minority position. But the intent of the Morrison government is still to play political games, even if the coronavirus has meant it engages with gamesmanship on a lesser level than usual. If Morrison does play obvious politics during the coronavirus crisis, the ramifications for him will not be so positive, especially at a time when the electorate prefers to see political leadership that addresses problems, rather than taking potshots at their opponents.

For example, a recent media conference commenced with all the achievements of his government, some of which skirted the boundaries of accuracy, perhaps relying on the short memories of the electorate. This, of course, is the mode of the Morrison government—spin, promotion of the positive news, and removing the negative news, as if any shade of negativity can be sprinkled away with a magic wand. And the electorate may forget these announcements, but they won't forget if they lose a family member or close friend to coronavirus, or if they feel the government isn't doing enough to manage the pandemic. Or the funeral they couldn't attend because of restrictions that were implemented because the government didn't act rapidly to stop the spread of coronavirus.

And the government only needs to look at the current events in Italy, where coronavirus cases and deaths have spiralled out of control, to see what can happen if governments act too slowly because of incompetence or being preoccupied with trying to create political advantage. In these situations, the task for a prime minister isn't to obtain the best outcome for their political party, it's about achieving the best outcome for the community.

During the Great Depression, Labor came into office in 1929, a government led by Prime Minister James Scullin. It was a difficult time, of course, and the Labor Party managed the Great Depression as well as they could: they alleviated the hardship on the community in so many different ways, and of course, they didn't play political games or take opportunity to create division. They did their best but their reward was a crushing loss in the 1931 election.

In 2020, if Morrison does everything that is needed to produce the best outcomes for the community and his reward ends up being an election loss, then that's the price that needs to be paid by a political leader. Sometimes, political partisanship and point scoring needs to be placed aside for the greater good, and this is one of those moments.

It's not exactly clear what type of economic systems are required at this time, whether it's a new hybrid of neoliberalism and small-scale entrepreneurship, a return to Keynesian economics, or new areas such as modern monetary theory, which is, more or less, based on Keynesian thinking. Whatever the long-term results are, the community isn't too concerned about what a different system might be, and might not be across the details of what the different systems are, but are more concerned about the government of the day acting in the interests of the broader community.

Governments need to support the populace and, depending on the circumstances, sometimes that means leaving the populace alone to continue with their lawful and ethical lives; sometimes, there's a need for government to intervene when there is a health crisis, natural disasters such as floods and bushfires, or when there is an external event, such as a terrorist attack. That is the purpose of government—to step in and support the community when that support is needed and expected.

But the Morrison government seems to have decided that governments are not needed during a time of crisis and has procrastinated for far too long while it decides which of these ideologically unpalatable programs it can implement, almost like a child choosing which medicine is the least awful.

The community wants good, clear and consistent messaging. People like to have reassurance, and people like help: they might not like to ask for it, but when the assistance arrives, they are grateful. And during these times, governments need to present good, centralised, co-ordinated and effective plans, and that's what the Morrison government has failed to do, up to this point.

*

The mysterious case of the Ruby Princess

8 April

One of the biggest scandals in Australia's recent history may be developing, and it's a scandal that has it all: a big ship in the harbour; surreptitious phone calls to captains in the middle of the night; ministerial blame games; departmental incompetence; denials; deaths at sea; deaths on the mainland; money; theft and cover-up. It's the mysterious case of the *Ruby Princess*, the large ocean cruiser that docked in Sydney Harbour, not once but twice, with passengers onboard that were infected with the coronavirus.

Over 900 coronavirus cases and twenty-eight deaths have been directly attributed to the *Ruby Princess*.[17] It's a sad public spectacle where NSW Health has blamed Australian Border Force; Australian Border Force has blamed NSW Health, which then went on to blame the crew of *Ruby Princess*, and then, the Minister for Home Affairs, Peter Dutton, went on to blame the company which owns the *Ruby Princess*, Carnival Corporation & PLC.

This is a serious mismanagement of a major health crisis, and these are matters of public importance: the public does have the right to know what happened on the *Ruby Princess* and how so many

---

17 State of New South Wales, 'Report: Special Commission of Inquiry into the Ruby Princess', Brett Walker SC, August 2020. https://www.rubyprincessinquiry.nsw.gov.au/report

passengers from an infected cruise ship managed to spread the coronavirus through to the public on the mainland.

The *Princess Ruby* is a crown-class cruise ship and has a maximum passenger capacity of 3,080 passengers, and 1,150 crew. The ship first arrived in Sydney early on 8 March after completing a cruise from New Zealand, and the ship's captain, Giogio Pomata, reported illnesses of 158 passengers and thirteen with 'high temperatures', one of the significant symptoms of coronavirus. As per protocol, these illnesses were lodged with NSW Health and, at this stage, the ship was considered a 'medium health risk'.

The typical rate of ships arriving to Sydney Harbour for influenza-like illnesses is 1.7 cases per 1,000 passengers. The *Ruby Princess* recorded a rate of 64.0 cases per 1,000 passengers. Despite this intensely high level of illness—thirty-seven times the typical rate—all passengers, aside from nine passengers who were tested for coronavirus on arrival, were allowed to disembark and return to their homes across Australia. And despite the assessment of a medium health risk and high rate of recorded cases of illness, the *Princess Ruby* departed Sydney Harbour with 2,647 new passengers later on that evening, with a crew of 1,151, for a thirteen-day cruise of New Zealand.

On 15 March, the Australian government announced a thirty-day ban on foreign cruise ships coming into Australian ports, but granted an exemption to four ships—*Ovation of the Seas*, *Celebrity Solstice*, *Voyager of the Seas* (owned by Royal Caribbean) and *Ruby Princess*, on the understanding they were already heading for Australia at the time of the ban, and considered to be at a low health risk.

These four ships arrived in Sydney Harbour over a three-day period: *Ovation of the Seas* and *Voyager of the Seas* on 18 March, *Ruby Princess* on 19 March, and *Celebrity Solstice* on 20 March.

The *Ruby Princess* was considered to be a 'low health risk' on this second entry back into Sydney on 19 March, even though it had been considered a 'medium risk' on 8 March and as at 14 March, five influenza-like cases had been identified on the ship. Back on the Australian mainland, passengers from the earlier cruise who disembarked on 8 March were testing positive to coronavirus, including one couple who had flown back to their home in Darwin.

There are many parts to the *Ruby Princess* incident to unpack, but there are also anomalies that need to be cleared up and questions of authorities and government ministers that need to be clarified—as well as ministerial resignations and an inquiry.

There were also many rumours about who was on the cruise ship and why the passengers were allowed to disembark with so many possible coronavirus cases onboard. Under international maritime law, Australia has an obligation to assist a vessel in distress, but it also has an obligation to ensure quarantine protocols are adhered to, and reducing the chances of infections of a serious nature entering the country. There should have been mandatory quarantine of at least fourteen days for all passengers, and there should have been a clearer understanding of how many passengers on the cruise ship were ill, and how many had coronavirus symptoms. This did not happen and, as with most issues this federal government needs to manage, the response has been far too little and far too late.

The shifting of the responsibility and blame from one area to another has also been unedifying and unbecoming of public officials and politicians with ministerial responsibility. The federal government has been blaming the NSW Government for this mismanagement, but the state of New South Wales doesn't control international borders; this is within federal jurisdiction. And then when neither government was prepared to take responsibility, both then went on to blame Carnival Corporation & PLC.

And this blame-shifting behaviour has been a hallmark of both the federal government and the NSW Government: they're keen to take credit for everything that goes well but nowhere to be seen when something goes wrong. This is the worst kind of official behaviour—the electorate expects governments to resolve problems, not to walk away from them and blame others. This is also a familiar narrative for these two governments: they were largely absent during the recent bushfire season, and on climate change, the NSW Premier, Gladys Berejiklian, declared "not today", when asked if it is the right time to discuss climate change and the relationship with severe bushfire activity.

Political leaders are in the business of accepting blame and responsibility: that's exactly what they're paid to do, and that's exactly why they are in their positions. It's not their role to look for others to blame and engage in playground-style political point scoring: real leaders are accountable for errors and problems and have to act swiftly to remedy them.

The NSW Police Commissioner, Mick Fuller, the self-appointed 'bin-man' for the Prime Minister and the person who decided not to investigate forgery allegations against the Minister for Energy, Angus Taylor, has involved the homicide quad to launch a criminal investigation into the *Ruby Princess* incident but, if previous form is a guide, not very much is going to be uncovered.

Whenever these investigations are stonewalled or covered up, the public has less confidence in the abilities of their governments and public officials to do their jobs but in the case of the *Ruby Princess*, too many people have been afflicted with coronavirus, too many people have died as a result of contracting coronavirus on this cruise ship, and it might not be possible to obfuscate or produce media spin for too long before the public demands concrete answers.

And the answers need to be provided for who authorised the entry of the *Ruby Princess*—not once but twice within a two-week period—why Australian Border Force overturned a decision to keep the vessel out of Sydney Harbour, and why it was allowed to dock at the International Terminal. Not only is it important for the public to know the answers to these questions, but in whose interests these decisions were made. Were there any relatives of key government ministers on board? Were there any commercial and corporate considerations that were taken into account that overrode public health concerns?

The owner of *Ruby Princess*, Carnival Corporation & PLC, is a company with a fleet of over 100 cruise ships, international revenue of $US21 billion in 2019, and staff of over 120,000. It's a massive company. It comprises a high-powered eleven-person board of directors, including the Australian businesswoman, Katie Lahey. Lahey was a long-serving CEO of the Business Council of Australia—a lobby group with long-established links with the Liberal Party—has a long history within the tourism sector and was chair of Tourism and Transport Forum Australia.

Up until September 2018, Lahey was a member of the Great Barrier Reef Foundation's Chairman's Panel—the same Foundation that received an unprecedented and controversial $444 million payment from the Liberal–National Government in 2018. She was also the Executive Chairman of the Australian arm of Korn Ferry, a global organisational consulting firm, up until 2019.

Also at Korn Ferry is Robert Webster, a former National Party politician, who was part of the Greiner and Fahey Liberal–National Party ministries between 1998–95, including a stint as Minister for Tourism in 1992. Although he was a member of the National Party up until his resignation from Parliament in 1995, he has been a member of the Liberal Party since 1996, a key fundraiser for the party, as well as making personal donations of almost $30,000 to the party over two donation reporting periods in 2016 and 2017.

Korn Ferry has strong links with the Liberal Party, and is often contracted to headhunt senior government positions, including a $71,500 contract to find a new chairperson for the Northern Australia Infrastructure Facility Board in 2015. It was also paid $160,000 to find a new ABC chairperson in 2018 after Justin Milne was forced to resign, even though the government overlooked their recommendations and opted to appoint Ita Buttrose.

Since the Liberal–National Coalition returned to federal office in 2013, Korn Ferry has received $2.9 million in consultancy fees, and currently holds a contract worth $616,000 for recruitment services provided to the NSW Government.

There are strong links between Lahey, Webster and the Liberal Party. Was favourable treatment provided to the *Ruby Princess* by the NSW Minister for Health, Brad Hazzard, because of these connections? Were there any passengers of interest on that cruise to New Zealand that could have influenced Hazzard's? In the interests of transparency, is there anything else the public needs to know?

There were also other rumours circulating that the parents-in-law of the Minister for Pacific Islands, Alex Hawke, were on board the *Ruby Princess*—and this influenced the decision by Australian Border Force to accept entry of the vessel into Australian waters—but this has been denied by Hawke and, so far, there has been no evidence to support this claim. There were other issues at play as well: was this scandal swept away too easily to cover over other issues in the management of the Sydney ports? There have been some allegations of theft of fuel, and payola to harbourmasters for favourable treatments to particular shipping companies to bypass illegal activities. Are there other issues of corruption that need to be investigated, but will they be covered over because they might be too politically difficult to handle?

The larger issue at this stage, however, is the *Ruby Princess* was allowed to dock in Sydney Harbor with 158 ill passengers on board. And in the context of what was happening with the *Diamond Princess* off the coast of Japan, where 712 of the 3,711 passengers and crew tested positive for coronavirus, an event which occurred just before the *Ruby Princess* incident, there is an expectation government officials and ministers would be monitoring similar events in other countries, learn from those experiences and ensure the same mistakes are not repeated. But this did not happen.

Almost 10 per cent of the 5,000 coronavirus cases across Australia originated from *Ruby Princess*. People have died. Ministers with the responsibility for avoiding this saga should have already typed up their resignation letters or sacked by Prime Minister, Scott Morrison, and NSW Premier Berejiklian. But they are still there, when they shouldn't be. It's essential for the public to know who was responsible for the mismanagement of the *Ruby Princess* incident, or if public health was compromised because of vested interests, ministerial incompetence and inaction.

Many coronavirus infections and deaths could have been avoided if the correct course of action had been taken. If the public is to hold confidence in the institutions deemed to protect the public, it's essential these ministers be stood down now, and an inquiry into their actions be held as soon as possible.

*

Politics and coronavirus: The issues flying under the radar

8 April

The coronavirus is a once-in-a-century event, and it's seriously affecting local and world economies. It's primarily a health threat and, of course, because of this, it is the focus of everyone's attention. But while most of the population is focusing on coronavirus, the business of politics continues, and there are several issues flying under the radar.

The NSW Government has approved a new coalmine under one of Sydney's most important drinking catchment areas—this is the first approval of this type for twenty years, and was a decision made just before New South Wales Parliament was suspended due to the coronavirus and, no doubt, it seems to have been a hastily-arranged approval to avoid proper scrutiny and attention.

The federal government is also attempting to make amendments to Fair Work legislation as well, using the coronavirus crisis and the effects on business conditions as a reason to reduce working rights and, supposedly, to protect jobs.

There have been some suggestions that careful scrutiny of political leaders is not needed at a time when they need to get on with the job of government and doing everything they need to do to protect the economy and the community. Of course, it could be seen to churlish at this time, but politicians rarely miss opportunities to use a crisis to their advantage and try to implement their specific agendas, irrespective of what the circumstances are. It is precisely at these times that more scrutiny should be placed on governments and their actions, not less.

Coronavirus is taking up most of the community's energy and time, and consuming a great deal of political time and resources. The business of politics continues, irrespective of external circumstances—laws have to debated and enacted; the management of society needs to continue but that also means these laws and parliamentary processes still need to be assessed and scrutinised.

Allowing a coalmine to be created near Sydney's water catchment areas would be one area that needs to be carefully scrutinised, especially in the context on the NSW Government selling off the Barangaroo site in the Sydney CBD region for a peppercorn amount to Crown Resorts and, according to former NSW Auditor–General, Tony Harris, an arrangement that could have cost the government millions of dollars in forgone revenue.[18]

It's also in the context of the NSW Government reducing funding to the Independent Commission Against Corruption after ten members of the NSW Government were forced to resign after the ICAC's Operation Spicer into the Liberal Party slush-fund, Eight By Five. The NSW Government is not a good government: it's a government that has spend eight years primarily building, or promising to build, but not finishing very much effectively: the Sydney–Randwick light rail system an excellent example of this. Ineffective and incompetent governments need to be continuously scrutinised, and the onset of a pandemic doesn't reduce the need for this.

Coalmining is an activity many people would assume to occur in remote areas but the NSW Government's mining proposal is to take place within the Sydney urban area, under the brand of Metropolitan Mine. The owner of the mine, Peabody Energy, is based in the United States and is the largest privately-owned coal company in the world. It's also a company that has been constantly attacking climate science and environmental protection laws in the countries in which it operates in and, in 2015, rebranded its coal production as the 'cure to poverty' in China and India, through its

---

18 *Australian Financial Review*, 'Ex-watchdog slams O'Farrell on Packer casino', John Kehoe, 30 October 2012.

'From Candles to Computers' campaign but, in effective, it's more than likely a campaign to cure their sagging share prices.

Peabody Energy has received approval for three new long walls under the Woronora reservoir in southern Sydney, where it will be able to extract vast amounts of coal. Woronora is large reservoir which supplies water to southern Sydney in the Illawarra region and there's great potential for coal mining activities to interfere with drinking water supplies. The NSW Government knew the approvals would create controversy and waited for the moment where the public and the media were focused on other overwhelming issues, such as the management of coronavirus. The other factor the government pointed out in a low-key announcement in the New South Wales Parliament was the Metropolitan Mine was all about creating scores of new jobs, but the mining industry is heading towards a low labour-intensive future and focusing more on automation, so this is a promise that won't actually come to fruition.

Miners have an unreasonably close tie with both the New South Wales and federal Parliaments: Scott Morrison infamously brandished a piece of coal during Parliament Question Time; the member of New England, Barnaby Joyce, and Queensland Senator, Matt Canavan, have both been calling for banks to provide more finance to miners, even though banks have assessed coalmining as an unsustainable industry and not worthy of investment.

It isn't improper or illegal for mining industries to have access to government ministers but their access shouldn't be any more than other key industries and their motivations and their influences should be kept in the public spotlight. Of course, governments will try to minimise attention on the issues they feel are contentious or may cause political problems and, with the media and public focused on coronavirus issues, it's obvious they'll force unpopular projects through when other issues are dominating the political landscape.

In the federal sphere, the Attorney-General, Christian Porter, wishes to amend the *Fair Work Act* and with Parliament currently in session, the government will prepare legislation to amend working conditions and the Award system, ostensibly, for businesses to be able to employ more staff. But the Secretary of the Australian Council of Trade Unions, Sally McManus, has suggested this kind of legislation—even if it is temporary—is unwarranted and is likely to lead to employers taking advantage of the legislation to reduce conditions for existing employees, rather than improve them.

Whenever legislative changes are made, it's very difficult to go through the political process of undoing them—there is the political time and capital involved in developing this, and the government is usually unlikely or unwilling to pass new legislation that supersedes their previous legislation, and McManus understands this. And it's the main reason why unions are resistant to these changes, because they're unlikely to be temporary.

There is a high level of electoral goodwill provided to governments during this coronavirus pandemic, but also an expectation governments will not use the opportunity to overreach and extend the more unpalatable parts of their political agendas. Goodwill is difficult to build but easy to destroy—reputations carefully built up over long periods of time can be quickly dismantled with unfortunate and careless actions, as witnessed during the Howard government's commitment to WorkChoices in 2005: a long-term government ruined its credibility with an unbridled enthusiasm for extremist workplace reforms that leaned too far towards employers, and was removed from office at the 2007 federal election.

These legislative proposals for workplace reform are a genuflection to the neoliberal contingent in Australia, which includes the Institute of Public Affairs, arguing the primacy of the economy in managing society and, to support this primacy, the role of government needs to be reduced, and laws that restrict human behaviours need to be removed and freedom of speech needs to be increased. But what the coronavirus has shown is that at this time of crisis, a strong and stable government is needed, and the economy by itself is too fragile. It took around three-to-four weeks for the coronavirus to damage the economy—possible irreparably—and to show that new economic thinking is required to guide the post-COVID-19 world. The economy is a central component of society, but it's also important for the economy to serve the people who make up that economy.

Neoliberalism as an economic philosophy has been failing for some time—it caused the global financial crisis in the late 2000s, and has been found wanting during the time of coronavirus. In the same manner of how neoliberalism introduced itself in the early

1980s—through a combination of leadership on both sides of the Atlantic that supported these ideas, Cold War politics, and economic thinking dominated by the Chicago school of economics—the end of neoliberalism will be a slow transition.

Economies move and change according to the human mores of the time. After World War II, economies were rebuilt, communities were rebuilt, countries were rebuilt, due to large-scale government investment into the economy. At that time, Nazism, fascism and chauvinist nationalism was defeated but in the 2020s, the world is seeing something different. Governments all around the world will need to intervene in their economies to restructure, stimulate and rebuilt but if governments are not careful and fail to calibrate the economy to the needs of the community, neoliberalism could possibly be replaced with form of economics that couples government intervention with right-wing nationalism, the opposite of the post-World War II era. That would be the worst of all options.

But what the pandemic has shown is that governments are crucial and the model of privatisation of social services has not worked. The fact that Healthe Care Australia, the third largest private hospital group in the country, cancelled surgeries and stood down 600 nurses at a time when COVID-19 cases have been surging across Australia is a key indicator of this failure. The public sector manages resources more fairly than the private sector and while there are areas where privatisation has resulted in more efficient delivery of some services, the profit motivator usually means social objectives are often misplaced or left behind.

The Liberal–National Coalition is in government today and is a strong proponent of neoliberalism. The irony is that even though it is more fanatical about conservative neoliberalist values than even the British government of Margaret Thatcher ever might have been, it is a government attempting to introduce programs and policies that a socialist might consider to be too extreme: $303 billion in stimulus spending is available to it; through the JobKeeper and JobSeeker programs, and an increase in Newstart funding, Australia is close to having a *de facto* social wage; free childcare has been introduced, albeit for a short period of time. Some private hospitals have been semi-nationalised; Qantas has received the bulk of stimulus support payment provided to the aviation industry of $715 million. These are radical interventions into the market from a government least likely to implement these kinds of interventions, but they are assuming that the stimulus support will be short-term, suggesting the economy needs to 'snap-back' to its pre-COVID-19 state, even though this return is unlikely.

In reality, economic recovery is going to take far longer and industries that have been seriously affected by this initial downturn, if they wish to survive in the longer term, will need to reform. And reform of these industries will need government support and stimulus for a much longer period of time.

Much of the rhetoric of economic 'snap-back' is a play to the Liberal Party's key allies and supporters, and a reassurance to those who voted for the Liberal–National Coalition in the 2019 election, that economic redemption is not too far away. But this is dishonest: it would be better if the government used this time, energy and resources as stepping-stone to a new and reformed economy, rather than a promise of a return to a false economic nirvana, an empty promise of the cruelest kind.

The economy needs to morph into an area diametrically opposite to the neoliberalism of the previous forty years: this is not to suggest the world is going to quickly move into a golden age of democratic liberalism that will be discussed in revered tones for the centuries to come but, more likely, an incrementalist movement. The teenagers of today—those who aren't in a position of influence—will be deeply affected by the economy over the next decade, similar to the way a generation of youth were affected during the time of World War I, the Great Depression, and World War II. These are the people who will bear the brunt of the economic damage caused by COVID-19.

The mainstream media has been quick to point out how the Prime Minister has traversed all parts of the ideological landscape to win over members of Parliament and convince his supporter base to implement actions that have been traditionally anathema to the Liberal Party. But, relatively speaking, it was an easy decision to make. The economy needed high-level stimulus, irrespective of the attitudes of the conservative rump of the Liberal Party: without stimulus, the economy would have died. And as a result of these ideological back-flips, Morrison has received a massive boost in opinion polls, along with every other incumbent political leader across the Australian states and territories. It was the correct economic move, as well as the correct political move.

As prime minister during a time of crisis, Morrison will be given great credit and great leeway, because Australia—as well as the rest of the world—is facing new and difficult circumstances. Morrison has had several opportunities to show his credentials as a prime minister and he has failed miserably. He may do better in the management of the coronavirus, because it seems he has started to take more notice of health and economic experts, and his more reckless actions have been hampered by the states and territories, through the National Cabinet process. And this is an obvious outcome: it is the premiers of the states and chief ministers of the territories who have responsibility for health and education, and will take the political consequences if any of these areas fail during this crisis; Morrison will not. This is a key issue in understanding the behaviour of the Prime Minister during this pandemic.

*

Pell Mal

8 April

The cardinal of the Catholic Church and former Archbishop of the Melbourne and Sydney dioceses, George Pell, has been released from prison, after the High Court recently overturned a court conviction of historical sexual abuse offences. Pell had been found guilty by a Victoria jury in 2018—a unanimous 12–0 decision, and a subsequent appeal was rejected by the Victoria Court of Appeal. Pell had been originally sentenced to a prison term of six years: although the High Court found that the complainant's evidence in the case was thoroughly credible and reliable, "the evidence did not establish guilt to the requisite standard of proof", and as a result, the conviction was quashed and Pell was released from jail. That's how the Australian legal system operates, and this is the end of the case—there's no avenue for the prosecution to take the matter to the British Privy Council; it's all over.

Pell's supporters within the Catholic Church and the media have compared his case to the infamous case of Lindy Chamberlain in the 1980s—accused and found guilty of murdering her baby daughter at Uluru, who also had her convictions quashed—but there are substantial differences. Firstly, Chamberlain's conviction wasn't quashed in the High Court, which initially dismissed her appeal; the conviction was overturned by the Northern Territory Supreme Court because the evidence used to convict her and her husband, Michael Chamberlain, was flawed, and did not support the case against them.

However, in Pell's case, the evidence has not changed, and no new evidence has been presented. The High Court decision was not based on the interpretation of law, but an interpretation of definition of 'reasonable doubt', and the summary by the High Court of their decision went to great lengths to point this out. Although the conviction against Pell has been quashed, it did not completely exonerate him and does not suggest he is completely out of legal reach: there may be grounds for civil cases against Pell and the Catholic Church, or even further criminal charges, as two new accusers have alleged they were abused by Pell in the early 1970s, and wish to pursue these matters further.

It has to be noted, however, these revelations were part of another court case—the so-called 'swimmers' trial—that was held concurrently with the case in 2018 which originally found Pell guilty. That case was dropped by the Victoria Director of Public Prosecution, after the Chief Judge disallowed crucial evidence from the defendants, and there was little chance of a conviction. It needs to be made clear that if these other cases do proceed, they will be civil and not criminal matters, and the defendants will be looking for financial retribution and compensation, and no criminal charges will be laid.

George Pell is currently seventy-nine years of age, and it's just a question of what kind of new legal material or allegations—if there are to be any—are made, and how long any new processes would take, considering it's very unlikely for the people who are supporting Pell—whether it be the Catholic Church or other interested parties—to run out of the financial resources required to defend these cases, or provide financial compensation in civil cases, if it ever comes to this. The Catholic Church is never short of the money it needs to protect itself or its leading figures within the church, and this would be one of those occasions.

This case, and any other new cases that do arise, will be defended by Pell and the Catholic Church, and that is their legal right to do this, as it their right to soak up the vast amount of church resources to defend themselves. And they may need it: during the Royal Commission into Institutional Responses to Child Sexual Abuse, there were many submissions that were redacted so the information presented to the Commission didn't become prejudicial to Pell's twin cases held in Victoria during 2018. This redacted material has never been made public, and now that Pell's criminal cases are over—for the time being—there is a reasonable expectation the Attorney–General, Christian Porter, will release these submissions un-redacted.[19]

Pell's case has highlighted the difficulties in prosecuting cases involving historical events of child sexual abuse and has provided an unsatisfactory conclusion: Pell was found guilty by a unanimous jury decision, a decision which was upheld by the Supreme Court of Victoria. But the High Court overturned a decision made through the cornerstone of the criminal justice system—trial by jury—and supported the evidence provided by the complainant but decided it was not to a sufficient level to justify guilt. Ultimately, it will be seen that this is correct legal decision but one key factor has been ignored by this process: where is the justice for the victims of child sexual abuse?

Pell has his supporters in the conservative media: he is a climate change denier, outspoken critic of same-sex marriage, regards homosexuality as a sin and "a much greater health hazard than smoking",[20] and was a guest of honour at the seventieth anniversary event of the Institute of Public Affairs in 2013. Pell will be looked after, no matter what happens to him.

For the victims, they are very much left to their own devices, in many cases, without access to legal resources or health support. The process for these types of cases needs to be reformed, but it's evident the reform of this nature will be a long and protracted process—detractors of Pell have called for the High Court to be reformed, whereas his supporters have called for the Victoria judicial system to be reformed[21]—it can't just be a situation where whenever a legal

---

19 The un-redacted submissions were released by the Attorney–General on 20 October 2020. Attorney-General for Australia and Minister for Industrial Relations, 'Un-redacted Royal Commission reports released', October 2020. https://www.attorneygeneral.gov.au/media/media-releases/un-redacted-royal-commission-reports-released-20-october-2020

20 *The Washington Post*, 'Opinion: George Pell and the end of the 'Melbourne Response', Richard Glover, 27 February 2019. https://www.washingtonpost.com/opinions/2019/02/26/george-pell-end-melbourne-response

21 *The Tablet*, 'The Cardinal Pell case highlights the serious need for legal reform', Frank Brennan, April 2020. https://www.thetablet.co.uk/features/2/17852/the-cardinal-pell-case-highlights-the-serious-need-for-legal-reform

decision fails to deliver an adequate or just response, the entire system needs to be scrapped and rebuilt but it is very clear that other avenues of redress need to be created for victims of child sexual abuse.[22] For the general public, Pell is a sideshow and it's hoped he disappears from the political landscape and is never heard from again. Whatever happens to him now—or through any future legal cases that may arise—will create divisions within the community, and with key and powerful supporters in the legal and media industries, Pell will always be exonerated by these players, even if he is ever found guilty.

The emphasis now should be focused upon how the community can support the victims of these crimes and provide for proper healing.

*

---

22 *Arena*, 'Judging Cardinal Pell: For Victims of Historical Sexual Abuse the Justice System Needs Further Reform', Robert Llewellyn-Jones, May 2020. https://arena.org.au/judging-cardinal-pell-for-victims-of-historical-sexual-abuse-the-justice-system-needs-further-reform

Government performance during the coronavirus crisis

22 April

Community lockdowns are continuing all across Australia and it seems the effects of the coronavirus will be here for some time to come—on the surface, the federal government seems to be managing the crisis but, on closer inspection, there's a massive gap between the rhetoric and action.

There have been many announcements related to the $303 billion in stimulus packages to be released over the next six months, but aside from the $750 one-off payment made to pensioners, not one cent has left the coffers of Treasury. At this stage, the JobKeeper and JobSeeker programs have been held up by bureaucracy and the funding needed to urgently stimulate and support the economy has been a small trickle so far.

The Prime Minister, Scott Morrison, did loudly announce he was going to leave ideologies at the door during this pandemic, but last week he suggested this is the perfect time to introduce industrial relations reform and company tax cuts as an essential part of a COVID-19 recovery program—this does sound like the talk of an ideologue: it's the free-market neoliberal talk from the Liberal Party conservative business base, and it's the drum many in big business have been beating for some time. This is classic right-wing economic philosophy and it's an outdated economic thinking that won't work at a time when the world is starting to work towards a new form of economy.

Trust is an essential part of government during a time of crisis, but it can't just be assumed political leaders will act in the best interests of the overall community. Rather than trusting the information put out by this government, it needs to be scrutinised carefully, because quite often, their actions are not exactly what they seem.

Implementing these kinds of extreme and ideologically-driven policies does not accord with the current circumstances, where the economy is extremely weak and has been for some time and has been exacerbated by the pandemic. The Liberal–National government wants a return to the moribund and unsustainable economy, because it's a system that favours its supporters in the business community and other vested interests. To use the state of the economy as a reason to implement harsher employment laws and reduce working conditions is extremely disappointing, it shows a government that is out of its depth, out of ideas and far from being a government that has 'left its ideology at the door', is trying to use the pandemic to ram through its ideology at precisely the wrong time to introduce it.

A prime minister needs to be in control of any crisis, but the issue here is that he claimed to be avoiding political gamesmanship when, in fact, it was precisely what he was doing—it's to be expected that politicians will play political games but this is not the right time. Morrison has been engaged in double-speak; raising expectations the economy will 'snap-back' and Australian borders need to be opened up urgently.

Morrison has also pushed the notion that the newly-introduced COVIDSafe app—produced by a Liberal Party-affiliated company at a cost of at least $3.8 million, and costing a further $64 million in promotion and advertising—can act like "a sunscreen" against coronavirus and if more people download the app, the economy will open up, people will be able to "go to the footy" again and life will return back to normal.[23]

But this is a false hope—COVIDSafe is a low-grade tracing app which has too many operational flaws and is not a panacea for anything at all. The Minister for Human Services, Stuart Robert, is responsible for the implementation of the COVIDSafe app, but

---

23 *The Guardian*, 'How did the Covidsafe app go from being vital to almost irrelevant?', Josh Taylor, 24 May 2020. https://www.theguardian.com/world/2020/may/24/how-did-the-covidsafe-app-go-from-being-vital-to-almost-irrelevant

has had as much success explaining the technical aspects of the app, as did the former Attorney-General, George Brandis, when inaccurately describing the functions of metadata in 2014.[24]

In essence, the government didn't understand how the COVID Safe app was operating—or not operating—and erroneously implied the app was actually a safeguard against the virus. Perhaps if there was a different minister involved here, the public might have more confidence in the messaging, but the Liberal Party has a failure of management of technologically-based projects: the roll-out of the National Broadband Network has largely been a disaster; the online management of the 2016 census was a disaster; there was a breakdown in the Centrelink website at the beginning of the pandemic.

All modern smartphones have the ability to be tracked through the mobile phone networks, and it seems many mobile phone users are happy to provide their mobile data to companies such as Facebook and Twitter, but distrusting of how the Australian government might use their information, for electoral gain or surveillance.

So far, the COVIDSafe has been ineffective, and it's not entirely clear what its goals are. The government changed its messaging about the app quite frequently, debating whether it would need to be mandatory or not; announcing that at least 50 per cent of the population would need to download the app for it to be useful, but then retracting that and confusing the information with other messaging.

It was then announced the app had to on at all times for it to be effective and, if a user contracted coronavirus, it was up to them to change the settings on the app. It seems there are too many user-based issues that come into play here: people forgetting to have the app open at all times; not updating their settings; forgetting to have the phone with them or switched on.

The app seemed to be a poor idea, and badly planned and badly managed—which could also be replicated as a mission statement for this government: bad planning and bad management. While these technical flaws are the major drawback within the COVIDSafe app,

---

24 ABC News, 'Attorney-General George Brandis struggles to explain Government's metadata proposal', Sarah Dingle, 7 August 2014. https://www.abc.net.au/news/2014-08-07/brandis-explanation-adds-confusion-to-metadata-proposal/5654186

the main issue as present is the politically disengaged audiences throughout Australia who show little interest in government, and low levels of trust even at the best of times. These suspicions seem to be based around the ulterior motivations by this government, especially when it comes to the handling of private digital data.

Some of these suspicions were evident during the creation of the My Health data system in 2018 where the Minister of Health, Greg Hunt, wanted to automatically place the health data of every citizen in Australia on the system, without supporting legislation that could protect privacy and personal data—without this legislation in place, the government could have sold off collated data to a third party, and the public would not have been able to do anything about it.

Aside from the issues about data management and privacy within the collation of private data, there are also issues related to public health messaging and the confusion arising from contradictory material provided by government. The Deputy Chief Medical Officer, Paul Kelly, was asked why it's acceptable for fly-in-fly-out workers to be crammed into interstate airflights from capital cities to remote mining towns, while the community messaging is for people to keep a distance of 1.5 metres from each other.

Kelly's response was to suggest these flights are short—which they are not—and there was close to no chance of acquiring the virus on these flights—which is contrary to current medical advice and current medical practice. It seemed to be more evidence of the government condoning actions that were in the interests of Liberal Party-supporters and donors—such as the mining sector—and further embed the notion that exemptions for any public health directives are always available, for the right people. Health and travel exemptions have been granted to the mining industry, and exemptions are also being requested by the horse racing industry, but these are industries where people congregate in close quarters.

There will always be a strong relationship between vested interests and this federal government—those that contribute directly to the Liberal Party, seeking to influence government action and policy, and ensuring whatever government-imposed activity is implemented for the rest of the community, doesn't apply to them. That's the nature of vested behaviour, and it's usually how the business of government and stakeholder management operates.

The conservative side of politics, in unison with national media proprietors, has called for an end to the lockdown—even acknowledging that ending the coronavirus is a major health risk and many people could die from ending the lockdown, imploring that the economy needs to survive, and suggesting the economy has been destroyed for the sake of saving an older generation of the community that is going to die anyway.[25] Is this really the type of economy that is worth saving?

The economy exists as a tool to assist society function efficiently, but it's just one of the many tools. Society and its economy also need a social contract to outline what are the duties, rights and responsibilities of citizens. Many of these issues are being pushed into the background and most of the efforts of this reactionary government are to protect the interests of the big players: the billionaires and captains of industry who brag about their resilience and strength of character to get to where they are but, as soon as conditions are not favourable to them and anything goes wrong, they're the first ones to call on the government to support them. A system that operates in this manner is a failed system. It's a system that has failed twice in 2020, first during the national bushfires and now during the pandemic. It's a system that cannot be sustained.

Unfortunately, conservative governments build their ideology on the economy first. The economy is an important part of the society, but it's essential for the economy to work towards the interests of as many people as possible within that economy. There are many factors to take into account when assessing the state of the economy: national government debt is heading towards $1 trillion, currently estimated to be around $850 billion, and this is an issue that will need to be resolved at some point. But lowering company tax rates and implementing industrial reforms that will reduce wage levels is probably not the best approach to tackling this issue.

National economies work best when there is a more equitable share of income spread throughout the entire economy, in exchange for fair prices for labour, goods and services. In those circumstances, coupled with an expanded middle-class, there is less poverty, less call on health services, less need for the law system and

---

25 *Australian Financial Review*, 'Lives matter but at what cost?', John Kehoe, April 2020. https://www.afr.com/politics/federal/lives-matter-but-at-what-cost-20200407-p54hox

courts and, ultimately, less call on the welfare system. But this is a government that wants different mechanisms in place: low wages, higher unemployment to keep wages low, lower company taxes so the business sector can increase their profits. The most successful economic period in Australia was during the last 1940s up until the early 1970s. Prices were high, but wages were higher. Employment was full and as Bob Hawke suggested, the leader of the Australian Council of Trade Unions at the time, there would have been permanent union strikes if the rate of unemployment reached the rate of 3 per cent, a level that is almost unthinkable today.

But if the post-World War II era is considered a most successful era, what can be made of the current era? Global health standards are at their best levels ever, and technological advances mean the world is at a far superior standard of living when compared to the 1960s—what can be made of these factors? Is it enough to simply assess economic performance on purely economic factors, and what will the economies of the future look like? Will the pandemic guide how these new economies will function, or is there a need for government intervention—or a point somewhere in between?

Currently, many people are working from home environments, rather than going into their offices. Although the state of Australia's internet is poor compared to world standards—currently ranked sixty-eighth in the Speedtest global internet index—the internet and online commerce have become large players within the economy.

Although long-term research is not available at this stage, short-term analysis suggests working from home has resulted in productivity boosts, and a better work–life balance[26]—not radical ideas, but concepts that were discussed both in Australia and the United States in the early 1970s.

These kinds of structural changes within the workplace and commercial behaviour rarely occur quickly, although the pandemic does mean these changes will be fast-tracked and, in many cases, have already been implemented. The value of work is moving outside of the relationship with dollar figures; the meaning of work and how it contributes to the overall society is also changing, away

---

26 *The Conversation*, 'Have we just stumbled on the biggest productivity increase of the century?', John Quiggin, 2020. https://theconversation.com/have-we-just-stumbled-on-the-biggest-productivity-increase-of-the-century-145104

from gross domestic product or per capita figures, which are blunt financial measurement instruments. Other factors need to be taken into account when assessing economic output and performance—environmental issues, social issues, relationships between people.

In 2008, the Kingdom of Bhutan introduced the Gross Happiness Index—this was ridiculed by many others in the developed world and the assumption was that this was an attempt by a very secretive and authoritarian government to mask a poorly performing economy. But there has been a groundswell of support to consider other factors in economic performances, and this includes the economists Amartya Sen, Joseph Stiglitz and Jean-Paul Fitoussi, who have argued that rather than being ridiculed, measuring 'happiness' and wellbeing will enable economies to become more sustainable and supportable into the future.[27]

The economy of Bhutan was one of the poorest world economies in 2008, and its GHI was easily ridiculed. However, a different country with one of the more sophisticated economies in the world, New Zealand, introduced a wellbeing index in their Budget last year, and included factors such as a life satisfaction index, human rights, housing standards, education and human relationships. Internationally, there is a measurable Human Rights Index, a World Education Standard: it's not such a huge leap to consolidate these indicators into an economic budget.

But new ideas are anathema to this Liberal Party and, after Labor's Shadow Treasurer, Jim Chalmers, suggested Australia's federal Budget should also include a wellbeing index, the Treasurer, Josh Frydenberg ridiculed the proposition: "Labor hasn't delivered a surplus since 1989 so it should surprise no one they're going to look around for some other way to measure economic output." Of course, this is standard and typical response from a treasurer who seeks opportunities for political byplay rather than seeking better solutions, but a wellbeing index is a concept that deserves serious consideration.

It should be pointed out that these initiatives have been recommended by international journals such as *The Atlantic*

---

27 *Harvard Business Review*, 'The Economics of Well-Being', Justin Fox, 2012. https://hbr.org/2012/01/the-economics-of-well-being

Monthly[28] and the New Zealand Prime Minister, Jacinda Ardern, has been praised for implementing a measure that takes a more holistic understanding of economic values. And it should also be noted the New Zealand economy is performing at a far superior level—using traditional economic measurement tools—than the Australian economy.[29]

Part of a transition to a new economy—and whichever economic tools are to be used to define the new economy—has to be the appropriate assessment of where critical infrastructure needs to be built and used, the management of essential services, and a transition towards universal provision of social services, and universal basic income. Small steps may need to be taken to achieve this, but the New Zealand experience has shown that a successful transition can be made.

*

---

28 *The Atlantic*, 'The Happiness Index', Justin Miller, January/February 2010. https://www.theatlantic.com/magazine/archive/2010/01/the-happiness-index/307866
29 Michael West Media, 'Australia v New Zealand: GDP just a fraction of the picture Mr Treasurer', Alan Austin, 29 September 2020. https://www.michaelwest.com.au/comparing-gdp-new-zealand-australia

The bigger picture of the Turnbull and Murdoch battle

22 April

Malcolm Turnbull has released his memoirs, *The Bigger Picture*, and it's filled with many accusations against those who brought down his prime ministership during the August 2018 Liberal Party leadership spill. The most interesting part of the debate has been his claim that News Corporation is in a symbiotic relationship with the Liberal Party—vetting candidates to run elections, deciding who they run positive campaigns for, those whose careers they can destroy—and the book also suggests it was the News Corporation empire that tore down Turnbull because he wasn't prepared to be "owned by Rupert Murdoch".

During his time in office, Turnbull amended media ownership rules, allowing Murdoch to have an even larger concentration of the media; he instigated an inferior National Broadband Network to offer protection for stranded News Corporation assets; and even gave a $30 million gift to Foxtel, with no questions asked and no answers provided. Contrary to Turnbull's claim, his behaviour doesn't seem like the actions of a prime minister who wasn't "owned by Rupert Murdoch".

Turnbull's behaviour was more akin to the behaviour of CEO in charge of government, with Murdoch acting out the part of the Chairman of the Board: Turnbull virtually provided Murdoch with everything he wanted. The installation of a third-rate NBN was an act of economic treachery. Australia could have had a first-rate, world best standard internet system, but it's currently ranked number sixty-eight: at least, Australia should be ranked within the top ten nations, or even the top five.

There were arguments put forward that Australia is geographically too large to adequately install a fast internet system, but the current copper-based network that was built in the 1940s has been used for voice transmission, fax data, general internet usage for almost seventy years and has outlived its usefulness. Fibre optic technology has the ability to provide all the needs for fast data transmission for the next fifty years, but the installation of a poor system now, means that it will need to be upgraded again in the short term. This is another key example of political decisions made in the interests of powerful conservative media players.

The relationship between the Liberal Party and News Corporation has existed for some time—Scott Morrison entered Parliament in 2007 with the assistance of the *Daily Telegraph*, which orchestrated a smear campaign against his preselection opponent, Michael Towke.

Currently, there is a wide range of News Corporation mastheads that actively campaign against the Labor Party: *The Australian* nationally, *The Courier-Mail* in Queensland; the *Daily Telegraph* in New South Wales; the *Herald Sun* in Victoria. News Corporation is malignant cancer on the Australian political landscape, and has a corrosive and corruptive influence on Australia's democracy.

There is also a symbiotic link between the Liberal Party and the Institute of Public Affairs, which in essence, are the political wings of News Corporation. It's a business whose behaviour is similar to that of a criminal enterprise, using its media outlets to incite hatred and division and, during the coronavirus pandemic, has been providing information that is medically negligent and may result in people dying. True to their form, News Corporation has been maniacally pushing for a removal of community lockdowns—primarily to protect their own business interests—and using their editorials to attack epidemiologists and health communicators who are pro-lockdown, such as the ABC's health reporter, Dr Norman Swan.

It's evident Murdoch is a reprehensible man. The business model of News Corporation is reprehensible; it's a model based on the worst of human instincts and it's a model that needs to be restricted and reformed. But this reform will never take place under a Liberal–National government, as the main beneficiaries of this form of media coverage, and in the position of the *de facto* political party of News Corporation.

Whenever the most favourable time arrives, there should be an inquiry into the actions of Murdoch and News Corporation in Australia, similar to the Leveson Inquiry held in Britain during 2011 and 2012. Although the Inquiry delved deeply into Murdoch's affairs, the only punishment for his misdemeanours was the closure of the *News of the World* newspaper, and the British Prime Minister, David Cameron, allowing Murdoch entry into 10 Downing Street via the backdoor, rather than the front.

Murdoch's assets should have been stripped; he should have faced criminal charges for the reprehensible and illegal behaviours of the *News of the World*. The Conservative Party's 2017 manifesto specifically stated the criminal charges arising from the Leveson Inquiry would be dropped completely, and that was the end of the matter.

In the interests of fair and balanced journalism, Murdoch's assets in Australia should also be stripped and broken up—no one enterprise should own more that 10 per cent of Australia's media market—to promote more independent media players. News Corporation has now been attacking the ABC over its reporting of the George Pell case, although it has to be remembered that it was the *Herald Sun* that actually broke the story about Pell and the child sexual abuse allegations, so some credit has to be given where it is due.

However, generally, News Corporation does more harm than good: it's not based on informing the public, it's a propaganda unit for the Liberal Party, which then feeds back into the interests of Murdoch. In a fair and competitive political system, given the number of scandals, instability, and poor economic management, Morrison should not have won the 2019 federal election. And there could also be an argument put forward that Tony Abbott shouldn't have won the 2013 federal election, although the inept and diabolical political performance of the Labor Party—removing Kevin Rudd in 2010 and Julia Gillard in 2013, on both occasions, several months before an election—certainly assisted.

Turnbull only won the 2016 federal election by one seat and the media support offered by News Corporation certainly had a role to play in that victory. Today, Turnbull is out of politics and living as an 'ordinary citizen', although he has stated he wants to be an 'activist citizen', pushing the ideas he's passionate about, including advocating for a Australian republic and promoting climate change issues.

However, action is primarily about acting when the power to act is available, and implementing ideas of conviction: Turnbull totally ignored republicanism during the three years of his prime ministership, he barely uttered a word on it. He also did very little about climate change during his time in office, except for working towards a National Energy Guarantee policy that was dumped as soon as he lost the Liberal Party leadership, and a surreptitious $443 million grant provided to the Great Barrier Reef Foundation, that had not been correctly tendered, failed transparency rules and was not even requested by the Foundation in the first instance.

If ideas that a prime minister is "passionate about" can't be implemented, or even barely discussed, at a time when they have the ultimate power in the country, there's not much chance of those ideas being implemented when they're not the prime minister and existing as the 'ordinary citizen'. Turnbull had the same issues in office that were suffered by Gillard and Rudd: a federal party comprising mediocre people with egos far greater than their capabilities, a classic example of the Dunning–Kruger effect, a type of cognitive bias where people believe that they are smarter and more capable than they are in reality. Going back further in time, former Prime Ministers Ben Chifley and Gough Whitlam had to deal with similar issues: surrounded by incompetent Caucus members who always thought they knew better.

The other key factor for any prime minister is that if they cannot control their own political party, they won't be able to effectively control the government and probably not going to be the leader for very long. The feature of Australia in the post-World War II period up until 2007, was longevity of prime ministers: once they reached the office, they were usually in office for a long time. After the four years of Chifley, Menzies was in office for sixteen years. There was some instability after Harold Holt disappeared at Sorrento Beach in 1967, and three changes of prime minister between 1967–1971 but, after then, longevity became a key factor: Malcolm Fraser, Bob Hawke, Paul Keating and John Howard all provided stable long-term leadership.

After 2007, Kevin Rudd couldn't control the Labor Party, so the Labor Party controlled him. Tony Abbott had issues with competence rather than internal issues within the Liberal Party, but Turnbull had virtually no control of internal matters within the party. One of the people he couldn't control within his party was George Christensen, the federal member for the north Queensland seat of Dawson. Although Christensen is a member of the Liberal–National Party of Queensland, he sits in National Party meetings and is notionally a National member, rather than a Liberal.

Between 2014–18, Christensen spent at least seventy days in each of those years overseas, mainly in Manila visiting his fiancé, for a total of 294 days and, according to the Australian Federal Police, had spent "substantial sums in Manila bars and nightclubs as well as making many small payments to women there". Turnbull has also alleged Christensen's activities and travels were "against the advice of our embassy in the Philippines, he had been staying in seedy hotels in Angeles City, which was not only recklessly unsafe but made him vulnerable to being compromised."[30]

Turnbull issued a 'cease-and-desist' instruction to Christensen when he became aware of this, but Christensen retaliated by suggesting he would use parliamentary privilege to attack Turnbull, allegedly sending him a message: "remember two words: parliamentary privilege; and two more years of it". After that exchange, Turnbull did nothing about Christensen.

A prime minister who didn't act on his passions, and a prime minister who had virtually no power within his own side of politics: a certain outcome of this arrangement is a short-lived prime minister, and Turnbull was in the position for under three years.

The other issue to take into account in this saga is: what is a member of Parliament doing spending so much time overseas?

---

30 *Sydney Morning Herald*, 'The hypocrisy made me sick: Turnbull reveals details about Christensen AFP probe', David Crowe, 17 April 2020. https://www.smh.com.au/politics/federal/the-hypocrisy-made-me-sick-turnbull-reveals-details-about-christensen-afp-probe-20200416-p54kfg.html

Anyone is allowed to travel overseas and spend their own holiday time in whichever way they wish to, but twenty-eight flights overseas each and every year for four years, outside of the normal travel between the seat of Dawson and Canberra doesn't leave very much time to represent the community and undertake all the activities a local politician usually becomes involved in: visiting schools, opening new buildings, meeting with constituents to discuss their concerns. Spending most the time overseas doesn't really allow for too much time to deal with these local issues.

Christensen argued he was in touch with the community while he was overseas through his mobile phone and iPad, but this is a seriously misguided approach to political representation. And, as it turned out, the National Party wasn't too concerned about Christensen's behaviour and absence from his electorate. Ultimately, the electorate of Dawson didn't seem too concerned about it either, rewarding Christensen with an 11.24 per cent swing towards him in the 2019 federal election, turning a marginal seat into a seat now held with a two-party preferred vote of 64.61 per cent. There were other factors in that seat, including debate about whether the Adani coalmine was going to proceed, and the employment that was going to arise from this development but it's now evident that the local member of Parliament spending so much time overseas was immaterial to the public in that region.

Christensen continues his role in Parliament but what is the future for Turnbull and what will his legacy be? It's hard not to think that Turnbull's duration as prime minister was a wasted opportunity: the country could have veered towards a far more ambitious and positive path if he had been a stronger leader but, unfortunately, it didn't turn out that way.

Turnbull did manage to introduce marriage equality, through the *Marriage Amendment (Definition and Religious Freedoms) Act*, but it was a process where the Liberal Party was brought along to it kicking and screaming, ultimately agreeing to a non-compulsory and non-binding postal vote plebiscite, as well as a drawn out parliamentary debate and conscience vote. These successes were few and far between, but the hallmark of Turnbull's leadership was not so much one of wasted opportunities, but rather, missed opportunities and not acting when he had a clear pathway for action.

When he first became prime minister in October 2015, Turnbull was riding high in the polls and should have called an election in November of that year: quick, decisive, stamp his authority over that party with an election victory, and move towards implementing his agenda. But Turnbull meandered for the next six months into a do-nothing prime minister and the more the public—and the Liberal Party—saw of Turnbull, there was less to be enthused about and the understanding that all those issues that people saw in Turnbull—republicanism, climate change, progressive government, renewables—were unlikely to happen.

Far from the decades that were predicted for Turnbull's prime ministership,[31,32] Turnbull lost fourteen seats at the 2016 federal election and by the end of 2018, had lost the leadership of the Liberal Party—and the position of prime minister—and left Parliament altogether. The public record will show Turnbull was just another privileged person who was handed opportunities before he entered politics and used them very well—the Rhodes scholarship; the brief but successful legal career, highlighted by his role in the infamous 'Spycatcher' case against the British government in 1988; the banking career; making $57 million through the internet service provider, OzEmail, by selling his stake at the right time in 1999. Turnbull made the most of these opportunities, but politics is an arena where opportunities need to be fought for and, in those circumstances, he floundered.

Political leaders do have a role to play in public life: US President, Jimmy Carter, is still active at the age of ninety-five: he serves as the Honorary Chair of the World Justice Project, and still teaches at the Emory University in Atlanta.

Julia Gillard has been involved with many projects since she left politics in 2013, including Visiting Professor of Politics at the University of Adelaide; chairwoman of the Global Partnership for Education; chairperson of Beyond Blue. Malcolm Fraser carried

---

31 ABC News, 'Turnbull settles into his most acclaimed role yet', Marius Benson, 20 November 2015. http://www.abc.net.au/news/2015-11-20/benson-turnbull-settles-into-his-most-acclaimed-role-yet/6957220

32 *Sydney Morning Herald*, 'Why Malcolm Turnbull will be our longest-serving PM since Robert Menzies', Elizabeth Farrelly, 25 November 2015. http://www.smh.com.au/comment/why-malcolm-turnbull-will-be-our-longestserving-pm-since-robert-menzies-20151125-gl7dy2.html

out duties with the United Nations; Stanley Bruce also worked with the precursor to the United Nations, the League of Nations. Kevin Rudd has also been actively involved, including a position with the Center for Strategic and International Studies in Washington, and a member of the Global Leadership Foundation.

There is a role for Turnbull in public life and this is to be welcomed. But post-political life could have been so much easier if he had fought much harder for those political beliefs that he held the passion for, rather than caving into the insignificant and insubstantial characters within the Liberal Party.

*

Back to school and the vexed question of opening up

7 May

For those in the community who thought there might be a political consensus during the time of the COVID-19 pandemic, that's turned out to be a false dawn, and it's back to politics as usual. There is a rift developing between the Prime Minister on one side and state premiers on the other, with a difference of opinion about whether schools should be fully reopened.

Scott Morrison wants schools fully reopened now, using limited medical data to force through his agenda, while the premiers want to adopt a more cautious approach, suggesting more medical research needs to be carried out before schools can open up again.

And that approach makes political sense—the state premiers and chief ministers are the ones responsible for managing schools, and if there are viral outbreaks at the schools when they do open up, they are the ones who will be cleaning up the mess and taking the political blame for it.

Education is important for school children, but so is public health for the rest of the community. Why would the Prime Minister be so keen for the schools to open up again so quickly?

There is an old adage: "if you don't have your health, you don't have anything" but in this case, there are several motivations for Morrison. First, it's about attacking the teacher's unions. The Minister for Home Affairs, Peter Dutton—speaking about an issue outside of his portfolio—suggested the Queensland Premier,

Annastacia Palaszczuk, was being cowered by the Queensland Teachers' Union into closing down schools.

Second, there's an ideological pursuit running underneath all of this messaging about the Prime Minister wanting the economy to return 'back to normal' after a series of poorly performing economic quarters. A strong economy wouldn't have large businesses holding out their hands for government-funded stimulus payments two weeks into the pandemic, and there has been a desire from the government to cover over the failures of their neoliberalist approaches to economic management. If the economy can't protect the community during a pandemic, what's the point of that kind of economy?

At this stage, Australia has recorded eighty deaths as a result of coronavirus and, compared to how the rest of the world is managing the pandemic, the management has been relatively successful. And the hard work that has gone into reducing the number of coronavirus cases could be jeopardised if the community is pushed back into workplaces too soon, and could also lead to disastrous outcomes.

The third issue relates to money: there are many big business supporters and donors of the Liberal Party who have lost income during this pandemic and want to start recouping revenue, and it's mainly in their interests for schools to be reopened, for people to return to the workplace, and for the economy to 'snap-back' to it previous state. But there's no real point to that economy if too many people are unwell and too many are dying.

A well-managed and functioning economy is very important to the wellbeing of society. But the economy needs to be reflective of the values of that society. Within neoliberalist economic philosophy, there seems to be a mismatch between the economy and the society and that has been exacerbated by the pandemic. The main reason Morrison wants a 'snap-back' is that he doesn't want the community to get to used to this new way of working.

Teleworking, or working from home, doesn't suit all workers, and there are different economic and flow-on effects that have an impact on the economy, such as a reduction of lunch-time trade in central business districts because of a lack of workers now going to work in those areas. But many teleworkers are having a better work–life balance. It's more complicated because of social distancing; for the time being, they're off the work treadmill. There is less air pollution due to the reduction of road and air traffic, which has obvious health benefits. But these modes of change are beyond the ideological capacities of Morrison and his Treasurer, Josh Frydenberg, and opening up schools will give the first impression of a return to normality and the gateway for the economy to fully open up again.

Many schools have adapted to online learning well, but it's not a clear substitute for traditional face-to-face learning at this stage, and there are many inequities across the digital divide: some schools have a set of academic tasks released to students at the start of the school day and, as soon as those tasks are completed, that's the end of the day for those students, sometimes before midday. Other schools have a comprehensive timetable, similar to online university courses—students logon at their usual class times through a combination of Moodle, Zoom, Microsoft Teams or Google Classroom, and their subject teacher appears on the computer screen. But not all students have access to a screen, some homes don't have the internet available to them—even in some of the more affluent areas—and many primary-aged children need to have parental support, or interaction with other children.

There have been many benefits to online learning, and some of these areas which have worked well could be adopted on a permanent basis. But the primary issue here is not so much the educational aspects—important as that is—but the health issues. What will happen if there are further coronavirus outbreaks when schools reopen?

As the country moves towards the traditional influenza season—although due to the lockdown and social distancing practices, the number of influenza cases has dropped down to 99 per cent when compared to a similar period in 2019—it's probably not the right time to open schools up fully. And there are so many longer-term issues about coronavirus that still remain unclear, with speculation that it may cause permanent damage to lungs, the heart, kidneys. Hopefully, that won't be the case, and at this stage, it's still unclear at what level children have the capacity to transmit the virus to adults, or to other children, as carriers of the virus. The countries that kept their schools open, such as Sweden, have had much larger community infection rates, compared to those countries that either closed their schools, or operated them at a minimal level.

Year 12—the final year of schooling—has been a challenge, but the lockdown and online learning has opened up new educational opportunities for older school students. The first *Education Act* in New South Wales was introduced in 1866 and, aside from some tinkering over the years, education is based on a model introduced in the nineteenth century. There might be some interesting dynamics to appear in the field of education, based on some of the experiences during this 'learn from home' period.

Looking at health outcomes, it's hard not to think there's a large degree of politics involved in the messaging from the Prime Minister and his entourage of chief medical officers. The Hippocratic Oath is practiced by medical doctors to uphold standards of ethics and practices and 'do no harm', but the Oath seems to have left behind. The public messaging of federal CMOs has been confusing, it has been contradictory, and seems to be more about balancing the political considerations of the federal government, rather than essential public health matters.

Dr Brendan Murphy is currently the Chief Medical Officer, and there are two deputy CMOs; Dr Nick Coatsworth and Dr Paul Kelly. Their supporting commentary to open schools fully is based on one piece of evidence: a five-page analysis from NSW Health and the National Centre for Immunisation Research and Surveillance,[33] as evidence for their case, as well as using the report as evidence to support their statements that social distancing is not required in schools, even though the report did not make that finding.

This report is documentary in its nature and outlines key events from nine school students and nine staff infected from fifteen schools: they went to hospital; the schools closed down for three days; the schools were cleaned and disinfected; the school reopened and the students eventually recovered. That's the extent of this report. Epidemiology cannot be based on one report, and public health actions cannot be based on one piece of evidence.

Dr Coatsworth also appeared on the ABC's *Q+A* program recently and was asked how schools could be considered safe for children

---

33 National Centre for Immunisation Research and Surveillance (NCIRS), *COVID-19 in schools – the experience in NSW*, April 2020.

when New Zealand's largest coronavirus hotspot was at a school where ninety-three cases were recorded. Dr Coatsworth responded by stating he wasn't fully aware of the circumstances, before quickly moving back to the contents of the NSW Health report.

It probably suited Dr Coatsworth's argument to open schools to not be "aware of the circumstances" of the school incident in New Zealand but shouldn't the community expect the second most senior chief medical officer in Australia to be fully aware of what was happening in a neighbouring country? Feigning ignorance or not being aware of a school contracting ninety-three coronavirus cases shows that either this medical officer is not doing the work required to earn his rather large salary, or is just pushing the political messages of his political masters.

This is not the time to be glib or ignorant of the details: the health of four million school children and 250,000 school teachers across Australia is at risk. These are not small numbers, and it would be wise to follow the advice of Victoria Premier, Daniel Andrews, who recently suggested more research needs to be considered and comprehensively understood before schools can make the full return to normal operations.

There is other international evidence from German virologist Christian Drosten cautioning against reopening schools.[34] Drosten suggests schools can act as hubs for COVID-19 transmission and although children seem to have less severe symptoms when compared to adults, the children that have acquired COVID-19 are as infectious as adults.

Schools in Denmark reopened on 15 April and their COVID-19 reproduction rate increased from 0.5 to 0.9 over the past two weeks (keeping the reproduction rate under 1.0 is essential in reducing the spread of the virus, and Australia's current rate is 0.8). Drosten's recommendation to the German government is not to open up schools at all. Why is this essential research and evidence ignored by the Morrison government?

The Chancellor of Germany, Angela Merkel, has been one of the outstanding leaders during the pandemic. Of course, she's a scientist

---

34 *Bloomberg*, 'New Reports on Virus in Kids Fuel Uncertainty on Schools', Jason Gale & Thomas Mulier, 30 April 2020. https://www.bloomberg.com/news/articles/2020-04-30/children-with-coronavirus-may-be-just-as-infectious-as-adults

and she can understand health numbers and research presented to her, critically analyse, and understand how important it is to listen to health experts. But in Australia, there's a Prime Minister who wants everyone to get back to work, except for himself: Parliament has been postponed up until August, at a time when Parliament needs to sit and collectively decide the future direction of the nation and how to manage an ongoing health problem.

It's obvious Morrison is not a scientist: he's a politician, and it's in these cases where politicians need to defer to the health experts and scientists. Instead, there's spin, bluff and blustering, at a time when there needs to be unified approach to resolving public health issues. There has been an uneasy veneer of public unity among the respective federal and state/territory leadership teams ever since the pandemic commenced in Australia, but that was blown away recently when the federal Minister for Education, Dan Tehan, decided now is the best time to start attacking Premier Andrews, on live television:[35]

> **Dan Tehan**: This is a failure of leadership by Dan Andrews. Let's be clear about this. And, you know where the impact is being felt? On the most vulnerable children, on those children from low socio-economic backgrounds, Indigenous children, rural and remote students, students with a disability—they're the ones being impacted on this. We've had now the Chief Science Officer of Australia out today, saying, backing in, that that's where the impact is being felt. You speak to [National Party federal member] Darren Chester in Gippsland, you speak to him. Those students there have been impacted by fires. Six months, now, they haven't been connected to a classroom. That's having a real impact on those students. I had a lady approach me in the supermarket last week. She's got a disabled child. The continuity of education for that child means that he's not violent towards her. He is now being violent towards her. I've been approached by a local mental health service provider, who provides mental health into schools. Now, they have to do that now by Skype.

---

35 ABC Television, *Insiders*, David Speers interviews Dan Tehan, 3 May 2020. https://www.abc.net.au/insiders/dan-tehan-joins-insiders/12209900

David Speers: To be clear, Minister, I don't think anybody wants this situation necessarily to continue. It's a question of when it's safe to reopen the classrooms, is the debate, right. Now, you've just accused Dan Andrews of a failure of leadership on this. Are you saying that the system, through the National Cabinet, is not delivering the right result?

Tehan: It's not, because we have one Premier, in particular, who is jeopardising the national consensus on this.

Speers: What about Gladys Berejiklian and what about Annastacia Palaszczuk?

Tehan: What has Gladys done? She now has a plan to open her schools, and she started opening her schools.

Speers: They'll start one day a week in a week's time...

Tehan: ...and if you have a look, the Catholic schools in New South Wales are committed to return to teachers in the classroom in the coming weeks.

Speers: What about Queensland?

Tehan: They have a plan to reopen their schools, as well.

Speers: When?

Tehan: They're hoping to do it by the end of the month. They have a clear plan. Yet, here in Victoria, we don't have one. We have nothing. And, it is the children, ultimately, in the end, and those most disadvantaged, who are suffering. And, I think it's time that we seriously called Dan Andrews out on this.

Tehan backtracked several hours after he attacked Andrews but the political damage had already been done. And this attack would not have taken place without the consent of the Prime Minister. This kind of criticism, if warranted, is best done behind closed doors, but Tehan—with the authority of Morrison—decided to telegraph this political attack publicly: it was uncalled for, it was unnecessary.

This issue cannot be repeated too many times: at a time of crisis, the community wants to see political unity, but this is a federal government that preferences political and ideological outcomes over good health and educational outcomes. Perhaps the adversarial political system—and the people who make up that system—means arriving at a broad consensus on important matters is too difficult to achieve in Australia.

Compared to many other countries, Australia's infection rates are low. Currently, there are 913 actives cases, though the reproduction rate has recently increased from 0.8 up to 1.5, and it needs to be kept below 1.0. The reproduction rate almost doubled in a short period of time, and the coronavirus infections can easily lead to an outbreak, and very quickly. And that's another reason which makes it difficult to understand why the federal government and his supportive CMOs are very keen to open up schools: if the current lockdown continues successfully for another month, the number of active cases could be eliminated entirely.

It's a difficult, and a boring process, but it seems the federal government doesn't have the stamina to persevere with a determined strategy to eliminate the virus but is very determined to take the easier option of just trying to make everything the way that it was before, even though this is a very unlikely outcome.

It's also essential for the federal government to consider the alternative, and the examples can easily be found in many parts of Europe and the United States, where coronavirus cases have spiralled out of control. And the other comparable global incident—although it's now part of folklore rather than the lived experiences from that time—is the 1918 influenza pandemic, also known as the Spanish flu. Although the 1918 flu and COVID-19 are different events, subsequent research suggests the numbers of deaths, estimated to be between 20 million and 50 million, could have been halved if measures such as banning public gatherings and mandating facemasks had been introduced.[36] The Spanish flu lasted for over two years, and arrived in four waves: the second wave was more deadly than the first, the third and fourth waves were not as severe, but still deadly. The number of cases moved from the tens of thousands, quickly into the millions. And this is a situation Australia really should be trying to avoid.

---

36 Proceedings of the National Academy of Sciences, 'The effect of public health measures on the 1918 influenza pandemic in U.S. cities', Martin Bootsma & Neil Ferguson, 2007.

COVIDSafe, not so safe

The Australian government has released COVIDSafe, an app that can be downloaded by citizens to trace their movements and be notified when they've been in close contact with someone who has tested positive to coronavirus.

This seems like it could be a good idea but, the world is not a perfect place: there is a conservative government in office that is very keen to keep people's data; there are privacy issues; trust in government issues; there is a wide range of technical issues that reduces the operability of the app; and, finally, there is one big problem—the app doesn't actually work.

The government has provided different messaging about the viability of the COVIDSafe app: initially, it suggested a download rate of 40 per cent across the entire population was necessary for the app to be successful. Then, they suggested a 20 per cent download rate was acceptable and then virtually suggesting it didn't really matter how many times the app was downloaded. Changing benchmarks, unreliable information; it seems the release of the COVIDSafe app is yet another government marketing exercise, and another attempt for the government to get the economy up and running again, and at the expense of public health.

It's a government that doesn't understand technology. It couldn't get the management of the 2016 national census right—creating the census package online is a large and a complex task, but it's not an impossible task and many countries around the world have managed the online collection of data very well. The low take-up of the COVIDSafe app might also relate to suspicions about whether the government will be able to hold the data securely, and what they intend to do with it. For example, data collected from the Opal travel card used on the Sydney transport network is accessible by NSW Police—yes, it can be used to combat crime and assist with the arrest of suspected criminals but it's not such a leap for governments to use this type of data against people who don't share the same values as that particular government.

The data collated from the COVIDSafe app is also being collated through Amazon cloud storage, private servers, rather than government controls servers, so there may be issues which doesn't inspire confidence with data security. According to the Office of the Australian Information Commissioner, there has also been 'incidental' collation of data from some of Australia's security agencies,[37] and with the 'five-eyes' agreement the United States, Britain, New Zealand, Australia and Canada, there's the possibility of data being shared outside of Australia's borders.

Technology, in general, should be a friend of government. Technology should also be a friend of the public too, but there are deep seated suspicions about the use of any data collated by government—is there a possibility the data mined through the COVIDSafe app will be used for direct SMS marketing by the Liberal Party during the next federal election campaign? Facebook uses data collected from mobile phone users in so many ways to boost its market share, and no one outside of Facebook Inc.—and perhaps many within Facebook Inc.—know exactly how this data is traced, collated and used. Without invoking too many 'Big Brother' and Orwellian overtones, there's a distinct possibility of a government that doesn't really know how to use technology constructively, and using technology for potentially nefarious purposes, as well as potentially losing control of that data.

The name of the app, COVIDSafe, is also a misnomer, and exploits misunderstandings of the nature of viruses within the community. Some people have assumed downloading the app will actually keep them 'safe' from coronavirus, when all it is intended to do is act as a tracing system. The Minister for Health, Greg Hunt, has also been pushing the message: "Want to go to the footy? Download the app", one of the more inane correlations between populism and health messaging, along with promoting the message of a return to the pub—all populist male-dominated areas. Interestingly, the messaging could have also pushed the message of a return to live music venues, or a return to bookshops but the government decided it was best to focus on populism, rather than the broader community.

And, as with most of the programs this federal government releases, the app was released too quickly, developed within a two-to-three-week period. App development is a fine art, with user-experience being a key focus. When the app was rolled out, the interface was clunky; there were too many flaws when the app was released; there

---

37   Inspector–General of Intelligence and Security, 'COVID app data and Intelligence Agencies within IGIS jurisdiction', November 2020.

were so many factors for the user to take into account, such as the requirement for the Bluetooth setting to be switched on for the app to actually function correctly. Again, the government seemed more concerned about getting the populist and political marketing messages out more rapidly than ensuring a viable health tool was functioning correctly and able to work in the public interest.

The app is still in its infancy, but it's yet to detect any contacts that weren't already identified using other means—and the prospects of being able to detect close contacts will remain low.

*

It's on: The Eden–Monaro byelection

7 May

The seat of Eden–Monaro is in a large regional area on the far south coast of New South Wales, and the electors there will be going to the polls in the near future. The sitting member, Mike Kelly, has retired due to ill health, and a byelection will be called for a contest between the current Mayor of Bega Valley, Kristy McBain, and either a Liberal or National Party candidate.

Eden–Monaro was considered one of the 'bellweather' seats and was held by the government of the day between 1972 and 2016. It's a very marginal seat and an unusually split seat geographically—there's a strong Liberal vote on the inland side of the seat, and that's balanced by a strong Labor vote on the coastal side.

This promises to be an interesting byelection—there has been the fallout from the recent bushfires which badly affected this region; the effects of the coronavirus; the practical part of being able to hold a campaign during these times in an area that does have a difficult terrain; and a popular and effective local mayor against a series of candidates offered up by the Liberal and National parties, who have been promptly dismissed almost as quickly as they've been nominated.

It will be a tough and hard-fought campaign—and it should be a tougher-than-usual byelection campaign. Both sides of politics have a good chance to win the seat; the government would be keen to add to its current wafer-thin majority in the House of Representatives and, for the Leader of the Opposition, Anthony Albanese, it would solidify his leadership of the Labor Party. Labor has preselected a good local candidate, and candidates with strong local affiliations tend to do better in this seat than those installed from outside the area.

The National Party toyed with the idea of preselecting the current NSW National Party leader, John Barilaro, but this was quickly canned after revelations that he may have breached COVID-19 restrictions by travelling to his country farm, two hours away from his house of residence, and leaks about how he was undermining the federal National Party leader, Michael McCormack, claiming he had "failed your team and failed as a leader" and "you will never be acknowledged by me as our leader, you aren't, you never will be."[38]

The current NSW Minister for Transport and Roads, Andrew Constance, was also a prospective candidate, announcing his intention to run in the seat, but retracting twenty-four hours later, claiming his original announcement was a "hasty decision".

Constance would have been a good choice for the Liberal Party—he performed very well as the local member during the bushfires towards the end of 2019 and shared his struggles with mental health during that time. Generally, he has been a good local member for the state seat of Bega for seventeen years and won plaudits for his appearances on the ABC's *Q+A* program, where he cast aside the usual political point-scoring that engrosses so many politicians, and outlined the practical solutions that needed to be implemented to reduce the bushfire risk in the region and how to heal the community in the recovery process.

However, he has been a relatively poor performer in the NSW Government, firstly as Treasurer, and then as Minister for Transport, in which he has presided over a number of poorly managed infrastructure projects, including the Sydney light rail project, which had a number of technical problems, legal cases and a budget blow-out of $150 million.

After Constance retracted his candidacy, the Liberal Party briefly considered the current Senator for NSW, Jim Molan, and there

---

38 SBS News, 'You have failed: John Barilaro unleashes on deputy PM in leaked text messages', 5 May 2020. https://www.sbs.com.au/news/you-have-failed-john-barilaro-unleashes-on-deputy-pm-in-leaked-text-messages

were even rumours former Prime Minister, Tony Abbott, could be parachuted into the seat, before wiser heads prevailed.

The other factor for consideration is, even though the seat is marginal, governments rarely take a seat off the opposition in a byelection, and this could possibly be playing on the minds of potential candidates in the Liberal Party. The last instance a seat swung from opposition to the government was in the 1920 byelection in the Western Australia seat of Kalgoorlie, so this certainly is a rare event. And to win this seat, the Liberal Party would also be keen to attract the best candidate possible.

Abbott—if the rumours are correct—on the surface, would be an excellent candidate: an experienced politician, an experienced campaigner, a recognised face, and a former prime minister. But a further inspection of his record shows he was not a top performer: in the position of prime minister for less than two years after a period of turmoil and chaos; guaranteed a seat in Parliament by landing in the safe seat of Warringah, losing the seat once he came across a tough campaigner in Zali Steggall during the 2019 federal election.

It also has to be taken into account that the Liberal Party does have a habit of preselecting inappropriate candidates in Eden–Monaro. Although he did win the seat in 2013, the former head of the Business Council of Australia, Peter Hendy, was a very poor member of Parliament, and lost the seat after just one term at the 2016 federal election.

The Australian electorate does have the habit of 'sending a message' to the government of the day during byelections; historically, there is an average swing against sitting governments of 3.8 per cent on a two-party preferred vote. But this byelection is a difficult one to assess: there are no reliable polls for the seat, and federal opinion polling has been widely discredited since the 2019 federal election. The Prime Minister, Scott Morrison, has been on a high personal approval rating since the coronavirus pandemic commenced; and the effects of the pandemic also make predictions for this byelection difficult.

Byelections are important for both sides of politics, and so it will be for the Labor Party. There have been a wide range of criticisms about the performance of Albanese, ever since he became the Leader of the Opposition in May 2019, but on this occasion, he's acted very swiftly. He nominated McBain the day after Kelly announced his resignation, and she was formally announced as the candidate within a matter of days.

There was some reporting within the media there were disgruntled Labor Party members who were annoyed about having their preselection processes removed and wanted a different candidate, but this always occurs in preselections: whether it's Labor, the Liberal Party, Nationals or the Greens, someone is always going be unhappy about the final selection. That's the nature of politics. So far, even though it might be another two or three months before the byelection actually occurs, the campaign hasn't started off very well for the Liberal Party.

Who will the Liberal Party turn to? There are further rumours Georgina Downer, the twice-failed candidate in the South Australia seat of Mayo, is being considered, although this rumour was started off by journalist Peter van Onselen through social media, rather than any serious deliberations by the Liberal Party. The Liberal Party candidate during the 2019 federal election, Fiona Kotvojs, has indicated she is considering nomination and, in the absence of any other serious contenders, the party may turn to her.

The area of Eden–Monaro was severely affected by bushfires towards the end of 2019 and earlier this year, and the federal government promised a $2 billion fund towards rebuilding the local economy and rebuilding the local community. So far, very little of that funding has actually come through, and that promise was made four months ago. The support that has been coming through has largely been through the NSW Government, the Red Cross, other charity organisations, and direct support from other members of the community. But now there is a byelection coming up in the middle of the area most affected by bushfires, there is an expectation the promised funding will be fast-tracked, as will be the appearance of temporary dongas and other reconstruction efforts.

Because nothing makes governments move faster than the allure of a rare byelection victory, and the gratification of taking something away from their political opponents.

*

Mismanaging the relationship with China

21 May

It's been a year since the Liberal–National Coalition won the federal election and much has happened during that time: Australia has witnessed severe flooding, bushfires, a coronavirus pandemic, and the collapse of the economy. Anniversaries and birthdays should be irrelevant in politics, but the media has been celebrating the anniversary of Scott Morrison's unlikely 2019 election victory so much, they've overlooked so many of the government's continuing errors and mistakes.

Federal Parliament still isn't sitting on a regular basis, which means there hasn't been enough scrutiny of the government's actions and behaviour, and now it seems there are international diplomatic mistakes which could lead to the long-term detriment of the Australian economy.

In this latest issue, there's been some old-fashioned China-bashing and political self-aggrandising on the world stage, where Morrison used his political megaphone to claim Australia was leading the way on a 'weapons inspectors' type of investigation into China's role in the origins of COVID-19—China feels it has been humiliated internationally and has retaliated by slapping an 80 per cent tariff on Australian barley imports, effectively removing this product from its markets. The Australia government has brought along a plastic fork to a political gunfight, and it's the local barley producers that are going to pay the price for the government's diplomatic ineptitude.

Although this action will damage local producers, the right-wing commentary in Australia has been 'dog-whistling' to its audiences, suggesting this is the right action for the government to take and, finally, someone is 'standing up' to the Chinese Communist Party. The commentary has wedded anti-communism with a racial component, implying that trading with China is not as strong as trading with Australia's traditional partners, such as Europe or the United States. For all the faults of the Chinese regime, it's actually quite stable at the moment—considering the Brexit issues in Britain, and the instability of the Trump administration in Washington— and humiliating trade partners internationally, especially such a large trade partner, is quite perilous for Australia.

International trade is a fickle process but if countries only traded with those nations that were fully compatible with their own, or agreed on every policy position, those countries might be pure, but they'd have very few trading partners. Australia does like to provide lectures to other countries but, based on its record on refugees and asylum seekers, and its human rights abuses of Indigenous peoples, if other countries applied the same protocols Australia wishes to apply to others, then there'd be very little international trade with Australia. But trade occurs because diplomacy ignores certain practices and beliefs.

But it's not quite clear what can be gained if Australia engages with a trade war with China, and based on Morrison's megaphone diplomacy, a trade war would be the likely outcome. And losing key Chinese markets would be disastrous for the Australian economy, with local producers then needing to source smaller and more inconsistent markets, which can't just be entered into overnight.

And the decision for the Chinese government to impose a tariff on Australia barley wasn't an overnight decision either. China believed Australia was price dumping into the Chinese market—where goods are sold at a lower price in the international market, when compared to the exporter's domestic market, and obtaining unfair advantage—launched an investigation in November 2018, and the Chinese Ministry of Commerce determined price dumping had occurred.

But withholding decisions until the best moment arises is typically how all countries act, and China made the announcement soon after Morrison decided to lead an investigation of China's role in the outbreak of COVID-19. And China then announced an increase of barley trade from the United States market, a lesson in the basic rules of international diplomacy to the Australian government: whatever unhappiness may exist between two countries, especially when one of those is China, it's best to raise any of those complaints behind closed doors for experienced diplomats to deal with, and shouting from the sidelines will usually leave self-inflicted wounds for the smallest player with the largest megaphone.

Of course, there may have been other international factors at play: Donald Trump is seeking re-election in November 2020, and Morrison may have been offering trade support. This notion may seem absurd, but Trump and Morrison have much in common, with similar policy aims and similar political philosophies. Trump's re-election prospects were looking solid before the pandemic commenced, but now it's more likely he will lose office, with the rising numbers of coronavirus cases and deaths suggesting poor public health management, as well as more instability and mismanagement surrounding his administration. Did Trump call on Morrison for a few trade favours during an election year to help him get across the line on election day?

In the lead up to the 1996 federal election, former Prime Minister Paul Keating told the National Press club that "when the government changes, the country changes"[39]—he said that as a warning to the Australian electorate that a change would see the country slip backwards economically, socially and culturally—the Liberal–National Coalition led by John Howard did win that election, and the country has changed dramatically since that time.

But when the American government changes, the world changes—whatever the political hue and ideology of the United States government, this tends to strongly influence the world in economic matters, geopolitics and, while it usually takes some time, those influences permeate through to the rest of the world. And perhaps this is a part of world history Morrison and Trump understand—elections losses for them would signify a swing against

---

39 *The Weekend Australian*, 'Change the government, change our lives', Tom Dusevic, 23 June 2012. https://www.theaustralian.com.au/national-affairs/change-the-government-change-our-lives/news-story/defa454a0c80e8e6e2ab078542bb3aba

their particular brand of politics and it would be understandable for them to be supportive to each other in whichever way possible.

Morrison's support for Trump adds to the President's international credibility, at a time where he has very few supporters on the world stage. And favours can be repaid in other ways into the future.

Calls for inquiries into other countries are always fraught with danger, especially when the outcomes are unclear. Although much focus has been placed on the wet markets in the Chinese city of Wuhan—which is where the first outbreak of coronavirus occurred—independent data has suggested this area may not have been the source at all.[40] There have been some suggestions the coronavirus may have appeared in Italy and France a month before it was reported.[41] Of course, that's why governments call for inquiries: to determine the cause of specific events based on the available evidence.

The last time there was a major pandemic was in 1918, known as the Spanish flu, even though it didn't originate in Spain. The origins remain unclear, although historical virologists have suggested it may have originated in the industrial zones of the United States, or transferred via China. The true origins will be difficult to track, but as it currently stands, the Chinese government has fully supported an independent inquiry into COVID-19, auspiced by the World Health Organisation—it's an inquiry initiated by the European Union, not the Australia government, as the Australian media keeps suggesting—and like any other country in its position, China doesn't want blame to be the starting point of an independent investigation.

While some in the international community wish to debate the origins of COVID-19, there is still very little known about the virus. Health experts know that it's a highly contagious virus, but are unclear whether infected people are immune from subsequent infections. As with any new virus, it's unclear what the long-term effects are and there are suggestions it may cause serious harm to lungs and other organs and, in some cases, debilitating and long-term

---

40 *Live Science*, 'The coronavirus didn't really start at that Wuhan wet market', Rafi Letzter, 28 May 2020, https://www.livescience.com/covid-19-did-not-start-at-wuhan-wet-market.html#xenforo-comments-2606

41 *New York Times*, 'New Report Says Coronavirus May Have Made Early Appearance in France', Adam Nossiter & Aurelien Breeden, 5 May 2020. https://www.nytimes.com/2020/05/05/world/europe/france-coronavirus-timeline.html

chronic fatigue. It's still unclear if certain types of people are more susceptible. The argument used by the advocates of fully opening up schools is that younger children are unlikely to be contagious, but other evidence suggests that while they may not display any symptoms, they could still be the carriers of the virus, so there are still many unknown medical factors that need to be explored further.

Australia is still managing the spread of coronavirus effectively, and there are currently 569 active cases nationally. These are relatively low numbers and, of course, the government will want to open up the economy and the society to a case load threshold that's acceptable to the community, both in terms of the number of infections, and any deaths that result from a rise of infections—but in this situation, the government that pushes forward for opening up will need to take responsibility when outbreaks occur.

Australia is only three months into the pandemic, but already there's talk about reducing Australia's reliance on Chinese manufacturing and defending "economic sovereignty",[42] even though successive governments in Australia have reduced the local manufacturing base significantly over the past thirty years, especially the Liberal Party since it returned to office in 2013. Government investment into manufacturing would be advantageous to Australia's economy, but with such an ideologically-driven government, and one which seeks nepotism and stakeholder management rather than industrial quality, it's questionable whether it would produce outcomes in the public interest.

And this suspicion of nepotism is based around the formation of the National COVID-19 Commission, a body in which it would be reasonable to expect would comprise leading epidemiologists, virologists, general practice doctors, nurses, other allied health professionals, but comprises mining and business executives instead.

These vested developments occur when there is a lack of scrutiny over government decision-making processes. Ironically, a prime minister who is pushing for the Australian economy to open up and

---

42 Australian Parliament House, Hansard, 8 April 2020. https://parlinfo.aph.gov.au/parlInfo/search/display/display.w3p;adv=yes;db=CHAMBER;id=chamber%2Fhansardr%2F247e20e8-7bbe-4712-afcb-c8833dc6a228%2F0013;orderBy=_fragment_number,doc_date-rev;page=0;query=Dataset%3Ahansardr,hansardr80%20Date%3A8%2F4%2F2020;rec=0;resCount=Default

'time to get back to work', is refusing to go back to work himself, still rejecting calls for Parliament to sit in Canberra and refusing to entertain alternatives, such as electronic meetings, teleconferencing and 'work from home' protocols, which many workers around the nation are practicing successfully.

It's essentially for Parliament to return as soon as possible, to inquire about the management of the China–Australia relationship; COVID-19 management and how large amounts of government funding is being spent; and other peripheral issues related to mismanagement of government spending and illegal actions, such as the "sports rorts" funding debacle involving the Prime Minister and the former Minister for Sports, Senator Bridget McKenzie.

The sitting of Parliament might not be something that enthuses the general public but, whether they like it or not, it sits at the apex of Australia's democratic system and a high level of scrutiny is reflective of a healthy and functioning democracy. The actions of the Abbott, Turnbull and Morrison governments since 2013—coupled with a compliant media—have shown that the structure of democracy can be paper-thin when eyes are averted and nobody checks up on it. And the media is part of this lack of scrutiny.

There wasn't too much questioning about Morrison's 'megaphone diplomacy' in the mainstream media. To be sure, the events and China's reactions were reported, but it's the depth that was lacking, generally, supportive of the government's actions and targeting their criticism of the Chinese government, instead of looking into the history behind the 80 per cent tariff on barley imports, as well as the geopolitics behind the decision.

But it's far easier to create an anti-China frenzy within the Australia community, rather than present a broader set of facts and material. Barley was dismissed as a product that isn't used very much and the Australian economy can easily do without, but the loss of a $5 billion export market over the next five years is incredible significant to the local barley industry, especially during the time of a severe economic downturn.

Perhaps the Australian barley industry will be able to transition into other international markets, but this is not an easy task. Those local producers can't simply make a phone call to other importers in Nigeria, North America or Argentina and suggest they have leftover barley that China won't take and politely ask if they'd like to purchase it. Large-scale international trade doesn't work in that way—relationships need to be developed with key members of government and importers; quotas need to be taken into account; deals need to be negotiated and signed.

Some trade contracts can take up to twenty years to negotiate, although some negotiations can be concluded within several months. For example, the current Brexit negotiations include over forty deals that need to be renegotiated with the other European Union members, and that may take many years after Brexit is finally concluded.

Entry into new markets or increasing trade within existing markets depends on so many factors: do those new markets need these products; if an importer in a country agrees to accept barley from Australia, what can an exporter from that country trade into the Australian market? The Minister for Trade, Simon Birmingham, has suggested barley producers should look elsewhere but it indicates a lack of understanding of how difficult these procedures are and what is involved for these new markets to be found.[43] The Australian government should have managed this issue in a far better way—but they didn't. Australia has one of the best foreign services in the world but it's difficult to downplay a crisis such as this if the Prime Minister makes a unilateral decision to attack the Chinese government, without too much care for the collateral damage, and more concerned about aligning himself with a failing US President and harvesting votes from a domestic audience that is only too happy to join the condemnation of the Chinese government, even if this loss of trade with China results in them losing their own jobs.

Perhaps incompetence in foreign affairs could reveal some more difficulties for Morrison. Perhaps the allegations of corruption within government could be Morrison's Achilles heel, as it would be for any political leader. His reactions to any problems—whether they are domestic or international problems—is to deflect the issue, move onto another topic, or claim that he's already answered

---

43 Nine News, 'Australia to seek alternative barley export markets after China hits farmers with punitive tariffs', 19 May 2020. https://www.9news.com.au/national/australia-to-seek-alternative-barley-export-markets-after-china-hits-farmers-with-punitive-tariffs/2598c332-f3bf-4dec-bac8-7bb3c0c7a093

the question. Morrison is a politician who does not wish to be questioned about anything or discuss any issues that may cause political embarrassment.

Media management is part of managing a successful government, but even a compliant media eventually tires of stonewalling on the bigger issues and feel like they're not being fed the answers they're satisfied with. And perhaps there has been a small but perceptible shift in the manner in which Morrison is being reported by the media. It's difficult to say whether this small shift will lead to anything greater but Morrison leads a government which is not very impressive, especially when compared to the Howard, Rudd and Gillard governments, which despite their flaws, were competent governments.

John Howard knew how to run government, and ran it well, despite the poor quality of ministerial talent, especially in the second part of his eleven years as prime minister. Kevin Rudd successfully steered Australia through the global financial crisis. Julia Gillard, despite all the internal problems within the Labor Party and difficulties managing the media, successfully passed 561 pieces of legislation, the highest ratio of any prime minister in Australian history.

Tony Abbott showed that he couldn't manage his government very well; Malcolm Turnbull was not much better and Morrison seems to be significantly worse. Corruption is systematic and overt, as is the level of nepotism. Since 2013, this favouritism and nepotism has always ended in failure and there always seems to be an endless supply of corruption and mismanagement. And one of the biggest risks is that during a time when so much funding is available to this government to spend on coronavirus spending, as well as the lack of scrutiny, corruption and mismanagement will continue for the foreseeable future. It's a not a good place for the country to be in.

*

The bad luck of being in opposition during a crisis

21 May

It's always difficult for opposition parties to remain relevant during a time of crisis, and there's not much for them to do except to offer their support to the government of the day, try to be constructive and useful, and hope that at some point in the near future, they'll be able to gain some traction for their own actions and political messaging.

The leader of the Labor Party, Anthony Albanese, was the preferred prime minister in opinion polls several months ago but since the coronavirus commenced, he's been relegated to a bit-part role in national politics, has barely been seen, ignored by the media and, with federal Parliament rarely sitting, he's also been denied a national platform.

The Labor Party risks being politically sidelined during this pandemic but is it a matter of waiting until society and the political processes returning to some semblance of normality—if that does ever happen—or a matter of being more proactive and developing different political tactics to work around the current political environment?

The task for any political party in opposition is difficult, even at the best of times but during times of national emergencies, security threats or major health concerns, the electorate tends to favour incumbent governments and opposition parties have to maintain a balance between supporting the government—and the community—during difficult times, but also maintaining relevance and still making a government accountable for their decisions.

If the ultimate goal of an opposition is to gain government, one of the most effective Leader of the Opposition was Tony Abbott between 2009–2013, but his behaviour was nihilistic, destructive and went through the process of opposing everything proposed by the Rudd and Gillard governments. It was a complete undermining of the structures and philosophies of the Liberal Party—and of the Australian Parliament. Certainly, Abbott did lead the Liberal–National Coalition into government and became prime minister but, history has shown he was one the worst prime ministers in Australian history.

The way a political party enters government usually defines how it will perform during its time in office and Abbott's behaviour as the Leader of the Opposition created a decade of instability in federal politics. An opposition's role is to oppose and scrutinise the actions of government, but it also has to take into account the interests of the community and be effective as a stepping-stone for a return into the position of government.

But maintaining relevance for an opposition is critical and it may need to be a process where Labor needs to be more aggressive in promoting its political messaging and creating more publicity for Albanese. After all, as Oscar Wilde pointed out, "there is only one thing in the world worse than being talked about, and that is not being talked about" and even negative media reports might be preferable to the very lukewarm and tepid responses he's receiving at the moment.

In the 2013 membership vote for the Labor Party leadership between Albanese and Bill Shorten, he promoted himself by saying "I fight Tories, it's what I do" but it's an attitude that seems to have gone missing since Albanese became Labor leader in 2019. And perhaps it's an approach he may have to reclaim if he wants to gain traction in the mind of the electorate.

These issues of relevancy aren't only restricted to the federal opposition: it's the same difficulty being faced by opposition leaders in state and territory politics as well. When the electorate is highly concerned about their own economic wellbeing and whether there will still be a job for them next week, they're hardly going to be too concerned about opposition parties discussing their policy platforms for a distant election campaign, and now is not the best time to start making key announcements or attempting to gain traction for key political messaging. But still, it's not just a case of simply giving the government *carte blanche* to do whatever they wish to, without repercussions. And in the theatre of politics, the performance for an opposition almost needs to be flawless and, at this stage, there is too much equivocation and mixed messages.

For example, Albanese recently made an announcement that JobSeeker payments needed to be reduced, but not to the levels of Newstart, which equates to the unlivable level of $40 per day. It was a clouded message where he argued "I don't think it should be kept at the level where it is, where JobSeeker is higher than the aged pension, that's not a reasonable proposition" and also criticised the JobSeeker payments where "875,000 [low income] people were paid more than they were earning before this crisis".[44]

This is more in line with conservative economic think-tanks— economically, it could be perceived to be the correct call in the long term but during a time of economic slow down and pandemic? It seemed like a foolish and convoluted message and resulted in several days of negative headlines for Albanese. Perhaps there needs to be more nuanced messaging, or being able to play both sides of the political divide without attracting the opprobrium from the media.

Are there any tactics Albanese could replicate from Abbott, one of the worst prime ministers in history, but an effective opposition leader who led his party into government? Many other effective Leaders of the Opposition, such as Gough Whitlam, Malcolm Fraser or John Howard, were brutal masters of attack but they had policies. There can be disagreement about whether their policies were effective or not, but at least they were ready for government, whereas Abbott was not.

Former Labor Party leader, John Curtin, was an excellent Leader of the Opposition in the 1940s, as was Robert Menzies, who both went on to become exceptional prime ministers for their respective side of politics. And the essential factor for all of these effective leaders of the opposition was maintaining that balance of opposing

---

44   ABC *Breakfast*, interview with Fran Kelly, 'Government's announcement of changes to JobKeeper and JobSeeker', 21 July 2020. https://bit.ly/2OV14IX

the government of the day, and pushing forward their own political agendas to the electorate. It's not easy, but it can be done.

Albanese has stated he wants to be a constructive opposition and offer support to the government to provide the best outcomes for the community during a crisis. This is a sensible approach and sometimes political opportunism has to be placed on hold during difficult times. But it's instructive to compare the behaviour of Albanese federally and the Labor Party, with the behaviours of the Liberal Party opposition in the states of Victoria, Western Australia and Queensland, almost existing in a parallel universe and replicating the worst political opportunism displayed by Abbott during his term in opposition.

Far from offering constructive support to those state Labor governments, they've been constantly attacking the premiers in those states, with incessant unhinged and maniacal attacks about the management of the coronavirus, opening up borders again, flaring up debates about masks or opening up schools, aided and abetted by right-wing media outlets—predictably, News Corporation, the Nine Network and, increasingly, the ABC.

There's also one member of the Victoria Parliament, Tim Smith, who has been raging in this pursuit of the Premier, Daniel Andrews. It's an unrelenting attack; it's juvenile, it's unhinged, it's maniacal; it's against the public interest and it's completely unacceptable. But, people are starting to listen to him and starting to take more notice of what he's saying which, of course, is being magnified by Liberal-friendly and anti-Labor mainstream media.

Smith's actions are part of process to become recognisable, and to claw back into the political game during a time of crisis, when oppositions are finding it difficult to focus and maintain relevance. But actions such as these are at the extreme edge of acceptable political behaviour and this factor is the one that becomes the dilemma for oppositions: should they adopt the extremist actions in the style of Abbott that could end up returning the political party to government; or the constructive support in the public interest, a support which ends up benefitting the government of the day? There might be short-term gain for extremists of this nature but, essentially, it becomes a test of political character. Sometimes, not all victories are worth pursuing.

Historically, the nuisance political 'rat-bag' character rarely occupies the centre of attention and if they do manage to gain that attention, they are even less likely to keep it. And there are many characters to choose from here: former Prime Minister Billy Hughes; Labor's Eddie Ward who rarely had friendly working relationships with any Labor leader; W.C. Wentworth and his 'bunyip aristocracy'; Pauline Hanson, who despite gaining great attention when she first arrived on the political scene in 1996, is a fringe-dweller at best. Tony Abbott: yes, he did become prime minister, but it wasn't for very long. He continued to cherish the role of political warrior and never grew into the role in the way someone like Paul Keating did, after years of assuming the role of political attack-dog, as the understudy to Bob Hawke.

It is, however, possible to maintain a level of public decency, and creating opportunities to maintain pressure on governments, while keeping a public profile and a reminder to the electorate that there are alternatives to the government of the day. One example of this is the performance of the NSW Labor leader, Jodi McKay, who seems to have a large amount of material to work with: the mismanagement of the *Ruby Princess* incident at the start of the pandemic; the deaths of at least nineteen residents at Anglicare's Newmarch House due to delays by the NSW Government to try and reduce the outbreak.

As a former newsreader and journalist, McKay does have an advantage in media presentation but one tactic she has adopted is to interview experts in the field of epidemiology, such as Bill Bowtell, and giving authority to the words that she would normally speak. It is an interesting strategy but perhaps at a time when the public is more interested in information, rather than political grandstanding, this is a political tactic that could develop as a meaningful tool for leaders. But whether this is effective as a political strategy, it is far more preferable when compared to the over-the-top rantings of Smith, the federal member for Bowman, Andrew Laming, or the Minister for Home Affairs, Peter Dutton, who seem more intent on scoring political points than seeking results in the public interest.

Another issue that helps define the role of opposition leaders across Australia is their engagement with the mainstream media, especially at time when the media is going through fundamental changes due to technology, viewer habits, and the economic downturn.

Foxtel is suffering from a loss of subscribers, declining revenues and is currently carrying over $2 billion of debt. *The Australian* newspaper is also in great financial difficulties, but it is a loss-leader ideological vanity publication that has never been profitable, cross-subsidised by other News Limited newspapers such as the *Herald Sun*, *Daily Telegraph*, *The Courier-Mail* and the *Adelaide Advertiser*, which are also having financial difficulties.

Over at the Nine Network, the recently-acquired *Sydney Morning Herald* and *The Age* are also suffering from shrinking revenues, and it's almost like these are the final kicks from an industry that is in its death throes, a far cry from the 'rivers of gold' of advertising and real estate revenue that propped the industry up until those 'rivers' ran dry, well over a decade ago. Many traditional news outlets have folded internationally, and have become internet-only businesses, but the way in which people are receiving news, and especially political news, has changed dramatically.

And with more news outlets being driven by opinion-based journalism and reporting, rather than the more expensive investigative stories to give a context to particular political events, it will become even more difficult for any opposition leader to get their messaging out. Independent media outlets are starting to proliferate, but these do not hold the same impact as traditional mainstream media, although that could change through aggregation software and the ability for audiences to curate the news media and political stories they wish to receive.

Media concentration is also another factor, as is the other assets owned by media proprietors: Rupert Murdoch also has substantial assets in oil and resources, as does the owner of Seven West Media, Kerry Stokes. And they've used their media assets to push climate change denialism. It's essential for the electorate to understand where their news and political information is coming from, and that Murdoch and Stokes traditionally push forward an anti-Labor agenda, as well as having close ties with the Liberal Party.

Taking all of these factors into account, it is hostile and difficult terrain for Labor to navigate through—being in opposition is always difficult but almost impossible when faced with a media that fails to engage with Labor, and does its best to negate any positive news coming from Albanese. That's why it's important for Labor to extract every political opportunity and be at the peak of its performance: even then, it might not be enough to win office.

But the other factor to point out is that the media bias against Labor is not new. The *Sydney Morning Herald* has endorsed Labor on only six occasions in federal elections: on the first occasion in 1961, and the most recent occasion, in 2019. Murdoch suggested Kevin Rudd "would make a good prime minister", before using his newspapers to endlessly attack him when he did become prime minister in 2007.

Labor needs to look at viable alternatives to circumvent the mainstream media that is primarily owned by proprietors who will actively wage a media war against the interests of the Labor Party. It's not an easy process but options need to be explored because, whatever they're doing right now, is just not working.

*

When will black lives matter?

4 June

The greatest stain on the Australian psyche is the unfinished business of Aboriginal reconciliation and the inherent discrimination many Indigenous people and communities still face in 2020. But for the key institutions of politics, law, police and media, reconciliation is a forgotten business where many structural impediments still exist and make it almost impossible for any meaningful change.

Certainly, many of these institutions have reconciliation action plans, statements of diversity and make all the correct statements about 'commitments' to advancing Aboriginal interests. But in most cases, these are perfunctory actions that assuage the guilt of authoritarian institutions more concerned about perpetuating the appearance of reconciliation, rather than implementing the real actions that could enable significant social change. And the real reason behind the lack of action by these key institutions? In reality, for them, black lives don't matter.

Political parties have long realised Indigenous people are not a substantial voting bloc that can make a difference to election results. It explains why Labor promises much about improving the lives of Aboriginal people, but actually delivers little when it sits in government. It also explains why the Liberal–National Coalition can afford to be openly hostile towards Indigenous groups, make significant cutbacks to frontline services—$500 million in one of its first acts after it won the 2013 federal election—knock back constitutional recognition at whim, and lose very little political capital over it. Electorally, Aboriginal and Torres Strait Islander people make up 3.3 per cent of the Australian population; politically, very few people are prepared to change their votes primarily based on Indigenous issues.

Of course, there is a substantial number of non-Indigenous people promoting reconciliation as a political cause, and have a strong desire to alleviate and correct the errors of Australian history. In 2000, 250,000 people walked across Sydney Harbour Bridge to show their support for reconciliation. According to polling from 2019,[45] a clear majority of the Australian community supports a treaty, constitutional recognition, and actions that will advance reconciliation with Indigenous people. Thousands of people across Australia—Indigenous and non-Indigenous—attended Black Lives Matter rallies, defying coronavirus restrictions to show their support, and AFL footballers were seen 'taking the knee' prior to bounce down last weekend, as a sign of solidarity.

But little progress will be made if one side of politics is openly hostile and dismissive of the political and social interests of Indigenous people; and the other side afraid of making courageous decisions, for fear of being dragged down into a quagmire by a conservative and hostile right-wing media. And for the other significant institutions controlled by the political system—law and police—they suffer from the same stagnation and cowardice. A fear of change, and a fear of ceding control. And a collection of systems that are almost impossible to change.

Double standards

There's a great deal to unpack from recent events. The catalyst for the Black Lives Matter rallies and protests in the United States was the murder of George Floyd on 25 May 2020 by a Minneapolis police officer. Arrested after using a counterfeit $20 bill in a local convenience store, Floyd was then held down by police for over eight minutes until he asphyxiated. Over the next week, there were

---

45 *The Guardian*, 'Essential poll: majority of Australians want Indigenous recognition and voice to parliament, Katharine Murphy, 12 July 2019. https://www.theguardian.com/australia-news/2019/jul/12/essential-poll-majority-of-australians-want-indigenous-recognition-and-voice-to-parliament

rallies and protests against police brutality and black incarceration, primarily in the United States, but spread to around 400 cities internationally, including a day of national action across Australia on 7 June.

In the lead up to the Australian rallies and protests, the Prime Minister, Scott Morrison, issued a warning that if these went ahead, "the whole track back to economic recovery [would be] at risk" and the movement was "taken over by other much more politically-driven left-wing agendas, which are seeking to take advantage of these opportunities to push their political causes". In addition, Morrison called on NSW Police to charge protesters.

Other ministers from the government were in unison with Morrison's sentiments. In an obvious pitch to a mainstream and disengaged audience, they fuelled the issue further when they claimed it was disturbing ANZAC Day ceremonies had been cancelled, and funerals had been limited during the coronavirus lockdown, yet protesters were taking to the streets, risking lives and the economy. Minister for Finance, Mathias Cormann, also suggested protesters were "incredibly self-indulgent" and "reckless," while Queensland Liberal–National MP, Andrew Laming, called for the removal of JobSeeker and welfare payments from participants.

But different causes bring out different responses, especially from conservative governments. From 9 May onwards, there was a wide range of protests across Australia hosted by fringe conspiracy groups, including the radical QAnon and anti-vaccination groups, calling for, among many other issues, an end to the lockdown, social distancing measures, self-isolation, tracking apps and 5G towers, and, bizarrely, the arrest of Microsoft founder, Bill Gates. There were many protests held over a three-week period in major cities and regional towns but the main events held in Sydney, Melbourne and Brisbane drew crowds of between 500 and 2,000.

When asked about whether he had any concerns about these numbers, Morrison deflected any concerns and offered sympathy: "I understand people's frustration, with the anxieties and the frustrations that they're feeling; it's a free country. People can make their protests and make their voices heard." Morrison made no warnings about how the anti-vax/5G/lockdown protests would place 'economic recovery at risk,' or if anyone was 'taken over by politically-driven agendas'. There were no calls for the police forces in those respective states to charge protesters or for Centrelink to remove JobSeeker benefits. And there were certainly no requests to the Supreme Court to classify them as 'illegal', as was the case for the Black Lives Matter rallies.

The anti-vax/5G/lockdown protests over several weeks received substantial media coverage, but no one in the media sought to query the Prime Minister or anyone from the government about the lapse in social distancing requirements, or whether there were any public health risks.

And for a full week after the Black Lives Matter rallies, no one in the mainstream media joined the obvious dots or even asked the obvious question: why were the anti-vax/5G/lockdown protests a democratic example of 'a free country,' yet Black Lives Matter rallies were 'self-indulgent,' placing economic recovery at risk, dangerous and needing the full force of the law and police to close them down?

The answer is simple, and the primary issue is skin colour: the anti-vax/5G/lockdown issues are predominantly white right-wing conservative niche causes; Black Lives Matter is a black social justice left-wing cause. And just like this Liberal–National Coalition government, the media clearly identifies and delineates according to skin colour, its own inherent subconscious biases and reflections of the world through a middle-class prism.

How the media encourages racism

The *Insiders* is the ABC's flagship political analysis program, broadcast every Sunday morning as a wrap-up of the weekly events in politics. It first aired in 2001 and, since that time, there have been nearly 800 episodes broadcast over a twenty-year period. The number of Indigenous 'insider' journalists who have appeared as panellists? Zero. Absolutely none.

On the morning of 7 June, an all-white *Insiders* panel debated the relevance of the Black Lives Matters rallies to Aboriginal people and, after a significant public backlash—which pointed out the obvious problem evident to everyone except for the ABC—the ABC finally acted.

A week later on 14 June, for the first time ever, the *Insiders* panel included an Indigenous journalist, Bridget Brennan. Brennan's career has flourished over the past few years, as National Indigenous Affairs and Europe correspondent for the ABC—she is an excellent journalist, articulate and clearly on top of the political issues of the day. There are many other excellent Indigenous journalists working for NITV, *New Matilda*, *Koori Mail*; they are out there, and they are easy to find.

Why has it taken twenty years and almost 800 episodes for an Indigenous journalist to appear on the *Insiders* panel? And why did it take a public backlash for the ABC to realise a panel comprising one white Anglo man, one white Anglo woman, and one Greek–Australian women might not be the best way to convey an Indigenous perspective?

It's the inherent biases at play. If politics is understood to be the domain of the white person, why would ABC producers even think about inviting a black person to interpret white persons' business, even if the topic is as black as Black Lives Matter? *Insiders* has had the few Indigenous parliamentarians as guests, but that's where it's ended. The real test will be if Brennan—or any other Indigenous journalist—is invited to participate on *Insiders* to discuss other political issues of the day, not just at the time when Indigenous issues are prominent.

Yes, the ABC does have a dedicated Indigenous Programs Unit but aside from those voices speaking to their own, how many Indigenous or non-Anglo people are executive producers of the ABC's many radio and television programs? There are over 4,900 employees within the ABC, yet only 103 are Indigenous, and most of these are from within the Indigenous Programs Unit. This represents 2.1 per cent of its overall staff, yet Indigenous people are 3.3 per cent of the overall population.

The ABC should be doing far better in its presentation and employment of Indigenous people. It's an embarrassment that it's so low but in other mainstream media corporations, it's far worse. For Seven West Media, Network 10, Nine Network and News Corporation, black lives don't seem to matter at all, unless it's a negative stereotypical news item used to boost ratings.

In the 2019 Seven West Media Annual Report, there are two references to 'Indigenous,' and they both refer to 'incarceration' and 'football'.[46] In the eighty or so photographs shown in the report, there is one slightly darker-skinned chef and one person of Asian origin, and the only other image of anything remotely dark-skinned is a brown racehorse and one muppet from the *Sesame Street* children's television series. This needs to be emphasised: the only dark-skinned images in the Seven West Annual Report are of a racehorse, and a muppet.

It's a festival of whiteness, which explains why Seven West Media constantly invites One Nation's Pauline Hanson to make regular and prominent guest appearances, and provides race-baiting entertainment on its *Sunrise* morning program.

It's a similar story at Nine Network: no mention at all of Indigenous people in their 2019 annual report, although there are two photographs of dark-skinned people, and one person of Asian origin. The Network 10 annual report: again, the only person of dark skin is Waleed Aly, but as one of their leading personalities, he would have been hard to ignore. And, of course, no reference to Aboriginal people, or what the corporation might be doing to improve Indigenous participation.

This is common within the mainstream media. And a media industry that ignores people of difference and Indigenous people is likely to reinforce its own prejudice and its own ignorance. A privileged middle-class white news journalist is unlikely to understand the issues of racism in Australia if they've never experienced it themselves and are a product of the white establishment that put them there in the first place.

Network 10 produces an off-beat news program which prides itself on 'news presented differently,' *The Project*. In early June, the panellists interviewed the actor/writer Nakkiah Lui, and academic/activist, Marcia Langton, who both talked about their experiences living in Australia as Indigenous people, the endemic and institutionalised racism that exists in Australia, deaths in custody and why the Black Lives Matter rallies were important as a focus on these many issues.

Two of the presenters, Peter Helliar and Carrie Bickmore, listened intently but seemed genuine shocked by what they were hearing, as if they knew nothing about deaths in custody or race

---

46 Seven West Media Annual Report 2019. https://www.sevenwestmedia.com.au/assets/pdfs/2019-SWM-Annual-Report2.pdf

relations in Australia. To their credit, they thanked Lui and Langton for providing their perspectives and 'letting them know' about these issues, but the encounter opened up other questions: the demographics for *The Project* are the twenty-to-forty year age group, and the presenters themselves are in their late-thirties, early-forties.

Surely Helliar and Bickmore should be more aware of these issues? Surely the teaching of Australian history had moved on from the inane and vainglorious representations of white explorers valiantly defeating the 'native savages', so typical of high school history education across Australia up until the 1970s.

Had they been so immersed in the pop culture of the past twenty years they haven't bothered to look into Aboriginal deaths in custody, or racism as an issue for many people in the Australian community? After all, they are news presenters presenting news differently but, perhaps, not differently enough.

The 'us and them' cancel culture

There are many examples of duplicity within Australian institutions when it comes to Indigenous issues. In May 2020, the mining company Rio Tinto detonated a 46,000-year-old Indigenous cultural site in the Pilbara's Juukan Gorge—during NAIDOC week—even though they had been aware of the site for at least seven years, and were advised by the local Puutu Kunti Kurrama and Pinikura groups about the significance of the site.

It's instructive to compare the destruction of this site in Juukan Gorge with the recent protection of monuments of Captain James Cook. During the recent rallies to raise awareness of Indigenous deaths in custody, a statue of Cook in Sydney's Hyde Park was protected by twenty police officers, including four on horseback, to ward off any potential desecration of the statue. Cook's Cottage in Melbourne is currently under 24-hour police guard. It's a cottage transported from England, and it's a dwelling Cook never actually lived in.

On one hand, the wanton and deliberate destruction of an Aboriginal sacred site by a multinational corporation with virtually no repercussions; on the other, a concrete simulacra of oppression and a house never occupied by Cook are afforded twenty-four-hour protection. Both the Aboriginal site and Cook are worthy and sacred symbols for different sectors of the Australian community, but why is only the one symbol always afforded the protection by the state and revered in a much greater level than the other?

And why is achieving equilibrium of history viewed within such a negative frame? The recent proliferation of 'cancel culture' is not a new development: Aboriginal culture and heritage has been destroyed, cancelled and ignored for well over 230 years.

Removal of statues and other monuments are not the 'vexed issue' the media keeps telling the public. Very few people cried or resisted removing the statues and busts of despots and dictators after the fall of communism across Eastern Europe in 1989. Even fewer were so concerned about the large statues of Iraqi dictator Saddam Hussein roped down by angry protesters in the streets of Baghdad in 2003.

Far from being 'vexed,' it's an easy decision: remove all the offensive colonial statues and place them in an outdoor museum, similar to Memento Park in the Hungarian capital of Budapest, which houses old communist and brutalist statues. Hidden on the outskirts of the city, it's part history, part *kitsch*, it's out of sight and out of mind. It's there for those who want to see, and if such a theme park was ever developed somewhere in Australia, it could be a small contribution to a post-COVID-19 economic recovery program.

And if the removal of these offensive colonial statues isn't acceptable to the community, perhaps the placement of alternative statues or 'counter-memorials' placed upon existing statues would be acceptable. Why not house a statue of the Aboriginal warrior Pemulwuy next to Cook's statue in Hyde Park? Or place a statue of the Aboriginal resistance fighter, Jandamarra, next to Governor Frederick Broome in the Kimberley region of Western Australia? Or a plaque at the base of existing colonial statues reminding the viewer that Australia's history is disputed and there are other versions of black history that have never been effectively presented?

One such example exists on the Explorer's Monument in Fremantle. Created in 1913 in the memory of three white explorers who were killed by Aboriginal people at Le Grange Bay in northern Western Australia—Frederick Panter, James Harding and William Goldwyer—the monument completely varnishes over the reality of these attacks.

The original plaque mentions they were "murdered" by "treacherous natives" but ignores the fact the three were well-armed and shot and killed over twenty Aboriginal people, and fails to recognise the right for Aboriginal people to defend themselves while under attack.

In 1994, a plaque correcting this history was placed at the lower part of the monument by "people who found the monument before you offensive," and indicated the original monument described the events at La Grange Bay from one perspective only.

In a society so enamoured with statues and monuments, a shared space or an opportunity to rectify history is a positive step in the right direction. But it's not so much the statues and monuments that need reform: these are collections of bronze and stone masonry that feel the whispers of wind and rain on their features, and provide resting spots for assorted birdlife, so they do have some use. Whether they stay or go can be debated by the many historical societies from around Australia.

The key issue is that none of the Australian institutions that created those statues in the first instance are fit for purpose.

Australia's institutions need to change

The current Australian political system was developed by men with long beards and wide moustaches from the nineteenth century who imagined an 'Australia for the White Man,' and it's a system no longer relevant for the needs of a country far removed from the federation world of 120 years ago.

But as inept and inappropriate as the system is, it's the system that currently exists and its ineptness permeates through to law, policing and the media. Modern Australia is trying to function on a system built for an antiquated time. It's a system that needs to change.

How does Australian society move from this point? For a start, the institution of politics is the sector that needs to take reconciliation far more seriously, starting from the branch level of all political parties, dedicated positions for Indigenous people within executives and working towards a representational model that removes barriers for Indigenous people—and other peoples currently excluded by Parliament.

Labor instigated a proactive female quota of 35 per cent in 1994 (raised to 40 per cent in 2002). While it hasn't achieve parity, its current level of female members is 47.8 per cent, far ahead of the Liberal–National Coalition, which currently has a level of only 25.8 per cent.[47] Based on these figures, it's evident political parties will not make positive change of their own volition, but the Labor quota system shows that it can be achieved.

Mixed-member parliamentary systems in Germany and New Zealand result in more inclusive parliaments, and those countries are regarded as the best and most responsive democracies in the world. There are solutions out there, if the will does exist.

Politics, the media, law and the police need to change radically, and improvements for Indigenous people—if any—will continue to move at a glacial pace, until radical change is made. It's no longer acceptable for these institutions for hold up their reconciliation action plans or their statements of diversity, like self-congratulatory trophies of their earnest intentions, if nothing changes in terms of representation in positions of real power.

And if nothing changes in these positions of real power, these institutions will continue to define an entire culture through criminalisation and negative stereotypes and after each cycle of public awareness drops off, the situation just reverts back to the way it has always been.

It's not acceptable for the NSW Police Commissioner, Mick Fuller, to claim a police officer was "just having a bad day" when he smashed the face of a seventeen-year-old Indigenous boy into the pavement of a Redfern park, and continue to gaslight the media by saying "most of the community" wouldn't want the police officer sacked. It's not acceptable for Morrison, as prime minister, to claim "there was no slavery in Australia," when there is clear recorded historical evidence to dispute this.

Key events influence the public mood momentarily, such as the murder of David Gundy by police in Redfern in 1989; the Royal Commission into Aboriginal Deaths in Custody in 1991; the *Mabo*

---

47   Parliament of Australia, 'Composition of Australian parliaments by party and gender: a quick guide', 2 December 2020. https://www.aph.gov.au/About_Parliament/Parliamentary_Departments/Parliamentary_Library/pubs/rp/rp2021/Quick_Guides/CompositionPartyGender

v Queensland decision from 1992 which overturned the legal concept of *terra nullius* in Australia; Paul Keating's Redfern Park Speech; the Reconciliation Walks in 2000; Kevin Rudd's Apology to Australia's Indigenous peoples in 2008; and now, the Black Lives Matter and deaths in custody protests.

These events pique the national conscience and lead to calls for further actions, but then recede into the distance until the next event of national significance occurs. And then the Australian communities goes through the entire repertoire again. More protests. More calls for action. More reconciliation action plans. But until there are significant reforms in the areas where the real power is held, in reality, very little is going to change. It really won't. And until that time, black lives won't really matter either.

*

Morrison: He's no Bob Hawke

4 June

Scott Morrison is being compared to Bob Hawke; a meeting of business leaders and unions to develop common ground on industrial relations has been dubbed the Accord 2.0 by the media; and he's been lauded for gaining an invitation to attend the Group of Seven summit in September.

As with most media massaging, it's time for a check on reality: Morrison is not Bob Hawke—the original Accord was a process that lasted eight years and totally transformed the Australian economy; Morrison wants his reforms implemented within three months and his ambitions are more related to the original WorkChoices agenda implemented by John Howard in 2005; Australia already has special observer status at G7, and attendance at this year's summit was guaranteed. The media is usually at hand to support the Prime Minister at most opportunities but have they pushed their support too far in their comparisons with Hawke and the Accord?

Hawke was a deeply flawed man in his personal life but did have the spark of greatness in his public life. Hawke had compassion: he didn't always use that compassion, but it was certainly genuine and he did want to make Australia a better place. There were also elements of Hawke's character, his undoubted charisma, his ability to persuade two hostile parties together for the sake of the nation and hammer out a compromise that each party could live with, as he did during the Accord process in the 1980s.

None of these qualities are evident in Morrison: he's not a charismatic leader; he doesn't have a clear vision of Australia but, then again, if it could be clearly articulated, it's a vision that no one would vote for. Hawke was also a humanitarian and this can be seen with the granting of permanent visas to resident Chinese students after the Tiananmen Square massacre in 1989; Hawke also advanced reconciliation with Indigenous Australia and supported a treaty—although he never went as far as he wanted to, and later expressed regret about not moving further with Indigenous affairs.

The Accord series of reforms commenced when Hawke and Labor won the 1983 election—the economy at that time was moribund after eight years of Malcolm Fraser's Liberal–National Coalition government—unemployment was at a rate of 10 per cent, inflation was high, industrial action was very common, and there was a recession where gross domestic product fell by over 6 per cent. There were many reforms Prime Minister Malcolm Fraser and John Howard, who was treasurer at the time, should have implemented, but they didn't.

Hawke believed good policy is good politics, and this would result in good election outcomes. Labor implemented what was best for the economy and for the public interest—receiving criticism from the left flank of the party for deregulating the economy and privatising public assets, a criticism that is still revisited by the left faction today—as a result, Hawke was prime minister for over eight years, and Labor remained in office for thirteen years, its longest stint in federal government ever.

For the current Liberal–National Coalition government, the reverse seems to be the case, where good policy development has been removed from the equation, and they've moved on directly to playing the political games to achieve good electoral outcomes for themselves. Morrison won the 2019 federal election, an election which all the evidence suggested he should have lost. But having won the so-called 'miracle election', he hasn't been able to do very much. Australia has been struck by two once-in-a-century disasters: the bushfires of 2019/20, which the electorate is starting to lose memory of, and the coronavirus pandemic.

Despite what the mainstream media has been suggesting, the federal government has not performed well in either of these events.

In the bushfires, it was the state and territory governments that performed all the work in managing this crisis; it was the federal government that went missing, with Morrison infamously going overseas during the height of crisis and refusing to indicate where he was.

It has, more or less, again been the states and territories that have managed the coronavirus pandemic: the South Australia Government functionally eradicated the disease; the Western Australia, New South Wales and Queensland governments have had very low case numbers, the exception being Victoria, which has had numbers spiralling out of control due to the mismanagement of their hotel quarantine system for overseas arrival. These successes have not been because of the federal government, although they have provided stimulus support through the JobKeeper and JobSeeker programs.

This is a sign of the Australian political system being able to manage difficult circumstances very well but it hasn't stopped the federal government wanting to implement what seems to be a new version of WorkChoices, an ideologically-driven workplace reform program the Liberal Party shares with the Business Council of Australia. The first part of this process occurred in 2018, when the federal government reduced penalty rates, on the promise this would lead to a surge in job creation, something that never actually occurred: even though corporate profits have increased since that time, wages have stagnated and very few new jobs have been created.

The coronavirus crisis is being used as a smoke screen for a clearly ideological pursuit—Morrison has been constantly saying the industrial relations system is broken, without saying what is actually broken about it. The arguments pushed by Morrison—that industrial reform will lead to new job creation—are the same arguments pushed by Malcolm Turnbull in 2018, even though the evidence suggests the opposite has occurred and reforms of this nature usually benefit corporations and businesses, rather than workers. If the reforms Morrison wishes to implement in the workplace ever come to fruition—at the worst possible time for the workforce—there'll be an entire generation of people who will lose their rights at work. This, of course, is more in tune with the requests of the business community, and corporate greed seems to be the motivating factor.

Private sector expansion within the economy since the early 1980s has distorted employment numbers and wages, where lower and stagnant wages have had a direct correlation with higher corporate profits. The reforms Morrison wishes to implement will result in even higher corporate profits and less income for the working population—which will result in less cash circulating through the economy.

The high level of government involvement in the economy through stimulus support may reverse this trend, but the Liberal–National Coalition that has consistently shown it does not have the ability to manage national finances fairly and effectively. This factor, coupled with the many allegations of misappropriation of funds, and a propensity to provide favours to corporate friends, means there is a strong possibility that this opportunity to reform the economy will be squandered, in the same manner the large proceeds from the mining boom of the 2000s was squandered by the Howard government on short-term and unsustainable middle-class largess, rather than long-term economic prosperity.

Parliament has approved in-principle spending of over $300 billion on stimulus-related programs—$130 billion was originally allocated towards the JobKeeper program, which has now estimated to cost only $70 billion due to a 'reporting error', but that means there is a $60 billion balance that can be used for other government largess on conservative pet-projects. And, of course, keeping track of monies that can be used with an eye on the next federal election.

The Liberal–National Coalition was devoid of any meaningful agenda at the 2019 election and a party without a firm agenda will always be managing policy in an *ad hoc* manner and, in the Coalition's case, spending vast sums of money on middle-class welfare. Their latest proposal, which is more like a thought-bubble, is the HomeBuilder program, which offers a grant of $25,000 for home renovations. This might seem like a fantastic program, all entirely marketable for a government which spends so much effort in promotions, but there are so many caveats, including many prospective recipients needing to provide $150,000 of their own funds to qualify.

And, as with many inappropriately targeted government programs, many unwarranted and unwanted home renovations will get underway, simply for the process of obtaining a $25,000 benefit, and the costs of tradespeople are likely to increase because of supply and demand issues. In addition, there might not be enough tradespeople to support the demand because the government has cut many apprenticeships and TAFE training. This is another example of poorly thought-out policy, poorly-targeted, and likely to assist the people who least need the support.

Simulating the building sector during an economic downturn, on face value, is a positive government action. Whether the money is wasted, or goes into the wrong hands, at least it stimulates the economy and perhaps that's what is motivating the government—get the money into the economy as quickly as possible, even though they've had several months to think this policy through. However, the public benefit of this type of program is limited: it's great for the residing family, but it doesn't have a longer-term benefit for the wider community. The school halls and buildings that were constructed from the Building The Education Revolution program in the late 2000s will benefit generations of children to come, and also be meetings points for communities.

The HomeBuilder program won't be anything like the Building The Education Revolution fund: it will be piecemeal, benefit only a small percentage of the community and even traditional government supporters have been critical, with *The Australian* economic editor, Adam Creighton suggests "forcing taxpayers to renovate other people's homes to aid some tradie, who probably earns more than the average taxpayer, is economic and political stupidity".[48] *The Australian* isn't a left-wing socialist rag, so when one of the government's major media supporters comes up with harsh criticism, it's a strong message that it's not a good policy and may need to be dropped.

HomeBuilder has been allocated $688 million, for approximately 27,000 house renovations across Australia or, on average, ten house renovations in every suburb. This is not a very high amount if the government's intention is to stimulate the sector, but it does relate

---

48   *The Australian*, 'We can't give in to stupidity', Adam Creighton, 3 June 2020. https://t.co/taAmAO6sG8?amp=1

strongly to how this government behaves: the main factor is to shoot the marketing flare high into the sky for as many people as possible can see it, and by the time people come around to arranging their renovations, the next election might be well and truly over. It fits perfectly into political marketing: even if only a few people access the HomeBuilder fund, and most people don't intend to, thinking they have the possibility of renovating their home at some point in the future—even if they don't—provides maximum political benefit to the government.

It's a similar political messaging the Coalition put forward during the 2019 federal election campaign, creating an environment where some people assumed they were going to lose share franking benefits under Labor's policy proposals, even though those people didn't own any shares for them to be able to lose franking benefits. The clear message is: the government will assist with home renovations, even if people never actually renovate their home.

One other factor to take into account: who is benefiting from the HomeBuilder program? Obviously, it will be the home owners, and the tradespeople within the economy, but it would be worthwhile to explore who else may benefit from the scheme.

Kerry Stokes is well known as the proprietor of Seven West Media but what is less know about his interests is that around 60 per cent of his wealth is within oil, construction and mineral resources. Recently, Stokes acquired a 10 per cent share of Boral Industries, a manufacturer of building construction materials and supplies. Stokes is close to the Liberal Party and can easily pick up the phone and have the Prime Minister at the other end of the line: how much information would he have known about the HomeBuilder program before it was announced and was it an issue that influenced his decision to purchase a share of Boral Industries?

Stokes purchased the stake on 2 June 2020, and the HomeBuilder announcement was made two days later. It is quite a remarkable coincidence, either a stroke of genius, good luck or a brilliant business move. Or it could be something else, which is an area that will always remain unclear.

The spluttering economy continues

In other economic news, the Australian economy is officially in recession, for the first time in twenty-nine years. Gross domestic product in the March 2020 quarter fell by 0.3 per cent, and the June quarter, while it won't be confirmed until September, is likely to be even worse. The December 2019 quarter resulted in a marginal growth of 0.5 per cent[49]—and this is usually a flourishing quarter because of Christmas spending and other seasonal factors, and the preceding September 2019 quarter recorded a growth of just 0.4 per cent.

The Treasurer, Josh Frydenberg, made the announcement that the Australian economy is in a recession, but he blamed the effects of COVID-19 and the severe bushfires towards the end of 2019. Based on its previous actions, this is not a government that takes responsibility for very much at all and will use other factors to deflect from their poor management. But the economy was struggling for a long period before the pandemic started, commencing with the disastrous Budget in 2014, six years ago. It's clear the Liberal–National Coalition are not the excellent economic managers they keep telling the mainstream media, who are only too happy to push this message to their audiences, but the economy has been spluttering for a long time and it has very little to do with external influences. What will it take for the mainstream media to realise external factors are not the cause of problems in the Australian economy?

Underperforming economies in recent times have been the hallmark of Coalition governments: the Fraser government presided over periods of high inflation and low growth. The Howard government, on the surface, performed well with the economy, but failed to manage it for long-term benefit. Incumbent conservative governments run the economy into the ground, eventually lose an election, only for the other side of politics to come in, clean up the mess, and wear the political pain.

The Coalition should have lost the 2019 election—primarily because of their poor economic management over the previous

---

49 Australian Bureau of Statistics, 'Australian National Accounts: National Income, Expenditure and Product', 4 March 2020. https://www.abs.gov.au/statistics/economy/national-accounts/australian-national-accounts-national-income-expenditure-and-product/dec-2019

six years in office—but they didn't, and now it's up to them to resolve deep-seated economic issues. As far as the economic figures are concerned, there seems to some distortion and 'smoke and mirrors' marketing being played out: there are many people in the unemployment queues, but the official unemployment figures for June 2020 are 7.4 per cent, a figure masked by the JobKeeper program, with some analysts such as Chief Economist at Bis Oxford Economics, Sarah Hunter, suggesting the figures could be much higher than those being reported.[50]

JobKeeper is one government program that needs to be explored closely. It is a stimulus support payment but not everyone can receive it and, anecdotally, some companies have not passed on the amounts fully to employees, and some companies that have been receiving JobKeeper subsidies, are not even eligible for the program. The university sector has been fully excluded from the scheme, even though it employs many seasonal academics who are now without an income, due to a fall in international enrolments and cancelled courses. The arts and entertainment sector has also been excluded, for reasons that were never fully explained by the government. And in the context of the government revealing its blunder in underestimating the JobKeeper package of $60 billion, this is inexcusable. The funding is available for these other sectors, and the funding has been approved by Parliament: why not use this surplus amount for the sectors that are really hurting at the moment?

This is a value judgement for the government: $688 million is being used up by the HomeBuilder program, which has dubious economic benefits for the economy and targeting the select few. And that compares with the $0 that has gone towards university casuals. Which option provides for a longer-term benefit? An educated population that is self-supporting and manages to resolve problems itself, or somebody's house that looks a little better than before? The government had a choice to fund education, or better looking backyard toilets—and it chose to fund backyard toilets.

---

50   ABC News, 'Australia's unemployment rate could be higher than 6.9 per cent according to analysis of welfare payments', Catherine Hanrahan, 23 October 2020. https://www.abc.net.au/news/2020-10-23/unemployment-figures-higher-than-reported-data-analysis-shows/12797226

These are the choices the government has made, and will have to deal with the consequences of these decisions at a later date. But the choices seem to targeting universities as a payback in the culture wars the Coalition seems intent on playing out, deciding this is a sector that does not traditionally support the Coalition during elections, and possibly as part of a gambit to privatise the tertiary education system, even though the example set through the privatisation of the polytechnical sector has been an abysmal failure, with many private colleges engaged with scams which exploit international students. Education is a sector which shouldn't be operated for profit.

Taking all of these current issues and mismanagement into account, it's obvious those in the media making favourable comparisons between Morrison and Hawke, or suggesting the combination of the JobKeeper scheme and a rebuilt WorkChoices collection of reforms is akin to the Accord, have no understanding of political history.

There were seven different stages of the Hawke's Accord program implemented over an eight-year period. Morrison has commenced his program of reform with a desire to implement programs entirely based on the needs of the business community, a process which has only been in place for several months, and has the potential to morph into outcomes that eventually become highly disadvantageous for employees. It will take more time to assess the work Morrison is attempting to implement and no level of waxing lyrical from his supporters in the media will be able to change this.

*

The cruel and brutal RoboDebt scheme

4 June

In 2016, Centrelink commenced an automated process of matching the records of welfare recipients with income data from the Australian Taxation Office, the Online Compliance Intervention program, and increased the amount of debt recovery notifications from 20,000 each year, to around 20,000 *per week*.

The federal government was warned at the time that an automated 'RoboDebt' process and the removal of human oversight was indiscriminate, possibly illegal, and could result in inaccurate assessments. Despite these warnings, the program was announced with great fanfare and expanded its reach in the 2018 Budget, as announced by then Treasurer, Scott Morrison.

In 2019, after a grassroots campaign was launched to investigate the legalities of the RoboDebt scheme, the High Court ruled the entire program was unconstitutional and illegal, and last week, the government announced it will pay back the $721 million it recouped.

The RoboDebt program cost $600 million to manage and recoup the $721 million from welfare recipients, so it was largely ineffective and cost-inefficient but, aside from the cost issue, it was hostile, inhumane, and a state-sponsored bureaucratic cruelty not even the master of bureaucratic entanglement, Franz Kafka could have written about. Overall, on the back of a class action instigated by Gordon Legal, the cost will be over $1 billion.

Despite all the warnings that were provided, despite the knowledge about the likely harm that would be inflicted on almost half a million people, it was a program that ran unchecked and was unaccountable for four years. RoboDebt is not the type of program governments should be implementing, programs that cause so much damage to the public.

It also relates to interpretations of the purpose of governments: they are there to assist people, not cause harm and damage to them. People do make mistakes, as do governments: sometimes they overclaim, sometimes there are inadvertent errors or incorrect claims made because of the complexity of the system. Of course, there are some people who will deliberately try to exploit the system but there are now enough checks and balances within the system to minimised these.

The Australian legal system has been based on the presumption of innocence until proven guilty but the RoboDebt reversed that onus of proof: welfare recipients were deemed to be guilty of receiving overpayments and were obliged to prove they were not liable for debt and, if they couldn't prove this, the debt would stand. For many people receiving RoboDebt notifications, it created too much stress and financial difficulty, and over 2,000 people died through suicide and other related causes after receiving debt notices. And these are not rumoured numbers, or manufactured figures found through social media outlets: these are official figures released by the federal Department of Human Services.[51]

RoboDebt was a program designed to brutalise welfare recipients, a program that should never have been introduced, was ineffective, and has wasted over $600 million in compliance and retrieval costs to recoup $721 million, which the government will now have to pay back. It was a program enabled by the media and the Liberal–National Coalition went to extremes in their desire to implement the program. They changed the statute of limitations, which made appeals against their decisions difficult: they imposed travel restrictions on welfare recipients; they employed private debt

---

51 Triple J *Hack*, 'Over 2000 people died after receiving Centrelink robo-debt notice, figures reveal', Shalailah Medhora, 18 February 2019. https://www.abc.net.au/triplej/programs/hack/2030-people-have-died-after-receiving-centrelink-robodebt-notice/10821272

collection agencies and armed them with incentives to chase down welfare recipients.

The government, with support from the media, tried to exonerate themselves by suggesting the problems were caused by automated intelligence, and 'the algorithm', the catch-all term to confuse people who know very little about how technology operates. But algorithms don't appear out of nowhere and initiate their own intelligence—humans are the ones who create the algorithm in the first instance, define the parameters they operate within, and then activate it. It was an intentional system designed by government, to create the exact outcomes that prevailed. They were simply caught out, and didn't even have the competence to confirm whether their actions were legal, ended up wasting over $600 million in recovery costs and caused the deaths of over 2,000 people.

This is a government that keeps the spectre of the 'dole bludger' in the public mind, so it can easily attack welfare recipients as part of their overall election strategy. But who are the real 'bludgers' in these circumstances? Morrison has never had a public job where he hasn't wasted other people's money, and his time at Tourism Australia between 2004–2006 is a prime example. What do other people within the Liberal Party actually do? Victoria Senator James Paterson has virtually done nothing outside of working with the Institute of Public Affairs, before appointed to the Senate in 2016, but is always keen to lecture people about how they should spend their money, as well as consistently voting against measures to increase welfare and disability support payments. The Minister for Human Services, Stuart Robert, couldn't even be bothered to negotiate a fair price for his home internet usage, charging taxpayers $37,975 over eighteen months.

Rupert Murdoch, keen to have his own massive wealth propped up by government subsidies, tax write-offs or direct no-questions-asked—and no-answers-given—payments such as at least $30 million paid directly to Foxtel, is another one to syphon off public funds, in contrast to the ways welfare recipients are berated and castigated by this government.

The dynamic of endless corruption, poor government management and incompetence is starting to reach its limits in the United States and Britain. There are frustrations with the system in those respective electorates, and it's evident US President, Donald Trump, will be the first to suffer the repercussions of these frustrations in the November 2020 Presidential election, and British Prime Minister, Boris Johnson, is facing great pressure for the mismanagement of COVID-19. There are no signs yet of any electoral pressure being placed upon Morrison and the Liberal–National Coalition, but there are potentially massive repercussions heading their way at the next federal election. In the perfect world, Robert and Morrison would be sacked, charged and arrested for their actions, actions which are more in keeping with the Chicago gangster era of the 1930s, rather than a Commonwealth government acting in the public interest.

Government's shouldn't be involved in chasing down relatively small amounts in a complex estimating process, and one in which many welfare recipients who did receive RoboDebt notifications, were found to be not in breach of their conditions and had not actually receive overpayments. The RoboDebt assessments were incorrect.

The announcement of the repayment of $721 million to welfare recipients and the failure of the RoboDebt scheme was announced during the traditional 'Friday news dump' timeslot, late in the afternoon, when mainstream media journalists have left their offices for the week, fraternising at the local Canberra bars, or wherever they can get a socially-distanced drink of alcohol. It's the time news deadlines have been dealt with and a time when no-one is listening.

During the announcement, the Attorney–General, Christian Porter, suggested it was a program created by the Labor Party, with Morrison and Frydenberg repeating the same sentiments which, of course, was duly reported by the media: this is how a mediocre media functions in Australia, simply repeating the talking points coming from a conservative government. But it wasn't a program initiated by the Labor Party—the Online Compliance Intervention program was initiated and implemented by the Liberal–National Coalition.

The government expressed "regret" about the way the RoboDebt scheme was implemented, but not the scheme itself. People died from the RoboDebt scheme; people were brutalised; some people couldn't eat, maintain their rental payments, or look after their children. And the government had the temerity to issue legalese in their apology and also announced they would continue with the program.

There was also an insight into the media management and the priorities of this government—detrimental news is announced late on a Friday night to minimise the amount of people who will hear the message. It was the same timing on the previous Friday when the announcement of the mismanagement of the JobKeeper program—where figures were underestimated by $60 billion—as well as the announcement of the first recession in twenty-nine years: Frydenberg announced the recession figures but this was quickly overshadowed with the HomeBuilder announcement—a controversial and ineffective program that deflected from the more serious issue about the first-in-a-generation recession and enabled the media to concern themselves with other matters.

There's also the issue about the depth of media reporting—certainly, poor economic news is duly reported and placed within the media cycle but the depth is shallow and the width is narrow. During the time of the global financial crisis, mining tax, and carbon reduction scheme—when Labor was in office—the negative reporting was relentless, without respite. In 2020, with the Liberal–National Coalition, it's almost as though there is not economic crisis to talk of.

The mining tax and carbon reduction schemes were repealed by the federal government soon after they returned to office in 2013 but the fiscal position would be much stronger today, if those mechanisms were kept in place. Australia has a government more intent on holding onto office, but it doesn't know what it wants to do once it's in office and because of this, retracts into ideological positions and whips up a frenzy within the electoral so it can remain in office. It's a style of politics that is destructive even at the best of times, but it's a style of politics Australia cannot afford to be engaged with during an economic downturn and a coronavirus crisis.

*

The closure of Murdoch's regional newspapers

4 June

Newspapers are no longer fashionable: 112 newspaper print editions will be moving online and thirty-six titles will be disappearing forever. It was only in June 2016 that News Corporation purchased these titles from APN News & Media—for a purchase price of $36 million—after amendments to Australia's media ownership legislation. The amendments were implemented by the Turnbull government and the rationale provided at that time was that the changes would strengthen newspapers as business ventures and boost the quality of journalism, but the reverse has occurred. Many of the newly-acquired assets were transformed into advertising vehicles and propaganda outlets for Liberal–National Coalition interests.

It's difficult to determine how these closures should be received: should the public be concerned about the loss of a wide range of newspapers—usually performing a vital information cog in regional towns—and the loss of many jobs in the media, or should the public—at least some—be satisfied that poor quality newspapers and right-wing propaganda are soon to be removed from the political landscape?

Regional newspapers have provided a vital service in informing the community about the events in their community; the good news, the bad news; what's going on within their local council or shire, and keeping track of the important issues occurring in their towns. But this level of reporting takes up resources and finances, and the demise of these newspapers, even if the bulk of them will be moving online, is not good for local communities. Will the *Daily Telegraph*, based in Sydney, report on the key issues at the Armidale local council in the Northern Tablelands? Will Melbourne's *Herald Sun* report on the events from Leongatha, a small regional town in the South Gippsland Shire? It's highly unlikely.

Traditionally, these newspapers have been more than just reporting the local political events; it's where local sporting teams can have their results published; families can see photographs of their children from key community events. Unfortunately, while many of these newspapers were struggling before they were acquired by News Corporation, many of them were run into the ground after the acquisition, and many of them were not much more than propaganda outlets for the local state or federal members of Parliament, and in most cases, National Party or Liberal Party members.

This is also in the context of the recent announcement of the closure of Australian Associated Press, which serviced these local papers through syndicated news reporting and photography. This is a major blow to these newspapers, although there is some speculation AAP may survive in another form.

Almost 500 jobs in the media sector will disappear across regional Australia and, with nowhere else to go, these jobs will more than likely disappear forever. Job losses in any sector are never good for the economy, and have a devastating impact in regional communities. In the context of the standards of journalism, other mainstream journalists have been suggesting these job losses are major blow to democracy,[52] but it's hard to argue the case for that, considering many of these lost titles comprised mainly advertising and political material that generally supported local Liberal and National politicians.

However, independent journalists have suggested it could actually improve the quality of journalism, and that if the brand of newspapers were not heavily swayed towards one side of the politics

---

52 ABC Southern Queensland, 'Cuts could 'compromise democracy', Caitlyn Gribbin, Marian Faa, 28 May 2020. https://www.abc.net.au/news/2020-05-28/news-corp-makes-regional-papers-digital-only/12295408

and the quality of journalism hadn't diminished so severely after the acquisitions by News Corporation, it might not have reached this point of massive newspaper closures.

There are wholesale changes taking place within the media landscape and for the largest proprietor of news media in Australia—Rupert Murdoch—to offload, close down, and digitalise a large collection shows that New Corporation is in deep financial trouble, certainly within Australia. And this seems to be technological transition News Corporation has failed to grasp: through the internet, it's possible to access every major news publication from around the world, either on a desktop computer, mobile phone, or tablet. And it's quite possible the stand-alone news ventures and the ones that are not spread out too thinly on the ground are the ones that will survive into the future. News Corporation is a behemoth that has become too large and too voracious for its own good.

Print media is in decline: it may not die immediately, but it's in a decline. Many people are surprised to hear the Encyclopaedia Britannica only ceased printing its large tomes in 2012, 244 years after it published its first edition. At the time, Britannica president Jorge Cauz, said "the print set is an icon. But it's an icon that doesn't do justice to how much we've changed over the years".[53] When asked why the print edition had continued for so long, even after the advent of the internet, his answer was simple: "we were still making money from it".

This is likely to be the case for newspapers in Australia: their proprietors are still making money from publishing newsprint. But over the next decade or two, the only way to read print newspapers will be through state library archives and microfiche. And even then, the public may wonder why it took so long for them to disappear completely.

*

---

53 *CNN Money*, 'Encyclopedia Britannica to stop printing books', Julianne Pepitone, 13 March 2012. https://money.cnn.com/2012/03/13/technology/encyclopedia-britannica-books/index.htm

Branch stacking in Victoria

18 June

There has been an exposé of the branch stacking antics in the Victoria branch of the Labor Party, where the Labor member in the Victoria Parliament, Adem Somyurek, has been accused of massive branch stacking to manipulate the preselection of Labor candidates—the ethics and legalities of *60 Minutes* making covert recordings inside a minister's office can be set aside for the time being—but affair has resulted in the intervention by the federal Labor Party into the Victoria branch, Somyurek has been expelled from the party and in the words of the federal Labor president, Wayne Swan, there'll never be a place for him in the Labor Party ever again.

Branch stacking is a blight on the democratic process and it's a practice usually associated with the Labor Party, but it does exist across all other parties: the Liberal Party, National Party, Greens, One Nation; it's the nature of a political system based on parties organising themselves to provide the right candidate in each seat. And, of course, it's not always the best candidate who gets into the seat. Some Liberal Party branches in Victoria have been influenced by right-wing Mormons, Catholic activists and neo-Nazis sympathisers such as Neil Erikson, and way back in 2007, Scott Morrison was the beneficiary of branch stacking activities in the preselection battle in the seat of Cook.

In the perfect world, branch stacking would not exist and the true members of a political party would choose their candidate but politics is an imperfect science, and it's not always the best candidate who wins the preselection. Every party has its back room people and heavy-hitters who try and manipulate the votes and the 'numbers' within its membership to get the candidate they prefer, rather than what the membership wants: they're the people who are not so much interested in policy matters but control of the party. Sometimes, this is a way of organising internal political or policy matters within each branch of the party, at other times, it's an outright abuse of power. There have always been infamous 'number crunchers' within politics, from Eddie Ward and Graham Richardson within the Labor Party, to Reg Withers and Tony Abbott within the Liberal Party.

'Playing the numbers' is quite often dismissed as a base political game but, essentially, working out who is going to vote in a particular way is important for the future direction of policy development or candidate selection and a guide for which issue will get the right number of votes—which is usually 50 per cent, plus one—otherwise, everyone's time is wasted and best to move on to other issues which will get support.

US President, Lyndon Johnson, didn't move on any issue until he was assured he had enough numbers to pass legislation, and making sure he put most of his political efforts into securing enough votes because, without this, nothing can actually be done. This seems like a basic part of the political process but others, such as former Prime Minister, Gough Whitlam, weren't so concerned about shoring up the support first, and that was one of his greatest failings: trying to implement what he thought was the best course of action, through his infamous 'crash through or crash' approach to politics.

Other former prime ministers, such as Bob Hawke, Paul Keating or John Howard, also understood the importance of securing 'the numbers': the numbers in themselves are intrinsically unimportant, but it's a mechanism for a political party, or political leader, to implement their policies.

Unfortunately, these numbers people can become too powerful. For Labor, there was Eddie Obeid in New South Wales, and now Somyurek in Victoria, and both had an influence far beyond their capabilities. Obeid was found guilty of misconduct in public office and sentenced to five years in jail in 2016. He used his management of internal party votes to amass a personal fortune—in some cases, such as his involvement with former Liberal Party Senator, Arthur Sinodinos, in the Australian Water Holdings scandals—his reach within politics was not restricted to the Labor Party alone.

Characters such as Obeid position themselves well and place themselves within the centre of activity within a political party and, as British Baron, John Dalberg-Acton once said, "power tends to corrupt, and absolute power corrupts absolutely"—not always, but certainly in this case, where Obeid stood to make $100 million from corrupt coal tendering processes.[54] Of course, Obeid ended up spending time in jail for his misdemeanours, but was released in 2019 after completing a three-year non-parole period.

The media does frame branch stacking as a 'Labor issue', but the Liberal Party has their players too: in New South Wales, there's Chris Hartcher and his involvement with illegal developer donations; there was Michael Photios and his lobbying activities and, of course, Sinodinos in the federal sphere. One other characteristic of 'numbers people' is they have a relatively low profile and do their work behind the scenes: they raise a large amount of money for their respective political parties, usually through their involvement with different ethnic groups within the community. And with this flow of money is a flow of power, and they're people usually left to their own devices, as long as they are drawing in the funds, and few questions are ever asked of them, even if they are using unorthodox or illegal methods.

Obviously, the existence of these people is not good for politics; it's a corrosive influence on politics and results in the people with the most wealth in a democratic system, having the most influence. But if it can be agreed that this is a corrosive problem, what can be done to resolve the issue? Perhaps fully publicly-funded elections is the solution—which is Australia is close to achieving anyway: for each primary vote received over the threshold of 4 per cent, a candidate receives $2.82. This is an advantage to the more established larger mainstream parties but it does mean smaller parties can still participate in the electoral process.

---

54 *Sydney Morning Herald*, 'Obeid family stood to make $100m from coal deal, court hears', Kate McClymont, 1 September 2020. https://www.smh.com.au/politics/nsw/obeid-family-stood-to-make-100m-from-coal-deal-court-hears-20200901-p55rb0.html

Even with a fully publicly-funded electoral process, party operatives are cynical and would manoeuvre towards obtaining a financial benefit in other ways. But it may limit these ways of exploiting the current system, in view of mining magnate Clive Palmer's recent involvement in politics through the United Australia Party, where large sums of money have been spent—$80 million during the 2019 federal election, which was primarily to aid the Liberal–National Party in key mining seats in Queensland. Perhaps other mechanisms could be introduced, such a cap of $100 per individual, or $5,000 in fundraising events, as well as real-time donations platforms, where the electoral can view political donations as they are made, rather than waiting for the Australian Electoral Commission to release their annual donations data. These reforms, while not completely clearing out corruption in political fundraising, would represent a good start.

While political donations are a real issue for reform within the political system, it has to be highlighted that while branch stacking receives a great deal of scrutiny and media attention, the act itself is not illegal. If any member of the public consents to being a member of a political party and someone else is paying the fee, then no electoral laws are breached. The illegal part of this process is in those cases where memberships are declared and paid for without consent—in some cases, people who have never had any intention of voting for the Liberal Party, found they were signed up for the party and voted for the preselected candidate, even though they'd never set foot in a branch meeting. But whether branch stacking is illegal or not, it does pervert the natural course of democratic processes.

While the cliché of branch stacking is of a shady Labor Party operative barking their instructions down the phone to a transactional go-between on the other end of the line, it should be noted the most recent Liberal Party prime ministers have been the main beneficiaries of branch stacking. In the lead-up to the 2004 federal election, Malcolm Turnbull undermined the sitting Liberal Party member in the seat of Wentworth, Peter King. Liberal Party membership rose dramatically in the seat, with Turnbull enrolling many people from the Jewish community in the eastern suburbs, and at one stage telling King to "fuck off and get out of my way", one of his many acts of besmirching King's reputation and prising him out of the seat.⁵⁵

Scott Morrison's entry into politics was also similarly anti-democratic manner where in the lead up to the 2007 election—soon after he was sacked from the position of managing director of Tourism Australia—he lost the initial preselection to Michael Towke, eight votes to eighty-two, but was subsequently overturned after Morrison launched a vicious media campaign against Towke. It's unclear exactly which type of branch manipulation Morrison engaged in but the seat of Cook has been beset with allegations of branch stacking over the past few decades, with Stephen Mutch losing his preselection to Bruce Baird in 1998, due to allegations of stacking, and another attempt in 2009 by Liberal Party moderates, ostensibly to 'protect Morrison' but with the strong intention to actually remove him.⁵⁶ In retaliation to Morrison's manipulation of the 2007 preselection vote, the Port Hacking branch of the Liberal Party refused to endorse his application to join their branch, and Morrison was forced to join another branch within the division of Cook.

In Towke's case, a democratically endorsed candidate was overthrown by the hard-right of the Liberal Party; eleven years later, Morrison becomes prime minister. It's not the way politicians should be elected to Parliament. In response to the allegations against Somyurek, Morrison made great political mileage out of event, claiming Albanese has serious questions to answer, even though it seems Morrison's preselection and branch manipulation is the area where more questions need to be answered, especially the role played by News Corporation in the downfall of Towke.

And the involvement of News Corporation and Nine Network should not be underestimated in the current allegations against Somyurek. It's interesting to note that these revelations—spread across national television and in news publications in New South Wales, even though Somyurek is member of the Victoria

---

55 *Inside Story*, 'The Battle For Wentworth', Brett Evans, 19 September 2015. http://insidestory.org.au/the-battle-for-wentworth

56 *Sydney Morning Herald*, 'Threat from right cited in Liberal branch stacking', Phillip Coorey, 13 June 2009. https://www.smh.com.au/national/threat-from-right-cited-in-liberal-branch-stacking-20090612-c68e.html

Parliament—were revealed the day before pre-polling booths open in the byelection in the federal seat of Eden–Monaro.

60 Minutes claimed their investigations had been running for almost one year but the Nine Network—chaired by former Liberal Party Treasurer, Peter Costello—decided the night before the booths open in a critical byelection was the most favourable time to air the program, with the allegations aired through electronic and print media for the rest of the week. It would take a brave soul to suggest the news about the allegations wasn't released to provide maximum damage to the Labor Party, and maximum opportunity for the Liberal Party in this byelection campaign.

Branch stacking undermines democracy but so too does the attempts by conservative media to favour the one side of politics based on innuendo, hearsay and gossip, and imply that it's only the Labor Party that engages in this type of activity. Politics would be better off if neither of these actions occurred within the national political debate.

*

Opening up too quickly

18 June

Is the Australian society and economy opening up too quickly, too slowly, or at an appropriate pace which balances economic and social needs, with good health outcomes? This issue has become pertinent over the past few weeks, just when it seems China may be on the cusp of a second wave of coronavirus cases. When the coronavirus first appeared in Wuhan in late 2019 and spread rapidly throughout northern Italy, Australia was able to witness these events from afar and adjust its reactions and policies to limit the spread locally. At the time, the Australian government didn't react as quickly as it could have and, with a second wave of coronavirus a distinct possibility, it should be looking at the unfolding events in other countries more closely.

New Zealand managed to completely eliminate coronavirus through a decisive and hard lockdown strategy and, because of the success of their fast action, recently removed all internal restrictions, although their international borders are still closed. In Australia, the only internal borders that are still closed are in Western Australia and Tasmania: should Australia remove all internal restrictions, as New Zealand has, or should it wait an extra period of time?

One of the arguments for fully opening up is that the hospital system across the states and territories is now equipped to manage any outbreaks that may occur and, based on the data that currently exists on coronavirus cases that have been recorded since the pandemic commenced, Australia now has enough hospital beds to deal with any influx. This is a good sign. But there are many aspects of coronavirus which are still unknown, and this is the nature of a new virus—it simply hasn't been around for long enough to be able to predict how it may behave in the future.

In the 1918 pandemic, the influenza came back in a wave much larger than any medical expert predicted and it was this second wave that killed millions of people, or between 1 and 2.7 per cent of the world's population.[57] In some regions of the world, it was a much higher percentage—30 per cent of local populations—although it does need to be pointed out that that world of 1918 is radically different to the world of 2020: health care generally is far superior, the means of media communication is faster, which means health messaging can be delivered instantly, and the 1918 pandemic commenced towards the end of the devastating World War I.

China was on the verge of opening up but has clamped down strongly with the onset of their second wave of coronavirus. Their first lockdown in Wuhan during January 2020 was severe, with authorities welding down apartment doors so residents couldn't leave, patrolling the streets and apprehending anyone who was found outdoors, and forcing people into ambulances. Australia's lockdown was almost voluntary: people could still go to supermarkets and hardware stores; they could still do their grocery shopping; they could exercise in small groups. It was a relatively mild lockdown which commenced in March, and perhaps it should have been more restrictive.

However, the federal government is one that is ideologically opposed to the notion of locking down individuals, even if there is a medical crisis or a pandemic that necessitates this. Because of this, perhaps Australia's response was the best that could have been delivered, and perhaps it was because of Australia's federated system of governments that allowed the premiers of the states and the chief ministers of the territories to create a more sufficient health response in the earlier stages of the pandemic.

Business groups and the many vested interests that depend on the Liberal Party for political support, have been pressuring the federal

---

57 *Our World In Data*, 'The Spanish flu (1918–20): The global impact of the largest influenza pandemic in history', Max Roser, March 2020. https://ourworldindata.org/spanish-flu-largest-influenza-pandemic-in-history

government to urgently open up the economy, even though this might not result in the best health outcome. Australia is still managing the case load well—the number of active cases around Australia has been hovering around the 390 mark for several weeks; suggesting an equilibrium between the numbers of cases being shed, and the new cases being acquired. It may be possible that this is the best that can be hoped for, within a relatively low-density population of over 25 million people. The key question for members of Parliament and medical officials is how to manage these numbers in the long term.

The debate about opening or closing borders and returning the economy to its former state has, predictably, navigated along political lines, irrespective of which part of the country is mentioned. There was a ridiculous situation where the Senator for Queensland, Amanda Stoker, attacked the Western Australia Government for keeping their borders closed, claiming their actions were damaging the Queensland economy, even though there is no evidence to support this claim. But these claims are in the context of the upcoming Queensland election, due in October 2020, where the Liberal–National Party has decided that any gross claim in the name of politics can be justified if it results in an increase in votes: the public interest falls back to a distant last. This is an issue that keeps being ignore by conservative politicians: an economy can't function efficiently if there are too many people in that economy that are unwell, or unable to work because of illness. And until the coronavirus dissipates or mutates into a less virulent variant, or an effective vaccine becomes available, the health of the public is an issue that will need to be prioritised.

*

The new McCarthyism in Australia

2 July

'McCarthyism' is the practice of making accusations of subversion or treason; it was prevalent in the United States during the 1950s, and saw many conservative politicians and community leaders make accusations of communist subversion against political enemies without any proof or substantiation—it was influenced by Republican Senator Joe McCarthy and gave rise to this infamous question: "Are you now or have you ever been a member of the Communist Party?", as well as influencing American foreign policy for well over thirty years.

Australia seems to be on the pathway towards the Third Red Scare, a new version of widespread fear of a potential rise of communism but in 2020, it's not the Soviet Union cast as the evil villain, but the Chinese Communist Party. It's not quite at the stage of blacklisting or public officials calling for executions for those with close links to communism—which was actually proposed in the United States in the 1950s—but with the current level of anti-China hysteria, that stage might be arriving soon.

Last week, the New South Wales Labor backbencher, Shaoquett Moselmane had his house raided by the Australian Federal Police, the media was tipped off, and Nine Network's *60 Minutes* program performed a large exposé. It has been confirmed that Moselmane is not under any suspicion, and it seems his biggest 'crime' so far has been to praise the Chinese President, Xi Jinping, and make favourable comments about the Chinese government.

He's been suspended by the Labor Party and virtually banned from attending the New South Wales Parliament. There may be a great deal to reveal within this story that the public might not be aware of, but it seems the legal principle of innocence until proven guilty—especially when it comes to issues related to China—has been completely removed.

It's not clear what the allegations against Moselmane are, although it seems his crime was praising the Chinese government for their swift response to their coronavirus outbreak—unlike the allegations that were made against federal Liberal Party member for Chisholm, Gladys Liu, where her clear connections with the Chinese government were downplayed by the media, as well as her fundraising activities—but there needs to be a presumption of innocence, unless a court of law finds otherwise. The raid on Moselmane's home was carried out with the media in tow, so there's a political dimension to this outside of whatever Moselmane is going to be accused of, although the Australian Federal Police has specifically stated that he is not a suspect.

This is more to do with political theatre than any actions of crime—many raids in recent times have resulted in charges quietly dropped with no further actions, implying a political motivation, incompetence or a combination—and, coincidentally, all of this material was released in the week leading up to the Eden–Monaro byelection.

Of course, Australia needs to be concerned about international influences in domestic politics but the public needs to be aware of all of these influences, not only the influences on *one* side of politics. The former Labor Senator for New South Wales, Sam Dastyari, was scrutinised for a $1,600 expenses claim and another $5,000 legal bill paid by a Chinese donor—all legally correct and within the current parliamentary entitlements rules—and eventually resigned from politics. This was a correct decision. But the rules—whether they are legal, administrative, or political—need to be applied to all sides of politics equally, and it seems the Liberal Party evades these types of rules entirely.

The member for the Victoria seat of Chisholm, Gladys Liu, raised over $1 million for the Liberal Party and there are many questions about where this money came from, including from a company that had received vast amounts of cash from a heroin trafficker.[58] There was also the case of Tony Abbott—just before he became prime minister—Stuart Robert and Ian Macfarlane receiving Rolex watches to the value of $250,000 from Chinese billionaire, Li Ruipeng.[59] There's also the Julie Bishop Glorious Foundation that was used to funnel money from a Chinese businessman to the Western Australia branch of the Liberal Party. Former member for Goldstein, Andrew Robb, acquired a $880,000 per year part-time consultancy with yet another Chinese billionaire, Ye Cheng, while he was still a member of Parliament.

While these issues were duly reported in the media, the depth of reporting was shallow and unsustained. Dastyari was headline news for weeks, had media crews parked on the doorstep of his family home for several days until the political pressure become too intense and forced his resignation. The actions of Liberal Party members of Parliament—which on the surface, appear far more serious and compromise national security to a much higher degree—resulted in no investigations forthcoming by the Australian Federal Police, and certainly no year-long investigation pursued by *60 Minutes* or any other news network: the news for Liberal Party misdemeanours was reported on a shallow level in the media and that was the end of the matter.

The irony of these events was the media insisted on journalistic freedoms when the Australian Federal Police raided the home of News Corporation journalistic Annika Smethurst, over publishing information that was deemed to be 'official secrets', and launched the 'Your Right To Know' campaign under the banner of: "Australia, you're being kept in the dark". Yes, Australia is being kept in the dark, not through some unfortunate raid on a journalist's home, but by the journalists themselves, who refuse to partake in balanced in-depth reporting and prefer to hold a Labor opposition to account,

---

58 *Sydney Morning Herald*, 'Gladys Liu demanded Liberal Party pay back her $100k donation', Anthony Galloway & Rob Harris, 5 December 2019. https://www.smh.com.au/politics/federal/gladys-liu-demanded-liberal-party-pay-back-her-100k-donation-20191204-p53gvp.html

59 *The Guardian*, 'Tony Abbott and other Liberals took Rolexes they thought were fake', Elle Hunt, 10 February 2016. https://www.theguardian.com/australia-news/2016/feb/10/liberals-took-rolex-and-other-designer-watches-assuming-they-were-were-fake

rather the government which is engaged in multi-level corruption and compromising national security.

Where is the curiosity of the media? Where are the raids on the offices of Stuart Robert's office; Angus Taylor's office; or Barnaby Joyce's office? These raids would be far more productive than searching the home of second-rate journalist, or scrutinising a lowly Labor Senator who didn't breach any rules or break any laws. It's a clear and obvious bias and, far from the 'holding power to account' message the media likes to promote about themselves, so many corrupt behaviours performed by the Liberal Party and the National Party fail to gain traction within their reporting.

Law enforcement officers and police departments do make mistakes sometimes and, when it comes to national security, it's better for a unit such as the Australian Federal Police to have some leeway in its activities but to enforce the law on one side of politics alone is completely unacceptable in a democratic system. For a politician to be publicly praising a government such as Chinese regime—in the way Moselmane did—is inviting unwarranted scrutiny, especially at a time when the federal government is viewing any relationship with China suspiciously, in keeping with the Trump administration in the United States.

All countries in the world will act according to their own interests, and Australia and China are not any different in this respect. Of course, China has a poor human rights record, it has consistently spied on other countries' commercial, economic and military operations—as does the United States, Russia, France, Britain and many other countries—no country is perfect and it's evident some countries are more imperfect that others.

Australia may have its suspicions about China's ulterior motivations but it has to be remembered that China is Australia's largest trading partner. Israel also has a poor human rights record but should the Australian government have the same ambivalence and distrust about the Israeli government? Israel's influence in Australian politics is an area of more concern but that is an issue that is never raised within the media.

The other factor in the raids on Moselmane's office and home is that there was a tip-off to the media and a camera crew and reporter arrived at the scene before the police. A journalist scoop or a handy relationship between the Australian Federal Police and conservative allies in the media? The former News Corporation political editor, Renee Viellaris, worked for *The Courier-Mail* in Brisbane, and is now the head of communications with the Australian Federal Police.

Soon after these raids were reported, *60 Minutes* aired promotions for a major story on Moselmane to air the following Sunday evening. Stories such as these take some time and high level of production resources and research for it to come together and it's evident *60 Minutes* would have had some time to prepare the story. The tip-off wasn't a 'spur-of-the-moment' decision by Viellaris at the last minute in the public interest, but a political hit-job by conservative media interests designed to maximise political damage to the Labor Party. There's a strong element of racism in these actions by the Australian Federal Police and the media; there's a strong element of acting in the interests of the Liberal Party, and promoting a message to a susceptible audience that is receptive to this kind of overt racism.

What will be the end game in these hostilities with China? It's very difficult to continue trading with a regime that is criticised on a daily basis from a government acting to boost its political stocks with some old-fashioned racism. Trading partners can set aside political differences or domestic political acts if that trade is beneficial to both partners but which markets can Australia go to if the trade with China is severely curtailed? What will become of the arrangements in the ninety-nine-year lease of the Port of Darwin to the Chinese-owned Landbridge Group if the relationship with China continues to sour? In hindsight, this was a poor decision made by the Country Liberal Party in 2015, and a strategic decision Australia may come to regret.

And what can be done about the continuing politicisation of the Australian Federal Police? They can raid with ease the homes and offices of journalists and Labor politicians, which seem to be conveniently positioned to favour incumbent conservative governments, but can't locate any fraudulent and illegal actions by Minister for Energy, Angus Taylor, or readily find the source of malicious emails that denigrated the Labor candidate in the byelection of Eden–Monaro, Kristy McBain, which claimed she was withdrawing from the campaign due to coronavirus and instructing the electorate to vote for her Liberal Party opponent,

Fiona Kotvojs. The Australian Federal Police seems to have good form to know where not to look, especially when something appears to be detrimental to an incumbent conservative government.

The public service has been politicised since the Howard government arrived in 1996,[60] although it was actually a Hawke government initiative to allow flexibility with contracts for heads of departments, instead of dominant public service Mandarin's holding their positions for over twenty years and allowing departments to stagnate. The Australian Federal Police has long been considered a politicised entity, originally being the creation of former Prime Minister Billy Hughes in 1917 as a *de facto* personal militia. Governments of all persuasions use federal police and the military for political purposes and this becomes dangerous when prime ministers use them with the wrong motivations.

Robert Menzies used commonwealth police resources and security organisations to generate a fear of communism and used it to great benefit in the 1950s, including the infamous Petrov Affair on the eve of the 1954 federal election, an election Labor was widely expected to win, but fell short by four seats, even though it received 50.7 per cent of the two-party preferred vote. Howard used national security issues in the lead-up to the 2001 federal election to generate a fear of Islamic terrorism and asylum seekers, and Tony Abbott infamously decided to stay at an Australian Federal Police training college in Canberra while the Lodge was renovated in 2013.

There is an undeniable link between the Australian Federal Police and conservative governments, as well as offering support to in the quest to promote fear of 'the other' and boost their domestic political stocks. And this fear of otherness and difference is a template used by conservative governments all over the world: different cultures, customs, appearances and languages, arise as an existential threat—people who look different, speak differently or arrive from a different political or cultural system are depicted as threats and only the government can offer protection against these threats. Menzies used this approach to great effect in the 1950s, Howard in the 2000s, and now Morrison.

---

60 Parliament of Australia, 'Politicising the Australian Public Service?', Richard Mulgan, Research Paper 3, 1998. https://www.aph.gov.au/About_Parliament/Parliamentary_Departments/Parliamentary_Library/pubs/rp/rp9899/99rp03

In the 1950s, the Soviet Union was the country that appeared to be the largest threat to the western world. Today, it's communist China and many of the tropes being used by right-wing politicians are continuing the battles of the Cold War period that ended in 1991 and, perhaps, it's a continuation of events that essentially commenced in 1917, towards the end of World War I. During the 1920s and 1930s, there were secret armies formed by establishment figures, as well as organised groups such as the New Guard, who attacked communist sympathisers and Labor Party members. Menzies continued this anti-communist rhetoric when he became prime minister in 1939.

There were riots in country towns and cities between left-wing and right-wing groups but by the time of the 1950s, these actions had settled down in relative terms, with a better performing economy and more stability in the post-World War II era. But communism was still presented as a lingering fear: Menzies continued when he introduced the *Communist Party Dissolution Bill* in 1950, which was invalidated by the High Court. This became the precursor to the 1951 Australian Communist Party ban referendum, which was narrowly defeated.

The fact that 49.4 per cent of the electorate voted in favour showed that there was a genuine and real fear within the community about communism; conversely, it also showed that 50.6 of the electorate didn't consider the Communist Party as a threat. The lineage of conservative threats can be seen all the way through to the 1983 federal election, when former Prime Minister, Malcolm Fraser, invoked communism as a reason for why Bob Hawke shouldn't be anywhere near government, and even used recently by Minister for Finance, Mathias Cormann in 2017, when he warned of Labor's "reds under the beds",[61] surely a reference most of the electorate would not understand.

The world has become more sophisticated since the time of Menzies but, clearly, conservative politicians still want to be defined through the enterprise of Cold War politics and cultural warfare that most of the world has left behind, but want to remind the

---

61 *Independent Australia*, 'Mathias Cormann warns of Labor's 'reds under the beds'", John Passant, 28 August 2017. https://independentaustralia.net/politics/politics-display/mathias-cormann-warns-of-labors-reds-under-the-beds,10658

electorate that, yes, there is still a bogeyman out there in the form of the Chinese Community Party that can threaten Australia's livelihood at any given moment.

There might be political opportunities in attacking a foreign government and stoking fear and racism among domestic audiences, but governments need to be careful in the way these issues are managed. Morrison announced a $270 billion ten-year program to acquire long-range missiles to be used in a "more dangerous and more disorderly" post-COVID world. This needs to be placed into the context of a byelection in the seat of Eden–Monaro, as well as the context of a government that makes many announcements but rarely delivers any of them, and it's a program unlikely to be delivered.

China wasn't mentioned by name, but it's clear who Morrison is referring to when he mentioned a "world that is poorer, more dangerous and more disorderly". A blustering announcement that was bellicose in nature but, in keeping with the philosophy of Menzies and Howard, reminding the public about a clear and present danger in faraway lands, but also a reminder that the Liberal–National Coalition is here to protect the community.

It was predictable; it was obvious; and it was clear who the target was: China. But it was also ridiculous and a reminder of how life can imitate art, or how politics can also imitate parody. In this sequence from the ABC's satirical series, *Utopia*, the head of the fictional Nation Building Authority is seeking answers at a meeting with defence chiefs about a soon-to-be-released defence white paper.[62]

> **Tony Woodford (CEO):** You know what? I'll name one [country], and you just nod. China.
>
> [nods from around the meeting table]
>
> **Woodford:** Yeah, okay. And what exactly are we protecting?
>
> **Colonel:** Strategic interests.
>
> **Woodford:** Specifically, Colonel.
>
> **Colonel:** Indo–Pacific strategic interests—
>
> **Woodford:** Really specifically...

---

62 ABC Television, *Utopia*, 'On The Defence', August 2017.

Colonel: Indo–Asia–Pacific strategic interests.

Woodford: You know what? I'll say it and then you nod. Our trade routes.

[nods from around the meeting table]

Woodford: And who is our number one trading partner?

Scott Byrnes (Project Assistant): Shall we use nods this time?

Woodford: Sure. China?

[nods from around the meeting table]

Woodford: So, under this scenario, we're spending close to $30 billion a year to protect our trade with China—from China. And that doesn't strike anyone at this table as odd?

[bemused head shaking from around the meeting table].

That episode of *Utopia* was produced in 2017 but the resemblance to Morrison's recent announcement is uncanny. For the Australian government to spend $27 billion per year for the next decade to protect Australia from its largest trading partner is a ludicrous proposition.

For the benefit of local exporters to the China market, it's hoped that Morrison antics are little more than ill-informed diplomatic shadow boxing on the world stage but in the event that China does further reduce trade with Australia, which other markets are available? The British Prime Minister, Boris Johnson, recently speculated that Britain could send Marmite to Australia, in exchange for Vegemite and Tim Tams, a trade conversation that could be most expected from a prime minister who is an equal to Morrison in terms of inane political speak and populist rhetoric. It was a suggestion from Johnson that these types of products are all the wonderful goods available because of Brexit, even though those goods are already available in British supermarkets.

Missile announcements are the standard fare of conservative governments, and these are messages that can be amplified by key players in the media, with Foreign Editor of *The Australian*, Greg Sheridan, suggesting foreign players would 'think twice' before invading Australia. The point here is that no foreign players will 'think twice' about an Australian invasion because they won't even be thinking once about it. A spend of $27 million per year is virtually the nuts and bolts of the armoury, and the Chinese army comprises 2.8 million active duty troops, compared to Australia's 58,000.

And if the $27 billion per year spend does eventuate, it will show the priorities of this government: it could be used for a temporary universal basic income or, failing that, universal services access, or fine tuning and extending the JobKeeper program. The expensive purchase of long-range missiles against an imaginary target that will never be used: it's an excellent metaphor for a government that doesn't seem to know any better.

*

Barbarians at the gate and reaching for their guns

2 July

The ABC is an important cultural institution in Australian life but for this federal government, perhaps it's not so important. A few months after the ABC performed essential news and communications during the bushfire season and was attributed with saving many lives with emergency updates and broadcasts, the ABC has implemented an $84 million funding cut, resulting in the loss of 250 jobs, including seventy in their news gathering services—and this brings the total of funding cuts to $783 million, ever since the Liberal–National Government returned to office in 2013, a further sign of their hostility towards cultural institutions.

The arts, screen and entertainment industries employ over 600,000 people and contributes $111.7 billion to the Australian economy.[63] These industries were the first to be impacted by the coronavirus pandemic, and will take the longest to recover, whenever society and the economy are stabilised.

The federal government has announced a $250 million rescue package for the arts—unlike the support offered to other sectors, $90 million of this amount is in loans—but it's far too late for this sector and, to place this amount into context, it's 0.2 per cent of the

---

63 Australian Industry and Skills Committee, 'Arts, Culture, Entertainment and Design', 2020. https://nationalindustryinsights.aisc.net.au/industries/arts-culture-entertainment-and-design

overall amount of $130 billion allocated to the JobKeeper program. For many artists, playwrights, actors and entertainers, whose work is based on short-term and piecemeal employment, the allocated funds are not going to be enough to save the industry.

And this is an area the Prime Minister and his government fail to understand. There are actually more people working in the arts and entertainment industries than the mining industry—over 300,000,[64] compared to 260,000 in the mining industry[65]—and Morrison seems to think that all he has to do is make a grand announcement with the performer Guy Sebastian, and that should be enough to satisfy the sector.

The arts and entertainment sector tends to support left-of-centre political parties and for some time, Labor has set the narrative for arts and creative funding since the time of Gough Whitlam in 1972 and, generally, arrives at elections with greater levels of funding support for the creative industries, and a pledge to restore funding to the ABC. The arts and entertainment sector is in desperate need of stimulus support funding, but the government's tardy and small response—which could ultimately be an ineffective support—shows antipathy towards a sector it doesn't support, a sector that doesn't support the Liberal Party either. But that's not the way governments should behave: in times of great and unusual difficulty, every industry needs support, not just the ones likely to offer political benefit to the government.

Morrison's understanding of popular culture—as far as what he is prepared to announce publicly—so far has been restricted to Tina Arena, Taylor Swift and making bawdy references to Sacha Baron-Cohen's alter-ego, Borat, in Parliament. Of course, these are his choices, but Morrison is clearly not attempting to define himself through popular music culture or the arts. During the announcement of the arts funding package, he made the ridiculous assertion that it was also a boost to the building industry, because carpenters would be able to create sets for movie and theatre productions, without understanding set design and construction is a different skill set to

---

64 Australian Bureau of Statistics, Arts and Culture in Australia: A Statistical Overview, 2014. https://www.abs.gov.au/ausstats/abs@.nsf/Lookup/4172.0main+features242014
65 Labour Market Information Portal, Mining, 2020. https://lmip.gov.au/default.aspx?LMIP/GainInsights/IndustryInformation/Mining

home building. On the surface, it seems like a poorly thought-out stimulus program which Morrison is trying to extract a political benefit and the amount of funding, when compared with the $303 billion in total stimulus support that has been approved by Parliament, is insulting and doesn't relate to the social, cultural and economic benefits provided to the community by the arts and entertainment sector.

And in keeping with the attitudes of the Liberal–National Coalition to the arts, the ABC has implemented another round of cutbacks: it's not a perfect organisation and there are many issues with it current style of political reporting, which seems to be more intent of highlighting problems within the Labor Party, and boosting the profile of the Liberal Party; it lacks diversity and although it is far better than commercial media, it is still unreflective of the Australian community and tends to reflect antiquated middle-class values. Despite these criticisms, the ABC is one of the more comprehensive broadcasters in the world.

The ABC has been a political play-tool of both sides of politics, but it's never as perfect as its supporters claim, or a terrible as its detractors in the government suggest. Although there have clearly been cutbacks—$84 million in this round, and $783 million since 2013—Morrison and the Minster of Communications, Paul Fletcher, have been claiming there have never been cutbacks, even though this is demonstrably untrue.[66]

The Liberal Party does have an agenda to privatise the ABC—their membership voted by a large majority in 2018 to break-up the ABC and sell off the areas deemed to be profitable—and a slow 'death-by-a-thousand-cuts' does seem inevitable under the Coalition government, and egged on by News Corporation and the Nine Network, who would be keen to acquire new audiences and new media assets at a time when their revenues are plummeting.

The government has been promoting the notion that as all commercial media players are suffering due to the coronavirus pandemic, the ABC shouldn't be exempt from cutbacks and other changes to the media landscape that are being forced by technological

---

66 RMIT ABC *Fact Check*, 'Paul Fletcher says ABC funding is rising each year. Is he correct?', 17 July 2020. https://www.abc.net.au/news/2020-07-16/fact-check-are-there-no-cuts-to-abc-funding/12417226

innovations and economic circumstances. But the charter of the ABC isn't about replicating the conditions faced by commercial providers, whether that be in the type of content produced, or its revenues. For many years, the revenues of commercial providers have far outstripped the financial resources available to the ABC, and there was never an argument put forward by governments that funding to the ABC needs to increase to the level of commercial networks. Why should they try and match it up now, when commercial revenues are in freefall?

The ABC, despite its imperfections and its attempts to align itself with the government in the way it reports political news, is an important organisation that needs to be funded adequately, not just so it becomes a replica of commercial enterprises, but a central part of Australia's intellectual, cultural and creative wellbeing. Clearly, the Coalition government sees this differently, viewing the ABC as key real estate that can be sold off to building developers, and an entertainment unit that can be purchased by friends of the Liberal Party; News Corporation, Nine Network and Seven West Media, so ending an institution that has been built with Australia's cultural and social capital from over the past ninety years.

And it's too obvious that a collection of politicians, and a political party, that has little understanding of how the community benefits from cultural creativity, is going to remove cultural creativity at any opportunity. The infamous words 'whenever I hear the word culture, I reach for my gun' first appeared in the 1933 play *Schlageter*, written by Nazi-aligned playwright, Hanns Johst. That was a different era, but the current band of Liberal–National Coalition members no longer reach out for the holster; they implement cutbacks; run institutions to the ground; and then sell them to their benefactors for a song, claiming that it all costs too much and better for private enterprise to manage them more efficiently.

The coronavirus pandemic has shown there is more to life than just counting the dollars and cents, and placing profit-making at the centre of a decent liberal democracy. Culture, creativity, arts and entertainment are at the heart of the community, but it's an issue the narrow neoliberalist way of thinking is continuing to ignore.

*

Are we really all in this together?

2 July

The coronavirus pandemic was meant to be a time when political gamesmanship was to be put aside and, as Scott Morrison said in April 2020, ideologies were to be "checked at the door" of Parliament but, far from being checked at the door, the pandemic has seen a sharpening of the ideological knife, and division in the community is more apparent than ever.

What started off as collective efforts and the catchphrase that "we're all in this together" has descending into national point scoring from the political class about opening up borders, opening up the economy, and whether schools should be open or not.

Australia was doing quite well with the number of coronavirus cases, getting down to as low as 380 cases nationally, but there has been a spike in Melbourne, and the national number of active cases is 724. But political blame is never in short supply—at this stage, the spike has been linked to the mismanagement of the state's hotel quarantine system, but conservative media outlets have also blamed social gatherings at the end of Ramadan as the cause—even though Ramadan ended in May—they've apportioned blame to Sudanese communities, Lebanese communities and the Black Lives Matter protests.

There had been political pressure placed on the Victorian government to ease their restrictions quickly—and this spike shows why it was wise to be cautious—and there has been even greater pressure on the Queensland government to open up their borders, and after sustained attempts from the Prime Minister, conservative politicians and business leaders to undermine her leadership, the Queensland Premier, Annastacia Palaszczuk has reached her threshold:[67]

> Annastacia Palaszczuk: I think for a start, these border wars have got to stop and I think a national leader should have been able to bring all of the states and territories together. Frankly, I'm a bit sick that Queensland has been singled out, as opposed to South Australia and Tasmania, just to name a few. I support the National Cabinet but what I don't support is people being friendly inside those walls and then sending out others to do their dirty work. At the moment, what we have is a bit of a confrontation where fights are being picked at different states and frankly, I don't think it's good enough, and I've been silent for a long time and I will not be silenced for standing up for what I believe to be right for the health advice that I'm being provided for.

The entire episode of these 'border wars', where Labor states have been attacked when they've actually implemented the same policies and procedures as Liberal states is a salient reminder that conservatives never miss the opportunity to play politics, irrespective of the circumstances.

The Liberal Party member for Kew in the Victoria Parliament, Tim Smith, has showered himself in humiliation and disgrace in his unhinged, immature and snarky attacks on Premier Daniel Andrews, attacks which might be more at home at internecine student political battles between naïve eighteen-year-old first year undergraduates. The Victoria Government seems to have mismanaged hotel quarantine for overseas arrivals but, for all these faults, it has to be remembered the NSW Government mismanaged the *Ruby Princess* disaster earlier on this year and, overall, as of 1 July 2020, New South Wales has a total of 3,203 coronavirus cases, while Victoria has 2,231—and the *Ruby Princess* also caused 443 additional cases in South Australia.

---

67 *Brisbane Times*, 'Premier, PM open fire even as Palaszczuk calls for end to border war, Lydia Lynch & Rob Harris, 30 June 2020. https://www.brisbanetimes.com.au/politics/queensland/premier-pm-open-fire-even-as-palaszczuk-calls-for-end-to-border-war-20200630-p557pa.html

No administration is going to be perfect, especially when considering the previous pandemic of this nature occurred a century ago: no one in any of today's political institutions or health departments was alive during the 1918 influenza pandemic. Smith is using a crisis to gain traction for his political leadership aspirations and, like many in the conservative mainstream media, is using coronavirus as a way of placing pressure on Labor state governments but ignoring the actions of Liberal state governments. The references to Ramadan or Black Lives Matter events as the causes of a spike is standard 'dog-whistling' reporting that occurs in the media, but there is no evidence to link these events to an increase in coronavirus cases, and Victoria's Department of Health and Human Services categorically ruled this possibility out.[68] But it hasn't stopped the media or conservative politicians such as Smith and his Liberal Party colleagues such as Sarah Henderson, Matthew Guy and Georgie Crozier making the link.

The Victoria Government has established an inquiry to investigate what went wrong with its hotel quarantine management. Governments of all persuasions need to take responsibilities for these matters when they occur, but Premier Andrews has been suggesting his main priority at this stage is ensuring the case numbers do not spiral out of control: apportioning blame and seeking retribution can be left for another time, irrespective of how much sensationalist media pressure is placed on political leaders to resign.

Andrews isn't responsible for causing coronavirus, nor is NSW Premier Gladys Berejiklian; Prime Minister Morrison isn't responsible either, nor is Queensland Premier Palaszczuk, or South Australian Premier, Steve Marshall. But the electorate can judge these leaders on their actions to the coronavirus pandemic and then to see what the consequences of their actions are. The blame-game so evident in the media, especially when it comes to placing pressures and responsibilities upon Labor leaders, is a hindrance to the public interest.

The other remedy that flowed into the spectre of the "all in this together" theme is the federal government JobKeeper program. It

---

68 RMIT ABC *Fact Check*, 'There's still no evidence Black Lives Matter protesters caused Melbourne COVID-19 surge', 25 July 2020. https://www.abc.net.au/news/2020-07-24/coronacheck-black-lives-matter-melbourne-andrew-bolt-masks/12481360

has been in place for several months and the original allocation of $130 billion has been reduced to $70 billion due to "accounting errors"—it was a program the Prime Minister was initially reluctant to introduce, but it was pushed forward by leader of the Australian Council of Trade Unions, Sally McManus, and former Labor Minister for Industry, Greg Combet. There have been discussions within government that the JobKeeper program must cease at the end of September 2020 and Morrison has received a report analysing the effects on the economy if this closure takes place: that report is yet to be released. And in the context of the Eden–Monaro byelection taking place on 4 July, it's quite possible Morrison is holding back the report until after this byelection is over: in keeping with the Prime Minister's propensity to highlight only the good news, if the report was favourable to the government and recommended extending JobKeeper past September 2020, he would have released it by now and used it a positive announcement during the Eden–Monaro campaign.

The JobKeeper scheme must be difficult for a government with an ideological aversion to such a program, to continue with. It is opposed to government support for welfare; it is opposed to government intervention in any part of the economy; it's a government that doesn't like to assist people in the community that can't look after themselves. There have been some messages within the media that some employees don't want to return to work because they're receiving JobKeeper and that is acting as a deterrent for people either returning to work, or looking for new work. But this is a pandemic: many people do wish to work, but they wish to work in an environment that is safe and coronavirus is making many workplaces unsafe.

These narratives ran for a while in the media, but as soon as they disappeared, they'd be replaced with a new narrative about 'job-snobs' and the 'dole bludger' syndrome; and starting to blame workers and the unemployed for high unemployment rates, even though there is not enough work at present. The heir to a multimillion-dollar hotel empire and former Liberal Party minister, Craig Laundy, claimed it wasn't "a global invisible virus" that was keeping people out of work, it was the unwillingness of people to "get off their backsides".

Unemployment is officially sitting at 7.4 per cent, but without JobKeeper support, the figures would be substantially higher.[69] It's not the most politically sensible or socially responsible move to start blaming people for not looking for work, when the work isn't there, or expecting them to move interstate into regional areas to pick fruit at sub-par wages and inferior working conditions. These narratives pushed forward by the media and political operatives are tropes used in a bygone era and is further proof that an ideologically-driven government is never going to leave its ideology "checked at the door". These are questionable tactics even at the best of times and it's certainly a series of tactics that shouldn't be used now.

Even the most patrician of Australian prime ministers, Stanley Bruce, never engaged in this type of banter or insidious tactics. He was prime minister at the beginning of the Great Depression, even losing office and his own parliamentary seat in 1929. But he never used those types of attacks against people who were underprivileged or had lost their jobs because of the changing economic circumstances. 'Job-snob', 'dole bludger' and any other term to denigrate the unemployed are terms of contempt: these are the terms used as part of bullying behaviour, terms of power and terms used against underprivileged people. Australian governments during the backend of the Great Depression from 1931 through to 1943 were conservative: the unemployed were looked upon as 'unfortunate'—problematic in itself, but at least there was a level of compassion and understanding that there was a compact between the government and the community: in times of severe difficulties, the government was there to help.

What this current Liberal–National Coalition government lacks is compassion. It has this understanding that if sometime can't find employment, then there must be something seriously wrong with that person. That can be considered an ideological position for a particular political party and attacking welfare recipients has worked politically for them in previous times. But to employ these political strategies and attacks during highly difficult circumstances

---

69 *The Conversation*, Jeff Borland, May 2020. 'Were it not for JobKeeper, unemployment would be 11.7%', https://theconversation.com/were-it-not-for-jobkeeper-unemployment-would-be-11-7-up-from-5-2-in-one-month-heres-how-the-numbers-pan-out-138268

for many people in the community shows that it's a government that also doesn't understand the shifting sands of political discourse.

The seat of Eden–Monaro for many years has been a litmus test for governments of the day, and was a 'bell weather' seat that swung with the government of the day, between 1972 and 2016. But it's still a highly marginal seat and the upcoming byelection will provide good 'real-life' opinion poll on how the Prime Minister and Leader of the Opposition, Anthony Albanese, are performing. Unemployment and under-employment in the south-coast region of New South Wales is high, and that was the case even before the pandemic commenced. It's also a region that is still dealing with a long-term recovery program after the recent disastrous bushfire season. Everything the government has been acting on should be held within the prism of the Eden–Monaro byelection, as it is seat that it keen to win. The result will prove whether Morrison has the right strategy in place—politically and economically—and it will be a test to see whether "we're all in this together" is a true sentiment of the community, or just another inane and meaningless political message.

*

Reading the tea leaves in Eden–Monaro

17 July

It's a result the Australian Electoral Commission will officially declare today, although the Eden–Monaro byelection has been virtually over for some time: the Labor candidate, Kristy McBain claimed victory last week when it was evident there weren't enough voters on the electoral roll to overtake her slender lead.

Ultimately, there was a slight swing against the Labor Party, but with the amount of resources the Liberal Party put into the campaign, as well the support the electorate is currently given to government incumbents during the coronavirus pandemic, it's a seat they should have taken off Labor, and it's a seat they should have won comfortably.

Prime Minister Scott Morrison was seen during the byelection campaign on a daily basis, he made regular announcements on defence spending for a seat that includes the Jervis Bay Military College, yet another announcement on the Snowy 2.0 project—which seems more like a marketing exercise than a project of substance—started pouring long-withheld money into the region still suffering from the effects of the last bushfire season, had massive media support behind him, as well as massive personal approval ratings in published opinions polls. Despite these advantages, it wasn't enough to translate into votes on the ground: it's a byelection the Liberal Party should have won.

Historically, the possibility of an election win was against them: no government has won a byelection off an opposition since 1920. The Liberal Party did have many external advantages but most politics is played out locally and what the world outside of the seat of Eden–Monaro saw in the media, was obviously different to what was happening on a local level. The Liberal Party had difficulties in preselecting a candidate, Fiona Kotvojs being the final choice after toying with the idea of choosing Andrew Constance—who withdrew his candidacy—Jim Molan, and even former Prime Minister, Tony Abbott. Procrastination over candidate selection rarely works out well, especially when played out so publicly, whereas Labor made an early selection with McBain, which provided her with a local campaign advantage.

It was a hard-fought campaign but, on election night, the Liberal Party was never ahead in the counting and after Labor received the preference flows from the Shooters, Fishers & Farmers Party, it was easier to predict the outcome, albeit it was a narrow victory. The dynamic between these two parties will be interesting to note in future election campaigns—the Shooters, Fishers & Farmers Party is relatively new and it seems they are attracting disaffected National Party voters who have seen the party they have traditionally supported move into tighter connections with larger agri-businesses and the mining industry, at the expense of smaller farmers and local enterprise.

There isn't enough research at this stage to make this definitive conclusion, but perhaps Morrison inserting himself so prominently may have helped to keep the vote closer than it otherwise would have been. And the Liberal Party bussed in so many senior government ministers and other backbenchers—it's not quite clear why the member for Wentworth, Dave Sharma featured so prominently in the campaign, at one stage described as a 'Liberal superstar'—but what was clear was the Liberal Party was determined to pick up an extra seat in Parliament, to add to their wafer-thin margin of one seat.

The seat of Eden–Monaro is considered to be a microcosm of Australian society: it has a mixture of wealthy and disadvantaged areas, it has a similar demographic structure to the rest of Australia, a combination of rural and semi-urban areas, manufacturing and farming. It's also a seat that is usually held by the government of the day, and because it is a seat that is so reflective of the rest of Australian society, it's acts as litmus test for the main political parties.

What are the motivations for the Liberal Party? Obviously, the party wanted to win the seat create a buffer in its majority in the House of Representatives but an added bonus would have been to destabilise the position of Labor leader, Anthony Albanese. Albanese has been under pressure from within some parts of the Labor rank-and-file membership for not offering enough opposition to the government since he become the leader in June 2019, but since the pandemic commenced early this year, these have been difficult times for any party in opposition. If Labor had lost the seat of Eden–Monaro, the pressure placed upon Albanese would have been intense and leadership speculation would have grown—perhaps if Labor had won the seat by a comfortable margin, the media would have complained that they should have won by more. In the current febrile and predominantly anti-Labor media environment, Albanese is in a position where the media decides he's a loser, irrespective of what he achieves.

If McBain had won the seat with a massive swing, the media would likely suggest it was all about her personal appeal, and nothing to do with Albanese. If Albanese had rescued young children from a burning orphanage in Cobargo at the height of the bushfires, the media would have complained about him not rescuing enough, or outlining what a show-pony Albanese is. He just cannot win in the eyes of the media.

The behaviour by the media after the Eden–Monaro shows how far the media has fallen over the past five years, with monopolised outlets and a compromised ABC swinging over to the conservative side of politics, and balance and fair reportage is difficult to find. Media conglomerates are facing severe difficulties, with News Corporation posting a $US1.5 million loss in the 2019 financial year, revenues in Australia declining by 16 per cent, and Foxtel subscriptions declining by 12 per cent.[70] News Corporation is

---

70 *The Guardian*, 'News Corp posts US$1.5bn loss driven by sharp declines in newspaper revenue', Christopher Knaus, 7 August 2020. https://www.theguardian.com/media/2020/aug/07/news-corp-posts-15bn-loss-driven-by-sharp-declines-in-newspaper-revenue

in financial trouble, as is the Nine Network, and perhaps they've decided to solidify their conservative political perspectives to attract advertising revenue from like-minded proprietors in corporate Australia, and producing editorial to appease this kind of advertiser is their new business model.

But there needs to be some level of standards within journalism. The day after Morrison and the Liberal Party lost a byelection they should have won, the *Sunday Telegraph* announced: "Scomo's Scorcher: Popular PM delivers Labor a brutual by-election lesson", also reporting there had been "a savage swing" against the Labor Party and the result was "a powerful endorsement of the Government's handling of COVID-19 with Scott Morrison's personal popularity driving the swing". The article, written by Annika Smethurst and Linda Silmalis, is an embarrassment to journalism and would be more at home in the editorial offices of the old Soviet Union's propaganda newspaper, *Pravda*, or *The North Korea Times*.

The Liberal Party did not win the seat of Eden–Monaro, it was won by the Labor Party: if anything, it was the Liberal Party that was taught a "brutal by-election lesson". The swing against the Labor Party was 0.45 per cent—not the "savage swing" depicted by the *Sunday Telegraph*—moving the two-party preferred vote from 50.85 per cent recorded at the 2019 federal election, to 50.39 per cent. The *Sunday Telegraph* reported its highly negative stance against Labor, even though the party actually won the seat—it would have been interesting to see how heavy their propaganda would have been if the Liberal Party *had* won the seat: the reports would probably still being announced in the years to come.

The reporting of the Eden–Monaro result and its heavy slanting towards the Liberal Party—even though they lost a campaign they should have won—is indicative of the mediocre standards of journalism and shallow pool of talent in Australian politics. In comparable political systems, British and American news outlets show the same level of tribalism and support for conservative politics but at least that can be balanced out somewhat by other excellent newspapers. In Australia, the balance to the tribalism of News Corporation is provided by mediocre publications such as the *Sydney Morning Herald*, or *The Age*, and the increasingly partisan ABC. There are some quality and experienced journalists in the mainstream media, but these are few and far between. Readers looking for different perspectives to the one-sided angles provided by News Corporation and the Nine Network are looking for their news in the independent sphere.

For Labor, it is about understanding how the much the mainstream media is stacked against them, and in Australian politics, this is not something new, but it has become more apparent in recent times. Despite the overwhelming approval ratings Morrison currently holds in published opinions polls; despite the entirely negative anti-Labor media headlines thrown against Albanese; Labor still managed to win the campaign and hold onto the seat. Sometimes, the influence of the media can be overblown in election campaigns, and it's evident that there are many factors and influences that play a part in voter intentions.

And after a byelection, there is always a great deal of analysis and navel gazing about what the result means for politics and if there are any portents for the next general election. The byelection result reflected the result in the May 2019 election—more or less the same two-party preferred vote—but so much has occurred in that region since that time. Severe bushfires decimated many parts of the Eden–Monaro region, which have received little government support; the onset of the pandemic. The result suggests that the electorate is still waiting to see the government's responses to the bushfire crisis and the management of COVID-19 measures before fully passing their judgement, and if the government does mismanage these issues, it's a government likely to be removed from office at the next general election.

The other key message to arise from the Eden–Monaro byelection is that choosing a strong local candidate with a presence in the field and strong roots with the community can make a difference. Both major parties chose local candidates with a strong community presence, but Labor acted swiftly, whereas the Liberal Party—and the National Party—acted indecisively and considered parachuting external candidates with little local knowledge or experience, before choosing Kotvojs. In a very close byelection, this indecision proved to be crucial, as well as the relative performances between the two main candidates, McBain and Kotvojs. Attempting to parachute has-been candidates and poorly-performing politicians from state politics—or a candidate of the low calibre of Jim Molan, the Senator for New South Wales—are not the solutions.

Strong local candidates can make a difference in a campaign, but the issue for all political parties is how to find the right people at the right time, that can seamlessly flow into the position, as well as being prepared to put themselves into difficult and arduous campaigns—as well as personal resources and finances—without any guarantees of success.

For Labor, McBain was front and centre of the campaign—as the case should be—but Kotvojs was overshadowed by the constant appearances of Morrison, senior and bit-part Liberal Party politicians, and was rarely allowed direct media conferences, or to speak without the presence of these other Liberal Party operatives. It could be argued that Albanese is unpopular when compared with Morrison's high approval rating, and that's the main reason why he didn't appear prominently in McBain's campaign material, but elections are played out on the local level: Morrison's appearances seemed over-the-top and unnecessary; perhaps Albanese struck the correct balance.

There can be endless opinion polls, media analysis and manipulation of the game of politics but nothing is more accurate than an actual election event. The Eden–Monaro byelection was a real-life event, and Labor performed far better than expected, and the Liberal Party failed to gain the victory so many in the mainstream media predicted and cheered on. While byelections can never accurately provide answers for a future general election—the Labor Party won five of nine byelections during the forty-fifth Parliament, with two seats won by independents, before going on to lose the 2019 federal election—it does set the scene for an election that could be far more competitive than many people are expecting, despite the messages that are coming out from a compliant pro-conservative media.

*

The release of the Palace Letters

17 July

It has taken almost forty-five years to see them, but the letters of correspondence between the former Governor–General, John Kerr, and the British Royal Family, have finally been released after a four-year legal battle to release the letters by historian, Jenny Hocking—211 letters exchanged between Kerr and Buckingham Palace between 1974 and 1977.

John Kerr sacked Gough Whitlam in 1975, and The Dismissal remains Australia's biggest political crisis in its history. It was a complex series of events—bastardry and intense skulduggery from the leader of the Liberal Party at the time, Malcolm Fraser, blocking of appropriation bills by the Senate, behind the scenes manipulation of the Governor–General by Fraser, and the sacking of a prime minister that should never have happened, followed by the infamous speech by Whitlam on the steps of old Parliament House in Canberra:

> **Gough Whitlam:** Ladies and gentleman, well may we say 'God Save the Queen' because nothing will save the Governor–General. The proclamation which you have just heard read by the Governor–General's official secretary was countersigned 'Malcolm Fraser', who will undoubtedly go down in Australian history from Remembrance Day 1975 as 'Kerr's cur'.
>
> They won't silence the outskirts of Parliament House, even if the inside has been silenced for the next few weeks. The

> Governor–General's proclamation was signed after he already made an appointment to meet the Speaker at a quarter to five.
>
> The House of Representatives had requested the Speaker to give the Governor–General its decision that Mr Fraser did not have the confidence of the House and that the Governor–General should call me to form the Government... Maintain your rage and enthusiasm through the campaign for the election now to be held and until polling day.

That was a big moment in Australian history and the release of the Palace Letters could be another big moment too. But will it see a shift in thinking about the relationship between Britain and Australia, and could it lead to another push for an Australian republic?

The 211 letters, comprising over 1,200 pages, represent a substantial collection. Hocking is one of Australia's best biographer and political scientists on these issues, having published a two-volume biography on Whitlam, and *The Dismissal Dossier*, a book outlining the collusion behind the scenes in the removal of Whitlam as prime minister, and a forthcoming book which will contain the contents of the Palace Letters. For many people, the release of the Palace Letters provide for a clearer picture of the background to the dismissal of Whitlam, and confirms the suspicions that Buckingham Palace was more involved than previously revealed.

There was a long ongoing debate about the actions of the Queen's personal secretary, Martin Charteris—whether he was operating as the go-between with Kerr and without the knowledge of the Queen, or whether the Queen was more actively involved, and the Palace Letters confirm that she was, as well as confirming a flaw in the relationship between the Australian and British political systems. In the mid-1600s, England was involved in a long, intense and brutal civil war in which thousands of people were killed over the question of who holds the sovereignty of the kingdom: is it the Parliament? Or is it the King? Ultimately, King Charles I was executed and a victory for the Parliamentarians proved the ascendancy of Parliament and that the monarch was more of an overall figurehead.

Who is the head of the Australian state? Technically, the Queen of England is still Australia's head of state, although her representative in Australia is the Governor–General. Since the *Australia Act* of 1986, British Parliament has no influence or right over Australian legislation, but the dismissal of Whitlam occurred eleven years before that Act was introduced. The key issue here is that Buckingham Palace was involved in Australian politics, in a way that it should never have been involved—there were discussions involving the Queen as early as July 1975, four months before The Dismissal, and there were also discussions with Prince Charles, the heir to the throne, and the possibility of Whitlam sacking Kerr and vice versa.

A constitutional event and political crisis of this nature may never occur in Australian politics again but it's certainly not an event the Labor Party will ever forget. Kerr died in 1991 and his death was publicly announced after he was buried—former Treasurer, Paul Keating, provided a motion of condolence in the House of Representatives, showing how the Labor Party and the labour movement felt about Kerr's actions in 1975:

> **Paul Keating:** Sir John Kerr was a person of substance. He was very interested in public affairs and public life. He is like a lot of frustrated people of quality: they want to be in public life, but never ever make the jump; they never quite take the chance. He was such a person. For him, it was always a dalliance at the edge of public affairs. He became Governor–General on the recommendation of Prime Minister Gough Whitlam because he was known to him and known also for his interest in public life and public affairs. It was with that in mind that I think the government of the day had great expectations of him at least having a role in public life, a role which otherwise had been denied to him over the course of his career. It was not that it had been a public life without distinction, because his service as the Chief Justice of New South Wales and as a barrister of note meant that he was a very well-regarded person. As the Prime Minister [Bob Hawke] said earlier, he was well regarded legally in all quarters. He had a reasonably close affinity with the labour movement; that is why he was trusted by the Australian Labor Party.
>
> The fact of the matter is that the Labor Party makes the political heroes in this country. When people cross the Labor Party, they wear the crosses it puts on them, whether it be Billy

Hughes or Joe Lyons—that is the truth of it. Sir John Kerr has worn the admonition of the Labor Party... He does so for one reason—he deceived his Prime Minister. He did not tell him that he was prepared to sack him.

I was at Government House with the then Prime Minister on the last occasion he saw Sir John Kerr, at an Executive Council meeting of three to appoint the Chairman of the Darwin Reconstruction Authority. The meeting was filled with bonhomie, cordiality and the like. As we left and walked down that long corridor at Government House, the Prime Minister was saying complimentary things to the Governor–General. The Prime Minister intimated to me that the Governor–General was a very proper person who would observe the constitutional position and prerogatives, including telling the Prime Minister what he intended for him.

Had the Prime Minister known that he intended to deceive him and dismiss him, another course of action would have been available to him. That is the nub of Sir John Kerr's problem with the labour movement and those who support it, and it will last forever. It is a sad thing for him, but it is a fact.

Anyone who has made a contribution to this country is to be admired. In a personal sense, Sir John Kerr did not come from privileged circumstances, but he surmounted any difficulties in those circumstances. He was a person of substance. But, in the end, one has to follow that substance with integrity. He lacked the integrity in dealing politically with the Prime Minister and he has suffered history's admonition as a result.

Kerr was 'a friend' of the Labor Party when he was installed as Governor–General by Whitlam—that's generally what prime ministers do: appoint a person with whom they can work with, who will follow the Constitution and the protocols of government, and act in the role of a figurehead and the Queen's representative in Australia. In Kerr's case, that did not occur: there were key misunderstandings of his role as Governor–General, Kerr was skillfully manipulated by the Leader of the Opposition, Malcolm Fraser, and Kerr's ego got the better of him.

As dire as Kerr's actions were in 1975, there's also the issue of the behaviours of the Liberal–Country Party Coalition: having been in government between 1949–72, for a political group that considered themselves to the 'natural party' of government, as well as intensely opposed to Whitlam's reform agenda, sitting on the opposition benches was anathema to many Coalition members. It didn't really matter how they returned to government, it was important to them that they returned to government as soon as possible, and to fulfil their *raison d'être* to 'keep Labor out'.[71] But it's not it's not up to an obstructionist Senate to change the government; it's not up to an opposition leader; and it's certainly not up to the Queen of another foreign jurisdiction or the Governor–General.

In Australian politics—as it has been in the British political system for over 300 years—the Parliament is supreme, and the Parliament is there because of the will of the people: the majority of people in the majority of seats elect the Parliament, and the leader of the party that has won the most seats in the House of Representatives becomes prime minister. The right to remove one government and install a different government is up to the electorate, that's how a democracy operates and that was the fundamental problem in Kerr's dismissal of Whitlam—it was a fundamentally undemocratic act.

The other factor that is often overlooked is that the Liberal Party had been in a state of disarray for many years before The Dismissal. Robert Menzies resigned as prime minister in 1966 and virtually handed the position over to Harold Holt, who was immediately undermined by Liberal Party operatives who criticised his leadership style and backgrounded journalists on potential health issues.[72] Holt drowned off Sorrento Beach in 1967; John Gorton became prime minister; who was then undermined by William McMahon and Fraser. McMahon then became prime minister in 1971—virtually undermining himself in one of the worst performances as prime minister in Australian history, losing office in 1972. Billy Snedden

---

71 *Inside Story*, 'Labor, the Coalition and the problem of political identity', Norman Abjorensen, 12 August 2014. https://insidestory.org.au/labor-the-coalition-and-the-problem-of-political-identity/

72 *Australian Dictionary of Biography*, Harold Edward Holt, I.R. Hancock, Volume 14, 1996. https://adb.anu.edu.au/biography/holt-harold-edward-10530

was leader of the Liberal Party for just over two years, before Fraser became leader in March 1975.

It's also instructive to view Kerr's statements after the dismissal of Whitlam, and especially after he resigned from the position of Governor–General in 1977: it's almost as though he knew what he was doing was not the correct course of action, using many odd precedents to justify his actions. But he followed through anyway, which makes his actions even more reprehensible: if he had announced that he stood up for principles that he genuinely believed in, that would have made his actions more acceptable. Another factor of note is that Fraser repealed very little of Whitlam's reforms the Liberal Party seemed to be so opposed to during Whitlam's tenure during 1972–75: Fraser kept the commitment to multiculturalism; free education; the infrastructure projects initiated by the Labor Party. The main policy Fraser reformed or removed was Whitlam's Medibank scheme, and attempted to reduce the influence of unions, which led to a high level of strike actions and lower productivity. But most of Whitlam's agenda remained in place.

The release of the Palace Letters, and the reactions to the letters, will help to define whether there will be a renewed push towards an Australian republic. While the contents of the letters won't provide the impetus, as much of the detail is confirming what many historians and academics had suspected, the publicity surrounding the release may place the relationship between Australia and Britain into sharper focus, especially in the context of the long drawn-out Brexit process, which will see Britain sever its links with the European Union.

The *Australia Act* legislated by the Hawke government formally terminated the scope of the British Parliament to legislate with effect in Australia, and Privy Council appeals as the final stage of appeal under Australian law, were also terminated. Royal assent is still provided for all legislation passed in the Australian Parliament, although the Governor–General does this in the name of the Queen. The Queen and the British Parliament have no legal influence in Australia, but the existence of this link acts as a legal and constitutional appendix attached to the Australian political system that has no need or requirement.

While the British monarchy has some support within the Australian community, that support is dwindling and the question for the Australian political class is: if Australia moves to become a republic, how is this to be achieved? Obviously, it can only be changed through referendum but at the heart of any change has to be an acceptance that the current constitutional arrangement is part of a bygone era and attitudes that no longer exist, and there is no need for the British monarch to be the head of state in Australia.

British power in the world sphere is declining and a poorly constructed Brexit agenda has hastened this decline. Does Australia really wish to link itself so strongly to a defunct empire and a nineteenth-century concept of the realm that is no longer serving its purpose? The world has moved on dramatically since those times but Australia clings onto this outdated imperialist symbolism—that many countries around the world have successfully shunned—because of a lack of political will and complacency.

But is a move to a republic—whenever that time arrives—the correct agenda for Australia? Many of the models for republicanism in Australia have suggested mere tinkering of the current system, and replacing the Queen as the head of state, with the Governor-General or renaming the position as a President, with debates about how this person should be installed into the position. Perhaps there should be a more ambitious platform for improving democratic outcomes and completely renovating the Australian Constitution, the method for electing candidates into Parliament and moving the political system away from mechanisms designed in 1901, and into a system more in tune with the twenty-first century.

The republic could be seen as a good first step to a superior system of government but the Australian electorate seems to be mistrusting of the concept and the 1999 republic referendum demonstrated how easy it is for opponents to discredit any republican model, when Prime Minister John Howard used the best of his political manipulations to ensure the referendum was defeated. And the many models available is sure to add to the confusion in any future debates about a republic: should the prime minister of the day appoint the President; should Parliament choose a candidate with a two-thirds majority; or an Irish or French model where the electorate chooses from a number of preselected candidates?

A majority of the electorate was supportive of a republic in 1999[73] but were distrustful of method of selecting the President, which was through the so-called 'minimalist model', where a person appointed by a two-thirds majority of the members of the Commonwealth Parliament would become President.

It's understandable why a 'minimalist model' was proposed: only eight of the forty-four referenda in Australia have passed—an 18 per cent success rate—and this model would have created the least disruption to the political system. But the Australian public prefer a different model, where 80 per cent of the electorate have stated they would support a republic if they could directly vote for a President.[74] While this arrangement could create other political issues, if this is the model the public prefers, and would help with the instigation of the republic, then this is the model that should be supported, with clear codifications of the role of the President to avoid a repeat of the 1975 dismissal of Whitlam.

The referendum on the republic occurred twenty-one years ago and, at the time, the leader of the 'Yes' campaign for the Australian Republic Movement, Malcolm Turnbull, suggested these opportunities do not arise often and if Australia wanted to become a republic, this would be the only opportunity in a very long time. So far, this has proved to be correct.

Perhaps the release of the Palace Letters will create another opportunity for change. Constitutionally, Australia could keep the British monarch as its head of state, even if Britain became a republic before Australia—as unlikely as that may seem—but it is an anomaly that needs to be cleared up and corrected. The Queen is now aged ninety-four and the Queen Mother lived to the age of 101. Will there be another impetus for change when the reign of Queen Elizabeth II ends? A confident country should be able to make decisions for itself and shouldn't need to wait for external events to force its hand on constitutional matters, or be enamoured with young future heirs to the throne who have little interest in

---

73 Newspoll, historical opinion polling on the Australian republic, January 2007. http://www.newspoll.com.au/image_uploads/0103%20republic.pdf
74 UMR Research, Australians Want a Republic: Quantitative and Qualitative Findings, November 2008.

Australia, except for the matter of continuing imperial interests from yesteryear.

The Palace Letters are an important part of Australian political history and their release is to be welcomed. It should provide an impetus for further change in the Australian political system, but that's a change that will need to wait for another future government to implement.

*

A prime minister at the football: Let's drink to that

17 July

Australia is still facing very difficult times—the economy won't fully recover until the coronavirus goes away; the rebuilding of the communities ravaged by bushfires has been stalled because of federal government inaction; climate change is an issue nowhere near finding a resolution; and the number of active coronavirus cases is starting to rise rapidly in Melbourne and Sydney.

This is a difficult period for every country around the world, and with the wide range of economic, medical and social issues that need to be managed and resolved, political leaders need to stay focused and ensure they're able to manage these issues that keep appearing at different intervals.

Last Friday, the Prime Minister decided it was time for a holiday, announcing he was taking a short break to spend time with his wife and two daughters during the school holidays. Perhaps for a prime minister managing the country during difficult circumstances, this might be acceptable to take a short break with his family but, on the following day Scott Morrison was sitting in the corporate box at a rugby league game played at Kogarah Oval in suburban Sydney, seen mingling with business leaders and Liberal Party donors. Morrison has done this quite often during a time of crisis, and he does seem to have unusual ideas about how to spend special holiday time with his family.

Prime ministers need to spend time with their families but it also has to be remembered that the position is like no other in Australia, scheduling time away from the job is critical, and sacrifices sometimes need to be made. Former Prime Minister Joe Lyons had twelve children with his wife Enid Lyons, and because he became leader during the Great Depression, as well as slower modes of transport at that time, he rarely had the opportunity to spend time with his family. Lyons died in office in 1939, at the age of fifty-nine. Bob Hawke was named Victorian Father of the Year in 1971—before he became prime minister—even though he spend so much time working, drinking heavily and sacrificing holidays. Kevin Rudd and John Howard had school-aged children during their time in office, and they all took holidays—which, of course, they are entitled to. But sometimes, the job of prime minister is larger than taking family holidays and, if it's not, then maybe that person isn't the right person for the position.

Morrison put out the message to the media that he was taking school holidays with "Jen and the girls"—his wife and two young daughters—and it's understandable for a prime minister to take time away from the job. But to then go to a football game the day after making such an announcement, and at a time when most people around Australian can't go to any form of recreational sport, seemed to be an ill-informed choice, especially after the opprobrium Morrison faced when he took his family to Hawaii—under a veil of secrecy—at the height of the bushfires crisis in December 2019. This was a massive blunder and almost destroyed his prime ministership.

Prime ministers need to choose their moments, and it's a skill Morrison seems to lack, oblivious to the requirements of the position. Gough Whitlam was criticised for going on overseas holidays twice in the one year—it wasn't a good look then, and it's not a good look today. Sometimes, the physical presence of the prime minister matters to the electorate and it seems Morrison hasn't learned the lessons from his Hawaii experience, which seriously highlighted his lack of judgement. There was justified anger coming from parts of Melbourne—a sports-crazed city that is not allowed to hold crowds at any sporting events, and in many cases, such as the Australian Football League, not even allowed to host any games at all.

A prime minister at the football: Let's drink to that

Morrison sat in the corporate box at the rugby league game between Cronulla and Penrith, and he could have watched from his residence at the Lodge or at Kirribilli House with a free Foxtel pay-television subscription provided by News Corporation. He was in the corporate box with key business leaders and Scott Briggs, a former Liberal Party director and a key Morrison ally. He is also a part of the Australian Visa Processing Pty Ltd consortium, a company keen to obtain a substantial contract if the visa system is privatised by the federal government, valued at around $1 billion, and he also donated $165,000 to the Liberal Party in 2018/19, even though he now denies the donation was ever made.

The other issue to point out is that Morrison made sure that he was visible to the media in the corporate box, as well as his substantial drinking of beer. He allowed television crews to record him talking to rugby league players on the ground. Then there was more drinking. Far from having schools holidays with "Jen and the girls", Morrison escaped to the football to create more media stunts. In the context of the many restrictions faced by many people around Australia, it was an insensitive act by Morrison.

Political leaders are engaged in many major positive actions to gain small movements of political support in their direction, but it's the small negative actions that can make all of that political capital fall away very quickly. Morrison's political capital almost diminished overnight because of his ill-fated and surreptitious family holiday to Hawaii, before the coronavirus pandemic created a lucky break for him and re-established support for his prime ministership in an overwhelming manner.

Morrison did suffer a substantial backlash on social media, but the mainstream media generally lauded his appearance at Kogarah Oval, advised by conservative 2GB radio broadcaster Ray Hadley to "take the phone off and just absolutely relax" and the public was urged by the *Daily Telegraph*, to "Give the PM a break". Perhaps it has reached a point where Morrison realises that irrespective of how many errors he performs, mainstream media will always be there to provide cover, in stark contrast to the negative media heaped upon Victoria Premier, Daniel Andrews, over the past three months.

A more stark example is the treatment of Christine Nixon, the former Victoria Police Commissioner during the Victorian bushfires in 2010, who was harassed by the media for having the audacity to have a modest pub meal with key fire services staff at the peak of the crisis. Morrison, at the time the Shadow Minister for Immigration, joined in the criticism at the time, appearing on the ABC's *Q+A* program to make the following observation:

> **Scott Morrison:** At the end of the day, whatever role we're in, the most important thing is about the job, not the individuals, and so there's a judgment call for her to make there—the Premier's [John Brumby] entitled to make the view he has made. But look, that was a very big event. She's [Nixon] clearly made a bad judgment call—that happens to people from time to time. But this was a very serious issue. And I think there are very serious concerns in the community about exercising judgment, and it's incumbent on all of us in public life to make decisions following that, in the best interests of the ongoing nature of the program.

It's not entirely clear what Nixon was meant to do in these circumstances: starve in solidarity? She was humiliated by former Victoria Premier Jeff Kennett, fat-shamed through social media, trawled through a Royal Commission into the bushfires and queried about her eating habits, a hairdressing appointment, and a meeting with her biographer. When Morrison was queried about his disappearance during the bushfires in 2019, he claimed that he didn't "hold a hose mate" and the media soon backed away from their criticisms of his performance.

Of course, there are party-political dimensions to the different treatments of players such as Morrison on one side, and Andrews and Nixon on the other—the latter are Labor, or Labor-aligned. In addition, the media support from conservative media now is the payback factor for Morrison's time as managing director of Tourism Australia during 2004–06, when he diverted large sums of advertising funds into News Corporation, as well as funds for publishing projects through the News Corporation custom publishing unit in Holt Street, Surry Hills. It was a form of payola from Morrison over fourteen years ago, and News Corporation has paid back in spades: they supported Morrison in smearing his opponent, Michael Towke, in the preselection contest in the seat of Cook in 2007; they've provided endless media support during his time as Minister for Immigration; as Minister for Social Security; as Treasurer; and now as Prime Minister. Morrison is the consummate 'transactional' politician and his actions of grafting Tourism Australia funds to News Corporation many years ago have paid handsome dividends today.

News Corporation is an insidious media organisation and although its influence is waning, it is still a powerful player within the political landscape and will be able to continue to offer support to the conservative parties and manipulate political dynamics. There are other independent media voices becoming louder, and younger demographics in the ages between sixteen and twenty-five—including new electors eligible to vote at the next federal election—who don't collate their news and political information through traditional mainstream media, and are more likely to access material through Reddit, Twitter and Facebook. This is a small but steady development but it seems that for as long as Morrison has the support of the conservative mainstream media, his position within the Liberal Party, and therefore his prime ministership, will be secure: Morrison is Rupert Murdoch's man in Australia.

*

The ghosts of Margaret Thatcher and Ronald Reagan

31 July

It has been a long time since the names of US President Ronald Reagan and former British Prime Minister Margaret Thatcher have been heard in the Australian media, but the Treasurer, Josh Frydenberg, decided that these are names providing his inspiration in repairing the Australian economy, which is heading toward national government debt of almost a trillion dollars, is currently in recession and facing depression-like conditions and high unemployment rates, and a generation of people with lost opportunities over the next few decades.

'Reaganomics' and 'Thatcherism' were shared ideologies that influenced politics on both sides of the Atlantic and became a prevalent form of economics for governments of all persuasions: cutting government spending, reducing taxes, deregulating markets, privatisation of government and social services. Frydenberg can muse about the merits of Reagan and Thatcher in his spare time or recall their virtues when he's writing up his memoirs, but these figureheads represent economic thinking of a bygone era. Neoliberalism and right-wing supply-side economic philosophies have had their time and new economic thinking is required in these challenging circumstances: it seems Frydenberg is channelling the wrong type of economic thinking at the wrong time.

It does suggest a great deal about the priorities of the Liberal–National Coalition government, where a relatively young treasurer is espousing the flawed ideologies of an economic system that is forty years old, and way past its use-by date. Reagan is fondly remembered in the United States but it's not because of these economic principles: he received credit for his role in ending the Cold War and the collapse of the Soviet Union, even though it was obvious communism was on the verge of collapsing in 1989 despite Reagan's rhetoric during his presidency. His economic legacy was disastrous: federal debt tripled from $US738 billion to $2.1 trillion; although there was a record period of economic growth during his tenure, this was mainly fuelled by recording military spending. Tax cuts were meant to increase revenue for the government, but this did not occur.[75] Job growth was lower than in preceding decades, unemployment was high, wages growth stagnated and the gap between higher and lower wages increased.[76] Society became more unequal.

Thatcher was a divisive, stubborn and thoroughly dislikeable prime minister, mainly remembered for her harsh economic policies that impacted working class people, and her economic performances in the British economy mirror those of Reagan's. Wage inequality increased; the public service was slashed; there was a failure of long-term investment in infrastructure, manufacturing and innovation.[77] Thatcher, like Reagan, led Britain into an unwarranted and unnecessary war with Argentina over the Falkland Islands (*Islas Malvinas*) in the South Atlantic Ocean, a cynical ploy to boost her electoral fortunes in the lead-up to the 1983 general election. It was a limited victory for a very limited purpose: Thatcher had actually considered ceding sovereignty to Argentina in 1980[78] and her about-face just eighteen months later resulted in the Falklands War and 904 deaths—and a crushing victory at the 1983 election, one that she had been previously expected to lose.

75 Miller Center, 'Ronald Reagan: Impact and Legacy', Lou Cannon. https://millercenter.org/president/reagan/impact-and-legacy
76 *Dollars & Sense*, 'Ronald Reagan's Legacy: His destructive economic policies do not deserve the press's praise', John Miller, 2004. http://dollarsandsense.org/archives/2004/0704miller.html
77 *Vox Eu*, 'Mrs Thatcher's economic legacy', John Van Reenen, April 2013. https://voxeu.org/article/mrs-thatcher-s-economic-legacy
78 *The Guardian*, 'UK held secret talks to cede sovereignty', Richard Norton-Taylor & Rob Evans, June 2005. https://www.theguardian.com/uk/2005/jun/28/falklands.past

Thatcher decimated the local British mining industry but didn't replace the industry. Coal mining communities during Thatcher's reign—almost a quarter of a million miners lost their jobs in areas of England, Scotland and Wales—without any transitional arrangements for the creation of new employment opportunities and, thirty-five years after Thatcher closed down over 180 working coalmines, most of those communities have never economically recovered. Almost six million people in those former coal mining areas are suffering from intergenerational unemployment, with little prospects for future employment and still dependent on social welfare payments.

In Australia, not many in the electorate would be fully aware of Reagan or Thatcher—they both finished their time in politics over thirty years ago—Reagan in 1989 and Thatcher in 1990—and half of the electorate might not have been born at this time, or would have been young children. They might not even have recollections of Australia's last recession in the early 1990s, primarily caused by Reaganism and Thatcherism.

Looking at the damage created by Reagan and Thatcher, both in terms of economics and sociology, it's perplexing why Frydenberg would use such examples for his economic inspiration, as it's not really a positive or successful model to build from. Perhaps it was Frydenberg's intention to invoke long-distant historical figures which the Australian electorate might not fully understand: almost like invoking the spirit of French leader Napoleon Bonaparte without understanding his tyrannical reign who, according to the British historian, Andrew Roberts, was "a megalomaniac who wrought greater misery than any man before the coming of Hitler".[79]

And for Frydenberg to invoke Reagan and Thatcher for ideological inspiration is fraught: it creates opportunities for his opponents to focus on the many negative impacts of their policies: an increase in homelessness, community upheaval, attacks on unions, the reduction of wages, the introduction of pro-business and anti-worker policies. The electorate doesn't need to receive a history lesson about either Reagan or Thatcher but once they gain an understanding of the ideas Frydenberg wishes to implement, there will be an electoral backlash against him.

---

79 *Napoleon: A Life*, Roberts, Andrew, Penguin Group, 2014, Introduction.

One of the weaknesses of this federal government is they haven't progressed from being a childish and immature opposition during 2007–13, into being a mature government from 2013 onwards. Frydenberg also referred to Reagan and Thatcher as being 'figures of hate for the left', as if he's announcing policy from an extremist think-tank such as the Institute of Public Affairs, rather than a treasurer who should be governing for all people, irrespective of their political persuasions: this kind of public utterance belongs to the discourse in student politics on a university campus.

If he'd supported his statements with intellectual rigour and outlined the facts and figures behind the economics of Thatcherism, or a grasp of supply-side economics and thinking, perhaps there could be some evidence of substantial thought that went into his commentary but, as it turned out, it was just a throw-away line to smear left-wing politics—politics is far more complex than just a left–right delineation anyway, but for Frydenberg, politics is always portrayed in black-and-white, rather than a multitude of shades.

This recent narrative commenced when Frydenberg gave an address at the National Press Club, where he outlined a pathway to economic recovery, but the commentary seemed like a recovery that will lead in the same type of economy as before the pandemic commenced—a spluttering economy, one that serves vested interests rather than public interests, inefficient, environmentally disastrous, and an economy ill-equipped to deal with the current circumstances. He did raise eyebrows when he mentioned Thatcher and Reagan as a source of inspiration, and followed it up with a discussion on the ABC *Insiders* program:

> **David Speers:** You did say when it comes to economic reform the other day that you'll be taking inspiration from Margaret Thatcher and Ronald Reagan. Really?
>
> **Josh Frydenberg:** Well, they dealt very successfully with the challenges that they faced, particularly stagflation, high unemployment, high inflation. But if you look at Margaret Thatcher after Labour's 'Winter of Discontent', she came in, she reduced the number of days lost to industrial disputation from thirty million down to two million, she cut taxes and she talked about every earner being an owner...

Speers: Also went for some sweeping IR reform that might scare some workers...

Frydenberg: Well, she had eleven and a half years, so she was doing something right by the people of Britain. And when it comes to Ronald Reagan, he used to talk about two economists having three opinions. But what he did say is that cutting taxes, cutting red tape, he created twenty million new jobs...

Speers: ...Doubled the debt...

Frydenberg: Well, he did spend the Soviets into submission, and that wasn't a bad thing for the world, so he was very successful...

Speers: Reaganomics is...

Frydenberg: Well, he boosted growth...

Speers: It sometimes known as trickle-down economics too, Treasurer.

Frydenberg: ...Thatcher and Reagan are figures of hate for the left because they were so successful. One got two terms, which was the maximum you can get in the United States, Margaret Thatcher got eleven and a half years...

Speers: So, they're the guiding light here?

Frydenberg: Well, you take inspiration from lots of different sources. I also take it from Howard and Costello. But the reality is that Thatcher and Reagan cut red tape, they cut taxes and they delivered stronger economies.

Of course, Thatcher and Reagan were major figures in political history—there is little dispute about that—and their brand politics was steeped in the history of Cold War politics and helped to bring about the end of the Soviet Bloc and communism in Eastern Europe. But for the Treasurer to start invoking these figures who were ideologues of the 1980s and Cold War warriors from a different era, it shows how out-of-depth Frydenberg's economic thinking is.

Economic philosophies need to suit the economic and political circumstances of the time and as the public keeps being told, these are unprecedented times: it's not just a matter of cherry-picking the policies that may have worked in the past—depending on ideological perspectives—and hoping for the same results. Global economics does not operate like that.

The Treasurer, and the Prime Minister, have been keen to talk up the prospect of 'snap-back', returning the economy to pre-COVID-19 conditions, but even with that prospect, there is no clear pathway or direction for how this might be achieved: it's the essential problem for a government intent on implementing *political* solutions, rather than *economic*.

Universal basic income is not a new idea, but it has been floated from outside of government as an economic program that could be useful—COVID-19 presents the right circumstances, but not the right government to consider this proposition, even though the JobKeeper program could be considered as a limited version of universal basic income. It is a policy that would be difficult to implement politically, and it's a theoretical idea that hasn't been fully tested, although the Republican administration of Richard Nixon had universal basic income as a serious policy proposition in the late 1960s.

And if universal basic income might be too difficult ideologically or politically for this government to implement, there is the concept of universal service provision, where key essential services are provided without personal cost to the public—health care, aged care, education across all sectors—early childhood education, primary and secondary, vocational and university education. These are some of the valuable economic and social ideas and programs Frydenberg could be considering and putting forward to his Cabinet colleagues, ideas that are relevant to the 2020s and beyond, not an old ideological-driven wishlist of ideas that should be consigned to the historical dustbin of the 1980s and 1990s.

It should also be noted that neoliberalism and supply-side economics was very successful for a small group of already wealthy people and captains of industry, and that type of thinking is prevalent for this federal government. A version of universal basic income, JobKeeper, was implemented and it worked: the government pushed forward the notion that it would stop people looking for work but it has the opposite effect: with basic bills paid for and the ability to sustain themselves, people had more mental and emotional energy to expend themselves again. It's not clear if this is a feasible long-term solution, but perhaps providing a universal basic income for all would provide a better outcome than the piecemeal and confusing JobKeeper program.

Stimulus payments worked during the global financial crisis, and stimulus payments have stopped the Australian economy from collapsing in 2020. It could be too much to expect a government that is too wedded to its ideological beliefs to fully comprehend this, but a good economy is an inclusive economy, one where every citizen has reasonable economic opportunities, and in those areas where economic opportunities are not favourable, those people should be provided with the financial support and the social support they need to be able to contribute to the economy. It's the basic premise of a civil society.

Thatcher and Reagan pursued policies that were the antithesis of an inclusive economy; they pursued policies that were divisive, and it's disappointing that the Treasurer has decided to hold up these distant figures as a model of excellence, at a time when different ideas are needed. Unfortunately, Australia is being led by the thinkers of the 1980s: to place that into perspective, solutions to the onset of the Great Depression of the 1930s were applied using the thinking of the 1890s and, as history has shown, the wrong ideas were implemented at the wrong time. These are salient lessons from history that should be listened to, not ignored.

*

Coronavirus politics fails to act in the public interest

31 July

Coronavirus cases are increasing all around the world, and Australia has had a spike during the past two months, almost doubling the total number of cases, with most of these coming from the city of Melbourne. Government leaders need to take responsibility in times of crisis and, whenever the exact causes for the outbreaks in Melbourne are uncovered, political costs will need to be paid. But those political costs can wait for another time.

Whatever opinions the public may have of the Premier of Victoria, Daniel Andrews—and he has his supporters and detractors—at least he fronts up every single day of the week, announcing to the public the bad news of increasing COVID-19 cases, and the deaths occurring in aged care facilities. But he appears at his daily media conferences facing all the pressure been thrown at him by the media and his political opponents, and implements whatever action he needs to take to resolve the crisis in Melbourne.

In contrast, while Victoria's citizens were facing a calamitous week, Prime Minister Scott Morrison was campaigning in Queensland on behalf of the Liberal Party—with the state of Queensland holding an election in October—declaring that the increase in COVID-19 numbers was a "Victorian wave", and offering political support to the High Court case instigated by the mining magnate and owner of Minerology Pty Ltd, Clive Palmer, in which he has taken legal action against the Western Australia Government for closing its borders to the rest of Australia.

It seems that state and territory leaders all across Australia, and of all political persuasions, are placing all their energies into containing the coronavirus and managing the economic crisis, whereas Morrison is doing his best to create division and maximise political opportunities for himself and the Liberal Party.

While the states and territories have been managing relatively well during this pandemic, Morrison's actions highlight some of the failings of federation. For Morrison—as leader of the federation of Australia—to target different states based on which political party the respective leaderships come from is unbecoming behaviour for a prime minister. He blamed Andrews for the viral outbreak personally, whereas he was quiet during the Sydney outbreak caused by the mismanagement of the *Ruby Princess* arrival, under the auspices of his government and the NSW Government. A prime minister's primary responsibility is to offer support and protection to all citizens of the nation, and not to use citizens of different states as political target practice and generate discord in those states.

Blame is never in short supply when something goes wrong, but Morrison has a propensity to blame others to deflect from his own shortcomings. But blame and electoral payback should always be played out at elections, and the electorate can then decide whether a leader was behaving irresponsibly or incompetently and install another government. Whether it's an issue that's developing from hotel quarantine mismanagement in Melbourne, or bureaucratic bungling that caused the *Ruby Princess* outbreak in Sydney, the community generally wants problems solved and practical solutions put in place to ensure the risk of those problems occurring again are minimised: electoral reckoning for a politician can take place at election time.

For certain political leaders and captains of industry, they're not so keen for solutions, especially where there are political or business opportunities to be found. Whenever Palmer appears in the public spotlight, self-interest is never far behind: he has a current case against the Western Australia Government in the Federal Court, which will end up in the High Court towards the end of 2020, a case which the Attorney-General, Christian Porter, and Morrison, have provide a high level of political and legal support.

Palmer's case will assess the merits of Sections 117 and 92 of the Australian Constitution—Section 117 relates to citizens of any state discriminated by another state, and Section 92 relates to free trade across Australia. It's difficult to know how the High Court will adjudicate in these matters—Morrison says the High Court is likely to uphold Clive Palmer's case, but that is exactly what former Prime Minister Malcolm Turnbull said in 2017, before the High Court ruled there was a number of members who were not eligible to hold office in the Australian Parliament. However, whatever the result may be in both the Federal Court and High Court, Palmer and Morrison are underestimating the *psyche* of the Western Australian community, which detests outside interference in state political affairs, especially when it arrives from 'eastern staters'. Even in the unlikely event the High Court rules in favour of Palmer, the Western Australia Premier, Mark McGowan, will have a high degree of local political support to keep their borders closed.

After his success in influencing the outcome of the 2019 federal election, Palmer seems to be keen to be a political player in the Western Australia election in March 2021, although his actions are not playing out well in the court of public opinion in that state, with 92 per cent of those polled supporting a hard border closure.[80] And Morrison's support—as the consummate 'transactional' politician—is returning political favours to Palmer who, through the United Australia Party, contributed to the Liberal–National Coalition victory through preference deals in key Queensland seats, and spending most of his time criticising Bill Shorten and the Labor Party during that campaign.

It's apparent Morrison does not have a full understanding of how the legal system works. A prime minister has never commented on a private citizen's case in the High Court, primarily because a prime minister should not be meddling in the affairs of the judiciary. Of course, Morrison can hold his private opinions about a High Court matter, but he shouldn't be commenting about a case until the

---

80 *Beaudesert Times*, 'WA premier talks down PM's hotspots plan', Michael Ramsey, 3 September 2020. https://www.beaudeserttimes.com.au/story/6908104/wa-premier-talks-down-pms-hotspots-plan/?cs=9397

High Court makes its final decision. Palmer is also facing charges for allegedly breaching company directors' duties and two counts of fraudulent behaviour—the Australian Securities and Investment Commission has alleged that in 2013, Palmer dishonestly obtained a benefit or advantage for two companies and his political organisation at the time, the Palmer United Party, and transferred $12 million, contrary to the purpose for which the funds were being held.[81] These are not light matters: Morrison would have been wise to retract any support for Palmer and let those matters play out by themselves, especially when it comes to matters in the High Court.

Contrary to the case pushed forward by Palmer that free trade and his personal rights are being discriminated against by another state, the Constitution is clear on self-determination of the states and territories and that if they wish to close their borders for extraordinary reasons—and it could be fairly assumed that a once-in-a-century viral pandemic would be one of those extraordinary reasons—they should be permitted to do that. Closing down borders is not a trade issue: it's a health issue, and governments should be able to enforce border closures in these circumstances.

The coronavirus pandemic has affected many people, not just in Australia, but all around the world. When unusual and difficult circumstances afflict humanity, there is usually an assumption that petty partisan political behaviour and self-interest is put aside for the public good and the national interest. But national characters such as Morrison and Palmer never put the personal aside for the public, irrespective of the circumstances. Morrison exploits political opportunities, at any cost—political leaders need to take the opportunities provided to them, but Morrison takes this to a new level, and relinquishes responsibilities and shirks away from problems.

It's not clear if his actions will cause electoral problems for him at this stage—at a time when opinion polls show around two-thirds of the electorate support Morrison's performance—but, ultimately, leaders need to take responsibility: it doesn't matter whether an

---

81 Australian Securities and Investment Commission, 'Clive Palmer charged over breaches of directors' duties and fraud', July 2020. https://asic.gov.au/about-asic/news-centre/find-a-media-release/2020-releases/20-163mr-clive-palmer-charged-over-breaches-of-directors-duties-and-fraud/

issue arises in Melbourne or Perth, Sydney or Brisbane, Adelaide, Darwin or Hobart. At a time when the state of Victoria was facing difficulties containing coronavirus cases, Morrison was campaigning for the Liberal Party in Queensland—his second visit within two weeks—throwing barbs from a distance at Premier Andrews. He also visited the fishing company, Walker Seafoods, a regular donor to the Liberal Party, inspecting the tuna fish catch, meeting and greeting donors and lapping up media opportunities.

Melbourne suffered a crisis, but Morrison was more keen to campaign on behalf of the Liberal Party in Queensland. There were other matters of national significance: outbreaks of the coronavirus at the Newmarch House aged care facility in Sydney, where seventeen residents died; in Melbourne, forty-five people died at St Basil's Home for the Aged and thirty-eight died at Epping Gardens Aged Care. Responsibility for private aged care facilities falls under the jurisdiction of the federal government. Why did Morrison deflect these issues to the respective state governments, when it was clearly the responsibility of his government?

A vast majority of coronavirus cases and coronavirus-related deaths in the aged care sector—on a percentage basis—have occurred in private aged care facilities, when compared to state-managed facilities.[82] The onset of coronavirus can't be held responsible for all of these cases and deaths—there have been issues of standards and regulations in the private sector for some time, ever since the Howard government encouraged the growth of private aged care through the Moran Group in the late 1990s. Aged care has been within the realm of vested interests and at a time when elderly residents should be supported in the latter stages of life, business people and captains of industry are keen to exploit the sector, highlighted by the revelations that Seven West Media proprietor, Kerry Stokes, owns a $100 million share of Estia Health, one of the largest for-profit aged care home operators in Australia.

There is also the matter of the $1.2 billion that was removed from federal aged care funding in 2017 by Morrison, who at that time was Treasurer. Advocates claimed that this would create a large shortfall

---

82 ABC News, 'Why are there are more COVID-19 cases in private aged care than the public sector?', Erin Handley, 1 August 2020. https://www.abc.net.au/news/2020-08-01/why-more-covid-19-cases-in-private-aged-care-than-public-sector/12503212

in staffing, resources and the quality of care in private facilities, and this was found to be the case when the pandemic hit this year.

These have been difficult times for the aged care sector, but it's yet another example of the failure of that relationship between the private market and social services. And it's another example of where these relationships need to change into the future, rather than having a government that is looking backwards and wanting everything to return to how society looked before the pandemic started. All sides of politics were persuaded by and adopted privatisation as an acceptable government practice, commencing in Australia with the Labor Party after they entered office in 1983. But it's yesterday's philosophy. Changing the Australian economy is a herculean task and it seems that the current government and, indeed, the collective political system, is ill-equipped intellectually, to provide the right guidance on this path.

The federal Parliament isn't sitting at present and four months after the pandemic commenced, the government still hasn't worked out a way of conducting the business of Parliament remotely—as the rest of the world seems to be doing successfully—and it seems there is little intention of doing this for the foreseeable future. Of course, the sitting of Parliament is more than just members of Parliament presenting bills in the House of Representatives or debating during Question Time: there are clandestine meetings; incidental meetings; meetings with stakeholders and lobbyists; and much of the other activities of political business that takes place away from the public view. But to not make any attempt at all is an issue that must be jarring for the public: the Prime Minister is imploring everyone in the community to work as much as they can, and many workers around the country are either working from their home offices and participating through online meetings and technological solutions to continue contributing to the economy, yet he's avoiding the important obligations of his position.

A parliamentary group has now been created to inquire how Parliament can work during the pandemic but to wait for three months to even get to an inquiry stage shows how little Morrison values the rituals of Parliament or scrutiny of his performance. And this has been another feature of Morrison's tenure as prime minister: avoiding as much scrutiny as possible, and ensuring that whatever actions he takes on, there is no one available to point out the errors of his ways. It's a blight on the processes of democracy.

Parliament is the centre of governance in Australia's federation: if it's not meeting, then government is not functioning correctly. A government doesn't need to be a legislative powerhouse like the Gillard government—the most productive government in Australian history[83]—but it needs to sit for around nine or ten months of the year. And it needs to sit so governments can be held to account, and for the alternative government to be able to proffer its own policy matters.

Instead, Morrison has created a range of committees that are representing vested interests and making decisions that not even freedom of information laws are allowed to access. The Australian Parliament sat during World War I, during the 1918 influenza pandemic and during World War II. Morrison's behaviours are thoroughly anti-democratic and while these might be seen within the Liberal Party as clever political moves, sometimes governments do need to be saved from themselves, and oppositions and crossbenchers often provide those checks and balances to ensure government actions are performed in the best interests of the public.

*

---

83 *The Guardian*, 'Was Julia Gillard the most productive prime minister in Australia's history?', Nick Evershed, June 2013. https://www.theguardian.com/news/datablog/2013/jun/28/australia-productive-prime-minister

The ongoing scandals in New South Wales

31 July

There's yet another scandal brewing in New South Wales politics—it's easy to lose count of the different misappropriations of funds and illegal activities over the years but just when the public could have expected there wouldn't be any further inappropriate behaviour by public officials, another scandal appears in the spotlight.

This scandal relates to iCare (Insurance and Care NSW), managed by the NSW Government: it's a scheme which replaced WorkCover in 2015 and collects over $3 billion per year in worker compensation insurance payments, but there have been claims of serious mismanagement, denial of claims to injured workers, underpayments to injured workers of $80 million, theft of funds by senior management and credit card fraud. The board of iCare is chaired by a prominent Liberal Party donor, Michael Carapiet, and the ultimate responsibility for this organisation is the NSW Treasurer, Dominic Perrottet, who obviously hasn't been keeping a close eye on these events.

Organisations such as these are supposed to be the gatekeeper of the public interest but a combination of low oversight by the NSW Treasurer and placement of the wrong type of people in these positions of responsibility has created these problems. There's a certain group of people with links to the Liberal Party who see organisations such as iCare as an opportunity to enrich themselves.

To be sure, people in senior positions within government corporations should be remunerated appropriately, and the ethical and competent management of these organisations depends on people of goodwill. Surely, there are enough people within the community that have the appropriate credentials to take on these roles, as well as being committed to strong public service.

But the issues arise when friends of any political party are preferenced over more credential candidates without those political connections, and it's obvious stronger corporate legislation needs to be enacted, because it's a situation that is becoming more and more prevalent. Theft, mismanagement, corporate neglect, illegalities; the opportunities for these to arise need to be minimised, and with the more recent examples of overt corruption in New South Wales—Eddie Obeid from the Labor Party, and Arthur Sinodinos from the Liberal Party; both involved with scandalous activities within Australian Water Holdings—there should be the expectation that governments will act to ensure scandals of this nature can no longer occur.

These incidents keep occurring because the cycle of political payback and favours continues in New South Wales: the wrong people arrive at the boards of these organisations for all the wrong reasons—self-aggrandisement and personal enrichment. They are not people of good calibre and they are not people of good character.

The philosophy of the Liberal Party—and this goes all the way back to the Greiner government in 1988 with the introduction of Harvard school business practices within government enterprises and offering large salary packages to the senior executive service—is that private enterprise should feature more prominently within government enterprises, even though the skills required to manage government services in the interests of the public are different to the skills required to make companies act in the interests of shareholders and private equity.

That's not to say that there can't be crossovers between the world of business and the world of government, but all sides of politics have been committed to an unsustainable slant towards business modelling within the public sector since the late 1980s and it's a debasement of what public institutions are meant to be all about: in the public interest. And, clearly, the management of iCare has been the responsibility of people—and a NSW Treasurer—who have little understanding of this concept.

*

COVID-style shape shifting and blame games

17 August

The fine art of politics is based around taking credit for all the positive news and making sure someone else takes the blame for all the negatives. It's the skill of deflecting, obfuscating and ensuring responsibilities always flow somewhere else, and doesn't land at a politician's own doorstep. But there are limits to this strategy: it may take a while for the public to detect the leaders who continuously shirk responsibility, but once the public's lived reality stops matching up to a political narrative, that's when all of the problems for a politician commence.

Since the start of the coronavirus pandemic five months ago, the federal government's behaviour has been more like a secretive star chamber, where decisions are made behind closed doors, scandals are swept away from public scrutiny and, recently, the Prime Minister, Scott Morrison, promised full co-operation with the inquiry into the *Ruby Princess* disaster earlier this year at Sydney Harbour, only for the public to discover he'd actually blocked two key federal public officials from appearing at the inquiry.

The US President, Harry Truman, had the famous sign on his desk—'The Buck Stops Here'—as the clear statement that he had the ultimate responsibility for government actions. But who are the people taking responsibility for the actions of this federal government? They're not so easy to find.

Based on his known history before he arrived to politics, Morrison clearly built a career looking good to outsiders but not actually being very productive on the inside. This approach has worked well for him in the sense that he has reached the highest office in Australia, and he had reached a number of prominent positions, most notably, managing director of Tourism Australia and, preceding that position, the director of New Zealand's Office of Tourism and Sport. Within both of these positions, it's difficult to find anyone who will publicly comment on his performances, and in both positions, he left over a year before his contract expired: he was sacked from Tourism Australia in 2006, and left the Office of Tourism and Sport in 2000 under mysterious circumstances.[84]

Of course, it's an essential management strategy, especially in politics, to manipulate news and information and meld that into a positive message but it needs to relate to personal experiences. Former Prime Minister Paul Keating announced the early 1990s economic downturn was "the recession we had to have" and tried to spin that into a positive at a time when many workers had lost their jobs, and the future employments prospects for many people were bleak. Keating wore the opprobrium for that comment for many years, although he did manage to win the 1993 election but many economists believe the recession created the conditions for strong economic performances in the Australian economy over the next three decades.[85] But at least there was some political honesty and acceptance from a senior political leader that bad economic circumstances were on their way.

Morrison spends most of this time as prime minister making announcements of specific government actions, re-announcing government actions dressed up with different figures, promising funding or, in the case of the recent bushfires, promising relief. Little of these announcements have actually been carried through, either as funding packages, or as relief packages. Recently, Morrison

---

84 *Michael West Media*, 'Where the bloody hell is it? Did Scott Morrison lie about the report that saved his bacon at Tourism Australia?', Jommy Tee, 18 November 2020. https://www.michaelwest.com.au/where-the-bloody-hell-is-it-did-scott-morrison-lie-about-the-report-that-saved-his-bacon-at-tourism-australia

85 *The Economist*, 'Clever reforms 30 years ago helped Australia's growth', Special report, October 2018. https://www.economist.com/special-report/2018/10/25/clever-reforms-30-years-ago-helped-australias-growth

announced a $400 million support fund for the local film and television industry at a high-profile media event at a Gold Coast film production studio, with the requisite comment that it would be a program that would assist 'tradies' but few details for this program have been released. A similar fund of $250 million in arts funding was also recently made, but the finer detail showed no funds were to be released until November 2020, with $90 million of this fund to be provided as concessional loans under difficult guidelines, unlike the free-flowing support packages made to other industries.

The key issue for a government-by-announcement process is that eventually, if too many promises are made to different sectors of the community without the forthcoming delivery or output, too many people in the community will end up disappointed, and too many disappointed people is bad politics. It is possible for political leaders to obfuscate to difficult parts of the community, or promise certain funding to the aged care sector, or to the arts community, or to the film production community but once the entire community realises the *modus operandi* of this government—announcement without delivery—then it's going to develop into a fundamental problem for the Prime Minister. If there's a dissonance between what Morrison announces and what he actually delivers, that's a strong political characteristic that's very difficult to undo once it becomes set in the public's mind.

A prime example of this dissonance is the current Royal Commission into Aged Care Quality and Safety. There is some very damning evidence being presented, relating to how underprepared the aged care sector was in dealing with the coronavirus pandemic, especially in Victoria. Morrison is adamant that nobody could have foreseen all of these problems—no doubt, to gloss over his act as Treasurer in 2017 of removing $1.2 billion of federal funding from the sector—and made sure that everyone heard of his plans… of a plan.

> **Journalist:** Prime Minister, when you established this Royal Commission, you said that it would uncover some uncomfortable truths. It has now found that there was no plan for the aged care sector in this pandemic, that none of the challenges were unforeseeable, and yesterday it said the

sector is still not prepared to handle the pandemic. Isn't this a gross failure of governance on behalf of your Government?

Scott Morrison: The Government has provided its response to those assertions and the Government maintains very strongly that the plan was in place. The plan was in place from March, and indeed, going back to January, preparations had been made and the plan had been updated twice. That's all on the record. I won't delay the press conference by going into the Government's very strong refuting of the points that you have made. There has been a plan... and it has been updated and so we completely reject the assertion that there was not a plan because there was a plan. So I think we have addressed that issue... There was a plan.

For Morrison, letting the public know that there was a plan—whether it was an effective plan or a well-known plan is another matter—seemed to be far more important than addressing the problem or the 188 deaths that had occurred in Victoria's aged care facilities in the preceding week. Announcing the existence of a plan, for Morrison, is far more preferable than accepting responsibility for people who have died in a sector in which the federal government has oversight. Obviously, Morrison or the Department of Human Services can't be held directly responsible for an outbreak of coronavirus in the first instance but they can take responsibility to ensure problems are rectified and minimise the chances of an outbreak occurring again. That's what leadership is, and that's what the public is interested in. But instead of showing that leadership, taking on the difficult tasks of government and accepting responsibility, Morrison is the consummate performer and classic narcissist, who deflects public responsibility and exonerates himself from the bad news, but gladly arrives to take the credit of other people's successes.

And that's how the political process operates but there are limits to how much of this behaviour the electorate can accept. Morrison's prime ministership just passed two years and once these perceptions are set in the public mind—that he makes announcements, but rarely delivers; and deflects responsibilities at all opportunities—it's difficult for this perception to be reversed. Morrison may have already reached this point with the public.

Another US President, Abraham Lincoln, said "you can fool some of the people all of the time, and all of the people some of the time, but you cannot fool all of the people all of the time", and it seems the electorate has been duped for past two or three elections and will continue to be duped by Morrison for some time to come.

One other area where Morrison has failed to deliver was in his promise to fully co-operate with the Special Commission of Inquiry into the Ruby Princess. The Special Commission inquired about the coronavirus outbreak at Sydney Harbour earlier this year—a scandal implicating the NSW Government, NSW Health, the federal government, Australian Border Force and the Department of Agriculture—2,647 passengers were allowed to disembark from the cruise ship without any medical checks, and resulted in over 900 coronavirus infections and twenty-eight deaths across Australia.

Despite Morrison making the offer of full co-operation with the Inquiry, lawyers from the federal government threatened to take the Special Commission to the High Court in a bid to stop two federal officers from appearing. These two witnesses are critical to the Special Commission—one is from the Department of Agriculture; the other one from Australian Border Force. It can only be assumed that the information from these two government officials would have been highly damaging to the federal government, and possibly resulted in criminal charges or implicate key government ministers. Threatening a Special Commission with a High Court injunction to resist the appearance of two government officials providing evidence doesn't seem to be the kind of co-operation Morrison initially promised and it's clear that the government had incriminating evidence to hide.

The report from the Special Commission was released on 14 August 2020 and there's no coincidence the federal government and the NSW Government were largely exonerated and most of the blame was placed onto NSW Health.[86] Certainly, NSW Health could have acted differently but it is extraordinary that a department from New South Wales takes all of the blame, when matters of border

---

86 State of New South Wales, 'Report: Special Commission of Inquiry into the Ruby Princess', Brett Walker SC, August 2020. https://www.rubyprincessinquiry.nsw.gov.au/report

control and quarantine falls under the jurisdiction—according to the Australian Constitution *and* in practice—of the federal government.

In shades of the BBC political satire, *Yes, Minister!*, the traditional adage is that a government should never create an inquiry or a special commission unless it already knows the results of that inquiry, or can determine the course of inquiry to create the results it is politically seeking. And this report has fulfilled the requirements of that satire in spades: the federal government wasn't held responsible; nor were any federal or NSW Government ministers. No-one has been removed from their positions or asked to resign.

It's difficult to believe a collective act of incompetence across two governments and three departments that seriously compromised Australia's health response during a pandemic, as well as directly causing the deaths of twenty-eight people, hasn't resulted in any resignations, or created any obvious practical changes in any of these institutions to ensure the same mistake cannot happen again.

Whether these events are still the public mind at the time of the next election—before May 2022 for the next federal election and March 2023 for the New South Wales election—is difficult to discern but it's the pattern of behaviour of these respective governments that is more likely to resonate with the electorate. The public primarily wants problems solved and, if these current actions of incompetence and mismanagement are still within the public consciousness at the time of the next elections, then those governments will suffer. After all, resolving problems and taking on responsibilities to ensure mistakes are not repeated, are signs of a good and competent administration.

Recently, the Lebanese government resigned after negligence and corruption issues that led to the accidental detonation of 2,750 tonnes of ammonium nitrate stored unsafely in the port of Beirut for six years, a blast which killed at least 204 people, injured over 7,000 people and caused over $US15 billion in property damage. In 2002, the Dutch government resigned after it admitted it could have done a great deal more through its peacekeeping forces to prevent the massacre of 8,000 Bosnian Muslims at Srebrenica by Serbian forces in 1995.[87] Responsibility still means something in other parts

---

87 *The Guardian*, 'Dutch cabinet resigns over Srebrenica massacre', Andrew Osborn & Paul Brown, 17 April 2002. https://bit.ly/3wphp9T

of the world, but Australia doesn't have a tradition of governments resigning when there has been serious maladministration or mismanagement of key events, such as the *Ruby Princess* disaster, mismanagement of aged care facilities, or hotel quarantine issues in Melbourne.

There have been calls for Victoria Premier, Daniel Andrews, to resign for flaws in Melbourne's hotel quarantine program for overseas arrivals: the calls have come from the members of the Victoria Liberal Party opposition, such as Michael O'Brien and Tim Smith, and business leaders such as Jim Penmen, the head of the Jim's Mowers Group. To be sure, there have been serious problems within the hotel quarantine program in Melbourne, which has resulted in a second wave of coronavirus cases in Victoria. But if no resignations were forthcoming from the *Ruby Princess* disaster, why should the Premier of Victoria resign?

For all the issues that have developed in Melbourne, Andrews is the one who has faced the media every single day since he commenced a second series of lockdowns on 3 July 2020; exhausted every question asked by the media; has accepted responsibility for the problems; and implemented a series of actions to resolve the problems. Despite these factors, Andrews still has a high approval rating in published opinions polls, although it is not as high as other national leaders.

Aside from dealing with a high level of media scrutiny and questioning, Andrews has come in for sustained attacks from senior federal and state Liberal Party figures: Josh Frydenberg, Dan Tehan, Tim Wilson, Matthew Guy, O'Brien and Smith, among others. Ironically, it was the former NSW Premier, Mike Baird, who gave Andrews the greatest level of political support, suggesting:[88]

> Leaders are making dozens, and perhaps hundreds, of big decisions every day. And not all of them will be correct in hindsight. Every leader around the world is learning on the run, and the stakes are impossibly high... Let's give them strength, not grief, as they try to make decisions for all of us. And it goes for Dan [Andrews], who I know is working his absolute guts out to save lives. Let's support him as he tries to do the impossible.

---

88 *The New Daily*, 'Daniel Andrews 'working his absolute guts out', says NSW ex-premier Mike Baird', Josh Butler, 9 August 2020. https://thenewdaily.com.au/news/2020/08/09/mike-baird-backs-andrews

For his efforts, Baird was criticised by former Victoria Liberal Party Opposition Leader, Matthew Guy, commenting that "Victorian Liberals are getting fed up with two-faced NSW Liberal cowards who back Daniel Andrews. Federal and state ones". Sometimes, the calls to stop playing foolish political games falls on deaf ears, and it's evident the Liberal Party—at the federal and state levels— has decided that there's no better time to stoke fear and division than during a pandemic, a time where the community is looking to leadership, rather than petty politicking and name calling.

Generally, seeking to gain political traction using such tactics is futile. It may produce the short-term results and gain the attention of the electoral, but after the furore drops and the issues that are creating problems are resolved—and, undoubtedly, the hotel quarantine problems in Melbourne will be resolved—the electorate will mark down those politicians who try to create havoc, rather than being constructive and seeking solutions. The Victoria Liberal Party suffered this fate during the 2018 Victoria election: for many months before that election, Guy, the leader at the time, exploited race relations within the community, and the death of Sisto Malaspina, who was murdered by Hassan Khalif Shire Ali in a street attack in the Melbourne central business district. The reward for Guy's incessant race-baiting and racist frenzy was a 5.31 per cent swing against the Liberal–National Coalition and the loss of eleven seats.

And the current projection for Liberal Party is they are likely to lose even more seats at the next state election, which is not due until November 2022. Some political operatives are very slow to learn from their past mistakes. The public can see through the charades and antics of politicians who are obviously creating political opportunities for themselves and their party through mischief-making and maniacal claims which bear little semblance to reality. Responsibility matters in public life: it may not create the ultimate rewards for those politicians and leaders who accept it, but it's definitely the trait many people in the community want to see.

Stimulus support and the post-pandemic economy

17 August

There are still many problems with coronavirus support payments, and some payments from JobKeeper, the government's flagship employment support program, are going into the wrong areas. JobKeeper is a good program in principle, but it's being exploited by some of Australia's largest companies, and other important industries are being left behind by not receiving the correct stimulus support.

There have been many companies that received JobKeeper payments, and then went on to pay dividends to their shareholders and bonuses to executive staff: seventeen companies receiving JobKeeper support, also paid out $250 million to their investors, and twenty-five other companies paid executive bonuses of $24 million.

The federal government did take a long time to implement JobKeeper, although payments were backdated to 1 March 2020, and the intention of the program was to maintain the relationship between businesses and employees, but it would have been enough time to create a fair and effective system that targeted the right parts of the economic, and to ensure it wasn't ultimately used for shareholders dividends or corporate bonuses.

Conversely, there are other industry sectors that have been excluded from JobKeeper and are still waiting for stimulus support. The promised arts funding package of $250 million is still months away from being implemented—November at the earliest time, and that's possibly an optimistic schedule—other packages are being delayed and there's no sign of any support for casual and seasonal academics in the university sector.

Other industry sectors have been fast-tracked: the federal government is still making a large push for a 'gas-led recovery', even though there are more jobs in the renewable energies sector. The gas market is a relatively smaller part of the economy and research from the consulting firm EY, suggests every $1 million spent on renewable energies and exports creates 4.8 full-time jobs, whereas the same amount spent on fossil fuel projects creates only 1.7 full-time jobs.[89] There are large profits to be made in the gas export market, and this only benefits a smaller part of the economy, but with the value of exports expected to drop from $48 billion in 2019–20 to $31 billion in 2020–21,[90] it opens up the accusations that it's a push by the federal government to support the interests of donors and vested interests, and return the export market to its pre-COVID-19 levels.

The billionaire, Solomon Lew, received over $24 million in dividends after his retail empire, Premier Investments, received almost $70 million in JobKeeper support, with profits for the current financial year surging by 30 per cent, up to $138 billion.[91] There have also been some large accounting firms receiving JobKeeper support payment—this is not to suggest they've committed any illegal actions, and if the program suggests eligibility is based around a 30 per cent drop in turnover in the previous month, compared to the previous year—if annual revenue is under $1 billion—then firms will exploit that and manipulate their accounting data, for example, by withholding invoicing or finding avenues to reduce their turnover, and increasing their chances of qualification.

---

89 WWF-Australia, WWF Report, 'Australian renewable export COVID-19 recovery package', 2020. https://www.wwf.org.au/what-we-do/climate/renewables/renewable-export-covid-19-recovery-package/securing-australia-s-future-renewable-export-covid-19-recovery#gs.s4dga2

90 *Offshore Energy*, 'Australia LNG exports to drop by $17 billion for 2020–21', Bojan Lepic, 28 September 2020. https://www.offshore-energy.biz/australia-lng-exports-to-drop-by-17-billion-for-2020-21

91 *The Guardian*, 'Solomon Lew to get $24m in dividends after retail group given $70m in Covid subsidies', Ben Butler, 25 September 2020. https://www.theguardian.com/business/2020/sep/25/solomon-lew-to-get-24m-in-dividends-after-retail-group-given-70m-in-covid-subsidies

The problem exists with the way the federal government created the program in the first instance, and there is little recourse for recouping funds that have been inappropriately gained or exploited. It probably would have been effective—and more ethical to implement a more extensive program of a basic income to the entire adult population. Maintaining a link between businesses and their employees was an important step but perhaps there would have been less corruption of the ideals of stimulus support if it was based on the premise of stimulating the entire economy, not just pockets of the economy and the areas the federal government considers are the 'winners', or favoured and vested interests. Economic stimulus should start at the lower levels of the economy and work its way up, not from the top down, and that's one area the government didn't really comprehend, nor did it fit in with its ideological positioning.

There have been certain types of sole traders that have been excluded from JobKeeper, especially those people in the arts and creative industries, where income is inconsistent and payments are sometimes received months after the work was performed. For example, in the film and television industry, many contractors and subcontractors in the field may receive zero income during the development stage of a production, but then receive all of their income in the next financial year. Larger projects may exist in the first three months of one financial year, but the final three months of the next financial year: it's inconsistent, but the JobKeeper program didn't take factors like these into account.

And although this is a federal government that distrusts the arts sector, inconsistent income is a factor in tourism and other seasonal ventures, especially in the tourism areas that had their markets wiped out during the last bushfire season, and many businesses in these areas have also been excluded from JobKeeper.

Despite these issues, JobKeeper has helped to stabilise the economy, and it's a type of deficit-inducing program that right-of-centre political parties have traditionally refrained from and used to attack the Labor Party to suggest that it's a sign of weak and inferior economic management. If anything, the federal government has not gone deep enough into deficit and should be looking for further measures to stimulate the economy.

While stimulating the economic is essential in the short-term period, governments should also be looking towards long-term factors and how a recovery process can benefit all sectors of the economy, and not just the select few. Not only is the 'gas-led recovery' mantra offering a false direction—especially when compared to investment in the renewable energies sector, as well as the environmental benefits that could be gained—there are clear conflicts of interest that have so far been ignored or brushed away.

The Chairman of the National COVID-19 Commission, Neville Power, also has a substantial interest—$2.4 million worth of shares—in an ASX-listed energy company, Strike Energy, and their primary business activity is gas production. There is no clear political or economic narrative or business case being put forward by Morrison or the federal government about what a 'gas-led recovery' actually means. Gas exports have been taxed at very low levels over the past two decades,[92] which means the government has not received the revenues it should have in the past and, unless the taxing structure of gas production is amended, it won't receive a great deal of tax revenue in the future. It's not a sector which employs a substantial amount of people—approximately 14,000 across Australia[93]—so it's unclear in whose interests the 'gas-led recovery' is in. How does it benefit the 7.5 per cent of people who are unemployed or those who have lost their jobs. How does a 'gas-led recovery' re-establish working opportunities for those whose sectors have been demolished by the coronavirus pandemic, never to return? How does a musician who doesn't have an opportunity to perform, benefit from the 'gas-led recovery'? Or the part-time sessional academic in the university sector?

It seems Power is someone who will benefit, it's a clear and obvious conflict of interest, and another sign Morrison is more intent on siding with the captains of industry and those close to the Liberal Party, than offering real economic reforms. During the pandemic, Australia has been provided with a unique opportunity to

---

92 *The Conversation*, 'In the midst of an LNG export boom, why are we getting so little for our gas?', Diane Kraal, 17 February 2020. https://theconversation.com/in-the-midst-of-an-lng-export-boom-why-are-we-getting-so-little-for-our-gas-131461
93 Australia Industry and Skills Committee, Gas sector, 2019–19. https://nationalindustryinsights.aisc.net.au/industries/utilities/gas

restructure its economy and diversify its interests away from the easy, but unsustainable, dependency on mineral and energy resources. For example, coal deposits in Australia at current production levels will only last for the next 125 years,[94] but perhaps only the next twenty years on economic and environmental grounds. What will replace this economic activity? Where is the economy of ideas? How can Australia build a service economy that is more reliable in the future, and sustainable in the context of environmental factors such as bushfire and flooding which are likely to become even more difficult to manage in the future?

In its insatiable desire to return and 'snap-back' to the pre-COVID economy—primarily because it lacks the creativity to imagine a different type of economy—the federal government has missed an opportunity to create pathways to a better economic system. It's not an opportunity that has been lost forever, considering Australia—and the world—is only six months into this pandemic, and it's unclear how long it will continue for—but it also has to remembered that long-term economic reform takes many years to be implemented and come to fruition. And perhaps this current government is not the one to implement these changes.

After World War II, the world collectively implemented the Bretton Woods agreement, the World Bank, the International Monetary Fund and a number of reconstruction programs dominated by Keynesian economic thinking: it took decades for many countries to reap the benefits of those reforms and government-induced stimulus spending. At the other end of the economic spectrum, the next wave of economic change through neoliberalism in the 1980s took well over a decade to filter through to other parts of the western world, and then fast-tracked after the demise of communism in the Soviet Bloc: economic reform is a slow moving process, but it does need to start somewhere.

It is evident that whatever economic thinking takes hold—globally or within the Australian economy, and whether is it a 'snap-back' to pre-COVID conditions or radical new economic ideas—there won't be any obvious changes in the lead up to the next federal election in 2021 or 2022, or even the election beyond that in 2025. The

---

94 Geoscience Australia, Black Coal, December 2016. http://www.ga.gov.au/scientific-topics/minerals/mineral-resources-and-advice/australian-resource-reviews/black-coal

panacea for a sluggish world economy might be so radical that it hasn't even been created yet.

The economy of the future needs to be more agile, and more creative. A one-in-a-century crisis can also present an opportunity to create a new future: perhaps Australia has also reached the end of the usefulness of the current political party system, a system that was built for the early twentieth century but seems to be out of touch with the realities of an Australian society in 2020 facing a world laced with uncertainties and a lack of clarity. A two-party system that so heavily favours an incumbent government, as well as a media ecosystem that so heavily favours conservative political parties and vested interests is fraying the edges of democracy and damaging the economy by ignoring alternative viewpoints and different methods for improving economic output and efficiency.

New Zealand implemented a mixed-member proportional representation system in 1993 and while it's difficult to compare their unitary system of government with Australia's federated system, it would be worthwhile considering a system that provides for more co-operative structures within government, and lessens the need for a combative 'winner-takes-all' approach to politics. But new systems of politics also requires all sides of politics to give up something in return, and it's unlikely the Liberal Party—which has held office federally for 64 per cent of the time since it was formed in 1944—would ever agree to a proposal which lessens its dominance over federal politics. And that represents the biggest institutional barrier to realistic change in Australia: the essential political and economic changes that need to be made to improve the country are unlikely to be made by a political party that is most opposed to those changes.

*

When money means absolutely everything in Canberra

17 August

Parliament hasn't been sitting ever since the coronavirus pandemic commenced and the last sitting day was on 23 March 2020, when the House of Representatives resolved to adjourn 'until a date and hour to be fixed by the Speaker'. The Prime Minister had resisted pressure from the Labor Party and the community to hold parliamentary sittings, whether that be in-person, by using teleconferencing or other technology, such as Zoom.

Then, all of a sudden, Morrison back-tracked and agreed to a new session in Canberra but then the real reason was exposed: it wasn't for any form of accountability or commitment to the ideals of Parliament, but because the federal Liberal Party scheduled not one; not two… but three party-political fundraisers at Parliament House, and at an entrance fee of $2,500 per person. In addition, these political fundraisers are being held contrary to medical advice recommending that large gatherings should be avoided and events such as these should not proceed, for fear of spreading coronavirus.

Australia has been fortunate in avoiding the coronavirus caseloads that have appeared in other countries and the numbers here have remained remarkably low. Of course, there is an ongoing risk within the community, and these risks should be minimised. But avoiding Parliament and not even attempting to look at other avenues to hold Parliament during the pandemic is regrettable. The former Liberal Party politician, James Killen, who was a straightshooter and had friends on all sides of the political spectrum, always maintained that 'Parliament is supreme' and if Parliament wasn't working correctly, the country was in trouble, and the governments which couldn't manage Parliament, couldn't manage the country. That might be considered an antiquated ideal, but it's unclear whether Morrison would agree to or understand those ideals: it's almost as though he considers Parliament as a perfunctory chore and a hinderance, rather than a system that provides the checks and balances on governments, as well as prime ministers.

It's a shame the traditions and conventions of Parliament have been so easily dismissed, ironically by a conservative party that is so eager to maintain traditions in so many other parts of society. It seemed there was no impetus at all for Morrison to hold Parliament, preferring the National Cabinet process with premiers and chief ministers where there was less scrutiny over decision making, but when the opportunity arose within the Liberal Party to prepare fundraising events and raise revenues for the next federal election campaign, he couldn't rush quickly enough to change his mind.

The other issue to consider is: should Australia Parliament House be used for political fundraising? The House is not like a sacred church, but it's unbecoming for it to be used for partisan events that generate income for partisan political purposes. The first occasion where any part of Parliament House was used for party-political fundraising—on the public record, at least—was in 2014, when the former Speaker of the House, Bronwyn Bishop, used her office suite to raise funds for the Liberal Party.

Parliament House is a public building and its sole purpose is for the business *of* politics in Australia, not for revenue raising and the business of one side of politics alone. No political party owns Parliament House, it has to *be* and *seen to be* politically neutral: it shouldn't be used for any type of fundraising for any political party. Aside from the obvious conflicts of interest at the annual Midwinter Ball—and it seems, opportunities for sexual harassment—where staffers, journalists, celebrities, and prominent members of the business community gather to raise funds for charities, even these kinds of events should be excluded from Parliament House.

The three fundraisers proposed by the Liberal Party are likely to raise around $150,000 in political donations: it might not be illegal to hold these events at Parliament House, but it does appear improper. Not everything in public life should have the 'for sale' sign prominently displayed. And these actions suggest that the Prime Minister and his government doesn't understand the full nature of Parliament, or issues of propriety and good governance, and see the entire role of government as an opportunity to revenue raise for their own political wellbeing. It shouldn't be and doesn't have to be this way.

*

The return of Parliament and a crisis in aged care

1 September

Federal Parliament has returned after its winter recess and it appears to be business as usual: the federal government is facing pressure for mismanagement in key policy areas and, they're calling on every political tactic available to them to deflect from the problems they're facing.

There are many ongoing problems within the aged care sector across Australia and the Minister for Aged Care, Senator Richard Colbeck, has come under severe pressure for his negligence in this portfolio. He has attempted to avoid scrutiny at every opportunity, even going to the extent of walking out from the Senate chambers when he was questioned about his performance.[95]

There was speculation the Labor Party would be able to force the resignation of Colbeck but by the end of the parliamentary sitting week, there was barely a scratch on the government. The concept of ministerial responsibility has changed dramatically over the past few decades, but what does a poorly performing minister have to do to lose their job?

In the Liberal–National Coalition, it seems the first requisite is to be a female minister: Senator Bridget McKenzie finally resigned

---

95 *The New Daily*, 'Disgrace as Aged Care Minister walks away from scrutiny', Josh Butler, 27 September 2020. https://thenewdaily.com.au/news/2020/08/27/richard-colbeck-aged-care-senate

after more allegations were made about her involvement in the infamous 'sports rorts' scandal. Many other male ministers have committed outrageous actions as parliamentarians—Angus Taylor, George Christensen, Stuart Robert—but in keeping with its image as the "boys' club", only McKenzie has been forced to resign when, in reality, all of them should have resigned. And, for McKenzie, she did lose her ministerial position, but she has kept all of her other positions: she remains as leader of the National Party in the Senate, as well as her Senate committee positions, so it's hard to see what the real punishment was.

As bad as McKenzie's actions were in distributing sports funding after the caretaker period had commenced, and the heavy bias towards government-held and marginal seats, Colbeck's performance has been far worse and with far greater consequences: during the coronavirus pandemic, many people have died in private aged care facilities, which fall under the responsibility of the federal government, and Colbeck seems to be unconcerned and incurious about the matter. This exchange at the Senate Select Committee on 21 August 2020, which explored the federal government's response to the COVID-19 pandemic, is indicative of Colbeck's poor performances:

> **Senator Katie Gallagher:** Thank you, Minister. How many residents of aged care facilities funded and regulated by the Australian government have passed away from COVID-19?
>
> **Senator Richard Colbeck:** I'll just have to look at my latest report. That might take me a moment...
>
> **Gallagher:** ...Could an official help if the minister is not able to find it? Ms Laffan?
>
> **Amy Laffan (First Assistant Secretary, Health):** As at 8AM on 20 August, 258 care recipients had passed away. Of those, 254 were residential care recipients. The remaining four were home care recipients.
>
> **Gallagher:** Minister, you weren't aware of that number?
>
> **Colbeck:** I was just trying to find my latest numbers. It wasn't in the frontline details of those things. I have got the details; I just couldn't find it at hand. I'm sorry.

Gallagher: Minister, how many residents of aged care facilities funded and regulated by the Australian government have COVID-19 today?

Colbeck: Again, I don't have the report with the actual detail in front of me. I'll have to ask…

Gallagher: …Minister, you don't know how many people have passed away. You are now telling many you don't know how many people have the infection. You are the Minister for Aged Care and Senior Australians. This is serious…

Colbeck: …I am looking for the report on my IT system…

Gallagher: But the numbers are not front of mind for you as minister for aged care? They're pretty important details as we are going through this pandemic and the heartbreaking scenes in Victoria. I am just struggling to believe that you are not aware of these details.

Colbeck didn't have the numbers at hand; he couldn't answer questions. He had clearly not done any preparation, he had not taken any duty of care in his ministry and has clearly failed under traditional Westminster protocols. And many federal government ministers have also failed these protocols as well. When the best performing minister of the government is Senator Simon Birmingham, it's fair to say that this is not one of the legendary and best performing Cabinets in Australia's political history: far from it. The public is entitled to feel angry about these underperforming ministers and, in the void left behind by this lack of performance, outside vested interests such as the Business Council of Australia, the Minerals Council of Australia, the Institute of Public Affairs and News Corporation, are coming in to fill the gap. It's the fault of the Liberal Party for permitting this to take place, but it's also the fault of the Australian electorate that keeps voting for this type of government—three consecutive federal election victories, and looking to secure a fourth in 2022—and the Labor Party for not effectively pointing out all of these disasters and gross incompetences.

Just because a minister can't recall a specific number in Senate Committees shouldn't in itself be a cause for resignation—members of Parliament need to deal with many facts and figures and the details of so much material, especially if they're a minister—but Colbeck's performances are appalling, especially in the context of 685 people dying in aged care facilities due to COVID-19. Ministers need to be competent to carry out their tasks, but they also have to appear to be competent as well. Being unable to recall such key material doesn't provide much confidence in the government being able to manage these issues well, or ensure conditions are created to reduce the chances of mistakes occurring again.

Another factor is—and this is a continuing feature of this federal government—blame shifting. Ever since the deaths in the sector were first reported, the Minister for Health, Greg Hunt, kept pushing the idea of shared responsibilities between state and federal governments, even though private aged care is specifically within the jurisdiction of the federal government. The issue then becomes someone else's problem and the problem remains unresolved: it's not the sign of good governance, or acting in the public interest. It might be beneficial politically to force responsibility elsewhere, but the community—especially those who have lost family members because of mismanagement—just want to make sure it doesn't happen again and for someone to take responsibility.

The collection of poor decisions, corrupt practices and incompetence has been growing larger and the Labor Party now has so much material to use politically against the government. Aged care is a key social policy issue and these recent events should be used to highlight these poor performances that are creating problems in the sector. Looking at the parliamentary performances of both parties, it seemed Labor couldn't gain any traction on this issues and were overwhelmed by the tactics used by the government, to close down debate and deflect onto other matters. But outside of Parliament, the issue seems to be brewing: in the most recent Newspoll opinion poll, the two-party preferred voting intention is locked at 50:50 per cent, which is a tightening of the vote when compared the vote at the 2019 federal election, where the final result was 51.53 per cent for the Liberal–National Coalition, to Labor's 48.47 per cent. Of course, there has to be the ongoing caveat that reliability in polling has decreased in recent times, but it's the only statistical report card that is publicly available.

The Labor leader, Anthony Albanese has released an eight-point plan for the aged care sector, including minimum staffing levels; better training for staff and infection control; and higher levels of funding for the sector, which did have a $1.2 billion cutback in the 2017 Budget, at the time when Morrison was Treasurer. Based on his previous behaviours and a 'bower-bird' approach to policy matters, it can be reasonably expected that Morrison will take Labor's ideas, implement them, claim they were his ideas all along, and then blame Labor for not having a plan for the aged care sector. In these types of circumstances, what else can the Labor Party do?

Morrison is assisted by a very soft mainstream media that would normally relish publishing material—on a sustained level—about all the mishaps, incompetence and corrosive corruption that has existed, ever since the Liberal–National Coalition returned to office in 2013. And the issue of corruption is not based on opinion or observations: the international Corruption Perceptions Index prepared by Transparency International, has seen Australia slip eight places in the index, going from third in 2013, down to eleventh in 2020.[96]

News of corruption in politics sells newspapers, or results in more online reader clicks. There are good journalists working in the field, but their work tends to be buried, and it seems that the material that could cause damage to the federal government—and boost circulations—is inevitably suppressed at a higher management level. It seems counter-intuitive to media corporations that are supposedly meant to be in the business of generating revenues for their shareholders.

With an aging population, and a life-expectancy rate that is increasing—from seventy-four years of age in 1980, up to almost eighty-four years of age in 2020—many families will have relatives in aged care, and have a closer experience with the sector today, compared to what it might have been forty years ago, and serious problems that occur in the sector have a greater resonance within the community. An aged care sector that has ongoing problems caused by ministerial incompetence is going to create ongoing political problems for the federal government, irrespective of how

---

96 Transparency International, Corruption Perceptions Index, https://www.transparency.org/en/cpi/2020/index/nzl

much deflection it creates, or how much it tries to blame others for their own failures.

The market-based mechanisms of privatisation of the aged care sector that have been pushed forward ever since the Howard government was elected in 1996, and have not resulted in better quality care, and the onset of the coronavirus pandemic has highlighted these failures. Of the 909 deaths that have been caused by COVID-19, 685 have occurred in aged care facilities: that is a damning statistic, and many deaths could have been avoided if systemic problems had been addressed in the past, and with proper ministerial oversight. Adequate policies have never implemented by the federal government, not even simple matters such as staff-to-resident ratios. And in response to this crisis, it seems Morrison took a loosely-based guidelines booklet and re-announced it as 'a plan', hoping that no one would notice.

The residents in aged care—the ones who have built today's community—their families, and the public, deserves far better than a concoction of media spin, blame-shifting and a lack of responsibility.

In keeping with the prevailing attitudes of the mainstream media, very few have been calling for the resignation of Colbeck: perhaps this is a better outcome, and it's essential for a minister to take responsibility for these matters, resolve them, and then after that, they can resign. And this compares quite differently to the attitudes of almost the entire business community and the conservative media who have incessantly called for the resignation of the Victoria Premier, Daniel Andrews.

Andrews has faced up to the media every single day since the second wave of coronavirus commenced in early July, has taken on responsibility and promised to resolve the issues and instigated an inquiry into the problems in Victoria's hotel quarantine management. It might not create the desired solution but this is the essence of leadership: in contrast, Colbeck walks away from Parliament, blames another government and doesn't understand the basics of his job. That is the antithesis of leadership. Colbeck is a serial underperformer: why is he still Minister for Aged Care or, to take it one step further, why is he still in the Parliament?

Politics usually abhors a vacuum but this federal government creates voids wherever it can, and fills the space with blame-shifting and deflection, leaving the public seeking more answers and hoping they won't be the ones that are affected by continuous problems that exist in the aged care sector. The public does deserve better, but is this what they will end up receiving?

*

The continuing saga of Australia's border wars

1 September

It's turning into a predictable but unedifying spectacle, with the federal government and other vested interests ramping up their push to open up state borders. The billionaire mining magnate Clive Palmer is racking up major legal losses in the courts but is still taking his appeals to the High Court to get internal Australian borders opened up as soon as possible.

The Liberal Party has traditionally been a firm believer in the rights of the states against the domination of the federal government but that history seems to have been thrown away, with the Prime Minister, Scott Morrison, now claiming Australia was designed to be a country without borders; borders weren't intended to be a barrier to internal interactions, and using an entire collection of emotionally-charged stories of people being denied medical care across the Queensland–New South Wales border, or not able to attend funerals or visit families and friends who live interstate.

There is a precedent for border closures, with many of Australia's internal borders closing during the 1918 influenza pandemic. And there is popular support for these closures: 72 per cent of Australia's population is satisfied with the respective state government decisions to close borders until the coronavirus threat is over, so the question needs to be asked: why is Morrison and the federal government even considering support Palmer's Federal and High Court challenges, when they are likely to result in defeat and public opinion is so heavily swayed against him?

Essentially, it's to send a message to key business people and quasi-political operatives such as Palmer, that the government is on their side and whatever the circumstances are, the Liberal Party is here to assist them and help to keep them in their place at the apex of society. The coronavirus has placed a halt on economic activity and, during this hiatus, the community has pondering the value of an economy that focusses so much on rapacious capitalism, low taxes, and a working life that exists at the expense of a personal life: the work–life balance that has been talked about for so long was swayed too far toward business and work, and there's been a perception that focusing on life factors is important and perhaps the economy is not as important as governments want society to believe.

Through more expansive work-from-home arrangements, businesses have realised that in most cases, it's not necessary to have the large and expensive office spaces overlooking the Sydney Harbour, the Yarra, or the Swan River, for workers to do their job effectively. More business can be performed collaboratively online and, in many cases, more productively. Business practices are beginning to change and perhaps that's one reason why the 'snap-back' philosophy of Morrison and Josh Frydenberg was pushed forward so vehemently: they don't have the creative philosophy or political intellect to imagine a different kind of economy and, for them, Palmer is a reminder of old economic thinking.

Palmer has been a negative influence on Australian political life: a billionaire who was campaign director of the National Party in Queensland during the 1980s and a politician in the federal Parliament between 2013–16. And it seems that through his experience of being a politician, even though it was only for one term, he's been savvy enough to realise he can gain more political power and influence outside of Parliament, which he did successfully during the 2019 election, through the United Australia Party: having deep pockets tends to fuel that belief.

Palmer has placed prominent two-page advertisements in *The West Australian* newspaper for several months to explain the reasons behind his challenges to the Western Australia Government's decision to close the borders. But there's also a contempt by Palmer to find fault with the Western Australia Labor government, and behave in a financially self-interested manner—as if rules enforced for the wellbeing of the entire community shouldn't apply to him.

The owner of Seven West Media, Kerry Stokes, is another businessman with close ties to the Liberal Party who also plays by different rules and laws. Early this year, Stokes and his wife Christine, were granted an exemption from hotel quarantine, even though they were arriving into Australia from a coronavirus hotspot in the United States. The exemption was granted on 'medical grounds', due to a series of medical procedures Stokes had undertaken, but apparently was well enough to travel to Canberra soon after for ANZAC Day commemorations, and then return to Western Australia, without completing the mandatory fourteen-day hotel quarantine. Obviously, there are different rules for different people.

Among these groups of businesspeople, and especially in the case of Palmer, there isn't enough acceptance about how difficult the coronavirus is to control and how deadly it can potentially become, and this illusion may have been created because of the relatively low case numbers in Australia. Even when the new daily cases reached a high point of 721 in Victoria on 30 July 2020, this was low when compared to the average daily case numbers of over 40,000 in the United States. The New Zealand experience showed the elimination strategy was probably the most effective approach to the management of the pandemic—and the open society approach in Sweden proved to be the worst—but that doesn't seem to have registered with the federal government, or some in the business sector calling for borders to be re-opened.

And there is also a deep political dimension to this, with the attacks from Palmer, and the federal government, predominantly against Labor governments in the respective state jurisdictions—Western Australia, Queensland and Victoria—while ignoring the two Liberal state governments that have exactly the same border closures, South Australia and Tasmania. In addition, New South Wales has been used by Morrison as an exemplar for not closing down its borders, even though the fact that the Queensland, South Australia and Victoria closures had meant New South Wales had a *de facto* closure, without specifically needing to do so.

Whenever the Liberal–National Coalition is in opposition—which hasn't been very often in recent history—the rights of state governments are sacrosanct but when they're in government, there's selective choices about which state they will uphold the rights of, and which states they will diminish. But, constitutionally, there is little the federal government can do: if a state wishes to close its borders on health grounds or quarantine, they can do that, and the debate about border closures needs to be seen through a political prism, not a legal one. These are diversions as well: pushing issues or deflecting blame onto other political leaders has been the hallmark of Morrison's leadership. This current action is a continuation of the same theme.

There also have to be questions over the calibre of politician that enters Parliament which is not that much better than the level that exists in student politics at universities: many parliamentarians have worked their way through student politics, and haven't yet realised that politics isn't some intellectual pursuit and trying to win battles against old political foes on campus; there are real-life consequences in federal and state politics, and the actions and decisions of members of Parliament have a tangible effect on people's lives. This is an area that tends to be forgotten.

And this kind of behaviour and political motivations extends into the media, where conservative commentators such as Adam Creighton, Andrew Bolt, Miranda Devine, Rowan Dean, Rita Panahi—all from News Corporation—tend to abuse those with whom they disagree with, rather than present logical and coherent arguments, and adopt a winner-takes-all approach to public discourse. People in politics or in the media can have their firmly-held believes and ideological perspectives but the winner-takes-all approach leaves too many people in the community behind.

One example of where conservative media goes too far in pursuit of party-political advantage, and at the expense of the Labor Party, was in their recent reporting of a Ballina women pregnant with twins, who was delayed in seeking access to a nearby hospital on the other side of the New South Wales–Queensland border, and lost one of the twins during the delay. People seeking travel from News South Wales into Queensland needed to apply for an exemption, and the woman assumed this is what she would need to do, but the current rules stipulate an exemption is not required for emergency procedures and the women and her family were unaware of this. However, the media trained all of their collective resources in attacking the Queensland Premier, Annastacia Palaszczuk, for a lack of compassion and prompted Morrison to add to the attack by claiming the situation was "terribly distressing", called for more compassion from states that were implementing hard borders and said that he would be "asking questions"—whatever that might mean.

Unfortunately, the woman had been provided with the incorrect advice: but that didn't stop the Prime Minister or the conservative media launching attacks against the Queensland government, even though the incident didn't have anything to do with the decision to close the border. It was just yet another level of political opportunism and another example of how this Prime Minister and the federal government feel the desire to win every political point and every political battle, even if it does end up being a Pyrrhic victory.

*

An international infrastructure program gets a belting

1 September

The Belt and Road Initiative is a global infrastructure development program implemented by the Chinese government in 2013, and it's considered the key foreign affairs policy initiative of President Xi Jinping. Its primary purpose is to develop better road, rail and sea connectivity around the world and address key infrastructure gaps, especially in the Asia–Pacific region, Africa and Europe, and also through a range of cultural exchange projects that aim to build mutual trust and understandings between nations.

In 2018, the Victoria Government signed a memorandum of understanding with the Chinese government to explore infrastructure investment projects of mutual interest—it's not a legally binding document and no projects have been agreed to so far, and there's no guarantee any projects will be developed—at this stage, it's only an agreement to only consider projects at some point in the future.

There has been some conjecture about the value of the Belt and Road Initiative and whether it is in the interests of Australia but in June 2019, Prime Minister Scott Morrison seemed to believe the Initiative would be significantly to Australia's advantage:[97]

---

97 Asialink/University of Melbourne, Address to Asialink: 'Where we live', Scott Morrison MP, 25 June 2019. https://bit.ly/3cTHITf

Scott Morrison: We would be mugs [to not accept the Belt and Road Initiative]; mugs! Only harming our own economic interests if were to deny our economy access to this capital. That is why we operate a non-discriminatory approach to investment screening—and investment screening is not exclusive to Australia, it's done by many countries—most in fact, including China. The infrastructure needs of our region are also enormous, and Australia welcomes the contribution that [the] Belt and Road Initiative can make to regional infrastructure, investment and to regional development.

Morrison did seem to think it was a very good idea at the time, but now Morrison is claiming he never believed in the Belt and Road Initiative, never supported the Victoria Government's memorandum of understanding with China—even though he never said anything at the time—and now wants to remove the right for Australian states to be able to engage with China within this project. Aside from the issue of needing to fact check everything Morrison says, it seems he's more intent in scoring political points against a Labor government, and engaging in some China-bashing for domestic political gain. Ultimately, his actions and commentary now are working against Australia's national interest.

The Liberal Party has traditionally been staunchly pro-United States in its understanding of how Australia's foreign policy should be managed. There was the 'all-the-way-with-LBJ' mantra from former Prime Minister Harold Holt and US President Lyndon Johnson in the 1960s; the relationship between former Prime Minister John Howard and US President George W. Bush in the early 2000s after the 9/11 attacks in New York and on the Pentagon. And now, the relationship between US President Donald Trump and Morrison, who referred to Morrison as the "man of titanium". Trump has initiated a trade war with China, for reasons which remain unclear, although there have been assumptions that it's to place a check on China's growing influence in politics and economics around the world.

While China is still the largest manufacturer in the world, with 28 per cent of global output in 2018, it's often forgotten the United

States is still a large manufacturer with 17 per cent of global output,[98] with most of its production occurring in petroleum, luxury cars, airplanes, chemicals and electronics. Perhaps Morrison's about-face on China is a reflection of Trump's economic and political ambitions and an attempt to veer trade away from China, as well as the reliance on China for the vast supply of consumer goods into the Australia market.

And, of course, there are the continuing issues of human rights abuses committed by the Chinese government, as well as its overreach in the South China Sea region and growing influence in West Africa and Pacific island nations; it's a problematic government, as most countries are around the world and there is a far-from-perfect government in Australia as well. Nonetheless, China is still Australia's largest trading partner. There may be a desire to increase trade with Britain, now that it is on the verge of completing the Brexit push to extract itself from the European Union; with North America; or with South Africa, perhaps with Western Europe.

Much of the world trade is transacted between countries that do not fully agree with each other, but they implement deals that are mutually beneficial, as well as traversing the fine lines that exist between opposing allies. Every country has a right to choose their trading partners, but to significantly damage the relationship with a large trading partner, without having new avenues to access, seems foolish and counterproductive. Morrison's about-face on the Belt and Road Initiative seemed to be just another one of his bizarre backflips, denying he'd ever supported the Initiative even though he is clearly on the record offering his enthusiasm.

One other factor that has been overlooked is the lack of consistency in foreign policy matters, and the involvement of the Liberal Party in other deals with the Chinese Government. In 2015, the Country Liberal Party in the Northern Territory established a ninety-nine-year lease of the Port of Darwin to Landbridge, a company with close links to the Chinese Communist Party—the deal is worth $506 million which, at $5 million per year, is an incredibly unfavourable deal for the Northern Territory Government—and also secured

---

98 World Economic Forum/Statistica, 'These are the top 10 manufacturing countries in the world', Felix Richter, 20 February 2020. https://www.weforum.org/agenda/2020/02/countries-manufacturing-trade-exports-economics

employment with the company for the former Liberal Party Minister for Trade and Investment, Andrew Robb, for a salary of $880,000. It's interesting to note Robb is also chair of Asialink, which hosted the event where Morrison made his enthusiastic speech about the Belt and Road Initiative back in June 2019.

If Morrison was seriously concerned about the Belt and Road Initiative, he'd cancel the Port of Darwin lease, as well as seek to terminate the salary contract between Robb and Landbridge. But, this won't happen: he's more concerned about petty party-based political point scoring and creating political problems for the Victoria Labor Party at a time when he should be focused on managing the coronavirus and promoting the national interest. Of course, there has to be a concern about the international reach of the Chinese government and its influence in key regions around the world, but the federal government shouldn't be creating situations where one program is deemed to be in the national interest if it is initiated by the Liberal Party, and another one is not, only because the Labor Party initiated it.

Several Australian electricity grids have been sold off to international interests and while foreign ownership of an essential energy service is not ideal, if problems ever arise with that service provision and a foreign owner becomes hostile towards Australia's interests, another grid can be developed or electricity can be accessed through other parts of the national grid: this, of course, is a problem, but there are solutions that can be implemented.

When ports are sold or leased out, there's little the host government can do. If a war-by-proxy is implemented with China, then anything is possible. One hundred years ago in 1920, there was a genuinely held belief that after the sufferings of World War I, there would never again be such calamitous events in world affairs: twenty years later, an even more disastrous event occurred with the onset of World War II in 1939. The world can change dramatically in a short period of time, and there is little understanding of what the relationship between Australia and China will be in 2114, when the current Port of Darwin lease expires: the notion of the nation–state could collapse by then; there could also be different understandings of world trade and supply-chain processes.

When the Port of Darwin lease was announced, it seemed like a very short-sighted and poor deal for the Northern Territory Government and it's questionable whether the national interest was well served in this instance. But as poor as that decision was, it seems even more foolish to initiate a trade war with China—which Australia has little hope of winning—and irritate Australia's largest trading partner, without providing or implementing alternatives.

Foreign investment can be a positive experience and political leaders should be able to traverse the fine line of walking a tightrope, able to advance Australia's interests in the field of politics and diplomacy according to domestic values, while maintaining close economic ties: after all, that's what the art of diplomacy is all about. And being hard-nosed about the economic benefits is essential as well, extracting every dollar possible: a deal which extracted the equivalent of $5 million per year—which in 2114 will probably be an average wage for a worker—means that key infrastructure has been leased for a pittance. Over time, this will be considered as one of the weakest arrangements ever made in Australia's history, and it's an error that will be with the Northern Territory Government for some time to come.

*

The interfering vested interests

24 September

A large schism has developed between the vested interests calling for the end of border closures—interests which include several national corporations and the federal government—and the general public, which according to recent opinion polls, is still highly supportive of the decisions by state governments to close their borders.

In Western Australia, an incredible 91 per cent[99] of all people surveyed are supportive of a hard border closure in that state and, in the other states, support is hovering between 60 and 70 per cent. There are many commentators in the mainstream media pushing for borders to be opened up as soon as possible—News Corporation, Seven West Media, Nine Network and, increasingly, the ABC—and they're pushing a corporatist agenda the public isn't interested in supporting.

And there are good reasons for this lack of public support: there are currently 7,000 new coronavirus cases occurring each day in Britain; 14,000 in France, and the United States has reaching a daily record of 46,000 new cases[100]—these countries do have much

---

99 *The West Australian*, 'Newspoll finds 91 per cent of West Australians think State premiers should have the power to close their borders', 30 August 2020. https://thewest.com.au/news/coronavirus/newspoll-finds-91-per-cent-west-australians-think-state-premiers-should-have-the-power-to-close-their-borders-ng-b881652861z
100 Worldometer.info, 26 September 2020. https://www.worldometers.info/coronavirus/#countries

larger populations than Australia but, in comparison, there have been sixteen new local coronavirus cases over the past twenty-four hours. With the same infection rate as the United States, Australia's daily case numbers would be over 3,500. The Australian public can see what is happening in other countries around the world and it's obvious they wish to avoid these numbers locally. If this is the case, why is the mainstream media and the federal government promoting an agenda to open the economy and increase people movement, when the public doesn't support this? Conversely, are the current case numbers low enough to realistically remove restrictions and border closures, or should Australia move towards complete eradication of coronavirus?

The answers lie in how much a community values lives when compared with how much it values money and it's evident throughout this pandemic, corporations and conservative governments have placed a higher value on the economy, with a subtext that the lives that are likely to be lost—older members of the community—don't matter that much. Eradication would be the ideal goal: New Zealand eradicated the virus, after being told that was an impossible goal. Queensland, South Australia and Western Australian haven't had any recent cases, and after their hotel quarantine problems, Victoria will eradicate the virus if it can hold its current levels for the next twenty-one days, and New South Wales is close as well. Case numbers are doubling every seven days in the United States and if Australia is so close to eradication when so many other parts of the world have seen the coronavirus spiral out of control, it's not surprising there is popular support for community lockdowns and border closures.

It's not a requisite for someone to be an epidemiologist to realise coronavirus can be a deadly disease, but the dichotomy between the public and the media, with its strong support of corporatists agendas, had been an interesting development, almost as if they've been reading a completely different set of figures and data to the rest of the world. The ABC's *7.30* program has consistently reported on the more negative stories about cafes and gym owners—as if they are the only business operators in the community—without offering any counter-perspectives, even providing examples of how a family in Perth was affected by a border closure in Tasmania, or a spurious and esoteric example of a food supplier in Brisbane not being able to supply goods to Adelaide. Of course, these concerns cannot be underestimated, and the media will always chase after the 'sad-sack' and 'woe-be-me' stories that bear little resemblance to reality, but the alignment of media stories, with the agenda of the federal government and corporate interests was stark.

There was also the *Herald Sun* in Victoria, a News Corporation newspaper, which published a daily fare of abuse and attacks on Premier Daniel Andrews, constantly pushing their agenda to end lockdowns and open up borders, despite the health advice that was provided. Part of this is a reaction to many of the freedoms that have been taken for granted for a long time, all of a sudden removed from the community.

And during a pandemic, the community has also developed an understanding of what is more relevant: overpaid CEOs and captains of industries are not as important as retail staff, health professionals, support staff such as cleaners, public transport drivers: all of the workers who are placing themselves at risk for the benefit of the overall community. These are the people who have provided value during the time of a pandemic, not the usual middle-management and proprietors who have been calling for state governments to behave in a way that protects their corporate interests, rather than the public interest.

And it's interesting to see who else is aligning themselves with these corporate interests. Recently, there were anti-lockdown protests in Melbourne, where seventy-four people were arrested for breaching restrictions.[101] Among the protesters were people also pushing conspiracy theories about how coronavirus was implemented to protect a well-established paedophile ring and children held against their will in underground locations in Melbourne,[102] theories espoused by the radical QAnon group and right-wing Christian

---

101 *The Guardian*, 'How Victoria's Covid lockdown protests are galvanising Australia's right', Michael McGowan, 19 September 2020. https://www.theguardian.com/australia-news/2020/sep/19/how-victorias-covid-lockdown-protests-are-galvanising-australias-right

102 *The Conversation*, 'What lies beneath: tunnels for trafficking, or just a subterranean service? Time to rescue these spaces from the conspiracists', Victoria Kolankiewicz, 14 September 2020. https://theconversation.com/what-lies-beneath-tunnels-for-trafficking-or-just-a-subterranean-service-time-to-rescue-these-spaces-from-the-conspiracists-144276

extremists. No-one from the federal government has admonished these people in the same way Prime Minister Scott Morrison labelled the Black Lives Matter protests in Sydney as "appalling" or asking "what gives people a ticket to not obey the law?",[103] primarily because they wish to harvest the votes of these people, irrespective of how extreme their views are. It's a similar strategy used by former Prime Minister John Howard, who surreptitiously attracted the votes of One Nation supporters by either not detracting their viewpoints or suggesting people have a right to freedom of speech in Australia, and a right that needs to be defended.

And attracting these votes on the periphery is always the key to holding onto government. These people are unlikely to vote against the Liberal–National Coalition, unless it's to register a protest vote, and perhaps this is part of Morrison's strategy: avoiding a protest vote against his government, because these extremists and conspiracy theorists are 'his people'. Although the next federal election is still far away—not due to be held until 2022—there are more immediate issues for the Prime Minister: the Queensland state election, coming up on 31 October.

With the reduction in case numbers across Australia and the threat of coronavirus slowly disappearing, the level of political point scoring has gone up. Last week, the Minister for Home Affairs, Peter Dutton, attacked the Queensland Premier, Annastacia Palaszczuk, for allowing the film actor, Tom Hanks, into Australia, even though it was his department, Australian Border Force, that formally approved his arrival, as well as his exemption from formal hotel quarantine protocols. Premier Andrews in Victoria has been attacked by the federal government, as has the Western Australia Premier, Mark McGowan. The federal Liberal Party, far from the 'all-in-this-together' rhetoric it pushed at the beginning of the coronavirus pandemic, is behaving more like a central political campaign unit that intervenes in state affairs, and assists state Liberal branches in their campaigns against the Labor Party.

This was the approach taken by the federal government in 2018—an election year for Victoria—where for most of the year, Malcolm

---

103 SBS News, 'Scott Morrison slams 'appalling' Sydney Black Lives Matter protest', 22 July 2020. https://www.sbs.com.au/news/scott-morrison-slams-appalling-sydney-black-lives-matter-protest

Turnbull and then Morrison when he became prime minister in August, railed against Andrews and the Victoria Government, claiming 'African gangs' had taken over the streets of Melbourne and pushed the threat of terrorism at every opportunity. And it's a similar strategy in 2020 in Queensland. Federal politicians and leaders can play a constructive and positive role during state election campaigns and, traditionally, they've risen above the fray and avoided the day-to-day political fights. But federal players such as Morrison and Dutton have inserted themselves into Queensland election, as though they were the ones running in that election as candidates.

There is a belief that Morrison is popular, and opinion polls support this idea through his current high approval rating, and that explains his involvement in the Queensland election campaign. But opinions polls, as was the case in the 2019 federal election, can be misleading and be interpreted incorrectly. The only real-life political test Morrison has faced since 2019—the Eden–Monaro byelection in July 2020—resulted in a loss for the Liberal Party. Is Morrison 'popular' in the same way John Howard was? And does it really matter as this stage of the electoral cycle?

During a time of crisis, it doesn't really matter who the prime minister is, or their personality: the critical factor is for them to be effective and perform as well as they can in their quest to unify the community. There are extenuating circumstances with this pandemic that are not just affecting Australia, but the entire world. Unity is critical, but unity won't be achieved by political leaders acting in a way that is contrary to professional health advice or attacking political opponents in state jurisdictions to gain political advantage. It seems the community is not "in all of this together" and, for this government, some people "are in this together", while many others are not.

*

Recycled political stories that are too good to be true

25 September

Recycling is generally considered to be a worthwhile practice in the community but the federal government seems to have a different understanding about this concept: it keeps re-announcing old ideas and, in some cases, the re-announcement is an exact repeat of previous announcements.

The government announced coronavirus vaccines would be available to all Australians, even though a vaccine hasn't been developed and is unlikely to be developed for some time. But that's not the issue here—the government announced exactly the same story from a few months ago—a 'letter of intent' with AstraZeneca was announced in early August—but the media cycle went through the same process as before, reporting as though the vaccine had already been prepared and ready for distribution, and creating a good news story for the government for an entire week.

More recently, the government made its third announcement of a 'gas-led recovery', even though it was virtually the same as the announcements from May and then June. There was nothing new in the announcement but it enabled the government to push forward and provide a public impression it had an agenda it was working towards when, clearly, it didn't really have one. A government that keeps recycling old news and brushing it up as new is a government that doesn't really have much of an agenda and it's a government that doesn't really know what it's doing.

The underlying philosophy of this government seems to be aligned with Ayn Rand's concept of objectivism, self-centred individualism and a form of *laissez-faire* capitalism where government has a shrinking or non-existent role. Neoliberalism refined Rand's crudes concepts and wedded them to the conservative economic philosophies of Friedrich Hayek: the reduction of government, the notion that 'tax is theft' as a response to the Marxist notion of 'property is theft'. As an intellectual pursuit, this can be a fruitful academic exercise but, in practice, this form of economic thinking has been disastrous for the world and has been found to be inadequately equipped to deal with an international pandemic.

It's the worst kind of political thinking even at the best of times, and it's apparent there is a group of people in government incapable of working out effective solutions because it's not within their ideological purview or political motivations to develop solutions that don't fit into their model of reducing the role of government at any expense.

This is a government that has the member for Hughes, Craig Kelly, among its ranks:[104] for sure, he is a backbencher for the Liberal Party, but has been pushing pro-conspiracy messages through his social media platforms about anti-vaccination, attacks on China, world domination by the United Nations and other theories more in tune with the QAnon conspiracy group. An inspection of Kelly's background prior to politics—a furniture salesman, a retailer and a director of a bankrupted business—should call into question his suitability for Parliament. Certainly, Parliament should be made up of a broad representation of society, but a character such as Kelly? James Paterson in Victoria: plucked from obscurity as a writer for the Victorian Employers' Chamber of Commerce and Industry before joining the Institute of Public Affairs as editor of the *IPA Review*, fills a casual vacancy in Senate in 2016. These are credentials for entering Parliament? Surely the Liberal Party can do better than this.

Political parties will generally promote the players they feel will be able to fulfil the agenda of that party, without pushback or

---

104 Craig Kelly resigned from the Liberal Party in February 2021, after repeatedly posting material about unproven coronavirus treatments on social media, and will be sitting on the crossbench as an independent member of Parliament.

questioning of the actions of that political party. And whether there is a real agenda or not, recycling old news to look like there is an agenda is a standard ruse in the political playbook: all political parties use this tactic.

The NSW Labor Party was in government for sixteen years between 1995–2011 and made a habit of announcing the development of a rail network in the north-western region of Sydney. In 2005, then Premier Bob Carr announced the development of the North West Rail Link. This was followed by a re-announcement of the project by Carr's replacement, Morris Iemma, in 2006, with yet another re-announcement in 2007. After Iemma was replaced by Nathan Rees in 2008, another re-announcement followed—this time rebadged as the North West Metro—with a promise to commit $4 billion to the project. After Rees was forced to resign and replaced by Kristina Keneally, another announcement was made in 2010.

Five announcements over five years by four different premiers, which essentially was the same project re-announced, rebadged and made to look as though a government was fulfilling its obligations and taking action. Ironically, it was the incoming NSW Liberal–National Coalition that actually implemented the project and the Sydney Metro Northwest scheme finally opened in 2019. Was there any political benefit to NSW Labor for continuously recycling old news and make re-announcements of major infrastructure projects? It's difficult to establish a clear link, although the NSW Labor Party did manage to win the 2007 NSW election, before being thrown out in a crushing loss in the 2011 NSW election, so perhaps it is fair to suggest there are positives and negatives in adopting such a brazen political tactic.

And the current federal government is using exactly the same strategy: the pre-announcement, the announcement of the announcement, and then, if the public is fortunate enough, the actual announcement of the project. At least in the case of the NSW Labor Government and their north-west rails links, there were different faces to make the announcement look and feel different, but the federal government uses the same people, the same ministers and, of course, the same Prime Minister. The announcements about the vaccine and the 'gas-led recovery': over several months, the key parts of the agenda are exactly the same—there are slightly different words or a minor change in the progress of the arrangement. In the case of the vaccine announcements, an early announcement of a 'letter of intent' with AstraZeneca, moved into an announcement of 'a deal' to provide vaccines. In the absence of a vaccine, either a letter of intent or a deal to manufacture a vaccine are essentially the same but the government decided it was best to extract as much publicity from this event as possible.

Does the public take much notice of the details of the previous announcements? Or even the current announcements? And is there a risk of oversaturating the audience with constant announcements that are not dissimilar to previous ones, and making the public think: 'hasn't the government already resolved that issue? Why are we hearing about it again?'.

Recycling of news and projects is a symbol of a tired government. The Liberal–National Coalition has been in office for seven years, although Morrison has only been prime minister for just over two years. All governments have a certain shelf-life and after they've achieved whatever it is they need to achieve, they look at easier ways of extending that shelf-life and the easier option is to keep up with the re-announcements and recycling of old ideas. And this relates to the motivations of governments, political parties and prime ministers: what is the purpose of government? Is it to implement worthwhile projects, implement agendas, or hold onto power for the sake of keeping an opponent out? After all, the prime motivation for 89 per cent of Liberal Party members, according to a 2014 survey, is "keeping Labor out".[105]

Power, in itself, is an insatiable aphrodisiac and prime ministers are removed from office or they die in office, as did John Curtin and Joe Lyons. Only two prime ministers in Australian history have resigned on their own terms: Andrew Fisher in 1915 and Robert Menzies in 1966. The British politician and author, Enoch Powell, suggested all political careers end in failure and even in the case of Menzies, he had been pressured to resign as prime minister, so his resignation wasn't as altruistic as it seemed.

---

105 *The Guardian*, 'Keeping Labor out: does the Liberal party stand for anything else?', Norman Abjorensen, 13 May 2014. https://www.theguardian.com/commentisfree/2014/may/13/keeping-labor-out-does-the-liberal-party-stand-for-anything-else

The duration of a prime minister also depends on the collective amnesia of the public, and of the media. Morrison has been in the position since August 2018 and although he's been in Parliament since 2007, there's still a lack of a deeper understanding of who Morrison is. He's difficult to define, in a political sense and when looking at this record prior to entering Parliament—essentially, roles in tourism, property management and marketing—there's not much there in terms of political thought, or intellectual interests or pursuits. Looking at the history of Australian prime ministers, most have been well credentialled, well known, and had a substantial public profile before becoming the leader, either within legal circles or the union movement: Morrison's resumé in comparison, is quite insubstantial.

Over the past fifty years, the least credentialled prime minister was William McMahon, whose ambitions far outstripped his talents, and a series of missteps and foolishness by his predecessor, John Gorton, resulted in McMahon stepping into the leadership. At the state level, there are many similarities between Morrison and former Queensland Premier, Joh Bjelke-Petersen, who used raw power, abuse, media manipulation and management to remain in office for nineteen years, only forced out of office after the findings of the Fitzgerald Inquiry into police corruption were released, resulting in his criminal trial over perjury.

Morrison seems to be curious about a hold on power and incurious about most other matters, and the process of announcement and re-announcement seems to be a key tool in maintaining that power. Perhaps during a time of pandemic, the electorate is taking a closer look at the events currently occurring in the political domain but the repetition of key policy matters that affects the public good is a cynical exercise that creates confusion within the community, and purely attempts to achieve an unwarranted benefit for the government.

*

Chaos and corruption in the Coalition

24 September

The leader of the NSW National Party John Barilaro—who is also the Deputy Premier of New South Wales—has taken four weeks of mental health leave, after threatening to dismantle the NSW Liberal–National Coalition over koala protection legislation, and there was another NSW National Party member of Parliament, Leslie Williams, who has resigned from the party and registered an application to join the NSW Liberal Party.

The National Party still attracts votes in federal and state elections across Australia, although they do not field candidates in every seat, which is a logical outcome for a political party focused on the interests of farmers and regional areas. But it seems the organisation is moribund and attracting the wrong type of person. Michael McCormack is the federal leader of the National Party, the member for New England, Barnaby Joyce, is constantly providing interference and trying to reclaim the leadership he lost in 2017. Senator Bridget McKenzie was forced to resign as a minister following the issues ensuing from the infamous 'sports rorts' debacle. What is the future for the National Party if low-calibre people are attracted to its parliamentary ranks?

These are the issues within the party, but now there is competition from outside: the Shooters, Fishers & Farmers Party and One Nation are providing the National Party with competition in the areas of the Riverina and Northern Tablelands of New South Wales, as are regional Greens. The Nationals have always been a collection of spivs, con artists and failed farmers which, on occasions, has had substantial figures such as Tim Fischer, John 'Black Jack' McEwen, Earle Page and Ian Sinclair. But these figures have been few and far between, and it would be difficult to place either McCormack or Joyce on the same pedestal.

A former National Party member of the New South Wales Parliament, who became an independent member of federal Parliament, Rob Oakeshott, recently commented that the koala protection legislation Barilaro was opposed to didn't have anything to do with marsupials, it was about protecting developers, and the National Party hadn't done anything substantial to defend farmers or farming lands for well over sixty years.[106] Wal Murray, the leader of the NSW Nationals in the early 1990s, was perhaps the last leader to effectively represent farming interests, even if it was simply to make a few minor amendments to market regulations.

Joyce was a suburban accountant in the Queensland town of St George before entering Parliament. The current member for Dawson, George Christensen was a failed publisher, with his business entities folding in 2013, before he entered federal politics. With the right networking and manoeuvring, they were able to leverage themselves into positions of power and influence, despite not having any obvious abilities, motivations or belief in what they thought would be best for the community or the country: politics for both of them was an option of last resort.

These are the calibre of candidates attracted to the National Party. The party receives around 6 per cent of the vote around Australia and only has a voter base in two states, New South Wales and Queensland, with some lesser support in Victoria. While it may seem that it's a party that's floundering, it's difficult to dismiss a long-established political entity, irrespective of the quality of leadership, or the external influences that may be affecting its level of electoral support. The issues affecting the Coalition in New South Wales are damaging to both the National and Liberal parties but it has to be

---

[106] *Brisbane Times*, 'To understand Barilaro's koala implosion you need to understand where power truly lies in regional NSW', Rob Oakeshott, 12 September 2020. https://www.brisbanetimes.com.au/politics/nsw/to-understand-barilaro-s-koala-implosion-you-need-to-understand-where-power-truly-lies-in-regional-nsw-20200910-p55uhw.html

remembered the next federal election isn't due until 2022 and the next NSW state election isn't due until 2023: whatever is happening on the ground right now might not have too much influence in a distant future.

Barilaro has been a controversial figure in New South Wales politics, and in 2017 called for Prime Minister Malcolm Turnbull to resign as a "Christmas gift to Australians". However, he displayed a level of political naïvety to suggest he could remove his confidence in the Premier, Gladys Berejiklian, as a Coalition partner, and still retain seats and positions in Cabinet—a completely unworkable arrangement. This is one of the basic tenets of the Westminster system, where positions within Cabinet depend on supporting the leader of the government, and the government itself: otherwise, governments falls apart when Cabinet solidarity is lacking. He also considered running as a candidate in the recent Eden–Monaro byelection, without thinking through the full ramifications of this decision, both in terms of how it would affect the National Party federally, and in New South Wales. He now remains within the NSW Coalition, but his trustworthiness within that arrangement must surely be diminished.

There are other matters in New South Wales that will put pressure on the Liberal–National Coalition and it's the evidence of corrupt behaviour within the federal government. The Commonwealth purchased twelve hectares of land in western Sydney from the Leppington Pastoral Company for $29.8 million, for which the Australian National Audit Office declared is valued at only $3.1 million, which means the federal government paid almost ten times the actual value of the land. The land was acquired for the Western Sydney Airport Corporation but won't be required until 2050. And if this wasn't unscrupulous enough, it was discovered that the Leppington Pastoral Company is a substantial donor to the Liberal Party: $58,800 in 2018/19, and $149,000 donated over the past eighteen years.

Scott Morrison promised his government would create a national corruption commission but, two years later, the public is still waiting. And with the revelations of the Leppington land deal, there might be a clearer understanding for why this commission has been delayed for so long. In the field of land acquisition, if a government is intent on purchasing essential property for industrial or building purposes, there could be argument to offer above-market rates to secure the property. Governments hold all the cards when it comes to forcing prices down and seeking the prices it wishes to pay for a purchase, rather than fair prices, as many residents would attest to when forced to sell their properties to the NSW Government for the WestConnex project in Sydney's inner west region.

Whether the amount was offered or negotiated has resulted in a poor deal for the Australian taxpayer and perhaps a deal of two or three times over the market value could be deemed to be acceptable. But ten times over market value? There is no utility or value in that, and it seems that it's an obvious act of blatant corruption, and certainly an area a national corruption commission could investigate. It's not corruption in the style of brown paper bags from the era of NSW Premier Robert Askin, or Queensland Premier Bjelke-Petersen: this is far more severe, far more pervasive, and performed in full view of the bureaucracy and at the stroke of a pen, rather than the rustling of wads of cash delivered in secrecy in late night locations.

While it took a series of Royal Commissions in those states to uncover this level of corruption, it seems the current brand of politicians in government has a failure of understanding of how the democratic system is meant to function, and are more concerned about the engagement of stakeholders and providing good outcomes to them, rather than good governance or working out what is in the interests of the public.

In 2003, the former Prime Minister, Tony Abbott, failed to explain where $100,000 in cash came from, ironically raised for his Australians for Honest Politics Trust, used to bankroll a political campaign against Pauline Hanson in 1998.[107] The instructions from Liberal Party elders were to put whatever cash he received into the trust, because it wouldn't be considered corrupt anymore, and whatever funds were received, he'd obtain benefit in other ways, mainly political. And this seems to be the mode of the Liberal Party: don't ask, don't tell, and the sands of time will help to wash away the memory of anything improper. The Minister with oversight for

---

107 ABC *AM*, 'Abbott linked with trust fund set up to fight One Nation', 26 August 2003. https://www.abc.net.au/am/content/2003/s931965.htm

the Leppington land deal, Paul Fletcher, has claimed he didn't know anything at all about the deal—this may actually be the case, but whatever happened to ministerial responsibilities? They have all but disappeared.

Good business deals and good governance doesn't result in a purchase price of ten times the value of the asset. Standards of propriety have been lacking in this deal and it would not have occurred had there been proper oversight, or at least an ethical understanding of contracts and deals made out in the public interest. It's yet another shocking example of corrupt actions without any institutional backlash or anyone being held responsible for poor decisions, an issue a national corruption commission would have been able to uncover—if one existed.

*

The NBN revisited

24 September

The National Broadband Network has been beset with so many difficulties ever since the Liberal–National Coalition decided to dump Labor's full fibre-to-the-premises plan and implement its own version in 2013, combining fibre-to-the-node, fibre-to-the-premises, hybrid fibre-coaxial and fixed wireless technology. The NBN is not so much an example of corruption—although there is some evidence to suggest the Coalition's version was implemented to mainly appease the interests of Rupert Murdoch[108]—but one of ineptitude and mismanagement, where a major piece of essential digital infrastructure was debased and used as a political playtool.

In keeping with this government's penchant for making announcements that are misleading and inaccurate, it has made a ministerial declaration that the rollout of NBN will be completed by December 2020, even though almost four million premises—25 per cent of total premises—will not be connected by that time, and with no timeline for when these premises will be finally connected to the NBN. Although it's clear the NBN project has yet to be completed, the federal government has announced they will now spend $3.5 billion to upgrade the system to a full-fibre network, which was the system Labor had proposed and commenced in 2011.

---

108 *The Conversation*, 'News Corp Australia vs the NBN – is it really all about Foxtel?', Emma Dawson, 8 August 2013. https://theconversation.com/news-corp-australia-vs-the-nbn-is-it-really-all-about-foxtel-16768

This decision—announced by the Minister for Communications, Paul Fletcher—is an acknowledgement by the Coalition that their hybrid system was a waste of time and money, and the original scheme proposed and implemented by Labor was the correct course of action. For the past seven years, many experts in the technology field had called on the government to implement a full fibre network, but they proceeded with the flawed model: so far, the government has spent $51 billion[109] for a flawed second-rate model, while Labor's original plan was costed at $45 billion.[110] In addition, there have been lost revenues and reduced productivity with the slower internet speeds and the world ranking for Australia's broadband is number sixty-one, and the average speed of 56 Mbps[111] is around one-third of the average broadband speed from the top twenty countries, 165 Mbps.

It has also been interesting to see the media reporting of this $3.5 billion, welcoming the news, rather than offering an analysis on how this is a complete about-face by the federal government, and how they are moving towards a policy that they previously rejected and used as a political blowtorch against the Labor Party for waste and mismanagement, even though the NBN has been a seriously mismanaged project by the Coalition, the cost has blown out substantially for a far inferior product and even more funds will now be spent on the project to correct the errors of the past.

Some of this motivation can be linked backed to the interests of Murdoch and News Corporation who would have considered online competitors such as Netflix and Stan—via a very fast broadband—a serious threat to their business model, especially after their efforts to build the pay television market in the early 1990s only would have started turning profits in the mid-2010s. The pay television model in Australia never reached the same levels of success as the cable version in the United States. News Corporation recently recorded

---

109 ABC News, 'NBN budget revised up again to $51 billion as higher costs and slower revenue bite', Peter Ryan, 31 August 2018. https://www.abc.net.au/news/2018-08-31/nbn-cost-revised-up-to-51-billion-dollars/10187108

110 *The Monthly*, 'What happened to broadband in Australia?', Micheal Quigley, March 2019. https://www.themonthly.com.au/issue/2019/march/1551445200/michael-quigley/what-happened-broadband-australia

111 World Population Review, Internet Speeds by Country 2020. https://worldpopulationreview.com/country-rankings/internet-speeds-by-country

a trading loss of $US1.5 billion, and the Foxtel service recorded a decline of 14 per cent in revenue, and a loss of 200,000 subscribers between March and June 2020.[112] It's a failing business model. Perhaps Murdoch has given up hope on continuing to recoup the costs of the original infrastructure rollout of Foxtel services in the 1990s—those unsightly thick black wires half-way up traditional telegraph poles—and decided News Corporation's own interests are best served through a full-fibre network.

The great shame here is that the Coalition could have continued with Labor's original full-fibre network, rebranded it, and claimed the scheme as its own. And by now, Australia would have had a world-class, top-ten internet broadband system and gained a competitive international economic advantage in the delivery of digital services, especially during times of lockdown and large-scale work-from-home and telecommuting. As it stands, Australia possesses a failing system that is more expensive and there are no guarantees that the additional spending of $3.5 billion will be sufficient, or a promised delivery date of 2023 will be achieved.

The only way to upgrade the NBN to full-fibre is to retrieve the old copper wiring—as well as the new copper wiring that was only recently installed—and install fibre optic cabling. Given that it has taken seven years to arrive at this point of a full rollout—even though these claims are dubious—reinstalling cabling all across Australia within a two-year timetable, and at a fraction of the original cost, seems highly unrealistic.

*

---

112 *The Guardian*, 'News Corp posts US$1.5bn loss driven by sharp declines in newspaper revenue', Christopher Knaus, 7 August 2020. https://www.theguardian.com/media/2020/aug/07/news-corp-posts-15bn-loss-driven-by-sharp-declines-in-newspaper-revenue

Unrealistic Budget expectations and lost opportunities

6 October

The first Budget of the Morrison government, elected way back in May 2019, has been released, and it's also the first federal Budget since the coronavirus pandemic commenced. Treasurer Josh Frydenberg's Budget will run at a massive deficit of $213 billion and even that figure is based on a number of key assumptions: a coronavirus vaccine fully implemented before October 2021; all internal borders within Australia opened, and the economy growing by 4.25 per cent in 2021, a figure that wasn't even achieved during the last mining boom and a figure that hasn't been reached since 1999—over twenty-one years ago.

There's no question about the Morrison government needing to spend money during this pandemic but despite the large amounts of funds available to them, there will be many people left behind within this Budget: there are tax cuts for people on higher incomes but not much for lower-income families or the unemployed; there's not much enthusiasm for women, childcare and early education; and the Higher Education Contribution Scheme fees for humanities courses at universities will double.

The Morrison government has been adamant about the 'snap-back' economy returning to the way it was performing before the coronavirus pandemic commenced but new economic thinking is needed to deal with the challenges of the future, not the old neoliberalist ways that haven't been able to support economies around the world during a time of crisis.

Several months ago, Frydenberg mentioned he was going to find inspiration from former British Prime Minister Margaret Thatcher and US President Ronald Reagan—this was ridiculed at the time but perhaps his intentions were serious. The problem for Australia is that Frydenberg might not hold the intellectual capacity to realise the flaws in the economic systems espoused by Thatcher and Reagan, systems that have been well tested for the last forty years and have been found wanting. The neoliberalist economic thinking excludes too many people; it enriches non-productive people; it encourages corruption; it encourages poor government; and it encourages the breakdown of necessary social services. It doesn't fit Frydenberg's agenda to accept this.

And providing this kind of analysis is not about adopting a 'right wing' versus 'left wing' perspective. Viewed objectively, conservative politics encompasses some very good ideas that, if applied correctly, can work well for the economy—the idea of individual and small-scale entrepreneurship is an area that should be encouraged, but this is a government that focuses on the other end of the economy: the areas of established money, power structures and the *nouveau riche*, based on non-productive economic models.

This Budget deficit of $213 billion, ultimately, will result in a $966 billion in national government debt, or 44 per cent of gross domestic product—it is a large figure but far more manageable when compared with other economies in the OECD, which hover between 50 per cent and 150 per cent of debt-to-GDP.

And there will be a change in the media dynamics about 'debts and deficits', accusations the Liberal–National Coalition levelled at the Labor Party for well over a decade after the global financial crisis. After all, it's a difficult argument to sustain if the Coalition is primarily responsible for this high level of national debt.

Two-thirds of this $966 billion of national government debt was accrued before the start of the pandemic, and the rate of debt grew dramatically after the Liberal–National Party returned to government in 2013, even with the onset of a lower-interest rate environment. And, of course, the government will try to use the pandemic to excuse these figures, but the poor economic performance preceded the pandemic.

Budgets in Australia are always highly political documents and they do have to boost confidence in the economy, especially at this particular point of time in history. But the Budget also has to target spending and stimulus in the areas that need it the most, and this one doesn't focus the money in the right areas.

When the coronavirus pandemic commenced in Australia, the federal government did say there was going to be a 'non-ideological' approach to economic and physical wellbeing for the population. But this is a very ideological Budget. It's an uncreative Budget. It's a Budget that's looking backwards to emulate the business models of the past, and the economy of the recent past, when all indicators are suggesting that new economic thinking needs to be implemented at this time. And in an act that has all the hallmarks of payback from student politics, the Budget has announced humanities courses at universities will triple in cost—$14,000 in HECS fees each year, and $42,000 for the standard three-year degree.

This decision has been couched within the notion of the government wanting prospective students to consider 'jobs-focused' courses such as science, nursing, teaching or mathematics—which is not the traditional function of universities. What will the prospective humanities student do if they have no experience at all in science or nursing, or lack the skills or desire to become a teacher? It seems to be an ill-thought out proposal, which won't have the intended effects, and leave a generation of students with a much higher debt when they graduate from university. It's also ironic the Minister for Education, Dan Tehan, possesses degrees only within humanities—but has now decided it's time to pull the drawbridge behind him and make these courses prohibitively expensive.

Generally, universities are not so much about training graduates up to an industry standard, they are more about conceptual development, critical and higher-level thinking, and the acquisition of skills transferable from one industry sector to another. This is based around contemporary educational thought that ensures students are not necessarily equipped with the skills required to perform in industry positions immediately after they graduate, but be able to adapt to industries of the future and skills-sets that haven't even been thought of yet.

Of course, the substantial increase in the HECS fees for humanities courses is only a minor component of the Budget, but it provides an insight into this government's political thinking and in contrast to its insistence of a 'non-ideological' approach; if anything, it has actually increased its ideological attacks on those groups that are traditionally hostile to conservative governments.

These HECS measures are not going to raise revenue for the government, and it may not necessarily push more prospective students into 'jobs-focused' courses. Again, it shows more about the ideological positioning of this government and, despite the economic and social circumstances, will always use any opportunity to engage in cultural warfare against imaginary enemies.

These measures also provide an insight into some of the other players in politics, including the Centre Alliance, who wholeheartedly supported these higher education measures, in conjunction with One Nation. And it's also instructive to see what the Centre Alliance received in return for their support. Within the Senate, Senators and political parties always need to go through a trading process with the government, where all sides negotiate and decide which areas of policy they can relinquish, in return for additional funds for their state, or a change of policy in another area.

But the Centre Alliance provided everything the government wanted with its HECS reforms and virtually received nothing in return. Centre Alliance achieved a 3.5 per cent growth in places for South Australian universities—which isn't a large increase—but the government's proposal included a 2.5 per cent increase across Australia. Although they also requested guarantees for failing students in South Australia to be exempt from penalties in units they've failed, and a reinstatement of the 10 per cent discount for upfront HECS payments—a system that benefits students from higher-income families—Centre Alliance effectively approved the government's HECS reforms in exchange of an 1 per cent increase in university places for South Australia.

There are similarities between the Central Alliance of today, and the Australian Democrats in 2000, where their leader at the time, Meg Lees, negotiated the introduction of the Howard government's

GST scheme—against the majority of her party—and agreed to what she considered to be 'a good deal'.

Within two years of making this deal, Lees was overthrown as the leader of the Australian Democrats, started the slow demise of the party and, by the end of 2007, the party no longer had representation in federal parliament.

The support from the Centre Alliance for the Liberal Party, however, should not come as a surprise. Rebekha Sharkie is the most prominent member of the Centre Alliance—she is currently the member for the Adelaide seat of Mayo, but was previously a member of the Liberal Party, and a former staffer for state Liberal leader, Isobel Redmond; federal Liberal Party member Jamie Briggs—who she actually defeated in the 2016 federal election—and state Liberal member, Rachel Sanderson. Perhaps Sharkie is not as independent as she'd like to think, and hasn't really forgotten her origins in the Liberal Party.

But the key factor is, that this increase to HECS fees for humanities is just a small financial issue, especially in the context of the overall Budget. Including all the 2020 Budget measures and other amounts agreed to in Parliament, this Liberal–National government will have $385 billion at its disposal for recovery measures for stimulus packages. That is a massive amount of money that has never been made available to any previous government, and provides an opportunity for this government to totally restructure the economy.

Frydenberg, however, does not seem to have the intellectual firepower or the economic thought processes to think creatively about where the economy could be over the next decade or so, and is so securely fixated on returning the economy to a pre-COVID-19 state. And this inability to focus on the possibilities of the future means conservative governments will continue to be wedded to a system that provides opportunities for a small number of corporate supporters.

The reason Australia hasn't embraced renewables as much as it should have is because companies such as Fortescue Metals, Hancock Mining and Rio Tinto benefit from the status quo, and they support the Liberal Party through direct donation, and promotion through think tanks such as the Institute of Public Affairs. The symbiotic relationship between conservative governments and corporations has kept money where it has notionally been for over 200 years in Australia. But economies do have to move on with the flow of history, and it's quite possible Australia's economy could be left behind.

Federal Budgets in Australia are usually received with great fanfare in the media, and it's almost like the business community's version of Christmas: there's great anticipation throughout the Budget lock-up, where journalists hand over their laptops and mobile phones and scan through the line items and policy implications, followed by the euphoria when the treasurer rises to speak in Parliament on Budget evening.

However, Budgets are normally here today, and gone by tomorrow. They do provide impetus for the government of the day and navigate an economic pathway for next twelve months and beyond, but they're usually forgotten about politically within few weeks' time. The most important factor for the 2020 Budget is how is the government going to sustain the economy into the future and keep it from collapsing? And what will happen with stimulus support after the JobKeeper program expires in March 2021?

Ideologically, conservative governments are opposed to this kind of stimulus program, and it will be interesting to see what happens or what replaces the JobKeeper program, but we can only assume that it will need to continue for some time into the future, if the economy hasn't picked up by the first quarter of 2021.

Although this Budget is largely on track with the government's ideological pursuits, and is a missed opportunity to create economic conditions more suited to the circumstances, there are other issues that may cause problems for the economy. For example, the Budget assumes a coronavirus vaccine will be available and implemented by October 2021. Certainly, it appears the vaccine will become available in the earlier part of 2021—a remarkable effort if this eventuates—but if the vaccine is effective, then there needs to be a method for manufacturing and distributing it in the most economically viable manner, and there's also the question of an intersection between competitive politics, finances and the pharmaceutical industry. Would it be technically possible to import or manufacture and distribute enough vaccines for every person in Australia by October 2021, even if the coronavirus vaccine did become available in early 2021? To vaccinate the entire Australian population of over 25 million people means around 3 million vaccinations per month, or 100,000 per day. And the cheaper AstraZeneca vaccine earmarked for most of the population requires two doses: these are large numbers but perhaps the government decided to get the political spin and benefit from the announcements in advance and worry about the practicalities when the time arrives, hoping the electorate will have forgotten about what was actually promised.

The full implementation of the coronavirus vaccination program by October 2021 is not unrealistic, but it is best to be cautious with Budget estimates that are based on the availability of something that has never been achieved before in human history, or a vaccination program that has never been implemented: there are so many roadblocks and peripheral factors that could stand in the way.

The other factor the Budget is widely optimistic about is the prediction of 4.25 per cent growth in GDP, figures last achieved in 1999, when the annual growth in GDP was 5 per cent. The growth rate in the March 2020 quarter—before the effects of the pandemic commenced—was -0.3 per cent, and then fell to -7.0 per cent in the July 2020 quarter.

Economies can rebound significantly after pulling out of a recession and boosting productivity, but the Australian economy is still in a recession and it's difficult to see when it is likely to pull out of this recession. Economics and budget forecasting is based on assumptions, but achieving a growth rate of 4.25 per cent within six-to-seven months is a heroic assumption, and many Australian economists agree with this sentiment, including economists such as Chris Richardson from Deloitte Access Economics and Jo Masters from EY.[113,114]

And the prospect of achieving 4.25 per growth has to be viewed relative to the performances of the past three treasurers—Joe Hockey, Scott Morrison and Frydenberg—who have presided over a long period of low economic growth since 2013. Overall, this Budget is a lost opportunity, at a time when the Australian economy

---

113 EY, July Fiscal Update: A Rock and a Hard Place, Jo Masters, 23 July 2020. https://www.ey.com/en_au/economics/july-budget-update

114 *The Canberra Times*, 'The 'super-heroic' assumptions underpinning the budget update,' Katie Burgess, 23 July 2020. https://www.canberratimes.com.au/story/6845969/the-super-heroic-assumptions-underpinning-the-budget-update

has to develop every opportunity available to it. It's based on some unrealistic assumptions—which may end up becoming reality—but it's essentially what a gambling addict might do if they're feeling lucky after some big losses at the casino.

Ultimately, there's a strong possibility it will cost the government a great deal more political skin than they've already lost.

*

Albanese and his Budget Reply

6 October

The Budget week in federal politics is all about the national numbers and finances but it's also a week steeped in politics and perceptions, and so it was with the Budget Reply, a tradition where the Leader of the Opposition can provide an alternative economic vision to the nation. Budgets are important documents for the future of a government and the Budget Reply speech for opposition leaders is also important, but in a far different way: it's not so much about numbers or even the economic ideas they might be presenting—they're not in government and their responsibilities are quite different.

Depending on the circumstances and the political cycle, it's usually about shoring up their leadership, offering a blueprint for change when they do return to government but also providing hope to other members of Parliament within their political party and their supporters in the electorate. It's usually a difficult task, even if they're performing well politically.

The leader of the Labor Party, Anthony Albanese, hasn't been performing so well since the coronavirus pandemic commenced, and his Budget Reply was an attempt to reverse those fortunes, a speech which focused upon Labor values, areas such as universal childcare and a focus on reforming the national energy grid, which has been beset by problems for many years. It was a competent Budget Reply: it ticked all the boxes of Labor values but it didn't seem to have the media sparkle or the salient moments the public could easily latch onto.

The 2020 year has been most unusual but time does not wait, even during a pandemic—this term of Parliament has almost reached its half-way point and 2021 could also see an early election—will the Budget Reply provide an impetus for Labor to work towards the next election and shut down Albanese's critics? This Budget Reply will be well forgotten by the time of the next election—as will the next Budget Reply, if there does happen to be one before the date of the next election—but the Labor Party needs to start gaining some much-needed traction.

Albanese has at least enervated some within the Labor movement and there were many who were very impressed with how he performed in his Budget Reply, claiming that the 'Albo of fighting Tories' seemed to be invigorated. Being in opposition is always difficult and can be made easier with fair and balanced reporting from the media, which the Labor Party doesn't get a lot of, and when it does, it's usually negative. For example, it seems every time the former New South Wales minister jailed for historical child sex offences, Milton Orkopoulos, is mentioned in the media, he is branded as an ex-Labor politician—and, that's fair enough, that's what he was—but when there's a scandal on the Liberal or Nationals side, they are usually only referred to as a 'politician', without the party identified. Of course, that's not the only reason why life in opposition is difficult for the Labor Party, but the media certainly doesn't help.

On the surface, Labor does have some very impressive members of Parliament—it's too early to suggest how promising they might be because this is an issue that tends to sort itself out once a party is in government: those that seem to perform well in opposition don't necessarily perform in the same manner once they need to deal with ministerial pressures and responsibilities of governing. But the basis of a good parliamentary team is there—whether there is enough 'cut-through' with the media and the public is a different matter.

The Australian political system has been stuck in a quagmire for some time and the generational restructuring of political parties that naturally seems to occur every twenty or thirty years is well overdue. The world now is quite different to how it was in 1990, and different forms of political thinking and economic philosophies are required for 2020 and beyond. The speed of modern politics is intense and with all sides of politics aspiring to win the next election, which is always a maximum of three years away, the structural reforms that need to occur to improve the system are unlikely to happen.

And a Budget Reply speech is going to be far more modest than attempting to reform a political party, or the political system but it does has to offer at least the basics to enthuse the public and the media. The focus of Albanese's Budget Reply was universal childcare, and a proposal to fund 90 per cent of all childcare and early education costs—so it's not actually 'universal' but it is close.

The sector, overall, is well managed and regulated through the National Quality Standards that were introduced in 2012 but the funding of early education and childcare all across Australia has been dysfunctional for well over two decades, commencing in 1997 when the Howard government removed direct operational subsidies to children's services. There is a funding mix between three tiers of government: local councils in some preschools; state/territory governments and federal governments, subsidies, payments made to parents, some subsidies made to directly to children's services. It probably would be better to restart the funding process and rethink the sector, with the end result being the attachment of early education to the primary school sector. That would seem to be the better outcome.

Childcare and access to early education is highly expensive across Australia yet, ironically, frontline workers in the sector are on the most lowly-paid salaries. There are many other expenses to take into account, such building rent and maintenance, and the cost of providing the best educational programs possible. But the major problem here is the majority of the sector is privately owned and managed, with some early education providers listed on the stock exchange: it's an essential social service that shouldn't be in private and for-profit hands in such a manner—if primary or secondary schools were managed in the same way, there would be a public backlash about profiteering from children's education. For issues of fairness, access and equity—and the ability to apply standards across Australia—early education should be brought under full government control, and Albanese was right push forward the idea of universal access for the sector. It won't stop the profiteering at this stage, but it's a good start.

One other area Albanese focused upon within his Budget Reply speech was streamlining the national energy and electricity grid—it's not to nationalise the grid but create a system that will harness all energy sources, including renewable energies, and melding them into a more efficient network, estimated to deliver $40 billion worth of benefits for the Australian economy. This was delivered as a response to the federal government's mismanagement of energy supplies over the past seven years and its inability to develop any meaningful or comprehensive policy for the energy sector—its previous attempt with the National Energy Guarantee ended in failure in 2018, and fast-tracked the demise of former Prime Minister, Malcolm Turnbull.

Although the cost of childcare is an issue that affects many families around Australia, and energy prices can always be used to whip up a state of public frenzy, these two themes are relatively low-key. It's also essential to remember Budgets and Budget Reply speeches are political documents, although one deals with the realities of governing, the other deals with the aspirations of what an opposition hopes to achieve when they return to government, aspirations that are rarely enacted.

And the day-to-day aspects of politicking is never to going to be too far away. The Prime Minister has already labelled Albanese's Budget Reply as 'divisive', an ironic response, considering Morrison is one of the most divisive and destructive political leaders ever seen in Australia. Albanese's main points are universal childcare and reforming the national electricity grid—hardly issues that are 'divisive'.

But Morrison engages in classic psycho–political projection, applying every derisory and negative label to his opponents, almost resorting to childish taunts and schoolboy tactics, and these are labels that dovetail neatly into the projections pushed forward by News Corporation, Nine Network and Seven West Media. If Morrison can posit Albanese and the Labor Party as 'divisive', irrespective of whichever policy they propose, he can then present himself as a sensible centrist figure of unity, even though he is a public figure who thrives on division, argument and chaos. Will the public see through this? It's difficult to say at this stage, but elections are the events which provide answers to these questions.

With the Budget Reply, Albanese—and the Labor Party—have started to work their way towards a sustainable political and economic narrative. There are still low-level murmurings behind the scenes about whether Albanese will lead the Labor Party to the next election—and he more than likely will—unless factors against him change dramatically, and that always has to be possibility in politics. The only Labor leader to not lead the party into an election campaign was Simon Crean, leader between 2001–03. Will Albanese become the second?

As has been noted many times before, Labor is not performing poorly within published opinions polls but it is the question of whether the right team is in place that can communicate their political and economic narrative in a way that connects more clearly with the electorate. Does Labor need to sharpen their attacks on the federal government? There is so much material to work with on this government; there's corruption, there's mismanagement, there's poor ministerial performances. Despite the undoubted benefit of political incumbency during the coronavirus pandemic, there is a feeling Labor could be doing so much more.

In the week during the lead-up to Albanese's Budget Reply, there was speculation within the mainstream media that this is a 'make-or-break' moment for Albanese: it had to signal a turning point for the Labor Party where they had to start 'taking it up to the government' if they wanted to have a solid chance of winning the next federal election.

The media will run its own narrative according to conservative interests but the question has to be: eighteen months into the electoral term—what has the Labor Party been doing during this time and why has it taken it this long to start 'taking it up to the government'? That's not to suggest the opposition and its leadership has done nothing since they lost the election in May 2019 and, it has to be noted that being in opposition is difficult, but why wait until now before ramping up pressure on the federal government?

There is the old adage in Australian politics that oppositions don't win elections, governments lose them and, perhaps, this is Albanese's understanding of political history. It might have been a tactic for the federal government to fall over on its litany of mistakes, but it's been apparent Morrison has made many errors and mistakes during his time as prime minister and there have been few consequences, so the 'waiting-for-the-government-to-fall-over' strategy may have to be reconsidered.

After the perception that Labor went into the 2019 federal election with too many policies that could be used against them, they've viewed the three years between elections more cautiously than their supporters would want them to. Albanese has consistently mentioned he doesn't want to adopt the approach used by Tony Abbott in opposition, which was to attack, destroy and oppose everything and let the consequences fall in whichever way they can, which was electorally a successful strategy: Abbott became prime minister in 2013, even if it was only for two years. But at least he returned his party to government, which is the ultimate goal for the Leader of the Opposition.

It's unrealistic for a political party, and its leader, to maintain the energy from the first day of an election cycle all the way up to the day of the election, three years later. And using up all of meagre resources available to an opposition in the early days of the electoral cycle is not worthwhile: at the point of the next election, how many people in the electorate will remember or be influenced by the events in early 2019 or 2020? That is a point that has to considered, but the essence of an opposition is to oppose what the government is doing, point out the errors—in the case of this federal government, there are many—and provide semblance of hope to its supporter base.

The competence of the government is the key measure that is up for consideration at elections, and it is a combination of the lived reality of the electorate, and also the battle of perceptions between a government keen to promote itself as a model of excellence, and an opposition that needs to highlight all the deficiencies of its opponents and highlight its own virtues. It's a difficult task for an opposition, but its task becomes far more difficult if it becomes almost invisible and doesn't make an offering that the public can vote for.

*

The Morrison recession

6 October

The Australian economy is now officially in recession but there are many in the mainstream media keen to let everyone know this has been solely been caused by the coronavirus pandemic, even though all the evidence suggests Australia was careering towards a recession due to the poor economic management provided by the Liberal–National Coalition ever since they returned to office in 2013.

The economy was already in a per capita recession in late 2019 and reached negative growth for the March 2020 quarter after narrowly avoiding a negative quarter in December 2019. Many economists were predicting a recession was unavoidable[115,116,117] and these predictions were made a long time before the coronavirus hit in March this year. Yet, the Prime Minister has been doing his best to deflect from these issues, suggesting to the ABC's *7.30* program that his government has had nothing to do with the recession:

---

115 *MacroBusiness*, 'Australian recession is certain', David Llewellyn-Smith, 6 September 2019. https://www.macrobusiness.com.au/2019/09/australian-recession-is-certain
116 AMP Capital, 'The odds of Australia going into recession', Shane Oliver, 9 October 2019. https://www.ampcapital.com/au/en/insights-hub/articles/2019/october/the-odds-of-australia-going-into-recession
117 *The Conversation*, 'Buckle up. 2019-20 survey finds the economy weak and heading down, and that's ahead of surprises', Peter Martin, 30 June 2019. https://theconversation.com/buckle-up-2019-20-survey-finds-the-economy-weak-and-heading-down-and-thats-ahead-of-surprises-119455

Scott Morrison: This is the why we've designed the Budget the way we have. This is why we've done it at such a scale, we're dealing with an enormous challenge when it comes to the coronavirus recession, and the pandemic that caused it.

The ABC—which could assumed to have a better understanding of recent economic debates and discussions about an impending recession, especially taking into account they actually asked the question themselves in early February if the economy was heading towards a recession[118]—supported Morrison in his quest to erase his responsibilities, by pitching these thoughts to the economist, Andrew Charlton, on Budget night:

Leigh Sales: Anthony Albanese use the term, the 'Morrison recession' again tonight and we've heard him using that in recent weeks. Is anyone really going to buy that all of this is Scott Morrison's fault? What's the Opposition Leader hoping to achieve with that line?

And then claimed the Labor Party is insulting the intelligence of the Australian public: here is Sales questioning Labor leader, Anthony Albanese:

Sales: You've been using the term, the 'Morrison recession' recently, you used it again in your speech tonight. Australian's aren't stupid, they see what's happening globally, who do you believe thinks it's all Scott Morrison's fault?

The Australian recession which commenced in 1990 was rightly referred to as Paul Keating's recession: no one ever referred to it as the "recession of ten years of failed international neoliberal policies", even though that's what primarily caused that recession and the high interest rates at the time. Despite what Morrison and the Treasurer Josh Frydenberg are publicly saying—with the strong support coming from the media—the current failure of economic performance can be rightly labelled as the Morrison recession.

Prior to the onset of the coronavirus, the federal government was keen to use the moniker of 'the bushfire recession' before that became redundant. The bushfires weren't the driving factors behind this recession: that's not to downplay the impact of the bushfires

---
118 ABC *7.30*, 'Is Australia headed for recession?', 6 February 2020. https://www.abc.net.au/7.30/is-australia-headed-for-recession/11941342

which according to some economic analysts, caused $5 billion in direct losses, reduced economic growth by between 0.2 to 0.5 per cent and cost the economy $20 billion in lost output.[119] This added to the effects of the economic downturn, but they weren't the primary cause.

And it's the same issue with the pandemic: they've exacerbated the poor economic conditions and fast-tracked the recession that Australia was already facing anyway, bringing forward the recession in the March 2020 quarter, when it was otherwise likely to be reported in the June 2020 quarter. That's the only realistic difference—and in November 2019, before the full impact of the bushfires, Australia had already reported the technical conditions of a 'per-capita recession'.

In the field of politics, the use of labels essentially becomes an issue based around semantics. Morrison, Frydenberg and like-minded media reporters have been very quick to preface the poor economic outcome as 'the COVID recession' or 'the coronavirus recession', whereas the other side of politics is keen to use the label of 'the Morrison recession', and there will also be the argument about which term is more correct.

But a closer analysis suggests that while external factors have played a part in the current economic circumstances, the economy was very close to recession-like conditions despite these external factors. The gross domestic product for the March 2020 quarter fell by 0.3 per cent: the December 2019 quarter grew by only 0.5 per cent, even with a traditional Christmas consumer spending spree, while in the September 2019 quarter, the economy grew by 0.4 per cent. Many economists had predicted two consecutive negative growth quarters for September and December 2019 and were surprised when the figures released by the Australian Bureau of Statistics showed small levels of growth.

A recession is defined as two consecutive negative growth quarters, and the Australian economy narrowly avoided three consecutive quarters of negative growth. A 'per-capita recession' is not a frequently used term—defined as economic output per

---

[119] C&D Restructure and Taxation Advisory, 'Ongoing Economic and Socio-Economic Impacts of the Australian Bushfires', Craig Dangar, 5 February 2020. https://bit.ly/3cW0LXq

person, rather than the total economy, declining for two consecutive quarters—but it is a predictive measure that allows economists and governments know that the economy is in poor shape and drastic measures need to be taken to turn it around. In March 2019, the Australian economy was in a per-capita recession for the first time since 2006,[120] so there is a great deal of evidence to suggest the economy was flagging and in poor shape for some time before the coronavirus pandemic commenced.

While there may be some dispute about this issue, it's fair to use the term the 'Morrison recession', rather than the 'COVID recession'.

But economic issues within the field of politics, especially in contemporary politics, are usually contained within media management, fabrications and contortions of language. For many years, the Liberal–National Coalition has made the claim the former Labor Treasurer, Wayne Swan, had baked in long-term national debt because of the policies and actions he implemented during the time of the global financial crisis in 2008. These claims are unfounded, but whatever the debate might be about who created Australia's long-term national debt issues, Swan's actions meant Australia avoided a recession at the time, and stabilised the national economy.

But this type of commentary, and one usually supported by conservative commentators in the media, is part of the ongoing process of the Coalition constantly looking to outsource responsibilities and ensure that whatever problems they create becomes the fault of somebody else. And, in this context, it can be seen why Morrison and Frydenberg want to keep referring to the dire economic circumstances as the 'COVID recession'.

And it's a message reiterated through the media landscape, where problems are always caused by external factors: during 2019 when many economists were predicting a recession was just around the corner, Frydenberg kept on playing up the world economy as a cause for poor economic circumstances, and "there are storm clouds

---

120 *Sydney Morning Herald*, 'Australia falls into per-capita recession as growth tumbles', Eryk Bagshaw & Shane Wright, 6 March 2019. https://www.smh.com.au/business/the-economy/australia-falls-into-per-capita-recession-as-growth-tumbles-20190306-p5122r.html

hanging over the global economy"[121] that would severely affect economic growth and domestic output.

Of course, this is how the game of politics is played out. For the Liberal Party, when they're in government, the global economy and every external reason is provided as an excuse for their poor economic performance; when the Labor Party is in government, as they were during the global financial crisis, there is never an acceptance that international "storms clouds" cause domestic economic problems: it's always Labor's fault.

Ultimately, the electorate can see what's happening with their own eyes, and their perceptions of economic performance is lived through their own circumstances. And no amount of political spin and media massaging can cover that up. Unemployment figures are being well hidden through the JobKeeper program—some estimates suggest an official unemployment figure of 6.2 per cent may actually be as high as 15 per cent[122]—there are many people who would have been classified as 'unemployed' during any other severe economic change but at least during this crisis, they have been provided with adequate financial support.

But the main issue here relates to economic competence and management and it seems this is the wrong type of government at the wrong time in office, or at least a government that is not prepared to implement the right solutions for the time. And that always tends to be the case when there is a government in place that values political outcomes at a greater level to economic outcomes. These are short-term solutions that may provide political benefits within the short-term electoral cycle, but will cause more harm than good in the long-term future of the national economy.

The next federal election—whenever it is held—will be based around which party can provide the best economic direction for the future. The Liberal–National Coalition has incessantly blamed the Labor Party for the prevailing economic circumstances in the 2016 and 2019 elections. But by the time of the next election, the

---

121 Nine News, 'Strong economy needed to withstand storm', AAP, 21 January 2019. https://www.9news.com.au/national/strong-economy-needed-to-withstand-storm/47bd09fe-8294-4ddc-a5b7-1642908439a3

122 The Australia Institute, 'Australia's unemployment figures mask a deeper reality', Ebony Bennett, 18 May 2020. https://australiainstitute.org.au/post/australias-unemployment-figures-mask-a-deeper-reality/

Coalition will have been in office for nine years and, at some point, the electorate wises up to these political performances and starts to ask questions about what has this government done to benefit the long-term future of Australia?

Of course, blaming Labor is part of the conservative mantra of 'keep Labor out', which is the poorest excuse ever for a political party wishing to hold on to office. They will keep trying to apportion blame onto the Labor Party, but it's not going to work for a third consecutive election.

Treasurer Frydenberg is a consummate media performer but his economic performance is another matter entirely, with a perception from the business community that he's more interested in political matters, rather that economic factors. It's also reflective of the performances of the longest-serving treasurer, Peter Costello: in office for eleven years and presiding during a time of Australia's greatest mining boom. And as time progresses after Costello's tenure, which ended in 2007, the less impressive his reign becomes.

He established a Future Fund which is a mere minnow to other national wealth funds, such as the Norwegian and Alaskan funds— the Future Fund is valued at $168 billion, compared to the $1.5 trillion value of the Norwegian sovereign wealth fund. With a more sophisticated performance as Treasurer, Costello's tenure would have resulted in a more stable Australian currency, higher royalties from mining, lower land prices, and a more diversified industrial base.[123]

After he retired from politics—at the relatively young corporate age of fifty-two—it seems he wasn't rewarded with the plum job so many other former senior politicians arrive in. In the end, he ended up as the Chairman of the Nine Network, a slowly decaying legacy media company. While Frydenberg has only been in the position of treasurer for two years, it remains to be seen whether he'll squander Australia's economic opportunities in the same manner Costello did.

The Coalition will push forward the idea of 'superior economic management' in the lead-up to the next election, but with the national debt heading towards $1 trillion, it's unlikely it will have the same impetus as in previous elections.

---

123 Prosper Australia, 'Peter Costello's indefensible legacy', David Collyer, 22 March 2016, https://www.prosper.org.au/2016/03/peter-costellos-indefensible-legacy/

While it might be too early to commence commentary on the next election, there has been some speculation the government will run earlier than the full term of May 2022, due to a perception the economy is going to take a turn for the worst after the current levels of government stimulus and JobKeeper support end in March 2021. There's also a feeling that unlike the current circumstances where incumbent state and territory governments are receiving high electoral support, the call to 'rally-around-the-flag' and the slogan of 'we're all in this together' is beginning to wear thin—especially now there's a realisation that not everyone is in this together and the federal government is behaving in a highly politicised manner. At the time of the next election, incumbency might not be considered to be such a natural advantage.

Morrison still has high personal approval ratings—63 per cent according to the October *Essential Report*[124]—but that's not translating into overwhelming support for the Liberal–National Coalition, which is evenly split at 50:50 per cent with the Labor Party in the two-party preferred vote, compared to the 51.53 per cent recorded at the 2019 federal election.

Many political commentators, such as Peter van Onselen, are suggesting the Labor Party needs to write-off its chances at the next federal election,[125] suggesting "one seemingly immutable certainty is that Scott Morrison will win the next federal election" and needs to start preparing for the next election after that. And keeping to the standard political timetable, that would mean the 2025 election, and the result of this would be thirteen years of an incredibly incompetent and poorly managed government.

However, no election should be considered unwinnable, and it's not over until all the votes in that election have been counted and seats declared. Commentators always do look at the political horizon, consider the future and can't imagine how the circumstances can change. It was said immediately after the 2004 federal election that Prime Minister John Howard was going to remain in office for

---

124 *Essential Report*, 2020. https://essentialvision.com.au/category/essentialreport
125 *The Weekend Australian*, 'Scott Morrison could retire as a Liberal legend', Peter van Onselen, 19 December 2020. https://www.theaustralian.com.au/inquirer/scott-morrison-could-retire-as-a-liberal-legend/news-story/6ffd9c4f151109ddc2913ba688a6d5ff

another decade, due to his crushing election win over the Labor Party, led at that time by Mark Latham: Howard lost the next election in 2007.

It was also discussed prominently that Malcolm Turnbull would remain in office until the year 2031,[126] and "looks good for two or three election wins from here"[127] after he became prime minister in 2015, but went on to almost lose the 2016 federal election and was removed as leader of the Liberal Party in 2018.

Sometimes in politics, events can overtake convention political thinking and, especially since the return of the Liberal–National Coalition to government in 2013, there has to be an expectation that the most unpredictable of events can occur in politics, especially when they are least expected.

The current polls can't be trusted though, especially in the context of almost every political commentator suggesting the Labor Party was going to win the 2019 federal election, based on the preceding three years of polling confirming this was going to be the likely outcome. Those polls were incorrect, as they were in the 2015 Brexit referendum, and the 2016 United States Presidential election. Of course, opinion polls are accurate in determining current and past electoral behaviour, but not the future: it's only a predictive guide for the future and too many commentators placed too much trust in the veracity of opinion pollsters, and they were caught out.

It is a cliché and many politicians use it: the only poll that counts is the election. But the only electoral assessment that is available to the commentariat and the political parties in between elections is opinion polling, irrespective of how flawed their methodology is at the present time. The don't offer the full perspective and they don't mean everything, but they do mean something: it's up to those consumers of those polls to accurately reflect upon what they represent and, perhaps, that didn't occur in the lead-up to the 2019 election.

---

126 *Sydney Morning Herald*, 'Why Malcolm Turnbull will be our longest-serving PM since Robert Menzies', Elizabeth Farrelly, 25 November 2015. http://www.smh.com.au/comment/why-malcolm-turnbull-will-be-our-longestserving-pm-since-robert-menzies-20151125-gl7dy2.html

127 ABC News, 'Turnbull settles into his most acclaimed role yet', Marius Benson, 20 November 2015. http://www.abc.net.au/news/2015-11-20/benson-turnbull-settles-into-his-most-acclaimed-role-yet/6957220

Whenever the next federal election is held—the earliest a standard half-Senate election can be held is 7 August 2021 and the latest date is 21 May 2022—the results will be based on which side of politics presents the best political and economic narratives the electorate finds more believable and more acceptable to the circumstances of the times. And this also needs to take into account whether the electorate—despite what the media messaging is—looks back at this time and decides whether this is the 'COVID recession' or the 'Morrison recession'.

*

The continuing corruption in New South Wales

27 October

Historically, New South Wales has always been the centre of political corruption in Australia—it commenced with the Rum Corp that arrived with the Second Fleet in 1789; it was the home of Thomas 'Lemonade' Ley, the only swindler and murderer ever to sit in Parliament; there's the widespread corruption within the NSW Police force; the corrupt era of Premier Robert Askin during the 1970s; Premier Nick Greiner in the 1990s was forced to resign after an investigation by the NSW Independent Commission Against Corruption; the corrupt era of former Labor minister, Eddie Obeid, which ended in 2011.

There was an expectation corruption had been cleaned up substantially in New South Wales but scratching the surface shows there's always something more to find: Premier Barry O'Farrell resigned over an undeclared bottle of Grange red wine and now, there's a new round of allegations against the current NSW Premier, Gladys Berejiklian—secret deals, covering up corruption, and shredding documents to remove a paper trail for $250 million worth of community grants to Liberal-held seats. It seems it's all too difficult for New South Wales to break its addiction to corruption.

It was the Greiner government, and with one of the better Attorneys-General from New South Wales, John Dowd, who initially created the ICAC in 1988 to break the cycle of corruption in the state, and Greiner considered it as a method of removing a few Labor members of Parliament he genuinely believed were corrupt. Greiner then ended up being a victim of the commission he created, when the ICAC found he had acted corruptly in 1992—the NSW Government was in a minority position after Greiner called a snap election in 1991—he offered Liberal-turned-independent member, Terry Metherell, an executive position in the Environmental Protection Authority, in exchange for resigning from Parliament. The expectation was that the Liberal Party would regain the Northern Beaches seat of Davidson, as well as regaining its parliamentary majority.

Greiner argued this was the type of political action taken on by Robert Menzies and other prime ministers and premiers, but the issue was that he had not followed proper processes, and was found to be technically corrupt, although it should also be considered that this type of political inducement is unethical and morally corrupt.

The corruption of Premier Askin was in a different league during the 1960s and 1970s. The illegal casinos operated by the racing identity Perce Galea were well established and well-known by the Sydney community, yet Askin claimed no knowledge and suggested there was no evidence of illegal gambling in New South Wales, even though he was visiting these sites virtually every night.

The 'brown-paper bag' type of corruption has moved on from the time of Askin and Neville Wran in the 1980s, but there's a more sophisticated type of corruption that exists in New South Wales, through the use of the senior executive service, external consultants and other white-collar methods that removed the need for shadowy late-night deals made in dark alleyways. The method of corruption has been cleaned up, but not necessarily the corruption itself: that's what the public hasn't quite gathered yet.

Berejiklian has been the NSW Premier since 2017 and presents herself in the media—and is presented *by* the media—as a cleanskin who is beyond reproach. But the business of politics in Australia is a dirty business: for governments to make their programs happen, there needs to be favours called upon from friends to ensure projects are delivered on time. A library building or a new train line, or a bridge that might need a little bit of extra payments to the right people so the project is delivered without a hitch. That's the nature of politics and it happens each and every day within government.

But it seems to be becoming worse as time moves on, and it seems there's one key factor in New South Wales politics: don't get caught.

Daryl Maguire is another person who arrived in politics for all the wrong reasons. Maguire was the member for Wagga Wagga in the Riverina region for almost two decades. He was essentially a non-performer in politics, never becoming a minister, although he did hold the position of Government Whip. In 2018, 'Operation Dasha' initiated by the ICAC found there was possible corruption involving Maguire and a local government councillor, where he acted on behalf of a Chinese client to purchase development-approved projects, in exchange for a commission from the developer, and it appears Maguire used his duties as a member of Parliament, Parliamentary Secretary, and as Chair of the NSW Parliament Asia Pacific Friendship Group to improperly gain a benefit for himself and his close friends. Maguire resigned from the New South Wales Parliament in 2018, but it has since been revealed that he was in a "close personal relationship" with Berejiklian between 2015–20.

The ICAC in New South Wales investigates corruption after it occurs—and this is its primary role—but there needs to be a far tougher system of oversight and penalties to deter the corruption before it occurs, as it seems the system to combat corruption in politics is more fragile than it has ever been. Corrupt occurs, but there are no real consequences. Former Premier O'Farrell resigned after he failed to declare a $3,000 bottle of Grange Hermitage wine—over a relatively insignificant misdemeanour suggests there was more to this issue beneath the surface and more to do with Liberal Party back room brawls and blackmail—yet Berejiklian remains in office after revelations that had she been in a relationship with a corrupt politician who was a part of her government.

It appears politicians and their officials in government are unclear what corruption is and what constitutes the act of corruption. Within political discourse and behaviour, it will always come down to semantics and word definitions, at one extreme, US President Bill Clinton asking the grand jury during the impeachment hearings in 1998, to define the word "is":[128]

---

128 *New York Times*, 'Excerpts From Clinton's Grand Jury Testimony as Quoted in Starr's Report to Congress', August 1998. https://archive.nytimes.com/www.nytimes.com/library/politics/091798clinton-text.html

Bill Clinton: It depends on what the meaning of the word "is" is. If "is" means "is" and never has been, that is not—that is one thing. If it means there is none, that was a completely true statement... Now, if someone had asked me on that day, are you having any kind of sexual relations with Ms. Lewinsky, that is, asked me a question in the present tense, I would have said no. And it would have been completely true.

If politics has difficulties defining the two-letter word "is", it's going to have infinite difficulties defining the act of corruption. In New South Wales in 2020, there are different attempts at defining simple words, in this case, the word "that", as revealed in a phone-tapped recording of an exchange between Berejiklian and Maguire:[129]

Gladys Berejiklian: Okay, that sounds fun...

Daryl Maguire: Yeah, I've been doing my books, my accounts, yeah! Counting my tax refund, hah, hah, hah, hah!

Berejiklian: Good.

Maguire: It's excellent!

Berejiklian: Given the size of it, it'll take you a week to count it all.

Maguire: That's true. And the good news is William [property developer Leong] tells me we've done our deal. So hopefully that's about half of all that's gone now.

Berejiklian: That's good. I don't need to know about that bit.

Maguire: No you don't, you do not. Anyway, so it's all good news, so we're moving ahead.

Berejiklian: Okay, good.

"I don't need to know about that": what is meant by "that"? What does Berejiklian know about Maguire's corrupt practices and dealings, a member of her government who was forced to resign

---

129 *The Guardian*, 'Former MP didn't know why he spoke in 'code' during conversation with premier – as it happened, Michael McGowan, 16 October 2020. https://www.theguardian.com/australia-news/live/2020/oct/16/icac-hearing-live-stream-inquiry-transcript-daryl-maguire-nsw-premier-gladys-berejiklian-future?page=with:block-5f88c0cd8f08ebac1a040a3a

during her tenure as NSW Premier? Berejiklian has also tried to downplay the nature of her relationship with Maguire, claiming it was an insignificant relationship, but then going on to claim that she was intent on marrying him. Of course, the private lives of public figures need to be kept private, until they become matters of public significance. Sometimes, these private matters need to be made public as a right for the public to know about the issues that may affect public probity and result in corrupt practices, as appears to be the case here.

Maguire was using his public office and the Premier's position for a personal business advantage when making government deals. This is the occasion when a personal private matter becomes a public issue. It is one issue for members of Parliament to overlook their own corruptive practices—as serious as that might be—but it's another issue for the media to play their role in hiding the corruption of a politician, as was the case when most of the media went into overdrive to cover over the errors of Berejiklian, claiming that all of the mistakes were caused by "a dud boyfriend", "Gladys is bad at love" and quickly became part of a feminist narrative that this debacle is an issue every woman experiences. The culmination of this nausea-inducing process was the appearance of Berejiklian at KISS-FM, with Kyle Sandilands and Jackie O:

> **Kyle Sandilands:** Premier of New South Wales had a tough week last week. Really? Everything I read, she actually went up in my opinion polls, I thought, Wow, look at this, this is what we want.
>
> **Jackie O:** This is really showed who are the Gladys supporters out there, and I don't know if Gladys is aware—huge amount of support for you and she joins us now. Hi, Gladys, how are you!
>
> **Berejiklian:** Hi, guys. I'm okay.
>
> **Sandilands:** What a week hey?
>
> **O:** It has been a horrible week, hasn't it? I know from you being in here on many, many occasions and having gotten to know you over the years, I know how embarrassed you would have been over this, and to have to front the media every day and hold your head up high must have been incredibly difficult.

Berejiklian: Oh, it sure was, and I don't wish that upon anybody. I guess when you have big traumas or big things that go wrong in your life, you don't have to tell the whole world which is what I had to do, and that was my responsibility. Because people needed to know from me, what happened. And it was a really, really hard week but I just feel very supported. And I actually am starting to feel even stronger, so I really appreciate the support.

O: They do make you stronger and to give people an idea of how private you are. Not even your family knew about this...

Berejiklian: No, I didn't because I thought to myself: if it was, if I thought it was a significant, you know, it was gonna go somewhere, definitely, I would have definitely [introduced Maguire]. But I didn't want to introduce someone and then not have it work because that would disappoint people because, and so you know, for that reason... and I'm also a very private person, and I kept it to myself.

KISS-FM doesn't involve itself with quality reporting and journalism but that exchange indicates how dire the relationship between the mainstream media and conservative politicians is. Serious allegations of corruption levelled at a NSW Premier is morphed into throw-away lines about a bad relationship gone wrong, and returning all the control of the media narrative to the male figures, as well as a return to pre-first wave feminism.

From the perspective of the suffragette movements of the late 1890s, this Berejiklian affair has come across as nineteenth century romance potboiler. The first inclination is to think about other prominent women in politics and how would they have reacted: the former NSW Liberal Party leader, Kerry Chikarovski—what would she have said? The Chancellor of Germany, Angela Merkel: would she ever announce she made a political error because she met a bad man, who'd 'done me wrong'? Or former British Prime Minister, Margaret Thatcher; or Hillary Clinton, even though more than most, she probably had good reason, after the behaviours of Bill Clinton in office. They wouldn't, because it's not in their nature, but also because if they did, they would be absolutely crucified by the media and their political opponents. But in Australia, things are done differently and conservative women in politics are not accosted with the same forces applied to women in the Labor side of politics.

By focusing on the relationship between Berejiklian and Maguire, the media has downplayed the effects and the role of corruption, as through it never occurred: two weeks after the ICAC hearings were held, very few people are discussing the corruption. But the other factor to take into account is that this is all for public consumption and putting any adverse findings against Berejiklian on hold. The ICAC won't be deterred by whether Berejiklian was in a "bad relationship" or not, or whether Kyle Sandilands and Jackie O think Berejiklian is "so popular" or how they tell their audience how fantastic she is: they simply look at the evidence placed in front of them.

The ICAC is not a court of law, and it cannot make any prosecutions, although it can make recommendations for prosecutions and then it's up to the public prosecutor to decide whether any charges should be laid. And Berejiklian's political future depends on the recommendations arising from ICAC's investigations, whether there are any adverse findings and if there is enough media pressure for her to resign—and based on previous media reactions, it will be minimal or non-existent.

Another issue for Berejiklian relates to $250 million worth of grants in the Stronger Communities Fund allocated just before the March 2019 NSW election, where it has been revealed there is no documentation to support how or why almost all the grants were made to local councils in Coalition-held seats, including $40,000 awarded by Berejiklian to the electorate of Wagga Wagga in 2017—a seat held by Maguire at that time, a person with whom Berejiklian was in a "close personal relationship" with.

Almost 95 per cent of these grants were made to Coalition-held seats; all of the documentation relating to these grants—paper and electronic—has been destroyed, although there will be attempts to retrieve the electronic data. It's a different version of the 'brown-paper bag' style of corruption of yesteryear, but it's a corruption far more prevalent and insidious, and involves larger sums of public monies: it's far more difficult to stuff $250 million in paper bags or hide it in a suitcase than it is to electronically transfer money to safe Coalition seats and then destroy all the evidence. Corruption in New South Wales, as it is was with the Rum Corp back in 1789, is still rife. It's just that in 2020, it manifests itself in a different way, and in a way far more detrimental to the public interest.

*

Investigating News Corporation

27 October

He's been out of Australian politics since 2013 but former Prime Minister Kevin Rudd has launched a petition calling on the federal government to hold a Royal Commission into the state of Australia's media and political reporting.

The petition is formally known as a "Royal Commission to ensure a strong, diverse Australian news media" but the main target within Rudd's scope is News Corporation and its proprietor, Rupert Murdoch, who controls at least 57 per cent of the media landscape in Australia,[130] and with Seven West Media and the Nine Network mimicking News Corporation, and the infiltration of the ABC by key News Corporation journalists and staff, Murdoch's influence over the media in Australia is in reality, closer to 100 per cent.

A Liberal Party government is never going to support a petition that scrutinises its main supporter and benefactor, and if anything ever arises from this petition—either a legislative response or a formal inquiry such as a Royal Commission, it's unlikely to arrive before the Labor Party returns to government.

Not that there would ever be any guarantees that the power and control of News Corporation would ever be checked: the British Leveson Inquiry in 2011 questioned the culture, practices and ethics

---

130 *The Guardian*, 'Australia's newspaper ownership is among the most concentrated in the world', Nick Evershed, 14 November 2020. https://www.theguardian.com/news/datablog/2020/nov/13/australia-newspaper-ownership-is-among-the-most-concentrated-in-the-world

of the media press and explored whether Rupert Murdoch was a fit and proper person to hold a media licence. It uncovered great details about phone tapping and other illegal activities used by the *News of the World* and other News Corporation mastheads.

Murdoch is too powerful to attack: the British Prime Minister at the time, David Cameron, declined to enact any legislation and the second part of the Inquiry investigating the relationship between journalists and the police force was completely abandoned in 2018. Instead of continuing as a global media mogul and cancerous influence on politics in Britain, the United States and Australia, Murdoch is someone who should be spending time in jail for his many corrupt and illegal activities.

Rudd once described himself as 'a determined bastard' when he first became the leader of the Labor Party in 2006 and if there is one person with the ability to force a Royal Commission, he would be the one. But it's not going to happen for a long time. At this stage, Rudd would understand that his petition for a Royal Commission is a symbolic gesture, and an act which will allow for a platform in the Senate to outline all of his concerns about the influence of Murdoch in the Australian media.

And it's also interesting to see another former Prime Minister, Malcolm Turnbull, also join in the campaign, even though when he was in office, he was more than happy to use the support of News Corporation when it suited him.[131] Former News Corporation journalists and editors such as Tony Koch are now happy to call out their former employer, bemoaning the decline of their political content and "shameful bias".[132]

The petition has galvanised the public—the largest ever in Australia—and over 500,000 people have signed up for it: most public petitions presented to the federal government might receive up to 10,000 petitions, although the climate change emergency petition from 2019 received over 300,000 signatures. There is no

---

131 ABC News, 'Scott Morrison and Murdoch's News Corp empire 'operating like a team', former PM Malcolm Turnbull says', Michael Vincent, 17 November 2020. https://www.abc.net.au/news/2020-11-17/scott-morrison-murdoch-media-like-a-team-turnbull-says/12891218

132 Pearls and Irritations, 'For 30 years I worked for News Corp papers. Now all I see is shameful bias', 10 May 2019. https://johnmenadue.com/tony-koch-for-30-years-i-worked-for-news-corp-papers-now-all-i-see-is-shameful-bias-the-guardian-9-5-2019/

legislation that stipulates a petition must result in an inquiry—only a small proportion of petitions are ever acted upon—but a government that receives a call for action from half a million people, ignores it at its own peril.

However, a Liberal–National government is the least likely to engage with a call for a Royal Commission into media ownership and political reporting in Australia and, even if it did, it would result a watered-down response. The value of Royal Commissions has also diminished ever since Tony Abbott became prime minister in 2013, instigating a series of politically-motivated Royal Commissions into trade unions and Labor's home insulation scheme when they were last in government—which revealed little—and there's also the consideration of the long-held belief that a government will only commission an inquiry once it already has the answers it's looking for.

How different would the public interest be served if the mainstream media acted according to agreed ethics and standards within journalism and political reporting? Of course, it's naïve to expect that the media could behave any differently when it's preoccupied with reporting according the conservative whims of their proprietors, but the outcome in the trials of George Pell could have been more fair if it wasn't for the constant undermining of the judicial process by News Corporation. The Victoria Government managed to flatten a major pandemic within eight weeks—no government in the world has managed to achieve this—yet all the public heard from News Corporation's *Herald Sun* was a tirade of political attack after political attack, in unison with the federal government.

Political outcomes are influenced when a monopolised media uses itself as a political weapon against its perceived political enemies—in this case, the Labor Party—and the lack of media diversity is a serious problem in Australian politics. With all of the material and evidence against NSW Premier Gladys Berejiklian, she is a figure that should have been hounded out of office by a fair and balanced media but, instead, there's a concerted effort by the media to overlook serious matters of corruption.

Although there is a domination of the media by Murdoch, this isn't necessarily translating into a domination of electoral support for conservative parties. The Queensland Premier, Annastacia Palaszczuk, has been lampooned and ridiculed at every opportunity by another News Corporation masthead, *The Courier-Mail*, yet the two-party preferred vote according to published opinion polls is roughly 50:50 per cent, so there are other factors that influence electoral perceptions. Also, the Liberal–National Party was led by Campbell Newman in office for one term only and removed in a large swing against it in the 2015 Queensland election, despite the media support provided to him for most of his term.

While the highly concentrated media may not mean everything in political outcomes, it does allow for outliers such as the mining magnate Clive Palmer to gain a foothold into the political market and have a greater influence on policy matters. It also allowed Palmer and his United Australia Party to launch a massive advertising campaign against former Labor leader Bill Shorten, resulting in many focus group sessions during the last term of Parliament where people would say they didn't like Shorten, without being able to articulate why. There are other subliminal messages that are received by the electorate: headlines on posters outside newsagents, where people don't need to buy the newspaper to receive the negative news in a short succinct message; or the negative ticker-tape message along the bottom of a television screen while Shorten—or any other Labor minister—delivers a key policy message. Collectively, all of these mini-messages have an effect.

What are the full effects of a highly concentrated media in Australia? It's difficult to determine exactly what the ramifications are, except to suggest it does have some influence on political outcomes. There are many factors that will come into play if an inquiry or Royal Commission is instigated over the short-to-medium-term period. US President Donald Trump is more-than-likely going to lose the November election to Joe Biden, so that will alter the relationship between the media and politics in the United States. Murdoch is no longer a young man; currently he is eighty-nine years old and by the time an inquiry does arrive—if at all—he might be ninety-two or ninety-three years of age, if he manages to survive until that time.

Due the dynamically changing media landscape, News Corporation in three or four years' time might not be the same dominant player that it is today and, if Murdoch dies in the meantime, it will become a different corporation, even if the reins are handed over to his son, Lachlan Murdoch. There's also the history of third-generation family corporations: built by the first generation, consolidated by the second, and destroyed by third. It happened with the empire built by the industrialist Andrew Carnegie; the newspaper empire of William Randolph Hearst. In Australia, Warwick Fairfax took over the Fairfax empire in 1987 and managed to send the company into receivership within three years. James Packer acquired the wealth of his father Kerry in 2005, valued at $7.1 billion, but valued in 2020 at $4.6 billion after a wide range of poor investment decisions, and removing himself from media ownership completely with the sale of Consolidated Media Holdings to News Limited in 2012.

While a personal value of $4.6 billion is substantial, Packer hasn't been able to consolidate on the wealth of his predecessors. Nor did Fairfax. What is in store for the News Corporation under a third-generation leadership? James Murdoch has removed himself from the business and there has been some debate that the children of the relationship between Rupert Murdoch and former wife Wendy Deng wish to be a part of the business. Lachlan Murdoch is reportedly even more conservative than his father but ultimately what matters is their management expertise and experience, of which Lachlan has very little of, when considering the debacle of the One.Tel telecommunications company, which folded in 2001 after a series of financial mismanagements, corporate breaches and cash flow problems.

All companies have a natural life span and very few in corporate history have a long-term existence: sometimes, businesses break up due to a wide range of confluent issues and events. News Corporation is still a dominant multinational company, but even large multinational corporations can arrive at an endpoint and, sometimes, that endpoint can arrive very quickly.

What are the motivations of Rudd? Is he settling old scores or does he genuinely see a public interest in calling for a Royal Commission into media diversity in Australia? It's difficult to accept that he would have been thinking about such an inquiry during the time of his prime ministership: why invite a political problem unnecessarily when Murdoch was, according to former British political adviser, Alastair Campbell, likened to a "wild dog in the corner of the room" that had to be managed rather than "fight against the power and influence that he held"?[133]

Rudd left politics seven years ago but, as with all people who have become prime minister, had the ego to match his ambitions. But this seems to be more of a public interest matter to Rudd, even if he wasn't prepared to do anything about the matter when he had the power to do so. The same could be said about Turnbull: couldn't act on the issues that were close to his heart but makes the right noises when he can't do anything about. However, this is an important issue that needs to be heard very loudly in the public arena, even if it doesn't result in an inquiry or a Royal Commission at this point of time. That time will come, but it's just that it will never occur under the leadership of a Liberal–National Coalition government.

*

---

133 *GQ*, 'The BBC's The Rise Of The Murdoch Dynasty says more about Nigel Farage than Rupert Murdoch', Stuart McGurk, 15 July 2020. https://www.gq-magazine.co.uk/culture/article/the-rise-of-the-murdoch-dynasty-bbc-review

Going postal: A deflection to cover up corruption

27 October

Senate estimates hearings in Canberra usually reveal material that quite often is in the public interest and, last week, it found excessive bonuses were provided to four senior executives at Australia Post—exclusive Cartier watches at the cost of almost $5,000 each, for a total of $20,000.

It seems like the days when staff received a box of chocolates or a lunch at a moderately exclusive restaurant to show appreciation for a job well done are well and truly over but with senior executives on such high salaries, there would be a public expectation that high quality work and performance should be achieved, without the need to resort to these types of incentives.

Australia Post is not managed by the federal government—it's an enterprise owned by government—but it was enough for Prime Minister Scott Morrison to vent his fury over the incident, claiming in Parliament that he was "appalled, and it is disgraceful and not on" and "on behalf of the Australian people… the chief executive… has been instructed to stand aside, if she doesn't wish to do that, she can go."

As a result, the CEO of Australia Post, Christine Holgate, has been stood down pending a four-week inquiry instigated by Morrison, and media was very keen to let the public know how furious he was, reporting that he was "outraged", "had acted swiftly" and "barely contained his fury".

But this action is a classic political deflection, and deflections have been the hallmark of Morrison's prime ministership. There has been recent pressure placed on Morrison about delays in the creation of a national corruption commission—the intention to create a commission was announced almost three years ago—pressure brought about because of the recent revelations of the federal government's $29.8 million purchase of land worth only $3.1 million in western Sydney, and resurfacing of the infamous 'sports rorts' affair, where over $100 million was granted in key marginal seats just before the 2019 federal election.

There are continuing misappropriations of money also occurring elsewhere in the federal government—the chair of the Australian Securities and Investments Commission, James Shipton recently made a $118,000 payment to KPMG to cover his personal legal costs for tax advice—and that's not the amount of his overall tax payable, it's only for advice—but Morrison was very quiet about this matter, just making sure all of his fury was directed firmly towards Cartier watches, Holgate and Australia Post.

A national corruption commission is well overdue, and the federal government is claiming delays have been caused because of the importance of managing the coronavirus pandemic and ensuring all of the focus of attention and resources are place there, but governments should be able to manage multiple issues concurrently. The US President Lyndon Johnson suggested politicians should be able to "walk and chew gum" at the same time, but it seems this government hasn't even been able to make the first step and get out of its chair yet.

One issue that has flown under the radar in the attacks on Holgate is that the Liberal Party-affiliated right-wing think tank, the Institute of Public Affairs, has long advocated for the privatisation of Australia Post—it sits at number forty-eight in list of items to 'radicalise' Australia[134]—and the best way to achieve this as a goal is to undermine the organisation, even if it does start with a public humiliation of its CEO.

---

134 Institute of Public Affairs, 'Be Like Gough: 75 Radical Ideas To Transform Australia', John Roskam, Chris Berg & James Paterson, 5 August 2012. https://ipa.org.au/ipa-review-articles/be-like-gough-75-radical-ideas-to-transform-australia

While it's a fair question about whether a publicly-owned entity should be providing $20,000 gift bonuses to its senior executives, the greater question is the public ownership of Australia Post: it's an essential public utility and while there are a vast range of business postal services that should be borne by the business sector, there are still many services of communications that are best kept within public ownership.

But the outrage displayed by the Prime Minister was completely out of proportion to his response to the $29.8 million purchase of land in western Sydney, or his response about a $118,000 payment by ASIC for personal tax advice to its chair. And it was this outrage the media was very keen to focus upon, rather than the more substantive issues of government mismanagement and corruption.

It's an issue that needs to be repeated time and again: the media in Australia is concentrated in the hands of few proprietors and they are too close politically to the federal government, and the symbiotic relationship between the two needs to be separated, especially the links with News Corporation—owned by a large benefactor of the Liberal Party and the Institute of Public Affairs, Rupert Murdoch—and the Nine Network, chaired by former Liberal Party member of Parliament and federal Treasurer, Peter Costello.

Compared to $100 million in the 'sports rorts' affair; or the $444 million grant allocated to the Great Barrier Reef Foundation in 2018 without a tender process; or even the $29.8 million purchase of land in western Sydney at 1000 per cent of the market value, $20,000 for Cartier watches to senior executives at Australia Post is relatively small but, once again, the mainstream media inserted Morrison as the hero into the national conversation. The impression was given that Australia Post was a corrupt and rorting enterprise that needed to be saved from itself, and Morrison was the man to sort it all out.

Although the Australia Post gift bonuses were revealed at a Senate estimates committee last week, the bonuses were provided two years ago in 2018, so it's hardly a contemporary issue. And while the gift bonuses might offend public sensibilities, providing bonuses to senior executives in a government-owned entity is not illegal or corrupt and was a bonus system actually approved by an Australia Post board stacked with Liberal Party appointees: the non-executive director,

Tony Nutt, was the Federal and State Director of the Liberal Party of Australia; Bruce McIver was recently the President of the Liberal National Party of Queensland; Michael Ronaldson was a former Liberal Party Senator and member of federal Parliament; Deidre Willmott was Chief of Staff for two Liberal Premiers of Western Australia, Richard Court and Colin Barnett.

It's clear Morrison blew the issue out of all proportion to avert the gaze from the many issues of corruption that are consuming his government, and to make the media and the public become preoccupied with other non-essential performative issues of politics, rather than the substance. And these are the areas Morrison excels at: purchasing an inflatable shark from the Bunnings Warehouse,[135] or building a cubby house or a chicken pen—essentially saying to the public, 'look how much like you I really am'. These are actions former Prime Ministers such as Paul Keating, John Howard or Malcolm Turnbull would never have stooped so low to achieve, but Morrison is a different type of political leader: it's the classic 'bread and circus' actions that keeps the populace amused with the trivial.

If the main aim was to deflect from the calls for a national corruption commission, it's easy to see why. Aside from all the other major matters that have occurred over the past few years, there are the smaller matters at the local level: several months ago, Assistant Treasurer Michael Sukkar and former minister Kevin Andrews were accused of misusing Commonwealth funds to recruit members to the Liberal Party, branch stack to boost key factional alliances in Melbourne and launch smear campaigns against their opponents. Instead of holding an independent inquiry, the federal Department of Finance provided $50,000 to Ashurst—a legal firm where Sukkar worked as a lawyer for seven years—to investigate the allegations. And *quell surprise!*: Ashurst found the allegations could not be substantiated and the pair were cleared.

Corruption in federal politics has been normalised: it does receive low-level reporting in the media, but it's soon forgotten about when it comes from the conservative side of politics. In a similar circumstance on the other side of politics, there were branch stacking

---

135 News.com.au, 'Scott Morrison's Christmas gift to himself, Anton Nilsson, 25 October 2020. https://www.news.com.au/finance/work/leaders/scott-morrisons-christmas-gift-to-himself/news-story/366d39d9e72b79d50c2e2a709c056cd8

allegations against Victoria Labor member, Adem Somyurek, and he was sacked on the spot by Victoria Premier Daniel Andrews. Even though there was a fast resolution in this matter, the media ran national headlines for several weeks, alleging what Somyurek had and hadn't done, all neatly primed to coincide with the opening of the pre-polling booths in the Eden–Monaro byelection campaign in June this year.

How far would the media have extending the headlines if Daniel Andrews instructed the Victoria Department of Treasury and Finance to pay $50,000 to a union-friendly legal firm to investigate and clear Somyurek of any wrongdoing? It would be the front page headlines in the *Herald Sun* and *The Age* on each and every day leading up to the next Victoria state election in November 2022. Yet the reporting on Kevin Andrews and Sukkar was perfunctory and quickly dispensed with.

For the federal Labor opposition, there is a strong message in this continual corruption by the federal government: weave the message of corruption into every political conversation it provides up until the next election until the public can no longer tolerate hearing the message—Tim Gartrell, the former Labor national president who is now Anthony Albanese's chief of staff referred to it as "the vomit principle"[136]—and half of their task of returning to government will be done.

Albanese does keep mentioning that he doesn't wish to adopt the destructive tactics of Tony Abbott when he was Liberal Party Leader of the Opposition between 2009–13, but for four long years, Abbott weaved the negative message of a "carbon tax" into every conversation: whether he was making an announcement on health, childcare, education or any other policy, he'd navigate and direct the conversation towards a carbon tax that didn't even exist. Was it political effective? Whatever the political debate was on whether a carbon tax existed or how much the body politic was destroyed by Abbott's constant harping and negativity, he did become prime minister and led the Liberal–National Coalition back into government in the 2013 federal election. And, seven years later, the Coalition is still in office.

---

136 *Crikey*, 'Time to test your gag reflex, 19 July 2010. https://www.crikey.com.au/2010/07/19/crikey-says-time-to-test-your-gag-reflex

How desperate is Albanese to become prime minister and lead the Labor Party back into government? He virtually threw away corruption as a key political attack point soon after he became Labor leader in June 2019: in response to an allegation by Tasmania independent member for Denison, Andrew Wilkie, that corruption was rife in federal politics, Albanese claimed he had "not seen any evidence of direct corruption… that has been proven in my time when I've been in Parliament". It was a peculiar statement to make by Albanese, in the context of the many corrupt practices that have been widely reported: certainly, no corruption has been found in a legal context—and, without a national corruption commission, it's unlikely to be found—but perceptions of corruption can be easily manipulated by a more wily political leader. It's difficult for a leader to make allegations of corruption against their opponents if they deny the existence of it in the first instance.

A Parliament can only be a good as the integrity of the institutions that support it and it's clear a national corruption commission would clear up the perceptions of politics in Australia, as well as acting as a deterrent against corruption, if it were to be correctly created. Currently, it's far too easy for federal members of Parliament to engage in corruption, with a compliant conservative media only too happy to ignore the poor behaviour of Liberal Party operatives, and magnify any failures on the Labor side of politics.

It's a system that needs to change substantially and the bellowing by Morrison about a relatively insubstantial issue at Australia Post is really not the big issue that he wants it to become.

*

Politics, Protest, Pandemic: Eddy Jokovich + David Lewis

The end of Trump and a change for Australian politics

12 November

It's the end of another presidential campaign in the United States—US President Donald Trump and the Vice President Mike Pence have been discarded by the US electorate, and the joint ticket of Joe Biden and Kamala Harris has been voted in. The Democrat candidate received the largest vote in United States history—over 81 million—and for just the third time in the past ninety years, a sitting president has been voted out of office.

Despite what Republicans are saying—that the voting was rigged, the election was fraudulent and the President will remain in office—Trump will leave the White House in January 2021, even if he has to be removed by security forces, or seeks exile in a remote part of the world.

Trump has influenced a wide range of right-wing populist nationalists around the world—British Prime Minister Boris Johnson; President Jair Bolsonaro in Brazil; Prime Minister Viktor Orbán in Hungary, and closer to home, Prime Minister Scott Morrison in Australia. But now that Trump is heading out of office, it will be interesting to see how world leaders react to a new United States administration, and how they adapt to Biden's agenda of climate change, education, economic reform and, importantly, the return of civility into the political system.

There is always debate about how the Australia–United States alliance traverses the political spectrum, but Morrison has lost a key political ally in the United States, and this Liberal–National Coalition government has a different world view to the incoming Democrat administration. Will Biden's victory influence Australian politics in a substantial way?

It should be noted that the second highest vote in a United States Presidential election, with 74 million votes, was recorded by Trump in this election: he's still the losing candidate, but it's still a substantial amount of electoral support. Morrison is a different type of politician to Trump, although he's very much made from the Trumpian mould of spin, deflection, outrageous lies and misrepresentation, belligerence and contempt for those who disagree with his world outlook. It's possibly the reason why Australia has been so belligerent in its accusations that China may have been responsible for the cause of the coronavirus, believing that the United States—with Trump as President—would provide cover.

This was always going to be a very high risk and problematic strategy, and the results of that failed strategy are evident, with China blocking or restricting key Australian imports. Morrison misunderstood the geopolitical interplay between China and the United States and the recent transitions that have occurred in those countries: China has moved rapidly in its economic development and world influence; the United States has been waning, even before the arrival of Trump in the White House. Using megaphone diplomacy with China and humiliating the regime has never worked in anyone's favour before, and it's unlikely to work now.

The Australia–United States alliance will always remain strong, irrespective of which government is in office, primarily because there are mutual military, strategic and economic interests and, historically, Labor administrations have worked well when Republicans have been in office in the United States, and the Liberal–National Coalitions have worked well with Democrat administrations. However, Morrison and Biden are different political leaders with radically different agendas: climate change is a major agenda for the Biden administration; virtually non-existent for Morrison. The management of coronavirus is critical for Biden, whereas Australia has managed this very successfully.

Trade will become another factor, where China and the United States will work towards mending their relationship, now that the primary creator of the bellicose rhetoric and trade war between the two countries—Trump—will soon be out of office. Where does that leave Morrison and the Australian government? Of course, there will always be tensions between two world super-powers who are jostling for the same power space but China will always gravitate towards the countries and leadership that it can work with. If that ends up being a more open, honest and less aggressive relationship with Biden, that doesn't bode well for Australia: more than likely, Australia will remain on the outer until there is change of prime minister, or a change of government.

Biden won't be able to completely ignore Australia's interests, especially in the context of strategic positioning in the Pacific region and military defence facilities but he's unlikely to do very much past what is absolutely necessary.

The United States needs key international markets for its wheat products. Pennsylvania is now a key state for Biden—not only in the sense of it being his home state that swung strongly towards him in the 2020 election, but it's also a key industrial state and he'll be looking to push production for renewable energy infrastructure and steel as much as possible.

A change in political tone, while not the most essential part of the political process, will also make a difference. Politics under Trump was too noisy, incessant, dramatic and chaotic. Biden and Harris gave inspirational victory speeches that provided a pathway towards a better standard of public discourse, and a sense that the adults had returned to the White House, after the four years of chaos and immature behaviour of not just Trump, but his entire administration. The United States economy was starting to perform markedly better before the coronavirus pandemic commenced in early 2020 and there was a strong belief that Trump would win a second term in office: the mismanagement of the pandemic and the mounting death toll—230,000 across the United States at the time of the election—as well as general perceptions of a disorganised regime, put an end to that prospect.

There were rumours that the entire Trump presidency was based on his desire to remove himself from financial difficulties and boost his television show, *The Apprentice*, to outperform *The*

Voice in the ratings.[137] The momentum of his 2016 campaign overtook everything, however, and landed him in office, almost like an accidental president. The head of state of any country is an important position but the presidency of the United States is a twenty-four-hours-per-day, seven-days-per-week position, and one of the most important positions in the world.

President Ronald Reagan come into the position at the age of sixty-nine, and as he become older in the presidency, he didn't work after a certain time of the day. But he looked tired and spent, even taking into account his age of seventy-seven when he left office. Barack Obama, much younger, still greyed considerably during his eight years in office, his eyes were haggard. Bill Clinton aged substantially, as did George W. Bush: it's a difficult job. Trump looked the same as he did on the first day of his presidency, spending most of his time on the golf course: it seems that he didn't ultimately really want the job and he wasn't up to it. 'Winning' is part the Trump business brand, and perhaps the claims that the election was rigged or stolen from him fits into that type of thinking—Trump is always a 'winner', unless ulterior motives come into play.

Once it was clear Trump had lost the election, the media stopped accepting the mistruths and outright lies that had punctuated his presidency for four years, and adopted the practice of commencing broadcasts of Trump speaking, cutting him off mid-sentence and correcting him in a form of live fact checking, as demonstrated in this report from CNBC anchor, Shepard Smith:[138]

> **Donald Trump:** There's now tens of millions of unsolicited ballots without any verification measures...
>
> **Shepard Smith:** ...well, we're interrupting this because what the President of the United States is saying, in large part, is absolutely untrue.

---

137 *USA Today*, 'Michael Moore claims Trump ran for president because of Gwen Stefani', Sara Moniuszko, 6 September 2018. https://www.usatoday.com/story/life/entertainthis/2018/09/06/michael-moore-claims-trump-ran-president-because-gwen-stefani/1210403002

138 *USA Today*, 'MSNBC, major networks interrupt Trump's falsehood-laden speech to fact-check', Bill Keveney, 5 November 2020. https://www.usatoday.com/story/entertainment/tv/2020/11/05/fox-cnn-covered-trumps-falsehood-laden-speech-msnbc-pulled-away/6182029002

> He began, and we're not gonna allow it to keep going, because it's not true. He began with: "there were legal votes, and if they only count the legal votes, I easily win. If they count the illegal votes, they're trying to steal the election". There is not a scintilla of evidence that this is true. None. There's only words here, no truth.
>
> He said, the pollsters knowingly got the polls wrong to create voter suppression. There is no evidence of any kind that this has happened, and he's provided none.
>
> He said that there is actually a red wave in this election—that is categorically false. He said there was election interference: there is no evidence to support that, and the president has offered none.

In many of Trumps statements, he'd mention he was robbed and that he'd actually won the election; widespread vote fraud and he was leading on the night of the election, how could he possibly be behind? And on the MSNBC, ABC, CBS, CNBC, and NBC networks, Trump's words would gradually fade out, the new anchors would correct the words and announce that what he was saying was completed wrong. CNN reporter Daniel Dale said that he'd "read or watched all of Trump's speeches since 2016. This is the most dishonest speech he has ever given". It's a news media tactic that should be introduced in the reporting of Australian politics, but perhaps most political speeches and media conferences would be drowned out by voiceovers correcting whatever a politician is speaking about.

Of course, manipulation of the truth is a critical part of politics but it's the part that most offends public sensibilities. And the media in Australia should be calling this out more often. Over the past four years in the United States, at least some journalists and reports have taken Trump to task and had the courage to call him out. In Australia, Morrison will hold a media conference and make statements that are clearly and demonstrably untrue: reporters will often repeat his statements as though they are fact, and this represents a serious problem within politics.

Journalists need to understand that it's part of their job to ask the Prime Minister difficult questions and correct him when he makes a statement which is untrue. It's part of the code of political journalism of holding power to account and there's not going to be very much accountability in public office if the right questions are never asked.

Generally, the Australian public doesn't take too much interest in national politics, so they're less likely to take notice of politics from the United States. To be sure, it is a large global event and there would be a recognition that Trump is on the way out, and Biden is on the way in but that's probably where the interest ends. There might not be too much interest but events from the United States will affect Australian politics: climate change, a change in the style of economic thinking, global trade and the management of the coronavirus pandemic. Australia is large enough and autonomic enough to act in a manner that suits itself, but political and social change in the United States does filter through to other parts of the world, even if it does seep through at a slow pace.

*

Sex in the city and the private lives of politicians

12 November

There have been more revelations about the misogyny and sexual misbehaviours of key federal government members of Parliament, with a series of inappropriate activities being alleged in the late-night bars of Canberra, sexual harassment of women working in Parliament, and ministers engaged in relationships with young female staffers.

The Attorney-General, Christian Porter and Minister for Education, Alan Tudge, have presented themselves to the electorate as 'family men'[139] and in Tudge's case, arguing against same-sex marriage and promoting the virtues of the nuclear married family but, behind the scenes, they're serial sexual harassers and quick to involve themselves in inappropriate relationships with a selection of young female staff members and advisers.[140]

There might be some naïvety about this perception, but the public would expect that the role of the parliamentarian is to advocate for the political causes they believe in, represent the interests of their

---

139 Mamamia.com.au, 'Here is a closer look at the people who have been lecturing us about family values', Billi Fitzsimons, 10 November 2020. https://www.mamamia.com.au/alan-tudge-christian-porter-family-values

140 *Four Corners*, ABC, 'Christian Porter was warned over public behaviour with young female staffer by then-prime minister Malcolm Turnbull', Louise Milligan, Peter Cronau & Lucy Carter, 9 November 2020. https://www.abc.net.au/news/2020-11-09/four-corners-investigation-christian-porter-alan-tudge/12862632

electorate in the best way possible and, hopefully, act as a role model for the community.

Instead, these are key members of the federal government, whose previous behaviour includes vomiting into plastic bags, 'smutting my way through law school', seducing young girls in public bars and behaving like sexualised bigots[141]—it's almost like they haven't been able to leave behind the frat party syndrome from their university days.

Man–children; arrested development; psychological immaturity; the Dunning–Kruger effect of cognitive bias where people with low abilities overestimate themselves: with these ministers, these are psychological characteristics that are all on public display, and symptomatic of selfish people of low character. Porter's situation is peculiar, especially when placed against the great conservative Attorneys–General throughout Australia's history: Robert Menzies, Isaac Isaacs, Henry Bournes Higgins, Garfield Barwick—all took on the role of the law and the interactions between the political and legal system seriously and were people of substance and intelligence.

It's not clear what Porter's credentials are in the context of being in the position of Attorney–General. Historically, he's come from a line of politicians, with his grandfather, Charles Porter, sitting in the Queensland Parliament during the era of Joh Bjelke-Petersen, and his father—Charles "Chilla" Porter—sitting in the Western Australia Parliament in the 1970s and 1980s. While he has worked as a commercial litigator and a public prosecutor, his main experience has been in the field of politics, not law. His current actions are more in tune with those of a politician: rather than upholding the law, it's according to the laws of politics which is being able get away with as much as possible, which is also an attribute of a privileged upbringing and an expectation that greatness is presented on a platter, rather than through hard work and industry.

And this factor has been the hallmark of the two Attorneys–General that have served during the time of the Abbott–Turnbull–Morrison governments: Porter and George Brandis, who worked

---

141 *Four Corners*, ABC, 'Investigation reveals history of sexism and inappropriate behaviour by Attorney-General Christian Porter', Louise Milligan, Peter Cronau & Lucy Carter, 10 November 2020. https://www.abc.net.au/news/2020-11-10/four-corners-investigation-christian-porter-sexism-inappropriate/12862910

primarily in trades practices law, and failing to become a Senior Council until he was virtually self-appointed in 2006 through a political process of payback, even though he hadn't practice law since 2000. Of course, the position of Attorney-General can only be filled from the parliamentary ranks of government and if the legal quality isn't there within the ranks, there's not much that can be changed there: Porter is there because of his ambition—as was Brandis—not because of his legal experience and credibility.

His position is untenable but the government will wish to hold on to him for as long as possible: losing a senior minister and the senior law office in the land will have far-reaching political consequences. There have been suggestions if Porter remains in his position, his seat of Pearce will be lost at the next election, although he holds the seat by a 7.5 per cent margin in the two-party preferred vote, having secured a 3.9 per cent swing towards him in the 2019 federal election. There have also been suggestions that because of Porter's profile—and the allegations that are being put to him—the seat of Pearce may become a target for a quality independent candidate, based on the success of independent candidate, Zali Steggall, in being able to unseat long-serving member and former Prime Minister, Tony Abbott, in the seat of Warringah.

And it's becoming more apparent that the only way for this type of parliamentary behaviour to be removed from politics is for the offending parliamentarians to be removed from office by the electorate: there are no consequences for members of Parliament who are caught out with this egregious behaviour. The member for New England, Barnaby Joyce, had sexual harassment allegations made about him in 2018,[142] left his wife for a younger female staffer—despite years of political grandstanding about the 'sanctity of traditional marriage'—yet remains in Parliament. When will the men who behave in this way ever change their behaviours?

Many excuses have been provided: Canberra is a dark, cold, lonely environment; members of Parliament are away from families and friends; the pressures of ministerial responsibilities. But the

---

142 *The Guardian*, 'Barnaby Joyce sexual harassment allegation: Catherine Marriott speaks out', Gabrielle Chan, 18 September 2018. https://www.theguardian.com/australia-news/2018/sep/18/barnaby-joyce-sexual-harassment-allegation-catherine-marriott-speaks-out

main issue for why these behaviours continue is because of a lack of accountability and rarely, if any, repercussions that result from their actions. If a serial womaniser and sex pest is never called to account and suffers no consequence, why wouldn't they keep offending?

It's also evident that instead of confronting the issue of sexual harassment and managing the human relations within parliamentary offices where great power imbalances exist, the Liberal Party has decided to manage the issue politically, and quick to call out politicians on the Labor side of politics, declaring former Prime Minister Bob Hawke was the greatest womaniser of all.

Hawke didn't behave well in his relationships, especially prior to becoming prime minister; he was a womaniser, a serial philanderer. It wasn't a well-kept secret—and this is not to condone his behaviours—but he never tried to hide it or cover it up in double-speak and hypocrisy about talking about the "sanctity of marriage", or the holier-than-thou approach typically adopted by conservatives while, behind the scenes, they're having sex with virtually everything that moves.

The federal government will try to ride this issue out and hope that it's replaced with something new, as it inevitably does within the news cycle. But these systematic problems with misogyny that constantly crop up within the Liberal and National parties won't disappear of their own accord. Perhaps the Liberal–National Coalition has considered that not enough people in the electorate have long-term concerns about men and their sexual harassment and affairs with young female staffers: there might be immediate outrage—as there is now in response to these events—but by the time of the next election, the outrage will dissipate and other matters might influence their voting preference. Which means the ongoing behaviour will continue and an opportunity to reduce this behaviour within Parliament will be lost.

Parliamentary practice is very difficult to change, and Australian Parliament House is not a family-friendly environment. Although the House does now include a childcare centre—ironically, at the site of a old staff bar—it was opened twenty-one years after the new Parliament House was built in 1988, after great resistance from the Howard government, and surviving an attempt by the Abbott government to close it down in 2014. It's an environment that tends to be structured around the old 'law firm' model of male domination—only 25 per cent of the Liberal–National Coalition Senators and members are women, and this compares with 48 per cent in the Labor Party. And within this context, the question needs to be asked: is Parliament House a safe working environment for women? It's a question that was asked of the Minister for Families and Social Services, Anne Ruston, during a joint media conference with Morrison on 11 November:

> **Phillip Coorey (journalist):** As a woman in government, your reflections on the culture inside: has it got better, worse or no change since the 'bonk ban'?
>
> **Anne Ruston:** Well, Phil, the only thing that I can…
>
> **Scott Morrison:** [interrupting] …How this ban is referred to I think is quite dismissive of the seriousness of the issue, Phil. And I would ask the media to stop referring to it in that way. We took it very seriously, and I think constantly referring to it in that way dismisses the seriousness of this issue. It's a very serious issue. Thanks – Anne.
>
> **Coorey:** What are your impressions on the culture?
>
> **Ruston:** Well Phil, obviously, I can only reflect on my own experience, since I have been in this place since 2012, and I have to say that I have always felt wholly supported while I have been here. And I'd particularly note that since becoming a member of the Cabinet and a member of the Expenditure Review Committee, there is nobody who has provided me more support and shown greater respect towards me as an individual than the Prime Minister.

Morrison's interruption typified the male domination of Parliament, his usual method of 'mansplaining' and interfering and answering a question that was asked directly of the woman at the media conference. It was pointed out that it probably wasn't a fair question from the journalist, knowing that the person who is, effectively, Ruston's boss was standing right next to her—she was hardly going to come out and say there are severe workplace issues and sexual harassment problems for the government in Morrison's presence—but Morrison should have waited until Ruston completed speaking first, and then provided his response. The days where the man answers the questions asked of a woman are well and truly over.

Generally, the public isn't too concerned about the affairs or private matters of members of Parliament, and nor should they be, unless those private matter affects their ability to carry out their work as a parliamentarian. When there's an affair or a relationship with a staffer within the workplace, that's an entirely different issue: there are power imbalances within the workplace; a relationship with a staffer can affect the dynamics of the ministerial office; there are sexual harassment issues that can arise and, finally, are male ministers in their positions to work on good government, policy development and the interests of the electorate, or think about who they can have sex with from their office? There are other issues of probity as well: how many members of Parliament are in secret relationships with key media journalists? Are there issues that the public should be made aware of as well?

In the case of the secret relationship between NSW Premier Gladys Berejiklian and disgraced former NSW politician, Daryl Maguire, if it had been with a businessman from Victoria with no involvement in New South Wales politics, then no one would have cared, but the fact Berejiklian kept the relationship a secret from colleagues and even her own family, suggests she knew it wasn't a relationship that was in the interests of good governance. If it was with anyone else, there's nothing of public interest, but a relationship with a disgraced and corrupt politician, from her own party, from her own government, who was organising land deals with government and skimming off a commission? That's definitely a relationship the public has a right to know about.

Is the private life of Christian Porter in the national interest? There are many factors that need to be taken into account: Porter is the Attorney-General and sits at the apex of Australia's legal system. He currently has the responsibility for the carriage of the national corruption commission—if that's ever to be introduced: the commission was announced in 2018 and, almost three years later, the public is still waiting—the Commonwealth Integrity Commission Bill 2020 makes no reference to sexual harassment and workplace exploitation, and the federal government does not want any commission to include retrospective actions, and insists on holding inquiries in private hearings.

Is his past behaviour guiding his actions as Attorney–General and the deliberations over the Commonwealth Integrity Commission Bill, knowing that he can tailor the legislation in a manner that will exclude his actions from the past? The character of the Attorney–General needs to be beyond reproach for the public to have confidence in the national legal system and the belief that laws are created in the interests of the community, not for the interests of the Attorney–General. It may explain why the legislation for the national corruption commission is taking so long to develop: an Attorney–General seeking a final piece of legislation that ensures that he is not the first one to appear in front of the commission on allegations of sexual harassment or other abuses. It's not the way laws and institutions should be created in Australia.

A national corruption commission is inevitable, it's just a question of which political party decides to implement it. For the Liberal–National Coalition, it's almost akin to the marriage equality legislation in 2017, where they had to dragged kicking and screaming to the legislative table, via postal vote plebiscite—over 61 per cent voted in support of marriage equality—and a laborious debate process in Parliament: a needlessly flawed and divisive process, but at least the legislation eventually came through.

The revelations about the relationships of Porter and Tudge still have some way to go politically, and it will be a question about whether any further revelations are put out into the public domain—for Porter and Tudge, or for any other ministers—and how the electorate perceives these matters. For many people, there is an assumption that ministers and politicians go into their workplaces to work, not to have sexual relationships with young staff members, or imbibe alcohol, of which a large amount is consumed within Parliament House. Surely the public can expect that male ministers in Parliament can adhere to a basic moral code: don't try to kiss young girls in the public late-night bars of Canberra; don't behave like sexualised bigots; keep hands away from female staffers. It can't be that difficult to implement a level of self-control and concentration on the role of minister.

Of course, the make-up of Parliament should be reflective of the rest of the community, but there should be standards and the people who are constantly in the public eye have a responsibility to act as role models for the community. It should be easy for politicians to not drink themselves to oblivion in public places, unless they have an alcohol problem and, if they have, they should seek help. If male politicians have problems keeping their hands to themselves, they need to work out a way of keeping their hands to themselves, and not force their way onto unsuspecting staff who are also there to perform important work, not perform the sexual favours for lustful and powerful male ministers. It's a pretty straightforward task for ministers to treat their female staff as professional colleagues, not as base and commodified sex objects.

It also has to be remembered that these male ministers are not young brash males with developing brains and laced with testosterone in their late teens or early twenties: these are grown men in their late forties with, supposedly, a wealth of worldly experience and experience of relationships. Instead, they're like unsupervised and out-of-control teenage boys that have privilege and never been taught the difference between appropriate and inappropriate behaviours. Perhaps it's a case where because they've behaved like this for all of their adult lives and never been called to account, they've continued that behaviour well into their parliamentary careers. It's clearly the results of men who have behaved badly over many years in their professional careers but have never had to face the consequences of their actions.

*

A Queensland victory for sensibility and decency

12 November

It's not as big as the recent United States Presidential election but in the recent Queensland election on 31 October, the Labor Party achieved a 4.1 per cent towards it and won an additional four seats, ultimately winning fifty-two seats in a ninety-three-seat chamber. There were many issues that played out during the campaign: leadership values; the power of incumbency; management of the coronavirus pandemic, health and safety, and the disputes over border closures.

The Queensland Premier, Annastacia Palaszczuk, had been in the position since 2015 and faced a poor leader of the Liberal–National Party—Deb Frecklington—who almost lost her position as leader just several months before the day of the election. Incumbency seems to have been a large factor in the Queensland election— many opinions polls have shown large approval ratings and electoral support for all leaders across Australia's nine jurisdictions but the Queensland election was the first real indication of whether these opinions are translating to actual results. After the recent territory elections in the Northern Territory and the Australian Capital Territory, the Queensland election was the first state to hold an election since the pandemic commenced.

It appears the management of the coronavirus pandemic and political stability will be the issues that affect the next batch of elections: Western Australia will hold an election in March 2021;

a federal election may occur anytime between August 2021 and May 2022; Victoria goes to the polls in November 2022; New South Wales in March 2023.

What's occurring in the political field right now won't have too much influence in those longer-term elections but with the election of the Democrats and Joe Biden in the United States, there is a small but discernible swing away right-wing do-nothing governments that steep themselves in empty nationalism and 'law-and-order' issues, towards a form of government that is more moderate and focusing on delivering outcomes that are favourable to the community, not to a special groups of friends and associates close to government.

For Palaszczuk to secure a third term of government, as well as secure a swing and four additional seats is quite a remarkable achievement: it has happened before in Australian politics, but it doesn't happen very often. Usually, an incoming government arrives on the back of a massive landslide, loses seats at its first re-election attempt, and then the second and, if it's lucky enough to still remain in office, try to secure another term. Longer-term governments at the state level have been less frequent in recent times and this victory will guarantee at least a nine-year stint in office for Queensland Labor.

Frecklington was ineffective as a leader, but was also too close to building developers[143]—actually reported to the Electoral Commission of Queensland by her own party—and clearly she wasn't a great candidate. But despite this, the media landscape dominated by News Corporation kept pushing the Liberal–National Party agenda and calling for the removal of Palaszczuk and the Labor Party at every opportunity. The Western Australia Government is highly likely to be returned in circumstances that are similar to those that were faced by the Queensland Government: a highly effect government, a highly popular Premier in Mark McGowan, against a highly unpopular and ineffective opposition.

What does the Queensland election—and the upcoming Western Australia election which is likely to result in another Labor victory—

---

[143] ABC Investigations, 'LNP Opposition Leader Deb Frecklington campaign in crisis after being referred by own party to election watchdog, Josh Robertson, 13 October 2020. https://www.abc.net.au/news/2020-10-13/lnp-crisis-as-deb-frecklington-referred-to-election-watchdog/12748400

mean for federal Labor? The common consensus now is that the electorate highly favours the incumbent, as shown by the elections in Northern Territory, the ACT and now in Queensland and, if a federal election was held now, it's fair to suggest that the federal government would win quite convincingly. The good news for Labor is the election isn't being held now and a normal election isn't to due be held until at least August 2021. Many events will take place between now and then, some of which are outside of the control of the federal government.

However, based on current performances, rather than the events that could happen between now and the next election, Labor is not going to do so well at the next election, unless it dramatically improves its tactics, strategies and media engagements. The federal government makes errors on a regular basis, but a compliant media tends not to magnify these errors, instead, focusing on what's happening on the Labor side, even though they're not the ones in federal office.

The Labor leader, Anthony Albanese, has picked up on that public mood that they're over the opposition-for-opposition-sake style of leadership that was adopted by Tony Abbott when he was the Leader of the Opposition between 2009–13, but that shouldn't mean that opposing the government of the day and pushing a Labor agenda needs to be eschewed completely: some level of oppositional behaviour would work in his favour and this definitely has a time and a place.

And it certainly doesn't help the Albanese's cause to have one of his shadow ministers deciding to resign just at the point when all the pressure is being placed on the federal government. The material about Christian Porter and Alan Tudge were revealed in an ABC *Four Corners* episode on the Monday night, and the fallout commence almost immediately, carrying through the evening, and morning news headlines the day after.

On this same Tuesday morning, the Shadow Minister for Resources, Joel Fitzgibbon, decided this moment was the best time to announce his resignation and his announcement deflected from the serious issues facing the federal government. Since the 2019 federal election, when Fitzgibbon's seat of Hunter moved from safe to marginal status, after a swing of 9.48 per cent cut the margin in the two-party preferred vote to only 2.98 per cent, he's been an outspoken critic of Labor's climate change policies, in the hope of warding off a challenge to his seat from One Nation, which secured 21.4 per cent of the primary vote in that election.

Fitzgibbon has never been an outstanding member of Parliament and a much stronger party leader would have been able to put Fitzgibbon back into his place. The media, predictably, commenced reporting on the pressures within the Labor Party, suggesting another round of climate change problems were going to arise, creating a schism between inner city elites and coal mining communities; which, of course, morphed into more speculation about Albanese's leadership and the possibility of facing a challenge to his position. Like all members of Parliament, Fitzgibbon understands how media management works in Australia and it was irresponsible—as a member of the Labor Party Caucus—to announce his resignation on that particular day.

The management of the political events as they play out is crucial for a leader, especially if they're in opposition during a time of immense crisis. The election result in Queensland shows that the Labor brand is palatable and acceptable to the electorate, provided there is the right leadership in place. Strong leadership is rewarded by the electorate, weak leadership is punished. That's the critical lesson of the Queensland election, and it's a lesson Albanese should heed.

*

Murdoch petition sealed and delivered

12 November

The petition to instigate a Royal Commission to ensure a strong, diverse Australian news media—initiated by former Prime Minister Kevin Rudd and, essentially, and inquiry into the assets of Rupert Murdoch and his media empire, News Corporation—closed on 4 November and has recorded 501,876 signatures of support.

It was tabled in the House of Representatives by Labor member, Andrew Leigh, subsequently tabled by Australian Greens Senator Sarah Hanson-Young, and the result of this has been the creation of the Media diversity in Australia Senate inquiry.[144]

Surprisingly, the federal government didn't vote against it: it's not the Royal Commission that Rudd requested but, given that the Liberal–National Coalition would never accept one while they're in government, perhaps it's the best that the public can expect at this point of time.

It's encouraging that over 500,000 people have supported the petition but it also has to be remembered that even if all of these signatures are *bona fide*, it only represents around 3 per cent of the 15 million people on the electoral rolls across Australia. But even so, it's

---

144 Parliament of Australia, 'Media diversity in Australia', 11 November 2020. https://www.aph.gov.au/Parliamentary_Business/Committees/Senate/Environment_and_Communications/Mediadiversity

a significant amount of people and the largest e-petition presented to Parliament, surpassing the 339,971 signatures calling for a declaration of a climate change emergency in 2019. It's reflective of a mood within the community that there is a media concentration in Australia that is not in the interests of good government practices and accountability.

The existing media power structures are breaking down and legacy media is looking out for other avenues of influence. That's not to suggest legacy media will disappear overnight or the *Daily Telegraph*, *Herald Sun* or *The Courier-Mail* are going to stop publishing anytime soon, but there is a sense that changes within the media publishing and news reporting industry will start to incrementally appear on the horizon soon.

It also suggests there's a level of anger—certainly for the 501,876 people who supported the petition, and certainly for Rudd—and another example of a federal government on the wrong side of history, as it has been since 2013. It may well turn out to be a very important Senate inquiry, given Rudd has previously stated that Murdoch is the "cancer eating the heart of Australian democracy" and an "abuse of media monopoly in Australia".[145,146] The Senate inquiry will complete its report by November 2021.

*

---

145 *Sydney Morning Herald*, 'Cancer eating the heart of Australian democracy', Kevin Rudd, 27 August 2018. https://www.smh.com.au/politics/federal/cancer-eating-the-heart-of-australian-democracy-20180826-p4zzum.html

146 SBS News, "Cancer on our democracy': Kevin Rudd calls for inquiry into Murdoch media dominance', 12 October 2020. https://www.sbs.com.au/news/cancer-on-our-democracy-kevin-rudd-calls-for-inquiry-into-murdoch-media-dominance

Not flying the Indigenous flag

12 November

NAIDOC Week (National Aborigines and Islanders Day Observance Committee) was held in November for the first time—moved away from its regular July slot because of the coronavirus pandemic—and there was a Senate motion proposed by the Labor Party to display the Aboriginal and Torres Strait Islander flags in the Senate chambers, alongside the existing national Australian flag.

This seems like a reasonable proposition, especially during a week that celebrates Indigenous culture, and the government had received three months' notice about this request—the Aboriginal and Torres Strait Islander flags have been recognised as national flags since 1995—but the federal government, with crossbench support, voted against the motion, indicating the only "appropriate" flag to be displayed in the Senate is the Australian flag.

The conservative viewpoint on these matters is that it's only "empty symbolism"[147] to fly an Indigenous flag at Parliament House but, despite these viewpoints, it's an important issue: if hoisting a flag is considered to be an 'empty gesture', what is the presence of the Australian flag in the Senate chambers meant to represent?

What is on the side of the federal government is that perhaps there aren't enough people in the community to feel that this is

---

147 *The Australian*, 'Vital step along the road to indigenous recognition', 14 November 2019. https://www.theaustralian.com.au/commentary/editorials/vital-step-along-the-road-to-indigenous-recognition/news-story/3c0c1318bc8f0aa033d2c10c3e8df329

an important issue, but if that is the case, then it comes down to national leadership to implement these types of actions. Sometimes, the smallest gestures can lead to the biggest impact, but this is a conservative government that has constantly worked against the interests of Indigenous people.

In 2014, Prime Minister Tony Abbott implement cutbacks of $534 million to front-line Indigenous services[148] and there have been consistent reductions of funding over the past seven years. The federal government refused to accept the Makarrata treaty process from the Uluru Statement from the Heart, claiming it would create and unwieldy 'third chamber' of Parliament, even though this is not even remotely a part of the Makarrata.

For the first time, the Minister for Aboriginal Affairs is an Indigenous person—Ken Wyatt—yet he's done very little for Indigenous Australia during his time, and actively worked against their interests as well. A small element of symbolism, that would have cost in the vicinity of a few hundred dollars to acquire the flags and hoist them in the Senate chamber, and the Minister couldn't even work the party room to have the motion passed in the Senate. It also shows the federal government is not prepared to cede half a millimetre on anything to do with Indigenous affairs, even if not doing something ends up being harder than actually doing the work itself.

It's also ironic that for all of the sanctity the government promotes about the Australian flag, it doesn't actually apply this sanctity correctly: wearing the Australian flag as a lapel, as Morrison is wont to do, is against national conventions; it shouldn't be worn as a mask, or a badge, or as a handkerchief, and these types of actions are considered to be 'defacing the flag' and reducing the dignity of the flag.[149] While it might be churlish to suggest all the acts of the Australian flags printed on beach towels and singlets are politically incorrect, at least politicians should be applying the conventions correctly and not displaying their ignorance.

---

148 ABC News, 'Budget 2014: $534 million cut to Indigenous programs', 16 May 2014. https://www.abc.net.au/news/2014-05-13/budget-2014:-$534-cut-to-indigenous-programs-and-health/5451144

149 Australian National Flag Association, Flag Protocol. https://www.anfa-national.org.au/flying-the-flag/flag-protocol

It's not a surprise the federal government failed to support such a simple gesture of flying the Aboriginal and Torres Strait Islander flags in the Senate chamber. It's a continuation of how lowly it perceives Indigenous issues and how reluctant it is to act on these important matters.

*

Mr Morrison goes to Tokyo and returns empty handed

27 November

Last week, Prime Minister Scott Morrison made a lightning visit to Japan and it's still unclear what the purpose of the trip was: ostensibly, it was to conclude a Reciprocal Access Agreement that remains unsigned. It was a twenty-four-hour visit and meeting with Japan's new Prime Minister, Yoshihide Suga, but it really could have waited for another time.

The eternal sticking point for concluding the Agreement for shared military activities between Australia and Japan is the reluctance of the Japanese government to remove the death penalty for any offence Australian troops may commit when they're stationed in Japan, although Morrison is reluctant to reveal this:

> **Jake Sturmer (journalist):** Prime Minister, under the Reciprocal Access Agreement, the in-principle agreement signed today, will Australian troops be subject to the death penalty in Japan?
>
> **Scott Morrison:** Well, what we've been able to achieve is that Australia will meet all of its obligations under its international agreements in relation to that matter.
>
> **Sturmer:** It's a yes or no question, what's the answer, sorry, I'm just not clear. That's always been the hurdle in this over the death penalty?

Morrison: No, we've been able to resolve it by ensuring that Australia could satisfy all of our international obligations in relation to that matter. And that has been a key factor for us as we work through this issue. And we're pleased that that was able to be worked through with the Japanese government. And I thank both Prime Minister Suga and his predecessor, Prime Minister Abe, for getting to that point.

Sturmer: So, there has been progress over the issue of the death penalty?

Morrison: The progress of ensuring that Australia is able to meet its commitments under its international obligations. Yes.

Sturmer: Can you just explain what that is?

Morrison: That's exactly what I just explained to you.

Sturmer: I'm not clear how the document sets that out?

Morrison: It is satisfied in the series of documents which are now finalised as we move to the conclusion of the agreement, which we hope to be able to put in place next year.

Sturmer: So, Australians won't face the death penalty?

Morrison: Australia will comply with all of their obligations in relation to the death penalty.

Morrison obfuscated in his responses and not much has changed in the progress of the Agreement, and his media release indicates the visit to Japan was more about a media opportunity, rather than anything of substance.[150] A last-minute overseas visit that really didn't need to take place at this point of time, an Agreement that has yet to be made. On his return to Australia, Morrison quarantined at the Lodge in Canberra with his official photographer, accessed Parliamentary Question Time remotely on his laptop from the comforts of his bedroom and, yet again, avoided scrutiny. Morrison is the consummate media marketing and performative prime minister and these recent events seem to be more about the appearances of

---

150 Prime Minister of Australia, Reciprocal Access Agreement, 17 November 2020. https://www.pm.gov.au/media/reciprocal-access-agreement

being a busy prime minister, rather than actually *being* a busy prime minister.

It's almost as though Morrison has acquired a travel bug and needs to go overseas at regular intervals, infamously travelling to Hawaii while bushfires were ravaging much of Australia in December 2019. Either that, or he feels that his time is finite as prime minister and has the need to fill in as much travel as possible before his time expires. In contemporary Australian politics, events can change dramatically when least expected, and perhaps there's something in his background that provides him with the impression that his position may be coming to an end, sooner rather than later. Of course, he may be in office for another decade, but his behaviours are not of someone who feels they'll be in there for that long.

Morrison has never liked the scrutiny of his office and his natural inclination is to bluff, bluster, deflect and tell outright mistruths. His sacking as the managing director of Tourism Australia in 2006; his departure from the New Zealand Office of Tourism and Sport in 2000; a brief stint with consulting group KPMG. All covered over in a shroud of secrecy and non-disclosure agreements. Unfortunately for Morrison, the job of Australian Prime Minister arrives with a higher level of scrutiny when compared with a job within Tourism Australia or an obscure position in an overseas destination.

Perhaps Morrison also considers any time after the May 2019 federal election as a bonus period, considering very few people expected the Liberal–National Coalition to hold on to government and there were suggestions at the time that he would be one of the shortest reigning prime ministers in Australian history. Morrison proved most people wrong by winning an election that even he possibly wasn't expecting to win. But he did.

In the years to come, historians will look back at this time and struggle to understand how Morrison came into the position of prime minister, and arrive at the conclusion that he was in the right time at the right place, rather than arriving into the position with any gravitas or intellectual abilities to perform well. Morrison understands power though, and perhaps that's where his credentials lie, as well as his desire to maintain this power, but not credentialled in many other areas.

The main area of contention within the Reciprocal Access Agreement is the access to death penalty: the conservative side of politics usually sees the death penalty as a viable punishment for egregious crimes but whether there's agreement or disagreement about this issue, it exists as law in the jurisdiction of Japan. If an Australian soldier did commit a crime punishable by death on Japanese territory, the Australian Department of Foreign Affairs usually steps in to diplomatically resolve the issue—except in areas such as those facing Julian Assange in Britain, which is more about politics rather than law—but in the context of the unlawful killings by Australian Special Air Service Regiment soldiers in Afghanistan, it's obvious why this might be a sticking point for the government of Japan, and why the Australian government would be worried.

Prime Minister Suga didn't seem to be so impressed with Morrison's aggressive 'elbow tap'—the equivalent of the handshake during the coronavirus era—but he may have been more bemused about why Morrison was in Japan at this point of time. The Reciprocal Access Agreement is an arrangement where the military of both countries can be engaged in war gaming and development of shared strategy and tactical knowledge, either on Australian or Japanese soil, as well as a military friendship exercise as well. These arrangements are not unusual—there is a similar arrangement with the government of Indonesia[151]—but they also help to solidify or establish better relationships between those countries in other ways, such as trade, medical research, tourism, education and cultural exchange.

But it does go back to the original question: why now, and why for only twenty-four hours? It could have been added to another series of diplomatic arrangements in the south-east Asia region at a later time, once the coronavirus pandemic is under control. And Morrison's decision to make a last-minute visit to Japan has caused great angst within China's diplomatic services, at a time of heightened tensions with both Australia and Japan. Morrison seems to be relaxed about the worsening relationship between Australia and China, without a strategy in place or an endgame. China has been placing tariffs on Australian imports—damaging to Australian

---

151 *Defence Connect*, 'Bilateral exercise to strengthen ties with Indonesia', Louis Dillon, 19 November 2019. https://www.defenceconnect.com.au/key-enablers/5167-bilateral-exercise-to-strengthen-ties-with-indonesia

exporters—and will continue doing this for some time to come, all primarily because of Morrison's poor diplomatic skills in appearing to blame China for causing the coronavirus.

There is a section of the wealth class and business community in Australia that prefers to see an expanded lower-income sector of the economy, which helps to drive Australian exports, forces wages and prices down, which also keeps the Australia dollar down and makes it more competitive on the international markets. But it also creates more misery and more poverty.

For those captains of industry and wealth in Australia, they're not too concerned about this: if they're doing well, they're not going to be too concerned about what's happening at this level of the economy, with businessman Gerry Harvey suggesting providing support to homeless and the unemployed was helping "a whole heap of no-hopers survive for no good reason", while his company, Harvey Norman, received $6 million in JobKeeper subsidies and doubled its profits.[152] And if this wealth sector is there to create as much wealth as possible—as well as antagonise those without wealth—then it's the role of government to ensure wealth is shared more equitably.

The business community has the government that it wants in power: there are shared values and agreement on promoting the wealth class, at the expense of the working class. But to create antagonisms with a global power and Australia's largest trading partner—$194 billion in two-way trade with China, compared to the second ranking of $77 billion in two-way trade with Japan[153]—is quite irresponsible and seems, on the surface, a very strange decision and perhaps shows a vestige of outdated 'white' Australia diplomatic thinking.

There doesn't seem to be an understanding that it is possible to have good strong relationships with two rival nations: that's the role of diplomacy. Australia maintained good relationships with Britain and the United States when those two countries exhibited difficulties

---

152 *Australian Financial Review*, 'Gerry Harvey no fan of wasted charity', Myriam Robin, 9 March 2021. https://www.afr.com/rear-window/gerry-harvey-no-fan-of-wasted-charity-20210308-p578u7

153 Department of Foreign Affairs and Trade, 'Trade and Investment at a Glance 2019'. http://www.worldstopexports.com/australias-top-import-partners/

over the Suez crisis in 1956[154] and during the 1970s, when British Prime Minister Edward Heath considered the United States as a "natural relationship" rather than a "special relationship", considered one of the lowest points in British–United States relations.[155] The relationship with Indonesia and East Timor—the push for East Timorese independence by Australia caused severe tensions in the Australia–Indonesia relationship—is also another example where issues can be managed and goodwill maintained. But it takes skill; it takes knowledge and it takes solid experience in being able to walk the fine line between good relationships and outright hostility between two or more countries.

Australia has very good diplomatic corps, but if Donald Trump had won the recent election in the United States, perhaps that might have provided Morrison with more cover. Since the demise of Trump and the end of the rhetoric of the trade war with China, Morrison now seems to be on his own. The incoming US President, Joe Biden, doesn't seem to have the same level of interest as Trump or Morrison in antagonising China, and he'll be keen to create the United States–China relationship according to his own line of thinking—which ultimately might not be any better than the way it currently exists—but at least it will be a different approach to the Trumpist style of war-mongering and megaphone diplomacy.

A manageable relationship between the United States and China is good for the world economy, and it's also good for the Australian economy. But the Australia–China relationship will be based upon some of the diplomatic problems caused by Morrison, despite what occurs between the United States and China. If Morrison considers that he's on borrowed time after the May 2019 election, he won't be too fussed about causing ructions with China and a further deterioration of that relationship, if the results of his actions and diminishing Australia's relationship with China accords with his personal ideologies and world view. Presently, there are over eighty Australian coal ships stranded near Chinese ports holding

---

154 *Critique 35.2*, "'Force is the Last Method': Eisenhower, Dulles and American Intervention in the Suez Crisis.", Richard M. Filipink Jr, 2007.
155 *New York Times*, 'Natural, Not Special Ties', C. L. Sulzberger, 14 January 1973. https://www.nytimes.com/1973/01/14/archives/natural-not-special-ties-foreign-affairs.html

$1.1 billion worth of coal,[156] held up, putatively over issues related to environmental standards and the low grade of coal, and many of the ships have been held up for several months. It was a similar situation with lobster exports—a $752 million per year market—where Chinese authorities decided to change their inspection protocols and screening processes, resulting in twenty-one tonnes of live cargo left at Shanghai Airport.

There might be an expectation from the Chinese government that Morrison needs to grovel or apologise for the humiliation he caused on the international stage but fanning the flames of anti-China sentiment always plays out politically for conservative governments in Australia, and he is unlikely to back down. And, given this situation, the impromptu acts of tariffs imposed on key Australian goods coming into the Chinese market, or consumable goods stranded at Chinese airports for a range of indiscriminate reasons, are likely to continue for as long as Morrison remains as the prime minister. Pre-emptively, Australian producers are seeking other markets outside of China, as it's unclear which goods or services will be targeted next.[157] But new markets are difficult to find and take years to cultivate so it's a problem Australian exporters may find themselves in for some time to come.

The other factor arising from Morrison's lightning visit to Japan is the need for him to go through a mandatory fourteen-day quarantine on his return to Australia. And being quarantined in the Lodge in Canberra provided excellent media opportunities documented by the Prime Minister's official photographer, Adam Taylor, a former News Corporation employee. Never one to miss an opportunity, Morrison was photographed in the *de rigueur* Zoom-era fashion of the day—a suit top and business shirt, board shorts and thongs below—followed up by another photograph of Morrison on an exercise bike, with legs suitable blurred to suggest a man-of-action peddling at break-neck speed; Morrison reading a

---

156 *7 News*, 'Australian coal ships held up off Chinese ports amid trade tensions', Daniel McCulloch, 26 November 2020. https://7news.com.au/business/finance/australian-coal-held-up-off-chinese-ports-c-1653183

157 *The Wall Street Journal*, 'Squeezed by China's Tariffs, Australian Farmers Cultivate New Markets', Rhiannon Hoyle, 25 February 2021. https://www.wsj.com/articles/squeezed-by-chinas-tariffs-australian-farmers-cultivate-new-markets-11614249003

newspaper; Morrison at a prime ministerial desk, about to put pen to blank paper, Trump-style.

Prime ministers have always had photographers working in some capacity documenting their work, and this is an important part of the nation's visual history and archive. The position of official photographer has only existed since 2013, coinciding with the time Tony Abbott became prime minister and it's essential to have the workings of the office documented in a way that is meaningful to the general public. In Morrison's case, however, the official photographer is producing outright propaganda[158] and not acting in the interests of the public.

In addition to the quarantine series of photographs, Morrison has been recently photographed at Bunnings Warehouses, purchasing hardware items, photographed building cubby houses and chicken coops at heritage-listed Kirribilli House in Sydney, where chickens are not permitted to be housed. It's a media narrative that seems to be endless, although there has been some skepticism, with Mick Tsikas, a veteran political photojournalist for Australian Associated Press, suggesting "we don't touch those photos… we view them as propaganda. Who knows with that chicken coop—did he nail the first nail and that was it? Or did he finish the whole thing. You wouldn't know."[159]

And that is the essence of Morrison's prime ministership: a prime minister with a raft of activity wouldn't need to promote himself as a man of action—the act of actually *being* busy and implementing government action should be the promotion and media opportunity in itself. Actions should speak louder than words, but in the absence of productivity, Morrison is engaged in endless publicity stunts and everyday-man-husband types of activities that have nothing to do with managing the country. This, of course, plays out to particular demographics and target groups within the electorate—otherwise Morrison wouldn't engage in humiliating engagements that would

---

158 *Inside Imaging*, 'Press photography infiltrated by "propaganda"', 6 August 2020. https://www.insideimaging.com.au/2020/press-photography-infiltrated-by-propaganda

159 *The Guardian*, "Daggy dad' or 'propaganda'? The media's growing use of official Scott Morrison pictures', Naaman Zhou, 25 November 2020. https://www.theguardian.com/australia-news/2020/nov/25/daggy-dad-or-propaganda-the-medias-growing-use-of-official-scott-morrison-pictures

put stuntmasters such as Russian President Vladimir Putin or British Prime Minister Boris Johnson to shame.

And pushing out these meaningless action photographs hides other political issues: while the media and public attention was preoccupied with the happy snaps of the Prime Minister in board shorts and thongs; on an exercise bike; building a coop; and reading a newspaper; the issues of RoboDebt, his performances as Treasurer, Minister for Social Services, and as Prime Minister all tend to be forgotten about.

RoboDebt was a complete tragedy, knowingly implemented by this federal government, and a time when Morrison was the Minister for Social Services. The High Court found that the program as implemented by Services Australia was illegal, and resulted in 470,000 wrongfully-issued debts—to people who had no debt. The mistakes created by the federal government will cost over $1.2 billion, made up of $721 million in repayments and a further $500 million to settle a class action lawsuit before it went to trial but that can never compensate for the over 2,000 people who died after receiving Centrelink debt notices.[160]

Whenever there is impending difficult news for this government, Morrison disappears. It's a well-formed practice by the Prime Minister, where he goes overseas on manufactured 'important' business, travels without telling anyone about it, engages in idiot media *shtick*—or all of the above—or simply disappears. And it's a set of classic engagements of a government that wants to avoid scrutiny and cover over its many poor performances, its poor governance, its corruption and its mismanagement. And while the public might lap up and crave these media management moments from Morrison—like the crowd at a zoo watching the performing seals, while the polar bears sneak out and terrorise all the other animals—ultimately, it's the public that suffers when incompetent governments remain in power.

Good government hasn't existed since 2013 and there's been a high level of instability in federal politics since former Prime

---

160 ABC Triple J *Hack*, 'Over 2000 people died after receiving Centrelink robo-debt notice, figures reveal', Shalailah Medhora, 18 February 2019. https://www.abc.net.au/triplej/programs/hack/2030-people-have-died-after-receiving-centrelink-robodebt-notice/10821272

Minister Kevin Rudd was deposed by his own party in June 2010. The arrival of the Abbott government in 2013 was essentially the continuation of the maniacal brand of oppositional politics from 2009–13 into government business and management, and the Morrison government is an extension of this thinking: an opposition party in government, with no wish to change this.

*

Cormann takes on the OECD

27 November

Senator Mathias Cormann has announced his retirement from politics and is the only person to support three prime ministers in a leadership challenge—during the Liberal Party leadership challenge in August 2018, Cormann was calculating the numbers for different contenders, and managed to pledge support initially for Malcolm Turnbull, switched over to Peter Dutton, before throwing his support towards Scott Morrison.

Cormann resigned from the Australian Parliament in early November after a thirteen-year stint as a Senator for the Liberal Party, including seven years as the longest serving finance minister and, as soon as he exited the door, he embarked on a taxpayer funded excursion to become the next Secretary–General of the Organisation for Economic Co-operation and Development. It has been revealed his quest has been supported by eight government staff members and escorted throughout Europe in a RAAF jet at the cost of $4,000 per hour.

Cormann has only a small chance of becoming the Secretary–General of the OECD but when asked about the cost of this venture, Morrison claimed the cost represented "value for money" and flying on commercially-available flight was deemed to be too risky during this time of the coronavirus pandemic. It's an extravagant outlay for what is, essentially, a post-politics job for a political friend who assisted Morrison to become prime minister in 2018.

Of course, Cormann has a right to seek whichever position he wishes to and having the experience in government enables him to spruik his credentials to whichever organisation or business is prepared to accept him.

Politics aside, Cormann personal story is fascinating. He came from a working-class family in a German-speaking community in a small city in Belgium, completing law studies and first learning the English language in 1993. When he first settled in Australia in 1996, he worked as a school gardener before working his way through the Western Australia Branch of the Liberal Party in various roles until he was selected as a Senator for Western Australia in 2007. It's an Australian migrant success story that should be celebrated. But when looking at any substantial policy gains and his political history over thirteen years, there really isn't very much to show: there are five Budgets that weren't passed by the Senate and two that were amended substantially during his time as Minister for Finance.

In a field of ten candidates for the role of Secretary–General of the OECD—a five-year term based in Paris—Cormann is perhaps a middle-ranked candidate but still considered a rank outsider, especially when compared against candidates such former European Trade Commissioner, Cecilia Malmström, experienced Greek politician and minister, Anna Diamantopoulou and President of Estonia, Kersti Kaljulaid, with Malmström favoured to take on the appointment.

Longevity in politics—or any field—shouldn't be considered as a key attribute of success, and while a thirteen-year career as a Senator is a marker of some level of success, Cormann's credentials should be viewed from 2013 onwards, when he first became Minister for Finance. While it's clear the position of finance is not the same as the Treasurer, who holds the ultimate political responsibility for the state of the economy, the two do work together in creating Budgets and developing the economic narrative for the government of the day.

But since 2013, the Australian economy has been underperforming, reaching a per-capita recession in 2019, narrowly avoiding actual recession for three consecutive quarters in the backend of 2019 and early 2020, before the onset of the coronavirus pandemic guaranteed the recession that had been predicted, in June 2020. This is not the sign of good economic management, and it has all occurred during Cormann's tenure.

As its name suggests, the OECD is primarily an economic organisation that acts as a forum, peak body and 'think tank' for its thirty-seven member countries, which represent 62 per cent of the world's economic output. Although it doesn't hold the power to enforce its decisions, it is an influential and important organisation in global economics. However, as part of its future thinking, the OECD has recommended world economies should move towards net zero greenhouse emissions as soon as possible, and effective global climate change action is urgent. Cormann's pitch to the OECD to bolster his bid has been reflective of these values, suggesting the OECD "can and must provide important global leadership to drive ambitious and effective action on climate change" and "help economies around the world achieve global net-zero emissions by 2050".[161]

Yet, during the time he was in office as a senior member of the Liberal–National Coalition government, Cormann did his utmost to deter climate change action: he was a part of a government that campaigned strongly against 'carbon tax' issues in the lead-up to the 2013 federal election; repealed Labor's carbon pricing legislation that had been the most effective tool in reducing greenhouse gas emissions; abolished the Climate Commission in one of the first acts of the Coalition government in 2013; repealed the *Clean Energy Act* in 2014; scrapped subsidies for renewable energy in 2017, failed to implement the National Energy Guarantee which would have resulted in lower emissions; and established a National Covid-19 Coordination Commission that championed a 'gas-led recovery' in Australia's post-pandemic economy.

These are not the signs of a candidate who wants to "drive ambitious and effective action on climate change", or "achieve global net-zero emissions by 2050", rather, a senior politician who has done his best to achieve the opposite. Cormann has little credibility on economic policy, and has no credibility on climate changes at

---

161 *The Guardian*, 'Mathias Cormann: the Australian OECD candidate trying to airbrush his climate record', Daniel Hurst, 20 February 2021. https://www.theguardian.com/australia-news/2021/feb/19/mathias-cormann-the-australian-oecd-candidate-trying-to-airbrush-his-climate-record

all: if Cormann does end up being the successful candidate and is appointed as Secretary–General of the OECD, it could either be a case where the OECD has seen qualities in Cormann that have never been on display in a thirteen-year political career in Australia; more credentialled candidates withdraw their nomination; or a sign that like most of the political world, their public commentary on climate change is essentially paying lip-service to an important global issue, and they're not inclined to recommend economic change that restructures world economies in an effort to address climate change.

In supporting Cormann's nomination, the Prime Minister has suggested that having an Australian citizen as Secretary–General of the OECD is important, but there is no direct relevance or advantage to the Australian economy in having an Australian in that position, and nor should there be. The position has a responsibility to all the economies of the thirty-seven member countries, and to the world economy overall: Morrison displayed a form of bureaucratic nationalism that was out of place, and is sure to use Cormann's appointment—unlikely as that might be—as a political weapon against Labor to suggest the world recognises the quality of Liberal Party ministers of finance, even though they've always ridiculed the award of the Euromoney Finance Minister of the Year to Labor Treasurers Paul Keating in 1984, and Wayne Swan in 2011. Cormann won't be able to provide 'favours' to the Australian government, if that's what Morrison is suggesting. Certainly, there is prestige for an Australian citizen to hold such a position on the world stage, but that's where it would end: he wouldn't be allowed to, or be seen to be favouring Australia in any way.

There also has been some controversy in the media about the cost of $4,000 per hour for the RAAF jet used to fly Cormann around Europe to lobby for his candidacy. But instead of focusing their attention on the acts of the federal government—after all, they are ones who have pushed through Cormann's nomination and made the decisions about the actions to be used for his nomination—they've criticised Labor leader, Anthony Albanese, for supporting the nomination in the first instance, albeit a qualified support, and suggesting if there are any criticisms of the federal government, then Albanese should share the responsibilities.

Albanese supported Cormann's nomination as Secretary-General of the OECD, as he considered it was the correct course of action, and the correct protocol to follow. In contrast, when former Prime Minister Kevin Rudd was seeking nomination to become Secretary-General of the United Nations in 2016, then Prime Minister Turnbull announced he would not support the nomination and after a "considered judgement"—including Cabinet discussions where Cormann spoke strongly against Rudd's nomination—he decided Rudd was not well suited for the role.

A failed Minister of Finance, who has actively campaigned against climate change and also campaigned against a former prime minister in his quest to become Secretary-General of the United Nations—also an appointment that would have provided Australia with prestige on the world stage—ends up with a nomination, even though he failed to support Rudd in a similar situation, who would have been a far more credentialed candidate for the position he was wishing to be nominated for. And that shows the nature of a partisan conservative Liberal Party: always seeking those personal benefits that suit themselves, and denying the opportunities for others, especially their opponents. Turnbull vetoing Rudd's nomination was a sheer act of political pettiness and shows they will act in their own interests, rather than the national interest.

Should Albanese have refused to support Cormann's nomination, as payback for the lack of support offer to Rudd in 2016? The federal government could have still continued with the candidacy if they wished to, but not receiving bipartisan support would have indicated a lack of confidence in that candidate, and there probably wouldn't have been any point in continuing with that nomination. Certainly, Albanese followed the correct course of action: if an Australian politician or diplomat is nominated for a senior international role, their candidacy should be supported, as they always have been—except for Rudd—and irrespective of which side of politics they come from.

There is a Confucian tenet that before embarking on a journey of revenge: dig two graves. These are wise words but, in this case, there is an element of politics that needs to be played out: the Liberal Party typically act as spoiler, break conventions and protocols, and reap all the political rewards; the Labor Party follows conventions and protocols, acts in the public interest and the national interest, and ends up empty-handed, rewarded with years in opposition and political oblivion. Albanese failed that political test: if he felt that Cormann was poor candidate, suggesting the government's position on climate change "has been so weak that it will undermine his [Cormann's] candidacy", he should have withdrawn the support from the Labor Party. Political action has to be based on rewards, and if Cormann is successful with his candidacy, it is the federal government that will accrue all the benefits and goodwill, not Albanese and the Labor Party. Albanese should have played harder in the game of politics.

Cormann's credentials are not without merit. But he is a poor candidate and gaining the appointment would be a reward for years of climate change denialism, poor economic management, and a politician who supported an 'It's OK to be white' motion in the Senate—even though he claimed it was an "administrative error"—and also negotiated a preference deal with the One Nation Party in the lead up to the Western Australia election in 2017. It would take an unusual turn of events for Cormann to be appointed as Secretary–General of the OECD.

> **Postscript:** An unusual turn of events did occur for Mathias Cormann and, progressively, eight of the ten candidates withdrew their nominations. Vladimír Dlouhý (Czech Republic) and Michał Kurtyka (Poland) withdrew their nominations on 13 January 2021; Christopher Liddell (United States) withdrew on 19 January 2021; Kersti Kaljulaid (Estonia) and William Morneau (Canada) withdrew on 28 January 2021; Ulrik Knudsen (Denmark) withdrew on 10 February 2021; Philipp Hildebrand (Switzerland) and Anna Diamantopoulou (Greece) withdrew on 2 March 2021.
>
> The final two candidates were Cecilia Malmström (Sweden) and Cormann, with Malmström still considered the favoured candidate. On 12 March 2021, the OECD appointed Cormann as the next Secretary–General, with his five-year term commencing on 1 June 2021.

*

Pizza lockdown in South Australia

27 November

How many pizzas does it take to cause a lockdown of an entire city? Several years ago, it's a question that would have been met with bemusement and ridicule but in the era of the coronavirus pandemic, it's now a question that can be easily answered. During the week, the South Australia Government locked down the city of Adelaide for seven days after a worker in a Woodville pizza bar provided misleading information about his relationship with the business that was misunderstood and misinterpreted by contact tracers, which led to an assumption that the coronavirus could be easily transmitted through cardboard pizza boxes.

Essentially, it was an issue blown out of all proportion and used to detract from another outbreak caused by flaws within the hotel quarantine system for overseas arrivals. The Parafield cluster of twenty coronavirus cases has been linked to poor management of hotel quarantine in Adelaide, and these problems are exactly the same as the problems that arose from hotel quarantine in Melbourne in June—albeit with a different final outcome. But the media responses, especially from the *Adelaide Advertiser*—another News Corporation newspaper—have been quite sympathetic to the plight of the South Australia Government, in complete contrast to their prolonged maniacal and hysterical attacks on the Victoria Government several months ago. The Premier of South Australia, Steven Marshall, applied an immediate lockdown of Adelaide but did he go too far, or did he act swiftly to protect the health of the public?

Coronavirus has been a terrible disease for many people who have been infected and there seems to be a different understanding of this across Australia. The governments of Victoria, Queensland and Western Australia have understood this differently to the government of New South Wales, which has placed the needs of business and commerce above the needs of public health—that's not to suggest they haven't worked hard to contain the virus—but their priorities have focused on the economy and causing political mischief over border closures in other states, making a mockery of Scott Morrison's claims that "we are all in this together".

The government of South Australia took the correct course of action, irrespective of how disadvantageous it was to the economy and the people of Adelaide. However, Premier Marshall was keen to apportion as much blame as possible onto the man who has become known as 'the Pizza guy'—a thirty-six-year-old Spanish national in Australia on a student visa—saying "the selfish actions of this individual have put our whole state in a very difficult situation... his actions have affected businesses, individuals, family groups and is completely and utterly unacceptable", which subsequently caused a social media boycott and outrage against the Woodville Pizza Bar.

Rather than focusing on the systemic problems that caused the outbreak, and the lockdown which was caused by the outbreak, Marshall wanted to bring up deflections to the lockdown which would have put him at ideological odds with Morrison and NSW Premier, Gladys Berejiklian, who have both taken potshots at Labor state governments for their versions of lockdowns and border closures: Marshall needed to find a scapegoat, and he found the solution in 'the Pizza guy': a non-Australian, a foreigner, a 'liar'; perfect fodder for a conservative media.

And it lessened the need to discuss the other consistent factor in all of the hotel quarantine outbreaks: a insecure and casualised lowly-paid workforce in the hotel quarantine system, where contracted staff work in multiple locations and multiple industries, increasing the chance of transmitting the coronavirus within the general community. It's surprising this critical link hasn't been made before, although the Victoria Government has announced it will overhaul its current system to ensure coronavirus outbreaks within hotel quarantine are eradicated or minimised.

'The Pizza guy' became the convenient fall guy: there'd be an expectation that health bureaucrats could have asked a few more questions or completed further investigations before recommending and implementing a full seven-day lockdown of an entire city but, of course, it's easier to blame others rather than take responsibility for poor acts of administration and mismanagement. And this fits into a pattern from the media: in July 2020, the names and faces of three women were splashed all over the front pages of the tabloid media after they made false declarations and travelled from Melbourne to Brisbane, via Sydney, with *The Courier-Mail* referring to them as "enemies of the state",[162] focusing on the colour and background of the women, rather than inadequacies within the system that failed to stop them from travelling. The same issue arose with 'the Pizza guy': otherness, Spanish, foreign, 'unlike-us-who-always-do-the-right-thing': it's the racist dog whistle that the conservative media and politicians always blow into at full throttle when it suits them the best.

Very few people—if any—would deliberately cause the coronavirus to spread, and every case so far in Australia has been inadvertent, caused by bureaucratic bungling, or the natural human response of not knowing exactly what to do during a pandemic that is a once-in-a-hundred-year event. If it can be found that people have behaved fraudulently, or acted as selfish criminals, then the law needs to be applied and actions to deter that kind of behaviour need to be implemented. But many people have transmitted coronavirus to other people in the community, without knowing they had the virus in the first place: surely, they can't be blamed for something they knew nothing about.

The main issue to point out is that every action to reduce risk during a pandemic needs to be taken, and the glaring issue of workers within the hotel quarantine system—usually casualised, low-paid, temporary or employed through a labour-hire arrangement without

---

162 *The Guardian*, 'Brisbane women charged over Melbourne trip as Queensland reports three new Covid-19 cases', 30 July 2020. https://www.theguardian.com/australia-news/2020/jul/30/queensland-covid-19-testing-blitz-results-best-we-could-have-hoped-for-as-three-new-cases-recorded

sick leave, holiday leave, superannuation or insurance—is one area that has not been acted upon. It is now being somewhat rectified but there is still a fundamental misunderstanding of how the 'gig economy' is failing the public interest and public health, especially during a time of crisis.

*

Afghanistan and the political killing season

27 November

Australia does have a tradition of putting its military forces on a public pedestal but their reputations took a sharp blow with the allegations of war crimes committed by Australian Special Air Service Regiment forces in Afghanistan, outlined in The Inspector-General of the Australian Defence Force Afghanistan Inquiry, led by Major General Paul Brereton. The Brereton report alleged thirty-nine Afghanis were murdered by personnel stationed in Afghanistan and has recommended nineteen of them should be prosecuted for war crimes.

The report also provided a historical context and found Australian military had committed war crimes in other conflicts as well: World War I, World War II, Vietnam, Korea. Further information about the current allegations will come out if there is to be a military trial but for the Australian Defence Force to provide this information suggests there is something very wrong within the military. Australia's military folklore is primarily based around the events of Gallipoli in 1915; others include the story of John Simpson and the donkey; Edward 'Weary' Dunlop; Nancy Wake, primarily people who provided medical assistance during wars. The Australian war tradition isn't merely about the Rats of Tobruk, the ANZACs or Gallipoli: it's the totality of the experience—the good and the bad—but the reports and allegations of war crimes committed in

Afghanistan is disturbing and disheartening, and resolution to this issue may take up to a decade.

Politically, many prime ministers have affiliated themselves with the military: Billy Hughes and the 'Little Digger' image he cultivated after World War I; Bob Hawke improved his relationship with the military and was quick to commit Australian troops to the Gulf War campaign in 1990; John Howard amplified the relationship; Tony Abbott was often photographed with military and federal police personnel; Scott Morrison was recently seen in a military tank during the recent Queensland election campaign.

Morrison does have the habit of draping himself in the Australian flag—appearing in front of the flag during media conferences, wearing it as a lapel on his suit, or as a facemask—but he also has the propensity to disassociate himself with any activity that holds a negative image: he made a quick announcement of the report, that it contained strong allegations of war crimes committed by Australian troops in a foreign country and then, it all ended, not to be discussed within the news cycle, or until it becomes absolutely necessary to provide an update in the future. And perhaps the Australian military will soon find out what a true friend Morrison is, as it appears the only use the military is to Morrison is in political terms and media opportunities: it's safe to assume the public won't be seeing the Prime Minister engaged in political stunts which involve army tanks and naval vessels for some time to come.

Justice in the military needs not only to be done, but also to be seen to be done and the military is best kept away from political partisanship and stunts which promote one side of politics over another. Often, when prime ministers become engaged with the military class, it's almost as though they're young children playing toy soldiers, acting out their fantasies from the school playground. It would be better if political leaders avoided the use of military props to boost their civilian image but as long as there are politicians, and as long there is a military, it seems the two will be intertwined.

Politics by other means

There is the infamous quote from the Prussian general and military theorist, Carl von Clausewitz, that "war is a mere continuation of politics by other means" and, in Australia, politically speaking,

December has been dubbed the 'killing season' in politics, where the final month of the year provides an opportunity for political parties to remove their leader—if they're considered to be underperforming or underwhelming—act as a circuit breaker, re-set, go into the Christmas break with new political leadership, and then be energised for the upcoming year in politics. On the Labor side, Mark Latham and Kevin Rudd launched successful leadership challenges in the month of December—2003 and 2006 respectively—as did Tony Abbott for the Liberal Party in 2009. Over in Western Australia, the Liberal Party commenced their killing season earlier, with the resignation of the Leader of the Opposition, Liza Harvey, just four months before the Western Australia election due in March 2021.

It's coming up to the final federal parliamentary session for 2020, and there has been some speculation in the media that if Labor wishes to make a change to its leadership team, this is the time to do it, especially in the context of the possibility of a federal election held in the second half of 2021. Albanese has been underwhelming as Leader of the Opposition, and some of this can be attributed to the effects of the coronavirus pandemic, but would there be an appetite for a leadership change now within the Labor Caucus?

Firstly, there are the Labor leadership rules which make it difficult for challengers to step up—it's difficult, but not impossible—and change would need to be orchestrated, rather than a messy Caucus process and rank-and-file ballot, in the case of more than one candidate. If this process was to be negotiated—and that's the only way that it could ever occur—who would be the likely replacement? There has been speculation that it could be the current Shadow Treasurer, Jim Chalmers, or the former deputy Labor leader Tanya Plibersek, with some outside focus on the Shadow Attorney-General, Mark Dreyfus, who has very little name recognition within the electorate.

The current parliamentary term is at the half-way point, and Albanese has followed the public interest in offering bipartisanship for coronavirus support packages during a time of immense crisis and community concern. This is commendable. Australia has managed the coronavirus very well and there are expectations vaccines will become available in early 2021, which is very good news for the community. But as a political party in opposition, it's difficult to keep offering support to the government of the day, keep doing this up until the day of the election, and not have any political capital banked up or anything to show for all of those efforts of support.

The other consideration is: when will the next election be held? Morrison may not have the courage to call a snap early election, considering he only holds onto government by one seat—or a majority of three seats—and recent polls have not provided a clear pathway to an election victory. A new leader needs time to solidify their position, and an election held as early as August 2021 may place a few handbrakes on those Labor Caucus members that may be pushing for a change now.

And this leads to the final factor: patience. Politicians of all persuasions don't want to sit on the opposition benches forever and they don't enter Parliament with an ambition to just arrive there and do nothing politically during their tenure: getting into government and beyond is the ambition of every politician that enters the doors of Australian Parliament House. If Morrison does call an election in the second half of 2021, that will have been eight years of Liberal–National Coalition government, which means eight years in opposition for the Labor Party.

Forty-one members of the ninety-four in the Labor Caucus have never experienced government. How impatient would they be to actually get into government? For the experienced Labor politicians, such as Plibersek or Senator Penny Wong, who are closer to the end of their political careers, rather than the beginning, how satisfied will they be of the prospects of another three-year term in opposition? Both have been long-term politicians—Plibersek since 1998 and Wong since 2002—but only in government office for six years. Opposition politics is incredibly difficult work and highly underestimated by the general public. If longer-term Labor politicians who recognise what it's like to be in government, as well as the hardship of opposition, if they feel they are unlikely to win the next election under the leadership Albanese, do they start agitating for change, or start thinking that perhaps it's time to tender their resignations and retire?

There are some talented people in the Labor Caucus and it's a reflection of what occurred after the 1949 federal election—

twenty-three years in the political wilderness, the Fraser and the Howard years—nineteen years in total, and currently eight years in opposition. That hunger for gaining government within Caucus is what will determine how long Albanese remains leader, and whether he leads Labor into the next election. It's likely that most opposition leaders would struggle to gain attention during such a time of crisis and perhaps that might end up being his saving grace: no one else can make a difference, so best to keep what is already there.

Quite often, politicians and political commentators in the media look out into the landscape and lack the imagination to think what can change, or what will change. Change can happen quickly, and in the least expected ways. Albanese is still likely to lead the Labor Party into the next election—whenever it is called—but something needs to change, because it doesn't seem to be working out right now.

*

The hard right-wing agenda and bad habits

11 December

There are more punitive legislative reforms being pushed through by this federal government: the Attorney-General, Christian Porter, wants to introduce legislation to change industrial relations; the Cashless Debit Card program which is enforced upon recipients of social security payments is one step closer to becoming a permanent program—although it has been blocked in the Senate for the time being—and after the failures and incompetence shown in the RoboDebt saga, an aggressive debt recovery program has been introduced to extract money from welfare recipients.

And there's no secret about their punitive right-wing agenda—several months ago, Treasurer Josh Frydenberg clearly stated that this agenda would be guided by the ideals of former British Prime Minister, Margaret Thatcher—and although she left office thirty years ago, the Liberal Party of today is keen to implement British Conservative Party nastiness, spitefulness, and the hateful and humiliating policies that attack working people, pensioners and social security recipients. From a progressive perspective, there is never the right time to implement these ideas but, from any type of perspective, these are the wrong policies at the wrong time. They are not in the interests of the public and the federal government keeps pushing for the policies and agendas that shouldn't even be reaching the discussion table.

This is a federal government that keeps pushing the idea of a smaller role for government within the economy and within the community, less red tape and making it easier for everyone until it arrives at the point of looking after the poorest parts of the community, those on the fringes and the people who don't fit into their ideological understanding of the world. Far from helping vulnerable people, they want to exploit these people for political purposes and promote downward envy within the electorate.

On the surface, many of the federal government's proposals have their genesis in Thatcherite ideas from the 1980s, and Porter has insisted the legislative reforms are necessary during the coronavirus pandemic: his message is that businesses have had difficulties, and the traditional conservative mantra, that it's better to have a job, than no job at all. But a job needs to have dignity as well, not a mad scramble to bottom to see who can be paid the least.

Porter's proposals include: a business being able to spontaneously change the duties of a worker; forcing workers to work additional hours without overtime pay; more casualisation of work; reduced levels of pay for at least the next two years and, in those circumstances where workers have been underpaid, the removal of the right to make a claim for backpay. Certainly, workers would prefer to have a job, but they also want job security and Porter wishes to implement punitive and unnecessarily harsh conditions that will result in more unsustainable and insecure work.

There are great similarities between Porter's industrial reforms and some of the more severe parts of the WorkChoices package former Prime Minister John Howard wanted to introduce back in 2005. But the thinking behind these reforms goes way past Howard, or Thatcher: it's the same conservative thinking from the 1950s, of the 1920s, or even of the 1890s. It's a notion that wages are always too high in relation to productivity, there isn't a need for a social wage and only the worthy should be lashed with riches and wealth.

There is a branch of Christianity that subscribes to this notion and it manifests itself in several ways: there is the prosperity theology of Pentecostalism; the Protestant 'work ethic', where there is strong relationship between working hard and being rewarded for the hard work. The issue here is that not everybody had the ability to fit into this religious model of 'hard work', and there are many different ways to contribute to the world, outside of the equation that 'working hard' equates to a high income. Most people work hard, but that doesn't mean everyone ends up becoming a millionaire. In most developed economies, employment, work and productivity should be based on social responsibility, paying fair prices and ensuring people employed by businesses and organisations are working safely. The Australia economy was an excellent model for this in the post-war period after 1945.

The antecedents for this were the Harvester case in 1907, a landmark Australian labour law decision of the Commonwealth Court of Conciliation and Arbitration. Justice Henry Bournes Higgins declared that "fair and reasonable" wages for an unskilled worker required a living wage that was sufficient for "a human being in a civilised community" to support a spouse and three children in "frugal comfort", while a skilled worker should receive an additional margin for their skills, regardless of the employer's capacity to pay. There wasn't a suggestion that the concept of "comfort" should be an extraordinary mansion with many servants and luxury cars, but a basic lifestyle: being able to own a modest house; affordable rent or mortgages; food and utility bills; an income base from employment that supported a decent and well-functioning society.

There's also the social contract that was developed by philosophers such as Jean-Jacques Rousseau in the 1700s, and Pierre-Joseph Proudhon in the 1800s, outlining the relationship that exists between rulers of a nation and the people within the realm: people have inherent rights and exercising these inherent rights collectively becomes more powerful than the rights of government. But this current federal government is not one that adopts these philosophies and it's evident that by proffering a policy agenda that removes substantial rights of working people, it had a desire to disrupt that social contract, remove powers and rights that belong to the general public, and move these rights over to the business class and the elite part of society.

There is other evidence where the federal government wishes to disrupt the social contract: the Minister for Superannuation, Senator Jane Hume, has been leading a campaign against industry superannuation funds, which is perhaps one of the more bizarre and incomprehensible campaigns in federal politics. Industry superannuation funds are those managed by not-for-profit groups and unions. Over a fifteen-year period, industry funds have outperformed retail superannuation funds—managed by banks and for-profit providers—by 21 per cent over the past fifteen years,[163] and have significantly outperformed retail funds in terms of returns over one, three, five and ten-year periods.[164]

Investing superannuation in industry funds, rather than retail funds, could have a massive difference over a working lifetime for those in retirement and, for a federal government that wishes to push self-funding in retirement and less dependency on government pensions, it seems to be a peculiar ideologically-driven agenda that is not in the interests of working people. It's seems the agenda is to syphon funds away from the traditional enemies of conservative governments—unions—and move it towards the vested interests affiliated with the Liberal Party. Also, there are many industry superannuation funds moving away from fossil fuels investments and with the strong support the federal government has with oil and mining interests, perhaps it's one way of creating a political difference with their opponents, and well as funnelling funds towards a resources industry they've been support of and, in return, an industry that supports them financially and politically.

Many industry funds have withdrawn from fossil fuel and coal investments, not for ideological reasons, but it's now considered to be better for business and returns. The traditional sources of energy are gradually being replaced around the world by renewables and investing now in a dying industry means that there will be a high level of stranded assets in the future, if a high level of investment is made now into an industry which is going to be replaced. Although there are new coal mines being opened, there are many more that are closing down. Many European countries are banning diesel and petrol case sales by 2040. North America and parts of Asia and Northern Africa have similar proposals on the table. There are substantial changes occurring in energy delivery and the federal

---

163 Australian Super, 'Retail or Industry super funds, what is the difference?', https://www.australiansuper.com/superannuation/superannuation-articles/2018/10/retail-or-industry-super-funds

164 *Money Management*, 'The never-ending story – industry vs retail super funds', Anastasia Santoreneos, 9 April 2018. https://www.moneymanagement.com.au/features/never-ending-story-%E2%80%93-industry-vs-retail-super-funds

government's approach to targeting industry superannuation will achieve two political and ideological agendas for them: removing the influence of unions within the superannuation industry—even though they are outperforming retail superannuation funds—and provide more support for fossil fuel industries. And who will be the main loser in these agendas? The general public, as they always have been whenever conservative agendas are implemented.

And, of course, the Liberal–National Coalition government will always attempt to introduce other harsh measures to attack those groups which it considers to be its enemies: the poor, the unemployed and underemployed, Indigenous people, people who are excluded from society and the economy through no fault of their own, and those who don't subscribe to their version of a prosperity philosophy. The Cashless Debit Card is one of those harsh measures.

The scheme, also known as the Indue card, is back on the government's agenda—although it never really dropped fully off their agenda—and it's a program they're fully committed to. The program has been trialled for the past five years and it's a forced welfare payments system that targets Indigenous people in remote communities and severely restricts what the recipients can spend their money on, with 80 per cent of their income—stored on the Cashless Debit Card—limited to retail locations determined by the Department of Human Services. It's a racist scheme; it's discriminatory; it's paternalistic. And, ultimately, according to research prepared by the University of Adelaide, it's a scheme that's ineffective.[165]

The federal government has been keen to make the program a permanent arrangement and legislation to enforce this was passed in the House of Representatives during the week, but blocked in the Senate by independent Senator Rex Patrick, who considered voting for the legislative bill but decided there was not enough evidence to suggest it should be introduced on a permanent basis. He has decided to implement his own fact-finding venture to Ceduna—one of the

---

165 The University of Adelaide, 'Evaluation of the Cashless Debit Car in Ceduna, East Kimberley and the Goldfields Region', Kostas Mavromaras, Megan Moskos, Stéphane Mahuteau & Linda Isherwood, January 2021. https://www.dss.gov.au/sites/default/files/documents/02_2021/fac_evaluation-cdc-ceduna-east-kimberley-and-goldfields-region-consolidated-report_012021.pdf

locations of the trials—but he didn't really need to worry about this: three Senate inquiries in 2015, 2017 and 2018 and already assessed the Cashless Debit Card and have arrived at the same conclusions: it's an ineffective program and the stated benefits were overstated and far from realised in the four trial locations. In lieu of permanent arrangements, the trials will be extended for another two years and the program will be reassessed again in 2022.

The government's persistence may relate more to achieving a legislative trigger—where a bill is rejected by the Senate twice and enables the government to call a double-dissolution election—but it seems there is another agenda in play, where once the Cashless Debit Card is implemented for marginalised welfare recipients in remote communities, it can then be applied across all social security payments, including age pensions, disability and sickness pensions, unemployment benefits. That's where all of this is headed—introduce the program on a small scale, develop acceptance within the community, and extend to all social security payments. It's an extreme conservative politician's dream-come-true: dictate what the poor and the unemployed can spend their money on.

One other consideration is the private company that has been managing the Cashless Debit Card—Indue—has been charging the federal government $10,000 for each recipient during the trial period. Of course, there would be economies of scale if there was a wholesale rollout of the scheme to all social security recipients, but this is an astronomical amount of taxpayer funds being locked up into one private company, for the management of an essential social service. There are also strong links between Indue and the Liberal and National parties.

The proposal for the Cashless Debit Card originated from the mining tycoon and businessman, Andrew Forrest, who delivered his *Creating Parity* report to Prime Minister Tony Abbott in 2014 and proposed the BasicsCard, first trialled in the Northern Territory. There might be an expectation that captains of industry would be too busy counting their dollars or investing in new projects to generate even more income for themselves—although quite often, they are the ones knocking on the doors of governments, seeking financial support and largesse—but these are the exact people who shouldn't be allowed anywhere near the development of social welfare policy.

Their involvement does become clearly, however, when it's revealed that former Liberal Party and National Party members of Parliament, such as the former federal member for Richmond who is also the current federal president of the National Party, Larry Anthony, holds substantial shares in Indue. Forrest launched an advertising campaign targeting the Kimberley region, through his Minderoo Foundation, without indicating he is the chairman of the Foundation, and would have a pecuniary interest if the rollout was implemented in the region.

The Cashless Debit Card is onerous and punitive and shouldn't be enforced upon any recipient of social security payments. If individuals choose to go onto the scheme, then that is another issue: choice should be the overriding factor. But it is quite offensive for one of Australia's wealthiest people—Forrest's current net worth is valued at $23 billion, up by over $15 billion during the year of a pandemic, when most other people and businesses have suffered dramatically—to be dictating social policy in an area that he has no expertise in, that is then used to discriminate against the poorest and most marginalised people in society. As a comparison, the current basic social security benefit Australia is $308 per week. Forrest's net worth during 2020 increased by $475 *per second*, and for each and every second for that entire year. In that week where the social security beneficiary received that small amount of $308, Forrest's net worth increased by *$287 million*. The comparisons are astronomical. Yet Forrest has been allowed to determine some of the most draconian social security measures ever implemented anywhere in the developed world. It's obscene.

The Labor Party did equivocate on the program when the trials were first introduced over five years ago, deciding they would wait to see the results of the trials before determining their final response, but they have now fully ruled out supporting the Cashless Debit Card, although they haven't stated what they will do with the program whenever they make a return to government.

Privatisation of social services and social security payments does not work. It has been evident for some time, but it's expected that a conservative government that has a predilection for selling off public assets and public responsibilities to corporate friends and donors at every opportunity, will continue to seek these opportunities, even if the times are not suitable. However, this is more about punitive measures rather than saving welfare costs.

There is a sizable level of support within the community for punitive measures introduced for social security recipients, and it's the conservative side of politics that speaks to this sector of the electorate. One Nation Senator Pauline Hanson, declared in a typically furious and maniacal speech to the Senate that "if you go on a welfare system, you've lost your rights" and anyone relying on social security had forfeited their right to decide how they spend their money.

It's up to governments to resist these kinds of attitudes for the public good, but when the government of the day is the one that implements policies that reinforce these attitudes, it's difficult to uphold the social contract that should exist between governments and the people who make up that society. People shouldn't lose their rights just because they're receiving a small stipend from the government so they can live day-to-day and eke out an existence. And these small amounts have to be placed into the context of the massive amounts of stimulus funding that's going directly into businesses in the form of JobKeeper payments. Profit growth for Domino's Pizza, Southern Cross Austereo, K&S Corporation, Adairs, ARB, Ingenia, and Korvest averaged 70 per cent during the time of pandemic during 2020, after they received a total of $57.5 million in JobKeeper support.[166]

Another example of a government tearing up the social contract is the RoboDebt scheme where the federal government settled a class action case with the people who had been wrongfully accused of owing debts to the government—when in fact, they didn't. The overall settlement will cost the government $1.2 billion and Morrison tried to turn the event into a good news story, even though it destroyed many people's lives and resulted in over 2,000 people dying through suicide, stress and other related illnesses after

---

166 *Australia Financial Review*, 'JobKeeper payments fuelling companies' profit growth', Matthew Cranston and Jessica Gardner, 22 August 2020. https://www.afr.com/policy/economy/jobkeeper-payments-fuelling-companies-profit-growth-20200820-p55nqt

receiving Centrelink debt notices.¹⁶⁷ There is a perception with this class action settlement that the RoboDebt era is over: it's settled and it's an inhumane and draconian practice that will never return.

But it seems the government hasn't learned from its errors and is not prepared to resign from their quest to terrorise social security recipients. There is a new program that has the potential to be even worse than RoboDebt and inflict even further damage upon the community. It doesn't have the catchy title of 'RoboDebt', but it's a different kind of debt recovery program: three major debt recovery companies have been commissioned to pitch for the work of chasing down welfare overpayments and the more debts they chase down, the more work they will receive from the government.

It's almost as though the Department of Human Services—in the best tradition of Orwellian names for bureaucracies—has commissioned its social policy team to develop a scheme that combines Darwinist theories, the dystopian *Hunger Games* and *The Maze Runner*, British fox hunting, Nazi experiments in pushing the boundaries of human punishment, with a smattering of Foucault's *Discipline and Punish* to provide intellectual credibility.

One of the biggest problems that arose from the RoboDebt scheme was the lack of human intervention and oversight. And it appears the government has corrected that problem, but has implemented the wrong type of oversight. It's a debt recovery program that has the potential to be far worse than RoboDebt and the potential to inflict far more damage upon people.

Perhaps it's Morrison natural inclination to implement such harsh policies against the people he sees no political benefit in, either for himself or for the Liberal Party. Perhaps he sincerely believes the best way to move people away from social security is to implement harsh policies in the hope that they never return to the social security system—certainly, if they die from a result of these policies, they definitely won't be returning. Perhaps because Morrison is still rating so highly in opinions polls—62 per cent approve of Morrison's performance, according to the December 2020 Essential

---

167 ABC Triple J *Hack*, 'Over 2000 people died after receiving Centrelink robo-debt notice, figures reveal', Shalailah Medhora, 18 February 2019. https://www.abc.net.au/triplej/programs/hack/2030-people-have-died-after-receiving-centrelink-robodebt-notice/10821272

Poll,[168] although the two-party preferred voting is virtually tied—he feels that he can implement long-held ideological beliefs without too many electoral consequences.

Incentivised debt collectors on steroids, trying to extract overpayments—if, indeed, they are overpayments, and RoboDebt showed that the government does have the propensity to harass welfare recipients, even when the debt isn't there—there is a feeling that this is going to be another program that doesn't work out well for the recipients, or for the government. It's difficult to see the logic in this but, then again, it's been difficult to see the logic in most of this government's behaviour, ever since they returned to office in 2013.

*

---

168 *The Guardian*, 'The Morrison government's handling of a difficult 2020 raises the bar for next year', Peter Lewis, 15 December 2020. https://www.theguardian.com/australia-news/commentisfree/2020/dec/15/the-morrison-governments-handling-of-a-difficult-2020-raises-the-bar-for-next-year

Labor's lack of success since federation

11 December

There has been a great deal of discussion recently about whether there will be an early election in 2021, and the likelihood of the Coalition winning, irrespective of when the election is held. Statistically, even without looking at the electoral fortunes at any given time, the chances are high: since federation in 1901, almost 120 years ago, centre-right parties have been in government for 68 per cent of that time; the Labor Party for only 32 per cent.

Conversely, since the Labor Party was formed in 1893, in the states and territories, it has held office for over half of that time. Why is there a massive discrepancy between the Labor Party's performance at the federal level, where it performs poorly, compared to the states and territories, where it has been relatively successful?

The easy analytical observation would be to suggest there is a strong media bias that acts against the interests of organised labour—and the Labor Party—but the same media operates in all of those states, and has done so since federation. Of course, there are different issues that play out in the state sphere when compared to the federal sphere but, quite often, there are overlapping areas of education, health, infrastructure, river management and environmental concerns, so that's an area that is also not so clear cut.

Another area is the Labor Party sees itself more as a state-based political movement, rather than a federal party, in the sense that it's six state branches, and two territory branches that unite at a federal level for the purposes of federal elections. There's also the nature of the different unions involved: the Shop, Distributive and Allied Employees Association, or the old 'shoppies union', whose leadership mainly comprises socially conservative men, even though their membership is possibly the most diverse within the Australian workplace. At the other end of the spectrum, the Construction, Forestry, Maritime, Mining and Energy Union—the CFMEU—is so socially and politically radical, the union has withdrawn from the left faction of the Queensland Labor Party, and federal Labor and the union have been at loggerheads for some time over political differences and the expulsion of the trade unionist John Setka from the Labor Party. Personnel-wise, there are radically different politicians across the states and in the federal party: Victoria Premier Daniel Andrews, and Queensland Premier Annastacia Palaszczuk are totally different types of leaders, very successful at the state level, but with skills that might not readily translate into federal politics. And vice versa for Anthony Albanese or Tanya Plibersek: they've performed well in federal politics, but might not perform as well if they entered politics at the state level.

There's also the state divide between different Labor branches: the 1916 split over conscription was fuelled by leadership in New South Wales—Billy Hughes—and Victoria, Fred Tudor, although the NSW branch did vote to expel Hughes. The 1931 Labor split saw James Scullin in Victoria to the left, and Joe Lyons from the right moving to create the United Australia Party. The great Labor split in 1955 was based around communism and along sectarian lines, but there were still state-based animosities, primarily Victoria and Queensland, pitched against the other states; and then the formation of the Democratic Labor Party in 1957 created a division which kept federal Labor out of office for another fifteen years.

Elections are based on winning a majority of the seats available, but statistically, there is little correlation between the popular support for Labor historically, and the amount of elections it has won. Since the 1919 federal election, when the two-party preferred vote was first recorded, the Labor Party has won 49.22 per cent of the vote, to the non-Labor vote (made up over time of the Nationalists, United Australia Party, Liberal Party and Country/National Party) of 50.78

per cent. In primary voting, it's similarly close: since 1919, Labor has won 43.15 per cent of the vote, non-Labor has won 45.68 per cent. There are not winning numbers, of course, but they bear no relationship to the result of twelve election victories for Labor during that time, and twenty-five election victories for non-Labor.

Labor is able to attract votes, but is lacking in national organisational skill to get it over the line in elections: winning 49.22 per cent of the two-party preferred vote should result in far more than the 32 per cent of election victories it has achieved since 1919.

National leadership in opposition, historically, has also been an issue for Labor. Although Labor leader Arthur Calwell almost won the 1961 federal election, his leadership was seen as dour and uninspiring, and was claimed by the *Daily Telegraph* to be led by "thirty-six faceless men" before the 1963 election (which he also lost).[169] More recently, Simon Crean was seen to be in a similar mould to Calwell: a leader who could work the back room, but not the front. In the Labor Party review of their 2019 federal election loss, it was understood that one of the defining issues—among others—was the unelectability of then leader, Bill Shorten. Party leadership does matter in federal politics, but it appears that it's more of an issue for the Labor Party: when the party does find an electorally palatable leader—Curtin, Whitlam, Hawke, Rudd—Labor tends to win elections, whereas underperforming leadership within the Liberal Party seems to be tolerated by the electorate.

It's evident that structural changes do need to be made to the Labor Party at a federal level, to bring about a parity it receives in two-party preferred voting—which is usually hovering around the 50 per cent mark—with the time it spends in office. These are not short-term processes that can be resolved within a six-to-nine-month period, but Labor could definitely adopt better political, campaigning and marketing strategies in winnable seats all across Australia.

The Queensland Labor Party holds fifty-two of the ninety-three seats in the Queensland Parliament, whereas in federal seats, Labor only holds six of the thirty seats in that state: that's a large

---

169 Australian Society for the Study of Labour History, 'Alan Reid and the thirty-six faceless men', Stephen Holt, 9 June 2010. https://labourhistorycanberra.org/2015/05/alan-reid-and-the-thirty-six-faceless-men

discrepancy. It's a similar situation in Western Australia, where WA Labor hold forty-one seats in a Parliament of fifty-nine, yet in federal seats, Labor only five of sixteen seats in that state. Also, Western Australia will hold a state election in March 2021, and polls are suggesting yet another landslide win for the Labor Party and if this is the case, that discrepancy between the federal and state vote for Labor is going to become even greater.[170] There isn't a great disparity between the historical federal and state voting patterns in South Australia, Victoria, New South Wales and Tasmania, so perhaps this inability to win the votes in the seats that can make a difference, is costing Labor dearly in federal elections.

And when Labor does win power, with the notable exception of the John Curtin era in the early 1940s and the Hawke–Keating era between 1983–96, it hasn't been unified. Gough Whitlam had problems within his own party, even before he led Labor back into office in 1972, and continued to have divisions during his term as prime minister between 1972–75. Kevin Rudd was brought down in 2010 by the large egos within the party who couldn't accept the fact they weren't ready for the types of positions they wanted in government, led by the likes of Senator Mark Arbib, National Secretary Karl Bitar, National Secretary of the Australian Workers' Union, Paul Howes, and Shorten, who would later be dogged by the claims he helped to overthrow Rudd. And these men installed a reluctant Julia Gillard into the Labor leadership, who was then overthrown by these same men, after they decided to switch their allegiances back to Rudd in 2013.

And perhaps because of the short periods of time Labor has spent in office since federation, there might be a level of impatience and desire to implement progressive agendas, because they might only have one or two terms in office before the Governor–General decides to take it away—as occurred in 1975 with The Dismissal—or if Rupert Murdoch decides he's had enough of a dalliance with Labor in power, and instructs the News Corporation battalion to recommence its eternal war against the Labor Party.

---

170 At the Western Australian election on 13 March 2021, WA Labor increased its two-party preferred vote by 11.9 per cent, up to 67.4 per cent, and won 53 seats of the 59 available, leaving the WA Liberal Party win only two seats, and the WA Nationals with four seats.

Federal elections are usually very close, usually within the band between 48-to-52 per cent of the two-party preferred vote for either side at any given election. But, too often, Labor has been on the wrong side of these results. Sometimes, it has been unlucky to lose—as it did in the 1954, 1961, 1969 or 1998 elections—or lost the unloseable election, as it did in 2019. But luck is created in politics and Labor needs to work out what it needs to do to create this luck, and push it over into a winning formula. This is easier said than done, but it's an issue Labor needs to resolve if it is to change its fortunes at federal elections in the future.

*

A most dramatic year in politics

11 December

The 2020 year is almost over, and it's not an understatement to suggest it has been one of the most dramatic years in human history. The onset of the coronavirus and its effect on the global community has overshadowed almost everything else in life but while there was a need for humanity to work towards a common goal—management of the effects of the pandemic and providing a medical response—the bad habits of partisan political behaviour were never too far away and, after the initial shock of the effects of COVID-19 to health, the economy and social behaviour, conservative politicians all around the world reverted to their usual actions: seeking to obtain political advantage and self-promotion at every opportunity. Politics doesn't have to be this way, but it is.

In Australia, federal Liberal Party ministers launched political attacks upon the Premiers of Queensland and Victoria and, from then on, conservative media, especially News Corporation, implemented their own unhinged attacks, especially against the Victoria Government, and doing their best to undermine public health messaging.

There have been massive stimulus packages that have missed their targets; promised funds for community support—such as bushfire recovery—that were never received; rewards for business friends of the Liberal Party; a wide collection of allegations of corruption against the federal and NSW governments; continuing poor performances from government and key ministers where they've been overpromising, yet underdelivering. It has been a very different year to many others, and a very difficult year for so many people in the community dealing with the effects of the coronavirus and bushfires, but it seems that in the field of political behaviour, not much has changed at all.

In politics, there's an understanding that a disaster should never be missed as an opportunity: there's probably two options in these cases, where there's an option to take stock, change and make the world a better place; or double-down and continue with business as usual. Conservative governments usually choose the 'business-as-usual' model, and it's unfortunate Australia has a government in office that chose the wrong option and sought to engage in divisive politics. It shows how wrong the priorities of the federal government are.

Wage differentiation: the CEO of IDP Education, Andrew Barkla, has a salary of $37 million in 2021; the CEO of CSL, Paul Perreault, earned $30 million. Philippe Wolgen from Clinuvel Pharmaceuticals—$20 million. Health workers at the front line defending the rest of the community—including those high-earning CEOs—from a highly dangerous and infectious disease, earn around 0.2 per cent of those incomes. Yet the government wants to increase the gap between lower-paid workers and those in the higher echelons.

The pandemic has shown society can still function effectively with a smaller economy, and a less profit-driven ethos within the business community. Through work-from-home arrangements, it was discovered that many workers don't have to get onto a train or a bus, or drive a car to get to work to be productive and, in many cases, were found to be more productive when they worked from home and had more flexibility in producing their work. Of course, these types of work arrangements aren't suitable for everyone, but the large-scale experiment to change working patterns has been largely successful.

There are many jobs that will need to be restructured into areas that could be more productive and instead of providing structural adjustment packages and rethinking an economy of the future, the government wanted to 'snap-back' to the old methods that weren't functioning adequately. The economy was performing poorly prior to the onset of the pandemic in early 2020, and the change of circumstances offered an opportunity for change—that's not to suggest that reform or a new economy could have been implemented over a six-to-nine-month period, but at least the building blocks could have been set in place for what would likely be a five-to-ten-year project.

The federal government has largely relied on marketing and media manipulation to promote a 'snap-back-business-as-usual' agenda, using contortions to the English language to confound the community, arguing that the 'technical recession' is over, implying the recession was only technical in the first instance. It's clear that the conditions for the recession were created by Morrison's government and the coronavirus underlined the recession, rather than being the sole cause of it.

Overall, the economy is still functioning poorly and a recovery is far from complete. Many key economic indicators are still low and, like the drowning man clutching at a straw in the water to save himself, the government misinterprets and amplifies any economic news that it can feature as a good news story. The gross domestic product for the September 2020 rose by 3.3 per cent, but when the economy is coming off a low-based—dropping by 6.4 per cent in the year up to the June 2020 quarter—any increase will look good. Comparing the performance for the year up to September 2020, economic output is down 3.8 per cent, so there is still a long way to go before the federal government can claim a successful economic recovery.

The unemployment figures are somewhere in the territory of 'lies, damn lies, and then there are statistics' that was cynically espoused by the British radical politician, Charles Dilke, in the nineteenth century. The OECD Working Party on Employment and Unemployment Statistics in 1983 suggested one hour of paid work in any form could be considered to be 'employed' and many countries have based their unemployment figures on this assumption, which would therefore include casual university academics, actors, writers, cleaners, contractors—many of these people are in atypical working environments and, in many cases, would be wanting to work or be gainfully employed for more than the "one hour or more for pay, profit, commission or payment in kind" that constitutes the current definition of "employed".[171] It's unclear what the current unemployment rate of 6.6 per cent constitutes, especially in the context of the number of workers attached to the JobKeeper program—3.5 million in July 2020—and how many of these will be added to the unemployment statistics once the program ends in March 2021. Other estimates suggest the real rate of unemployment in Australia is anywhere between 12 and 16.8 per cent.[172]

The headline unemployment figure affects the workforce psychologically, as well as the confidence of the economy—if the perception of high unemployment is strong, people are less likely to apply for work if they feel their chances of obtaining work are slim. Perhaps that's the benefit of the concept of the one-hour-per-week employment figure, a lower numerical figure sustains confidence in the employment market and the economy, even if it is an overvalued confidence. And perhaps that was another aspect to JobKeeper—paying workers to keep them off the unemployment statistics.

However, the JobKeeper program was the correct type of stimulus required by the economy, even if the government did implement it in the wrong manner. A great deal of JobKeeper support payments ended up in the pockets of company directors, used by businesses for reinvestment, or propping up inefficient businesses that in any other economic cycle would have closed down. The JobKeeper program was too easily manipulated by businesses and there should have been tighter controls on the program in the second and third phases of the package—the government certainly had enough time and data to evaluate the targeting of the program.

Generally, Australia has managed the coronavirus pandemic well, although there have been some clear deficiencies, and it would be churlish to highlight these in the context of current coronavirus cases: there is one case in New South Wales; one in South Australia. Victoria hasn't recorded any community transmissions for over forty days and Western Australia hasn't had any transmissions for over five months. And if it became a choice of living in Australia, or the United States, or Europe, or many other parts of the world where

---

[171] Australian Bureau of Statistics, '6102.0.55.001 – Labour Statistics: Concepts, Sources and Methods, 2006', 15 December 2015. https://bit.ly/39Pkk1F

[172] Roy Morgan Research, Roy Morgan Employment Estimates (1999-2021), http://www.roymorgan.com/morganpoll/unemployment/estimates-detailed

the coronavirus cases are still rising exponentially, most Australians would choose to be here.

The First interim report from the Senate Select Committee on COVID-19[173] has suggested although Australia avoided the worst of the potential health outcomes, the national health strategy was not explained clearly to the public until late July and, throughout most of March, the Prime Minister appeared reluctant to fully embrace social distancing measures and confused the public with messages suggesting life could carry on as normal. This led to the states and territories deciding to proceed in their own directions, and ultimately did most of the work in managing the coronavirus, despite the lack of a clear national strategy from the federal government, and its continuous insistence that internal borders and the economy remain open and politicking against state Labor governments in Victoria, Queensland and Western Australia.

The federal government did implement the JobKeeper program, but even that was a mechanism proposed by the Secretary of the Australian Council of Trade Unions, Sally McManus, and former Labor Minister for Industry, Greg Combet, implemented reluctantly by the Prime Minister and the Treasurer, Josh Frydenberg.

What were the main actions of the federal government? After they implemented the JobKeeper package, there was a sense their job was done and it was back to behaving like political warriors, engaging in their culture wars again, and avoiding responsibilities for issues that were developing as a result of the coronavirus pandemic. Their attacks on Premiers Daniel Andrews and Annastacia Palaszczuk became increasing more unhinged and desperate, as though they couldn't resist these opportunities, even in the face of a national crisis.

The NSW Government has had several border breaches, especially on an international arrivals, but the way the federal government has responded to these, compared to the incidents in Victoria has been stark. When breaches occur in Melbourne, there's outrage in the conservative media, headlines about 'debacles' and incompetence from Andrews—messaging encouraged by federal government

---

[173] Senate Select Committee on COVID-19, First interim report, December 2020. https://www.aph.gov.au/Parliamentary_Business/Committees/Senate/COVID-19/COVID19/Interim_Report

ministers—but when the same types of breaches occur in Sydney, and because it's under the purview of a Liberal Party government, these breaches are brushed away as a 'human error' that was always inevitable.

Recently, NSW Police incorrectly allowed two German–Australian nationals to board a flight to Melbourne, without undergoing mandatory hotel quarantine when they arrived in Sydney from an international flight.[174] In contrast to the vitriol endured by Andrews in Victoria, this was promoted within the media as an incident that was an 'honest mistake by a good cop'. It's remarkable to see the difference in media report of similar incidents that occur under a Liberal Party government, when compared to incidents that occur under a Labor administration, and the reporting would have been totally different if the two German–Australian nationals arrived in Melbourne first, and then incorrectly allowed to travel to Sydney without hotel quarantine: News Corporation would have reported the incident as a major news item, framing it as yet another example of Labor incompetence, and would still be reporting this every day up until the day of the next Victoria state election in November 2022. But when it's a Liberal government that performs the breach, it's an 'honest mistake' and the issue goes away.

This is an immature federal government, managed by an immature Liberal Party, and supported by immature media conglomerates, headed by News Corporation. The NSW Liberal Party and the media has periodically referred to NSW Premier Gladys Berejiklian as the 'school captain'[175] and 'head prefect',[176] but managing government is different to managing a school debating team. Quite often, it appears as though the federal and New South Wales governments acquired their political skill at the campus clubs at university but didn't actually learn how to engage in politics outside of university,

---

174 ABC News, 'NSW Police admit they 'incorrectly' let German nationals fly to Melbourne without quarantining', 6 December 2020. https://www.abc.net.au/news/2020-12-06/nsw-police-admit-wrongly-letting-german-pair-fly-to-melbourne/12954984

175 Nine News, 'Gladys Berejiklian rescues the site of her old high school', 1 December 2017. https://www.9news.com.au/national/gladys-berejiklian-goes-back-to-school-with-opening/99871203-b14c-4cd3-9ca6-dd6ef8f87609

176 *Australian Financial Review*, 'NSW's head prefect shows how politics is done', Aaron Patrick, 24 March 2019. https://www.afr.com/politics/nsws-head-prefect-shows-how-politics-is-done-20190324-h1cqb7

with a mentality that is based around putting the party and vested interests first, and the public interest last.

It's a problem that is becoming more apparent in Australian politics, but especially since the time Tony Abbott first became leader of the Liberal Party in 2009, the main game has all been about winning at every opportunity. The trouble with always 'winning' in politics is that this ultimately registers as a loss—sometimes in politics, it's necessary to have the loss, because it might be the right thing to do in the public interest, or it's an ethical solution. This is a government that still hasn't worked out that every time it pushes through with a so-called victory, it loses more and more political capital in the long term.

The China crisis continues

One other major issue during 2020 in Australian politics has been the management of the diplomatic relationship with China, and it's a relationship that is continuing to sour with no end in sight. Another Australian beef producer has been targeted, with imports from Meramist Pty Ltd suspended until further notice,[177] along with five other producers banned earlier in the year. Timber exports have also been blocked from the China market and it seems there will be a slow release of tariffs and suspensions on other Australian goods, for as long as Scott Morrison remains as prime minister—whether this be another month, two years, five years or ten years—and it's a retaliation for the humiliation Morrison inflicted upon the Chinese government when he called for an investigation into the origins of the coronavirus and implied it was caused by China.

Chinese diplomats have been provided with a *carte blanche* in their attacks on Morrison, and the Chinese media has depicted him as "Lao Youtiao" (老油条) which translates into English as "old fried doughstick", referring to someone as a "slick customer, lazy, untrustworthy, slippery, ass-kissing, and really, anyone who's being an all-around dickhead".[178] It's a delicately Chinese way of hurling a deep insult to an Australian prime minister.

---

177 ABC News, 'China suspends importation of more Australian beef as trade battle escalates', 8 December 2020. https://ab.co/3xdZWlc

178 *Happy Mag*, 'Chinese state media label Scott Morrison an "old fried dough stick"', Mike Hitch, 8 December 2020. https://bit.ly/3dndCSW

In diplomatic stoushes, it's easy to look at home-town nationalism, and this is one aspect Morrison would be hoping to touch on—whipping up a frenzy with a country that has historically been an easy political target for many centuries—but this is a problem which is all of Morrison's own making, and it's Australian exporters who are going to pay the financial penalty. Of course, there will be a core group within Australia who suggest trade with China should be halted, in the context of its poor human rights record, as well as believing Australia's international trade is too lop-sided with China and it should diversify. But Australia's human rights record is imperfect too and if every country ceased trading with every other country with which it didn't agree with, there would be very little global trade. That's where foreign relations and diplomatic ties come into play, to gloss over these issues and develop relationships that are mutually beneficial.

Australia is in a position where it can constructively criticise and disagree with allies and trading partners due to the calibre of its diplomatic corps. There was the incident at the first Asia–Pacific Economic Cooperation summit in 1993, when Prime Minister Paul Keating labelled Malaysia Prime Minister, Dr Mahathir Mohamad, as a 'recalcitrant' for failing to attend the meeting—a term Mahathir later agreed with[179]—which created all kinds of diplomatic problems for Australia and Malaysia, but was massaged over through strong behind-the-scenes diplomacy.

However, Morrison's ill-timed and ill-informed actions have tested the skills of these corps, and it's difficult to see how the Australia–China relationship will improve, except for a departure of Morrison from the prime ministership. The fact that the relationship has deteriorated so badly speaks volumes of the incompetence of the Australian government.

*

---

[179] *The Interpreter*, Lowy Institute, Graeme Dobell, 21 October 2011. https://archive.lowyinstitute.org/the-interpreter/mahathir-agrees-he-was-recalcitrant

Incumbency and the year ahead

11 December

During 2020, there has been massive support for political incumbents: Scott Morrison has had high approval ratings, hovering between 60–68 per cent; the Queensland Government was returned with an increased majority in the state election in October; despite the hotel quarantine issues and the spiral in coronavirus cases and associated lockdowns that occurred in Victoria, Daniel Andrews still has a high level of support; Western Australia Premier Mark McGowan personal support levels have hovered in the high-eighties, and as high as 91 per cent.

Every year in politics is different and the end of year usually provides a political reset, for governments and opposition parties. But will a reset provide different perceptions and understandings of the coronavirus? Most of the support behind incumbent governments and leaders has been the support that usually arises during a time of crisis: the electorate looks to stability in political leadership, and looks to the government of the day to provide the support and the protection it feels is necessary to both stabilise the crisis, and ensure the welfare of the community is attended to. But a crisis alone is not the only aspect of high electoral support for governments: there has to be an understanding within the electorate that the coronavirus pandemic has been managed well, and if there is a perception that governments are not fulfilling their responsibilities and carrying out their duties adequately, then they will suffer politically. The 2020 year has been one of the most dramatic ever in world history but will the public use the Christmas break as a reset as well, and be looking for different responses and behaviours from the political class in 2021?

It has to be remembered that there is still a long way to go with the coronavirus pandemic: the development of a vaccine will certainly help, but the vaccination program will take almost a year to distribute and implement—the announcements from the federal government suggests the release of the vaccine in February 2021 and completion of vaccination by October 2021—and then there are issues related to variants of the coronavirus which seem to be transitioning into more severe and contagious versions of the virus. Morrison has consistently suggested Australia is at "the front of the queue"[180] when the vaccine becomes available but, realistically, due to the low case load across the country compared to many other countries around the world, it's quite possible Australia will be one of the last countries to receive the vaccines. Already in New South Wales, there have been coronavirus hotspots caused by inadequacies in the Sydney hotel quarantine program, and there is a possibility of a third wave, or ongoing lockdowns to deal with these outbreaks, so there will be ongoing issues that will need to be managed, irrespective of when the vaccine become available.

If there is a different perception from the electorate about how the coronavirus should be managed throughout 2021, what are the political dangers for Morrison? At the moment, his approval rating is high—even though there isn't a relationship between this high support and the two-party preferred opinion polling, which suggests the government and opposition are equally balanced at 50 per cent each—is there a possibility of the Liberal Party turning against Morrison in the same way the Labor Party turned against Kevin Rudd in 2010? Of course, Morrison does have his supporters but, anecdotally, there are many within the party that loath his leadership.

That point for Tony Abbott arrived exactly two years into his prime ministership in 2015, replaced by someone considered to be his ideologically opposite—Malcolm Turnbull, who was then deposed by Morrison three years later, in 2018. Whichever person

---

180 *The Conversation*, 'Scott Morrison to announce two new COVID vaccine deals', Michelle Grattan, 4 November 2020. https://theconversation.com/scott-morrison-to-announce-two-new-covid-vaccine-deals-149458

the Liberal Party has in place, there will be agitators in the 'wets' and 'dries' group to make the leader more like them, and will work towards implementing a change: it's the eternal leadership conundrum within the party. It will be three years of Morrison's prime ministership in August 2021—will the cycle continue? He is protected by his own leadership rules: if a leader wins an election and becomes prime minister, they will remain prime minister for the full parliamentary term; and can only be challenged by a special majority of two-thirds of the Liberal Party parliamentary team.

Sometimes, a political party needs to remove its leader, and under these rules, it's difficult for Morrison to be removed, and it's impossible to see how a prime minister such as Morrison would resign, unless it was under terms of illegality or misleading Parliament, although it's not clear if even this would be enough. But the Liberal Party ignores so many rules and so many conventions that it's easy to imagine they could change the rules if and when it suits them. If Morrison becomes a political liability, the Liberal Party will work to remove him, rules or no rules.

Very few people expected Morrison to come this far and, ironically, he's likely be the main beneficiary of the revolving door of prime ministers Australia has seen since 2010, perhaps the least deserving. Any prime minister who wins an election has to take credit and Morrison surprised most pundits and defied many opinion polls to win the 2019 federal election, with many suggesting he would take his place as one of the shortest-serving prime ministers in Australian history. With these new Liberal Party leadership rules, he now has the potential to be one of the longest-serving prime ministers.

His strategy is to surround himself with the good-news stories and vacate himself from the public's view whenever negatives issues arise: and when he's confronted with those negative issues, he places a special media spin upon the issue, deflects responsibilities to others, or simply tells outrageous lies. If his goal is to remain prime minister and 'keep Labor out', rather than act as a creative government, this strategy might work in the short term, but will damage the long-term body politic in Australia. Of course, prime ministers need to play to their strengths and minimise their weaknesses but, ultimately, leading the country isn't like a marketing SWOT analysis, although it's been the hallmark of Morrison's time as prime minister: it explains his penchant for a wide range of insignificant social media engagements—building a cubby house or a chicken coop; pulling a beer in a boutique bar in Melbourne; drinking a beer in another location; riding an exercise bike; donning a Cronulla Sharks jersey—all quickly posted onto Instagram, Facebook and Twitter.

Prime ministers should be able to manage all issues, whether they are difficult or not: Morrison runs away from problems. And this situation creates a political opportunity for the Labor Party: focusing on these areas of neglect and reminding the electorate that Morrison avoids responsibilities, blames others for problems he created in the first instance, such as the RoboDebt disaster, should be areas of focus for the opposition during 2021. Scandal after scandal, incompetence after incompetence, mismanagement after mismanagement, many of these problems can be traced back to Morrison. The moral failure of the Murugappan family spending their third Christmas in immigration detention—a Sri Lankan family seeking refuge in Australia, successfully living in the regional Queensland town of Biloela, but attempt after attempt by the federal government to deport them. Failure after failure, yet defended at every opportunity by a conservative media. How many failures will the electorate tolerate?

And how many more opportunities does the Labor opposition need to be provided with before they can gain traction? Does Anthony Albanese need to be looking over his shoulder, or do the Labor leadership rules—introduced after Kevin Rudd returned to the leadership in 2013—stipulating a Labor leader in opposition can only be removed through a 60 per cent vote in the Caucus, mean he is immune from a leadership challenge as well? In the final week of Parliament, the federal government left Albanese alone, but fired a severe personal and brutal attack on Shadow Treasurer, Jim Chalmers. It's a signal Morrison believes he might be facing Chalmers at the next federal election, rather than Albanese, and feeling that he is the greater political threat.

It's also reminiscent of the conversations the retiring Robert Menzies had with his successor, Harold Holt in 1966 when he suggested "look after Artie"—referring the long-term Labor leader, Arthur Calwell, who was ineffective as Leader of the Opposition, and it was thought to be better for the Liberal Party if they had a weaker opponent, than someone such as Gough Whitlam, who was deemed to be the heir-apparent, and a far more ferocious opponent.

Albanese has been ineffective as a leader so far, but the coronavirus pandemic has made it difficult for many opposition political parties all around the world. It may be a case where he's also decided to keep his powder dry for the lead up to the next election and possibly be underestimated in the same manner Joe Biden was in early 2020, before winning the United States Presidential election in November. That might be a brave strategy to adopt, because the Labor Party is usually impatient with this type of approach.

But politics is an unpredictable business and as former British Prime Minister Harold Macmillan was alleged to have said when he was asked how governments can be toppled, his response was: "events, my dear boy, events". The severity of the bushfire season in the summer of 2019/20 almost destroyed Morrison's leadership, before he was rescued by the calamity of the coronavirus pandemic. The government has had one-too-many policy disasters, and these have the potential to escalate. The Attorney–General, Christian Porter, wishes to implement a harsh and highly destructive anti-worker scheme that could replicate the political damage caused to the Howard government by the WorkChoices system in 2007.

There are many ongoing problems with the management of the National Disability Insurance Scheme; the welfare cashless debit card, which the government is keen to implement across all social security recipients; attacks on Medicare. As shown during 2004–07, when the Howard government had control of both the House of Representatives and the Senate, when a leader feels they can act without any hinderances, there is a tendency for ideological overreach, even if the political circumstances aren't suitable for the implementation of these agendas. Or will there be other unforeseeable events that affect Morrison's ability to lead and govern?

Events can change quickly in politics and often arise when least expected. The pandemic has made politics unpredictable and created the need for adaptable and creative thinking in government. But this is a federal government that finds it difficult to break the shackles of its ideological past and freely talks about espousing the values of a long-gone British Prime Minister, Margaret Thatcher, for directing its pathways for the future. In 2021, there are many areas the government can exploit to pursue its agendas, most of which seem to be politically motivated and punishing its real and perceived enemies. It's a time where accountability has never been more important in Australia's political history.

*

Index

A

Abbott, Tony 18, 24, 27, 39, 55–56, 61, 99, 101, 118, 125, 127, 129–132, 164, 174, 177, 193, 276, 294, 314, 322, 331–333, 340, 345, 354, 356, 368–369, 377, 393, 396
Abetz, Eric (Senator) 25, 46
Aboriginal deaths in custody 140–141, 145
The Accord 146, 154
accountability 30, 32, 35, 46, 48, 50, 62, 243, 329, 333, 343, 400
Adairs 379
Adani coalmine 102
Adelaide Advertiser (newspaper) 133, 363
Afghanistan war 350, 367, 368
African gangs 267
The Age (newspaper) 133, 195, 322
Albanese, Anthony
    anti-Labor media 133, 194, 196
    approval ratings 10, 52, 128, 197
    avoiding negative tactics 322, 340
    Budget Reply 289, 290–293
    coal mining 36
    critique of JobSeeker levels 130
    direct corruption 323
    'I fight Tories' 129, 290
    leadership 117, 293, 369, 371
    nomination of Mathias Cormann 360
    standing orders 62
Al Qaeda 55
Aly, Waleed 140
Andrews, Daniel 10, 109–111, 131, 187, 209, 219, 235–236, 251, 265, 322, 383, 391, 395
Andrews, Kevin 321–322
Anthony, Larry 378
anti-vaccination 11, 137, 138, 269
ANZAC Day 137, 255
apartheid 67
APN News & Media 160
Arbib, Mark 385
Ardern, Jacinda 96
Arena, Tina 183
Ashurst (law firm) 321
Askin, Robert 276, 304
AstraZeneca 13, 268, 271, 287
The Atlantic Monthly (journal) 95
Australia Act 199, 203
Australia–China relationship 120–126, 352, 394
Australia–Indonesia relationship 352
The Australian (newspaper) 17, 41, 57, 60, 64, 98, 113, 118, 126, 133, 150, 156, 177, 180, 225, 264, 290, 295–296, 344, 367
Australian Associated Press 161, 354
Australian border closures 222, 253, 255–256, 263–264, 338, 364
Australian Border Force 58, 62, 72, 75–76, 233, 266
Australian Broadcasting Corporation (ABC)
    Four Corners (television program) 12, 330–331, 340
    funding cuts 182–184
    Indigenous Programs Unit 139
    Insiders (television program) 110, 138–139, 215
    Q+A (television program) 108, 117, 210
    7.30 (television program) 53, 264, 295–296
    Utopia (television program) 179–180
Australian Communist Party 178
Australian Constitution 14, 46, 201, 204, 221–222, 234
Australian Council of Trade Unions 80, 94, 189, 391
Australian Defence Force 367
Australian Democrats 284–285
Australian Electoral Commission 166, 192
Australian Federal Police 22–26, 101, 172–177
Australian Football League 208

401

Australian Greens 26, 119, 163, 274, 342
Australian National Audit Office 18, 21
Australian Republic Movement 205
Australian Securities and Investment Commission (ASIC) 222
Australians for Honest Politics Trust 276
Australian Taxation Office 155
Australian Visa Processing 209
Australia Post 318–320, 323

B
Baird, Bruce 167
Baird, Mike 235
Bankstown Observer (newspaper) 27
Barilaro, John 117, 273
Barkla, Andrew 388
barley industry 120–122, 125–126
Barnard, Lance 47
Barnett, Colin 321
Baron–Cohen, Sacha 183
Barwick, Garfield 331
Belt and Road Initiative 258–261
Berejiklian, Gladys 28, 74, 77, 111, 188, 275, 304, 305–310, 314, 335, 364, 392
Bergson, Henri 15
Beyond Blue 103
Bhutan 95
Bickmore, Carrie 140–141
Biden, Joe 69, 315, 324–326, 329, 339, 352, 399
The Bigger Picture (book) 97
Birmingham, Simon (Senator) 126, 248
Bishop, Bronwyn 33, 244
Bishop, Julie 174
Bitar, Karl 385
Bjelke-Petersen, Joh 50, 54, 272, 276, 331
Black Lives Matter 2, 11, 135–136, 138–140, 145, 186, 188, 266
Bolsonaro, Jair 324
Bolt, Andrew 256
Bonaparte, Napoleon 214
Boral Industries 151
branch stacking 163, 165–167, 321
Brandis, George (Senator) 91, 331

Brennan, Bridget 138
Brereton, Major General Paul 367
Bretton Woods agreement 14, 63, 66, 241
Bretton Woods Mark II 66
Brexit 36, 121, 126, 180, 203–204, 260, 302
Briggs, Jamie 285
Briggs, Scott 209
Broome, Frederick (governor) 142
Browne, Frank (journalist) 27
Bruce, Stanley 33, 104, 190
Brumby, John 210
Building the Education Revolution 40–41
bushfires 9, 42–43, 51, 56–57, 70, 93, 116–117, 119, 120, 147–148, 152, 194, 196, 207–210, 230, 296–297, 349, 388
Bush, George W. 259, 327
Business Council of Australia 75, 118, 148, 248
Buttrose, Ita 76

C
Calwell, Arthur 384, 398
Cameron, David 99, 313
Campbell, Alastair 316
Cam, Scott 48
Canavan, Matt (Senator) 80
Canberra bubble 52, 149
Carapiet, Michael 226
carbon pricing 359
carbon tax 322, 359
caretaker convention 45
Carnegie, Andrew 316
Carnival Corporation & PLC 72, 74–75
Carr, Bob 270
Carter, Jimmy 103
Cashless Debit Card 372, 376–378
Catholic Church 85–86
census 91, 113
Center for Strategic and International Studies 104
Centre Alliance 284–285
Centrelink 59, 91, 138, 155–156, 355, 380
Chalmers, Jim 95, 369, 398
Chamberlain, Lindy 85

Chamberlain, Michael 85
Chandler, Raymond (novelist) 23
Charlton, Andrew 296
Charteris, Martin 199
Chester, Darren 110
Chicago school of economics 82
Chifley, Ben 100
Chikarovski, Kerry 309
childcare 62, 82, 281, 289, 291–292, 322, 333
China trade war 121, 259, 262, 326, 352, 393
Chinese Communist Party 121, 172, 260
Chinese government 121, 123, 125–126, 172–173, 258, 260–261, 353, 393
Chinese Ministry of Commerce 121
Christchurch massacre 43
Christensen, George 101–102, 247, 274
Christianity 373
Churchill, Winston 14, 63
Clean Energy Act 359
climate change 14, 22, 36, 43, 74, 87, 100, 103, 133, 207, 313, 324–325, 329, 341, 343, 359–362
Clinton, Bill 306, 307, 309, 327
Clinton, Hillary 309
Club of Rome 67
Clueless (film) 59
coal mining 36–37, 79–80, 165, 214, 241, 341, 352–353, 375
Coatsworth, Nick (doctor) 108–109
Colbeck, Richard (Senator) 246–249, 251
Cold War 55, 82, 178, 213, 216
Combet, Greg 67, 189, 391
Commonwealth Court of Conciliation and Arbitration 374
Commonwealth Integrity Commission Bill 335–336
Community Sport infrastructure program 16, 18
Conan Doyle, Arthur 68
conflict of interest 240
Consolidated Media Holdings 316
Constance, Andrew 117, 193

Construction, Forestry, Maritime, Mining and Energy Union (CFMEU) 26, 383
Cook, James (captain) 141
Cook's Cottage 141
Coorey, Phillip 167, 334
Corbyn, Jeremy 36
Cormann, Mathias (Senator) 47, 137, 178, 357–362
coronavirus
    active cases 112, 124, 171, 186
    blamed for recession 152
    deaths caused 251
    economy 56, 64
    existential crisis 67
    infection rate 264
    management 326, 387, 390, 395
    northern Italy 169
    onset in Australia 51
    outbreak in Wuhan 36
    pandemic 38
    political opportunism 69, 219–223, 229
    post-COVID 81, 142, 179
    pre-COVID 68, 83, 217, 238, 241, 285
    public gatherings 112
    Ruby Princess 73
    state governments management 148
    vaccination 137, 269, 287, 396
    vaccines 171, 268, 270–271, 281, 286–287, 396
corruption 16, 27–28, 79, 127, 250, 304, 310, 321
    'act of grace' payment 47
Corruption Perceptions Index 250
Costello, Peter 168, 300, 320
The Courier-Mail (newspaper) 98, 133, 176, 315, 343, 365
Court, Richard 321
COVIDSafe (app) 90–91, 113–114
Crean, Simon 293, 384
Creating Parity (report) 377
Creighton, Adam 64, 150, 256
Crown Resorts 79
Crozier, Georgie 188
Curtin, John 14, 63, 130, 271, 384, 385

D

The Daily Telegraph (newspaper) 22, 98, 133, 161, 209, 343, 384
Dalberg-Acton, John 165
Dale, Daniel 328
Darwin Reconstruction Authority 201
Dastyari, Sam 173–175
Dean, Rowan 256
death penalty 347–348, 350
debt recovery program 372, 380
Democratic Labor Party 383
Deng, Wendy 316
Devine, Miranda 256
Diamantopoulou, Anna 358, 362
Diamond Princess 77
Dilke, Charles 389
The Dismissal 198–200, 202, 385
domestic violence 48
Domino's Pizza 379
Dowd, John 28, 304
Downer, Georgina 18, 119
Drosten, Christian 109
Dunlop, Edward 'Weary' 367
Dunning–Kruger effect 100, 331
Dutch government resignation 234
Dutton, Peter 54–56, 72, 105, 132, 266–267, 357

E

early education 62, 281, 291
East Timor 352
economic depression 65
economy
    Budget 38–41, 95, 152, 155, 250, 281–293, 296, 345
    Budget assumptions 287
    Budget surplus 38–39, 40
    casualisation of work 373
    debts and deficits 282
    economic reform 215, 241, 324
    economic sovereignty 124
    economic weaknesses 298
    fall in export earnings 238
    gross domestic product 42, 65, 95, 147, 282, 297, 389
    national government debt 93, 212, 282
    negative growth 42, 65, 152, 295, 297
    per capita recession 295
    recession of 1990 230
    'snap-back' 12, 83, 90, 106, 217, 241, 254, 281, 388–389
    superannuation 366, 374–376
    supply-side economics 212, 215, 217
    tariffs 120–121, 125
    technical recession 389
    trade with China 351
    trade with Japan 351
    universal basic income 96, 181, 217–218
    working from home arrangements 94, 106, 254, 280, 388
Education Act (NSW) 108
Eight By Five (slush-fund) 79
elections
    1919 federal election 383
    1920 byelection 118
    1931 federal election 70
    1949 federal election 370
    1954 federal election 177
    1961 federal election 134
    1983 British election 213
    1983 federal election 147
    1993 federal election 56, 230
    1996 federal election 122
    1999 republic referendum 204
    2001 federal election 177
    2004 federal election 166, 301
    2007 federal election 81, 167
    2007 NSW election 270
    2011 NSW election 270
    2013 federal election 99, 135, 322, 359
    2016 federal election 100, 103, 118, 285, 302
    2018 Victoria election 266
    2019 federal election 16, 18–21, 38, 40, 45, 47, 50, 69, 83, 99, 102, 118–120, 147, 149, 151–152, 166, 195–197, 221, 249, 254, 267, 293–294, 301–302, 319, 332, 340, 349, 352, 384, 386, 397
    2020 Queensland election 8, 267, 338–341
    2021 Western Australia election 8, 338, 369

2022 Victoria election 236, 339, 392
2023 NSW election 234, 339
Eden–Monaro byelection 116, 118–119, 168, 173, 176, 179, 189, 191–197, 267, 275, 322
federal election due in 2022 13, 56, 114, 149, 158, 211, 234, 241, 244, 266, 275, 293, 299, 301, 303, 339, 370, 398
publicly-funded 165, 166
United States election 158, 302, 325, 338, 399
Electoral Commission of Queensland 339
Encyclopaedia Britannica 162
English civil war 199
Environmental Protection Authority (NSW) 28, 305
Erikson, Neil 163
Essential Report 301
Estia Health 223
Euromoney Finance Minister of the Year 360
European Union 39, 123, 126, 203, 260
Explorer's Monument 142

F
Facebook 52, 91, 114, 211, 398
Fairfax, Warwick 316
Fair Work Act 80
Fair Work legislation 78, 80
Falklands War 213
fascism 82
Federal Court 220–221
Female Facilities and Water Safety Stream program 16, 19
Fierravanti-Wells, Concetta (Senator) 54
Fischer, Tim 274
Fisher, Andrew 271
Fitoussi, Jean-Paul 95
Fitzgibbon, Joel 36, 340–341
Fitzpatrick, Ray (journalist) 27
'five-eyes' agreement 114
Fletcher, Paul 184, 277, 279
Floyd, George 11, 136
Forrest, Andrew 377–378
Fortescue Metals 67, 285

Foxtel 48, 97, 133, 157, 194, 209, 278, 280
franking credits 151
Fraser, Malcolm 101, 103, 130, 147, 178, 198, 201
Frecklington, Deb 338–339
French Revolution of 1789 55
Frydenberg, Josh 39, 40, 95, 107, 152, 158, 159, 212, 214–217, 235, 254, 281–282, 285, 287, 296–298, 300, 372, 391
Fuller, Mick 75, 144
Future Fund 300

G
Gaetjens, Philip 18, 53, 67
Galea, Perce 305
Gallagher, Katie (Senator) 247
Garrett, Peter 61
Gartrell, Tim 322
'gas-led recovery' 14, 238, 240, 268, 270, 359
Gates, Bill 137
Gillard, Julia 33, 61, 99–100, 103, 127, 129, 225, 385
Global Business Network 67
global financial crisis 38–42, 60–61, 64, 66, 81, 127, 159, 218, 282, 298–299
Australia avoids recession 39
Global Leadership Foundation 104
Global Partnership for Education 103
Goldwyer, William 142
Gordon Legal 155
Gorton, John 202, 272
Great Barrier Reef Foundation 75, 100, 320
Great Depression 64–65, 70, 83, 190, 208, 218
greenhouse gas emissions 359
Greiner government 28, 227, 304
Greiner, Nick 28–29, 76, 227, 304–305
Groom, Littleton 33
Gundy, David 144
Guy, Matthew 188, 235–236

H
Hadley, Ray 52, 209
Halton, Jane 67

405

Hancock Mining 285
Hanks, Tom 266
Hanson, Pauline (Senator) 132, 140, 276, 379
Hanson-Young, Sarah (Senator) 342
Harding, James 142
Harris, Kamala 324
Harris, Tony 79
Hartcher, Chris 165
Harvey, Gerry 351, 369
Harvey, Liza 369
Hawke, Alex 76
Hawke, Bob 44, 94, 101, 132, 146, 164, 178, 200, 208, 333, 368
Hayek, Friedrich 269
Hazzard, Brad 76
Healthe Care Australia 82
Hearst, William Randolph 316
Heath, Edward 352
Helliar, Peter 140–141
Henderson, Sarah (Senator) 188
Hendy, Peter 118
Henry, Ken 39, 66
The Herald Sun (newspaper) 98–99, 133, 161, 265, 314, 322, 343
Hewson, John 31, 32, 51
Higgins, Henry Bournes 331, 374
High Court 85–87, 155, 178, 219–233, 253, 355
Higher Education Contribution Scheme 281, 283–285
His Last Bow: Some Reminiscences of Sherlock Holmes (novel) 68
Hocking, Jenny 198–199
Holder, Frederick 33
Holgate, Christine 318–319
Holt, Harold 100, 202, 259, 398
HomeBuilder program 149–151, 153, 159
Horne, Donald 49
horse racing industry 92
hotel quarantine system 148, 186–188, 220, 235, 236, 251, 255, 264, 266, 363–364, 365, 392, 395–396
House of Commons (Britain) 32
Houston, Brian 53
Howard, John 44, 101, 122, 127, 130, 146–147, 164, 204, 208, 259, 266–267, 301, 321, 368, 373
Howes, Paul 385

Hughes, Billy 132, 177, 200, 368, 383
human rights 95, 121, 175, 260, 394
Hume, Jane (Senator) 374
Hunter, Sarah 153
Hunt, Greg 92, 114, 249
Hussein, Saddam 142

I

iCare (Insurance and Care NSW) 226, 228
Iemma, Morris 270
illegal casinos 305
Indigenous Australians 110, 121, 135, 136–141, 143–145, 147, 344–346, 376
Indigenous flag 344
Indonesia 350, 352
Indue card 376–378
influenza 73, 107, 112, 170, 188, 225, 253
Inspector-General of the Australian Defence Force Afghanistan Inquiry 367
Institute of Public Affairs 81, 87, 98, 157, 215, 248, 269, 285, 319–320
International Bank for Reconstruction and Development 14, 63
International Monetary Fund 14, 63, 241
Isaacs, Isaac 331
Islamic terrorism 55, 177
'It's OK to be white' (Senate motion) 362

J

Jackie O 308, 310
Jandamarra 142
JobKeeper 82, 89, 130, 148–149, 153, 154, 159, 181, 183, 188–190, 217, 218, 237–239, 286, 299, 301, 351, 379, 390–391
JobSeeker 82, 89, 130, 137–138, 148
Johnson, Boris 14, 63, 69, 158, 180, 324, 355
Johnson, Lyndon 164, 259, 319
Johst, Hanns 185
Jones, Alan 52
Joyce, Barnaby 28, 36, 80, 175, 273, 332
Juukan Gorge 141

K

Kaljulaid, Kersti 358, 362
Keating, Paul 31, 32, 44, 56, 101, 122, 132, 145, 164, 200, 230, 296, 321, 360, 385, 394
Kelly, Craig 269
Kelly, Paul (doctor) 92, 108
Kelly, Ros 17
Keneally, Kristina 270
Kennett, Jeff 210
Kerr, John 198, 200–201
Keynesian economic thinking 11, 63–65, 70, 241
Killen, James 243
King Charles I 199
King, Peter 166
koala protection legislation 273–274
Koch, Tony 313
Koori Mail (newspaper) 139
Korn Ferry 76
Kotvojs, Fiona 119, 177, 193
K&S Corporation 379

L

Labor Party
    brand recognition 341
    Caucus 100, 341, 369–371, 398
    climate change 341
    female quotas 144
    lack of federal success 382–386
    leadership rules 398
Laffan, Amy 247
Lahey, Katie 75
Laming, Andrew 132, 137
Landbridge Group 176
Langton, Marcia 140–141
Latham, Mark 302, 369
Laundy, Craig 189
League of Nations 63, 104
Lebanese government resignation 234
Lees, Meg 284
Leppington Pastoral Company 275
Leveson Inquiry (Britain) 99, 312
Lew, Solomon 238
Ley, Sussan 24
Liberal Party
    fundraising 244
    leadership rules 397
    superior economic management 300

Lincoln, Abraham 233
Li Ruipeng 174
Little, Paul 67
Liu, Gladys 173, 174
lockdown 58, 68, 93, 98, 107–108, 112, 137, 138, 169–170, 265, 280, 363–365
The Lucky Country (book) 49
Lui, Nakkiah 140
Lyons, Enid 208
Lyons, Joe 201, 208, 271, 383

M

Mabo case 144
Macfarlane, Ian 174
Macmillan, Harold 399
Maguire, Daryl 306–310, 335
mainstream media 32, 50–51, 83, 125, 131–134, 138–140, 147, 152, 158, 188, 196–197, 209, 211, 250–251, 263–264, 293, 295, 309, 314, 320
    in decline 162
The Makarrata Project 345
Malaspina, Sisto 236
Malmström, Cecilia 358, 362
Manuatu, Josh 23, 25
Marles, Richard 36
marriage equality 87, 102, 330, 336
Marshall, Steve 188
Marx, Karl 64
McBain, Kristy 116, 176, 192
McCarthyism 172
McCarthy, Joe 172
McCormack, Michael 36, 117, 273–274
McEwen, John 274
McGowan, Mark 10, 221, 265–266, 307, 339, 395
McIver, Bruce 321
McKay, Jodi 132
McKenzie, Bridget (Senator) 18–19, 28, 46, 125, 246–247, 273
McMahon, William 202, 272
McManus, Sally 80–81, 189, 391
media concentration 343
media diversity 314, 316
Medibank 203
Medicare 399
Memento Park 142
Menzies government 27

Menzies, Robert 178
Merkel, Angela 109, 309
Metherell, Terry 28, 305
Metropolitan Mine 79–80
Milne, Justin 76
Minderoo Foundation 378
Minerals Council of Australia 248
Minerology Pty Ltd 219
mining 37, 67, 79–80, 92, 124, 141, 149, 159, 166, 183, 193, 214, 219, 253, 281, 300, 315, 341, 375, 377
minority government 35
misogyny 330, 333
mixed-member proportional representation system 242
Mohamad, Dr Mahathir 394
Molan, Jim (Senator) 117, 193, 197
Moore, Clover 22, 24, 25
Moran Group 223
Morrison government 16, 34–35, 48, 60, 69, 71, 109, 281, 356, 381
Morrison, Scott
    aged-care 223
    aged-care cutbacks 223, 231, 250
    'all in this together' 266, 364
    approval ratings 83, 118, 197, 267, 301, 380, 395
    avoiding scrutiny 224
    behaviour during bushfires 57, 208–209, 349, 399
    Belt and Road Initiative 259
    black lives matter 266
    Budget 38, 41, 296
    'bushfire' recession 296
    campaign against Michael Towke 98, 167, 210
    China investigation 122
    China relationship 180, 325, 350, 353, 394
    Christine Holgate incident 318–319
    coal in Parliament 80
    comparisons with Bob Hawke 146, 154
    divisiveness 55, 292
    economic recovery 137
    foreign affairs 126
    High Court 221
    ideology 62, 83, 89, 186
    industrial reform 148
    Japan relationship 347–348
    'Jen and the girls' 208–209
    land purchase in western Sydney 320
    media management 50–52, 69, 115, 127, 151, 189, 192, 219, 231, 272, 321, 328, 348, 353–355, 368, 396
    'megaphone' diplomacy 120–122, 125, 325, 352
    'Morrison recession' 295–302, 297–298, 303
    narrow majority in Parliament 69
    national corruption commission 275
    national flag 345
    Office of Tourism and Sport 230, 349
    official photographer 348, 353–354
    'old fried doughstick' 393
    opening borders 253, 257
    political fortune 43
    political fundraisers 243
    populism 324
    postponing Parliament 110
    rejecting comprehensive National Cabinet 66
    reluctance on social distancing measures 391
    Ruby Princess inquiry 233
    rugby league 43, 207
    schools fully reopened 105
    secrecy 53, 349
    'sports rorts' 17
    Tourism Australia 28, 157, 167, 210–211, 230, 349
    understanding of popular culture 183
    with Donald Trump 259
Moselmane, Shaoquett 172–173, 175–176
Murdoch, Lachlan 316
Murdoch, Rupert 97–99, 133–134, 157, 160, 162, 211, 278–280, 312–317, 320, 342–343, 385
Murphy, Brendan (doctor) 108
Murray, Wal 274
Murugappan family 398
Mutch, Stephen 167

Index

My Health (data system) 92

N
NAIDOC Week 141, 344
National Broadband Network (NBN) 91, 97, 278–280
National Cabinet 62, 66, 84, 111, 187, 244
National Centre for Immunisation Research and Surveillance 108
National COVID-19 Coordination Commission 67, 124, 240
national crime and corruption commission 28
National Disability Insurance Scheme 399
National Energy Guarantee 100, 292, 359
National Family Violence Prevention and Legal Services Forum
 removal of funding 48
National Indigenous Television (NITV) 139
nationalism 82, 339, 360, 394
National Party
 future of the organisation 273–276
National Press Club 215
National Quality Standards (early education) 291
natural disasters 64, 70
Nazism 82, 185
neoliberalism 11, 63–65, 68, 70, 81, 82, 83, 89, 217, 241, 296
Network 10 54, 139, 140
Newmarch House 132, 223
New Matilda (news service) 139
News Corporation 41, 97–100, 131, 139, 160–162, 167, 174, 176, 184–185, 194–196, 209–211, 248, 256, 263, 265, 279–280, 292, 312–316, 320, 339, 342, 353, 363, 385, 387, 392
News of the World (newspaper) 99, 313
New South Wales Independent Commission Against Corruption 28–29, 79, 304–306, 310
New South Wales Parliament 78, 80, 173, 274, 306
Newspoll 205, 249, 263

Newstart 42, 82, 130
Nine Network 131, 133, 139–140, 167–168, 172, 184–185, 195–196, 263, 292, 300, 312, 320
Nixon, Christine 209
Nixon, Richard 217
Nolan Meats 21
Northern Australia Infrastructure Facility Board 76
Northern Territory Supreme Court 85
Norwegian sovereign wealth fund 300
NSW Health 58, 72–73, 108–109, 233
NSW Police 25–26, 75, 113, 137, 144, 304, 392
Nutt, Tony 321

O
Oakeshott, Rob 274
Obama, Barack 327
Obeid, Eddie 164, 227, 304
O'Brien, Michael 235
Occupy activists 30
OECD Working Party on Employment and Unemployment Statistics 389
O'Farrell, Barry 28, 79, 304, 306
Office of Tourism and Sport (New Zealand) 230, 349
One Nation Party 26, 140, 163, 266, 273, 276, 284, 341, 362, 379
One.Tel telecommunications 316
Operation Dasha (ICAC) 306
Operation Spicer 79
opinion polls 191, 249
Orbán, Viktor 324
Organisation for Economic Co-operation and Development (OECD) 282, 357–362, 389
Orkopoulos, Milton 290

P
Packer, James 316
Packer, Kerry 316
Page, Earle 274
The Palace Letters 198–199, 203, 205, 206
Palaszczuk, Annastacia 10, 106, 111, 187–188, 257, 266, 315, 338–339, 383, 391
Palmer, Clive 10, 166, 219–222, 253–255, 315

409

Palmer United Party 222
Panahi, Rita 256
Panter, Frederick 142
Papandreou, Georgios 66
Paris Peace Conference 63
Paterson, James (Senator) 157, 269, 319
Patrick, Rex (Senator) 376
Peabody Energy 79–80
Pell, George 85–87, 99, 314
Penmen, Jim 235
Perreault, Paul 388
Perrottet, Dominic 226
Perth Airport Corporation 67
Petrov Affair 177
Pezzullo, Mike 67
Photios, Michael 165
'the Pizza guy' 364–365
Plibersek, Tanya 23, 369–370, 383
police force corruption 23–24
Pomata, Giogio 73
Porter, Charles 331
Porter, Charles "Chilla" 331
Porter, Christian 12, 80, 87, 158, 221, 330–332, 335–336, 340, 372–373, 399
Port of Darwin lease 176, 260–262
Powell, Enoch 271
Power, Neville 67, 240
Pravda (newspaper) 195
price dumping 121
Prince Charles 200
privatisation 82, 154, 212, 224, 251, 319, 378
Privy Council 85, 203
The Project (television program) 140–141
Protestant 'work ethic' 373
Proudhon, Pierre-Joseph 374
Putin, Vladimir 355
Puutu Kunti Kurrama 141

Q
QAnon 137, 265, 269
Qantas 82
Queen Elizabeth II 198–205
Queensland Teachers' Union 106
Question Time 30–32, 35, 80, 224, 348
　　Dorothy Dix 33–35

R
Ramadan 186, 188
Rand, Ayn 269
rape allegations 12
Rats of Tobruk 367
Reaganomics 212, 216
Reagan, Ronald 212–213, 215–216, 282, 327
recession 38–39, 42, 51, 56, 65, 147, 152, 159, 212, 214, 230, 287–298, 303, 358, 389
　　1982/83 147
　　in Australia 65
Reciprocal Access Agreement 347–348, 350
reconciliation 135–136, 143–145, 147
The Red Cross 119
Reddit 52, 211
Redfern Park Speech 145
Redmond, Isobel 285
Rees, Nathan 270
renewable energies 43, 238, 240, 292, 326, 359
republicanism 100, 199, 203–205
Richardson, Graham 164
Rio Tinto 141, 285
Robb, Andrew 174, 261
Robert, Stuart 59, 90, 157, 174–175, 247
RoboDebt (Online Compliance Intervention) 155–156, 158, 355, 372, 379–381, 398
Ronaldson, Michael 321
Roosevelt, Franklin 14, 63
Rousseau, Jean-Jacques 374
Royal Caribbean 73
Royal Commission into Aboriginal Deaths in Custody 144
Royal Commission into Aged Care Quality and Safety 231
Royal Commission into Institutional Responses to Child Sexual Abuse 86
Royal Commission into the Home Insulation Program 61
Royal Commission to ensure a strong, diverse Australian news media (petition) 312–317, 342
Royal Family 198
Roy Morgan 52, 390

Index

The *Ruby Princess* (cruise ship) 58, 62, 72–77, 132, 187, 220, 229, 233, 235
Rudd government 39, 60, 61
Rudd, Kevin 38–40, 44, 60–61, 99–101, 104, 127, 129, 134, 145, 208, 312–313, 316–317, 342–343, 356, 361, 369, 384–385, 396, 398
Rum Corp 304, 311
Ruston, Anne 334

S
Sales, Leigh 53, 296
Sanderson, Rachel 285
Sandilands, Kyle 308, 310
Sarkozy, Nicolas 66
Scullin, James 70, 383
Sebastian, Guy 183
Second Fleet 304
Sen, Amartya 95
Senate Select Committee on COVID-19 391
Seven West Media 133, 139–140, 151, 185, 223, 255, 263, 292, 312
sexual harassment 12, 244, 330, 332–336
Shanks-Markovina, Jordan (Friendly Jordies) 52
Sharkie, Rebekha 18, 285
Sharma, Dave 193
Sheridan, Greg 180
Shooters, Fishers & Farmers Party 193, 273
Shop, Distributive and Allied Employees Association 383
Shorten, Bill 37, 61, 129, 221, 315, 384–385
Silmalis, Linda 195
Simpson, John 367
Sinclair, Ian 274
Sinodinos, Arthur 165, 227
60 Minutes (television program) 163, 168, 172, 174, 176
Sky News 54
Skype 62, 110
Slipper, Peter 33
Smethurst, Annika 174, 195
Smith, Shepard 327
Smith, Tim 131, 187, 235
Smith, Tony 33
Snedden, Billy 202

social contract 93, 374, 379
social services 82, 96, 212, 224, 282, 378
social wage 31, 82, 373
Somyurek, Adem 163–164, 167, 322
Southern Cross Austereo 379
Soviet Union, the 172, 178, 195, 213, 216, 241
Spanish flu (1918 pandemic) 112, 123, 170, 188, 225, 253
Special Air Service Regiment 350, 367
Special Commission of Inquiry into the Ruby Princess 58, 72, 233
Speers, David 110–111, 215
Sports Funding 45
'sports rorts' affair 9, 17, 28, 53, 125, 247, 273, 319–320
Spycatcher case (Britain) 103
St Basil's Home for the Aged 223
Steggall, Zali 118, 332
Stiglitz, Joseph 95
stimulus spending 40, 43, 59, 61–62, 82, 241
Stoker, Amanda 171
Stokes, Kerry 133, 151, 223, 255
Strike Energy 240
Stronger Communities Fund 310
Sturmer, Jake 347–348
subprime lending market 64
Suga, Yoshihide 347–348, 350
Sukkar, Michael 321
The Sunday Telegraph (newspaper) 195
Sunrise (television program) 140
Swan, Norman (doctor) 98
Swan, Wayne 163, 298, 360
Swift, Taylor 183
Sydney City Council 22
Sydney Harbour 58, 62, 72–73, 75, 136, 229, 233, 254
Sydney Morning Herald (newspaper) 54, 61, 101, 103, 133–134, 165, 167, 174, 195, 298, 302, 343

T
Tanna, Catherine 67
Taylor, Adam 353
Taylor, Angus 22, 24, 28, 75, 175–176, 247
Tehan, Dan 110–111, 235, 283
terra nullius 145

Thatcherism 212, 214–215, 373
Thatcher, Margaret 82, 212, 215–216, 282, 309, 372, 399
Third Red Scare 172
Thodey, David 67
Tiananmen Square massacre 147
Tourism and Transport Forum Australia 75
Towke, Michael 98, 167, 210
Truman, Harry 229
Trump, Donald 8, 14, 63, 69, 121–123, 158, 175, 259–260, 315, 324–329, 352, 354
Tsikas, Mick 354
Tudge, Alan 330, 336, 340
Tudor, Fred 383
Turnbull, Malcolm 27, 39, 54, 56, 97, 100–104, 125, 127, 148, 160, 166, 205, 221, 267, 275, 292, 302, 313, 317, 321, 330–331, 357, 361, 396
Twitter 52, 91, 211, 398
2GB (radio station) 54, 209

U

Uluru Statement from the Heart 345
unemployment rate 56, 65, 153, 390
union raids 26
United Australia Party (1931–45) 383
United Australia Party (Clive Palmer) 166, 221, 254, 315
United Nations 63, 67, 104, 269, 361
United States–China relationship 352

V

van Onselen, Peter 54, 119, 301
Victoria Court of Appeal 85
Viellaris, Renee 176
von Clausewitz, Carl 368

W

Wake, Nancy 367
Walker Seafoods 223
Ward, Eddie 132, 164
Webster, Robert 76
wellbeing index 95
Wentworth, W.C. 132
The West Australian (newspaper) 254, 263
WestConnex 276

Westminster system of government 30, 46, 60, 248, 275
'white board' affair 17
Whitlam, Gough 47, 100, 130, 164, 183, 198, 200, 208, 385, 399
Wilde, Oscar 129
Wilkie, Andrew 323
Williams, Leslie 273
Willmott, Deidre 321
Wilson, Tim 235
Withers, Reg 164
Wolgen, Philippe 388
Wong, Penny (Senator) 370
Woodville Pizza Bar 364
WorkChoices 81, 146, 148, 154, 373, 399
work–life balance 94, 106, 254
World Health Organization 38
World War I 63–64, 68, 83, 170, 178, 225, 261, 367–368
World War II 12, 63–66, 82–83, 94, 100, 178, 225, 241, 261, 367
Woronora reservoir 80
Wran, Neville 305
Wuhan (China) 36, 123, 169–170
Wyatt, Ken 345

X

Xi Jinping 172, 258

Y

Ye Cheng 174
Yes, Minister! (television series) 234
'Your Right To Know' campaign 174

Z

Zoom 62, 107, 243, 353

www.ingramcontent.com/pod-product-compliance
Lightning Source LLC
Chambersburg PA
CBHW050258010526
44107CB00055B/2083